Animism in Southeast Asia

Animism refers to ontologies or worldviews which assign agency and personhood to human and non-human beings alike. Recent years have seen a revival of this concept in anthropology, where it is now discussed as an alternative to modern-Western naturalistic notions of human-environment relations.

Based on original fieldwork, this book presents a number of case studies of animism from insular and peninsular Southeast Asia and offers a comprehensive overview of the phenomenon – its diversity and underlying commonalities and its resilience in the face of powerful forces of change. Critically engaging with the current standard notion of animism, based on hunter-gatherer and horticulturalist societies in other regions, it examines the roles of life forces, souls and spirits in local cosmologies and indigenous religion. It proposes an expansion of the concept to societies featuring mixed farming, sacrifice and hierarchy and explores the question of how non-human agents are created through acts of attention and communication, touching upon the relationship between animist ontologies, world religion, and the state.

Shedding new light on Southeast Asian religious ethnographic research, the book is a significant contribution to anthropological theory and the revitalization of the concept of animism in the humanities and social sciences.

Kaj Århem is Emeritus Professor in Social Anthropology at the University of Gothenburg, Sweden. His previously published books include: *Makuna: Portrait of an Amazonian People* (1998); *Ethnographic Puzzles* (2000) and *The Katu Village* (2010).

Guido Sprenger is Professor at the Institute of Anthropology, Heidelberg University, Germany. He has previously published on ritual, exchange, human-environment relations, kinship and social morphology, cultural identity, and sexuality.

Routledge contemporary Southeast Asia series

1. **Land Tenure, Conservation and Development in Southeast Asia**
   Peter Eaton

2. **The Politics of Indonesia-Malaysia Relations**
   One kin, two nations
   Joseph Chinyong Liow

3. **Governance and Civil Society in Myanmar**
   Education, health and environment
   Helen James

4. **Regionalism in Post-Suharto Indonesia**
   Edited by Maribeth Erb, Priyambudi Sulistiyanto and Carole Faucher

5. **Living with Transition in Laos**
   Market integration in Southeast Asia
   Jonathan Rigg

6. **Christianity, Islam and Nationalism in Indonesia**
   Charles E. Farhadian

7. **Violent Conflicts in Indonesia**
   Analysis, representation, resolution
   Edited by Charles A. Coppel

8. **Revolution, Reform and Regionalism in Southeast Asia**
   Cambodia, Laos and Vietnam
   Ronald Bruce St John

9. **The Politics of Tyranny in Singapore and Burma**
   Aristotle and the rhetoric of benevolent despotism
   Stephen McCarthy

10. **Ageing in Singapore**
    Service needs and the state
    Peggy Teo, Kalyani Mehta, Leng Thang and Angelique Chan

11. **Security and Sustainable Development in Myanmar**
    Helen James

12. **Expressions of Cambodia**
    The politics of tradition, identity and change
    Edited by Leakthina Chau-Pech Ollier and Tim Winter

13. **Financial Fragility and Instability in Indonesia**
    Yasuyuki Matsumoto

14 **The Revival of Tradition in Indonesian Politics**
The deployment of *adat* from colonialism to indigenism
Edited by Jamie S. Davidson and David Henley

15 **Communal Violence and Democratization in Indonesia**
Small town wars
Gerry van Klinken

16 **Singapore in the Global System**
Relationship, structure and change
Peter Preston

17 **Chinese Big Business in Indonesia**
The state of the Capital
Christian Chua

18 **Ethno-religious Violence in Indonesia**
From soil to God
Chris Wilson

19 **Ethnic Politics in Burma**
States of conflict
Ashley South

20 **Democratization in Post-Suharto Indonesia**
Edited by Marco Bünte and Andreas Ufen

21 **Party Politics and Democratization in Indonesia**
Golkar in the post-Suharto era
Dirk Tomsa

22 **Community, Environment and Local Governance in Indonesia**
Locating the Commonwealth
Edited by Carol Warren and John F. McCarthy

23 **Rebellion and Reform in Indonesia**
Jakarta's security and autonomy polices in Aceh
Michelle Ann Miller

24 **Hadrami Arabs in Present-day Indonesia**
An Indonesia-oriented group with an Arab signature
Frode F. Jacobsen

25 **Vietnam's Political Process**
How education shapes political decision making
Casey Lucius

26 **Muslims in Singapore**
Piety, politics and policies
Kamaludeen Mohamed Nasir, Alexius A. Pereira and Bryan S. Turner

27 **Timor Leste**
Politics, history and culture
Andrea Katalin Molnar

28 **Gender and Transitional Justice**
The women of East Timor
Susan Harris Rimmer

29 **Environmental Cooperation in Southeast Asia**
ASEAN's regime for transboundary haze pollution
Paruedee Nguitragool

30 **The Theatre and the State in Singapore**
Terence Chong

31 **Ending Forced Labour in Myanmar**
Engaging a pariah regime
Richard Horsey

32 Security, Development and Nation-Building in Timor-Leste
A cross-sectoral assessment
Edited by Vandra Harris and Andrew Goldsmith

33 The Politics of Religion in Indonesia
Syncretism, orthodoxy, and religious contention in Java and Bali
Edited by Michel Picard and Remy Madinier

34 Singapore's Ageing Population
Managing healthcare and end of life decisions
Edited by Wing-Cheong Chan

35 Changing Marriage Patterns in Southeast Asia
Economic and socio-cultural dimensions
Edited by Gavin W. Jones, Terence H. Hull and Maznah Mohamad

36 The Political Resurgence of the Military in Southeast Asia
Conflict and leadership
Edited by Marcus Mietzner

37 Neoliberal Morality in Singapore
How family policies make state and society
Youyenn Teo

38 Local Politics in Indonesia
Pathways to power
Nankyung Choi

39 Separatist Conflict in Indonesia
The long-distance politics of the Acehnese diaspora
Antje Missbach

40 Corruption and Law in Indonesia
The unravelling of Indonesia's anti-corruption framework through law and legal process
Simon Butt

41 Men and Masculinities in Southeast Asia
Edited by Michele Ford and Lenore Lyons

42 Justice and Governance in East Timor
Indigenous approaches and the 'New Subsistence State'
Rod Nixon

43 Population Policy and Reproduction in Singapore
Making future citizens
Shirley Hsiao-Li Sun

44 Labour Migration and Human Trafficking in Southeast Asia
Critical perspectives
Michele Ford, Lenore Lyons and Willem van Schendel

45 Singapore Malays
Being ethnic minority and Muslim in a global city-state
Hussin Mutalib

46 Political Change and Territoriality in Indonesia
Provincial proliferation
Ehito Kimura

47 Southeast Asia and the Cold War
Edited by Albert Lau

48 Legal Pluralism in Indonesia
Bridging the unbridgeable
Ratno Lukito

49 **Building a People-Oriented Security Community the ASEAN way**
Alan Collins

50 **Parties and Parliaments in Southeast Asia**
Non-partisan chambers in Indonesia, the Philippines and Thailand
Roland Rich

51 **Social Activism in Southeast Asia**
Edited by Michele Ford

52 **Chinese Indonesians Reassessed**
History, religion and belonging
Edited by Siew-Min Sai and Chang-Yau Hoon

53 **Journalism and Conflict in Indonesia**
From reporting violence to promoting peace
Steve Sharp

54 **The Technological State in Indonesia**
The co-constitution of high technology and authoritarian politics
Sulfikar Amir

55 **Party Politics in Southeast Asia**
Clientelism and electoral competition in Indonesia, Thailand and the Philippines
Edited by Dirk Tomsa and Andreas Ufen

56 **Culture, Religion and Conflict in Muslim Southeast Asia**
Negotiating tense pluralisms
Edited by Joseph Camilleri and Sven Schottmann

57 **Global Indonesia**
Jean Gelman Taylor

58 **Cambodia and the Politics of Aesthetics**
Alvin Cheng-Hin Lim

59 **Adolescents in Contemporary Indonesia**
Lyn Parker and Pam Nilan

60 **Development and the Environment in East Timor**
Authority, participation and equity
Christopher Shepherd

61 **Law and Religion in Indonesia**
Faith, conflict and the courts
Melissa Crouch

62 **Islam in Modern Thailand**
Faith, philanthropy and politics
Rajeswary Ampalavanar Brown

63 **New Media and the Nation in Malaysia**
Malaysianet
Susan Leong

64 **Human Trafficking in Cambodia**
Chendo Keo

65 **Islam, Politics and Youth in Malaysia**
The pop-Islamist reinvention of PAS
Dominik Mueller

66 **The Future of Singapore**
Population, society and the nature of the state
Kamaludeen Mohamed Nasir and Bryan S. Turner

67 **Southeast Asia and the European Union**
Non-traditional security crises and cooperation
Naila Maier-Knapp

68 **Rhetoric, Violence, and the Decolonization of East Timor**
David Hicks

69 **Local Governance in Timor-Leste**
Lessons in postcolonial state-building
Deborah Cummins

70 **Media Consumption in Malaysia**
A Hermeneutics of human behaviour
Tony Wilson

71 **Philippine Politics**
Progress and problems in a Localist democracy
Lynn T. White III

72 **Human Trafficking in Colonial Vietnam**
Micheline Lessard

73 **Conflict Resolution and Peacebuilding in Laos**
Perspective for Today's world
Stephanie Stobbe

74 **Urbanization in Vietnam**
Gisele Bousquet

75 **Social Democracy in East Timor**
Rebecca Strating

76 **The Politics of Aid to Burma**
A Humanitarian Struggle on the Thai-Burmese Border
Anne Décobert

77 **Animism in Southeast Asia**
Edited by Kaj Århem and Guido Sprenger

Animism in Southeast Asia

Edited by
Kaj Århem and Guido Sprenger
With an End Comment by Tim Ingold

Routledge
Taylor & Francis Group
LONDON AND NEW YORK

First published 2016
by Routledge
2 Park Square, Milton Park, Abingdon, Oxon OX14 4RN

and by Routledge
711 Third Avenue, New York, NY 10017

Routledge is an imprint of the Taylor & Francis Group, an informa business

© 2016 Selection and editorial matter: Kaj Århem and Guido Sprenger; individual chapters: the contributors.

The right of the editors to be identified as the authors of the editorial material, and of the authors for their individual chapters, has been asserted in accordance with sections 77 and 78 of the Copyright, Designs and Patents Act 1988.

All rights reserved. No part of this book may be reprinted or reproduced or utilised in any form or by any electronic, mechanical, or other means, now known or hereafter invented, including photocopying and recording, or in any information storage or retrieval system, without permission in writing from the publishers.

Trademark notice: Product or corporate names may be trademarks or registered trademarks, and are used only for identification and explanation without intent to infringe.

British Library Cataloguing in Publication Data
A catalogue record for this book is available from the British Library

Library of Congress Cataloging in Publication Data

Animism in Southeast Asia / edited by Kaj Århem and Guido Sprenger
  pages cm. — (Routledge contemporary Southeast Asia series; 77)
Includes bibliographical references and index.
  1. Animism—Southeast Asia. 2. Ethnology—Southeast Asia. 3. Southeast Asia—Religious life and customs. I. Århem, Kaj, editor. II. Sprenger, Guido, editor. III. Howell, Signe. Seeing and knowing. Container of (work):

GN471.A54 2016
306.60959—dc23   2015022435

ISBN: 978-0-415-71379-5 (hbk)
ISBN: 978-1-315-66028-8 (ebk)

Typeset in Times New Roman
by codeMantra

Printed and bound in Great Britain by
TJ International Ltd, Padstow, Cornwall

Contents

Lists of figures and table   xi
Preface and acknowledgements   xiii

Part I
Introductory

1 Southeast Asian animism in context   3
  KAJ ÅRHEM

2 Dimensions of animism in Southeast Asia   31
  GUIDO SPRENGER

Part II
Case studies – Mainland and the Philippines

3 Seeing and knowing: Metamorphosis and the fragility of species in Chewong animistic ontology   55
  SIGNE HOWELL

4 Graded personhood: Human and non-human actors in the Southeast Asian uplands   73
  GUIDO SPRENGER

5 Animism and the hunter's dilemma: Hunting, sacrifice and asymmetric exchange among the Katu of Vietnam   91
  KAJ ÅRHEM

6 Wrestling with spirits, escaping the state: Animist ecology and settlement policy in the Central Annamite Cordillera   114
  NIKOLAS ÅRHEM

7 Actualizing spirits: Ifugao animism as onto-praxis   138
JON HENRIK ZIEGLER REMME

Part III
Case studies – Insular Southeast Asia

8 Relatedness and alterity in Bentian human-spirit relations   157
KENNETH SILLANDER

9 The dynamics of the cosmic conversation: Beliefs about spirits among the Kelabit and Penan of the upper Baram River, Sarawak   181
MONICA JANOWSKI

10 Animism and anxiety: Religious conversion among the Kelabit of Sarawak   205
MATTHEW H. AMSTER

11 Boundaries of humanity: Non-human others and animist ontology in Eastern Indonesia   219
TIMO KAARTINEN

12 Gods and spirits in the Wetu Telu religion of Lombok   236
SVEN CEDERROTH

13 Impaling spirit: Three categories of ontological domain in Eastern Indonesia   257
DAVID HICKS

Part IV
Concluding

14 Southeast Asian animism: A dialogue with Amerindian perspectivism   279
KAJ ÅRHEM

15 End comment: To conclude in the spirit of rebirth, or, a note on animic anthropo-ontogenesis   302
TIM INGOLD

Notes on contributors   311
Index   315

Lists of figures and table

Figures

1	Southeast Asia showing the distribution of ethnic groups and localities described or discussed in the book.	xiv
5.1	The dual figure of the Katu Animal Master.	100
6.1	The Mraang basin in the northern part of the A'vuong commune (Tay Giang district, Quang Nam province). The map shows villages and settlement in 2004.	117
6.2	The distribution of pre-war village territories in the Mraang basin and the effects of the 1975 resettlement campaign (FCSP) in the area.	119
6.3	The return of the Dövil and A'urr groups to the upper Mraang basin and ensuing settlement moves 1988–2010.	123
14.1	The spectrum of possession.	294

Table

13.1	The seven narratives: motifs, occurrences and frequencies.	268

List of figures and Tables

Preface and acknowledgements

This volume is the result of a panel with the same name that we organized at the 6th conference of the European Association for Southeast Asian Studies (EuroSEAS) in Gothenburg, Sweden, August 26–28, 2010. The book has taken a long time to complete; several important works relevant to our topic were published or came to our notice in the passing years, and we have tried, as far as possible, to take account of these works – particularly in the two introductory chapters. Of particular significance in this respect was the publication in English of Philippe Descola's *Beyond Nature and Culture* (2013). We felt that it was necessary for us to relate to Descola's book and, specifically, discuss his notion of analogism since it bears directly on our topic – animism in its prototypical Southeast Asian form. This is done in the introductory part of the volume, especially in Chapter 1.

Our thanks go, first and foremost, to all the contributors to this volume for their patience and unwavering trust that the volume would eventually be completed. We also want to express our gratitude to the two anonymous reviewers who helped us to develop important themes in the introductory and concluding parts of the book – thus providing a frame around the case studies – and, at Routledge, to Dorothea Schaefter, who first approved our book proposal, and Jillian Morrison, Rebecca Lawrence and Sophie Iddamalgoda for their support, flexibility and encouragement throughout the project. Finally, we would like to thank Felix Bregulla who helped in the final stages of preparing the manuscript and the index.

Kaj Århem
Guido Sprenger

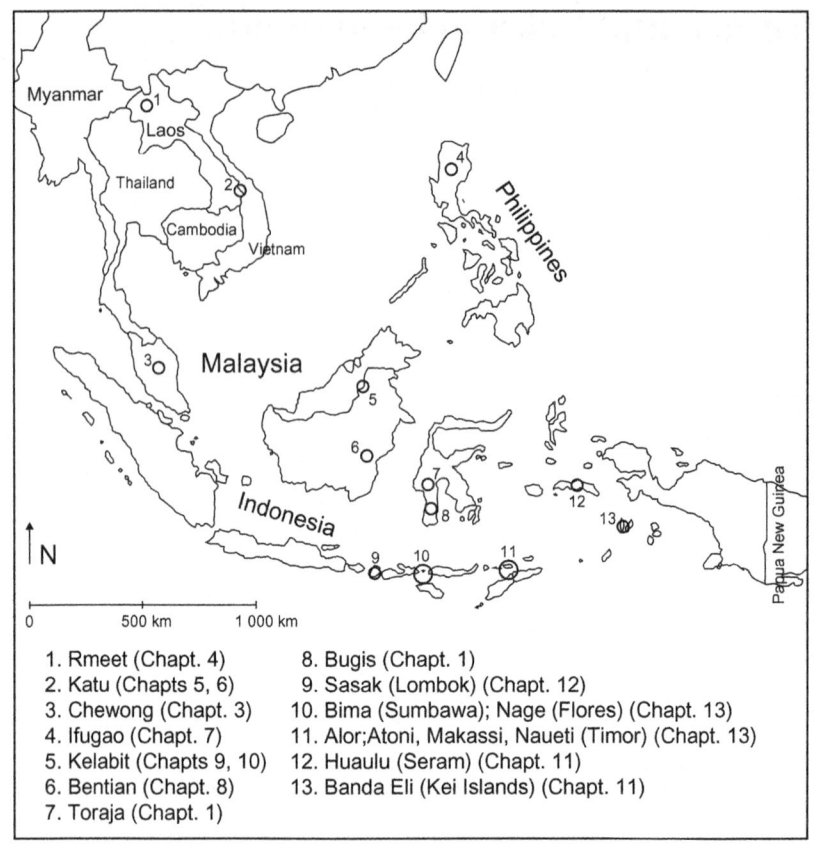

Figure 1 Southeast Asia showing the distribution of ethnic groups and localities described or discussed in the book.

1. Rmeet (Chapt. 4)
2. Katu (Chapts 5, 6)
3. Chewong (Chapt. 3)
4. Ifugao (Chapt. 7)
5. Kelabit (Chapts 9, 10)
6. Bentian (Chapt. 8)
7. Toraja (Chapt. 1)
8. Bugis (Chapt. 1)
9. Sasak (Lombok) (Chapt. 12)
10. Bima (Sumbawa); Nage (Flores) (Chapt. 13)
11. Alor;Atoni, Makassi, Naueti (Timor) (Chapt. 13)
12. Huaulu (Seram) (Chapt. 11)
13. Banda Eli (Kei Islands) (Chapt. 11)

Part 1
Introductory

1 Southeast Asian animism in context

Kaj Århem

Over the past two decades, the old concept of animism has been resurrected and given new meaning.[1] Divested of its obsolete evolutionist connotations, animism has come to stand for an alternative, non-modern ontology, a counterpoint to naturalism – the hegemonic cosmology of modernity. As such, it has travelled beyond the disciplinary boundaries of anthropology and religion and is now a widely used critical concept in the humanities and social sciences at large.[2] In anthropology, a host of studies on animism has emerged mainly dealing with indigenous peoples of the Americas and Northern Eurasia.[3] Old ethnographic texts are resuscitated and interpreted anew in light of the revitalized concept, yielding fresh insights into non-modern ontologies and epistemologies as well as contributing to the reshaping of the concept itself.

As opposed to naturalism, which assumes a foundational dichotomy between objective nature and subjective culture, animism posits an intersubjective and personalized universe in which the Cartesian split between person and thing is dissolved and rendered spurious. In the animist cosmos, animals and plants, beings and things, may all appear as intentional subjects and persons, capable of will, intention and agency. The primacy of physical causation is replaced by intentional causation and social agency. This preliminary outline of the concept will be fleshed out and critically examined in the course of this introductory chapter.

It is against the background of this refigured notion of animism that the ethnographic cases presented in the present volume should be read. The fact that ideas and practices conventionally identified with animism are still highly pertinent in Southeast Asia makes the topic all the more relevant. This pertains not just to the indigenous and local religions that are subject of most of the chapters in this volume, but also to non-doctrinal practices in societies adhering to world religions (e.g., Cederroth, Kaartinen, this volume; Endres and Lauser 2012), or to modern states and cities (e.g., Ong 1988; Johnson 2014), which are not covered here.

Yet, the new animism discourse has made little impact on anthropological scholarship in Southeast Asia. With few exceptions, (e.g., Allerton 2009; Aragon 2000; Bovensiepen 2014; Tsintjilonis 2004; and notably Howell, this volume), ethnographers of indigenous Southeast Asia have showed little interest in the theoretical and comparative issues raised by the ongoing animism debate. This is unfortunate although, to some extent, explainable; as will become evident in

4 *Kaj Århem*

the ensuing chapters, what we refer to as Southeast Asian animism, and what is known by this name in the classical regional literature, is quite different from the current understanding of animism.

However, this discrepancy should not detract Southeast Asianists from engaging with the concept. On the contrary, we suggest that a critical engagement with the current theoretical work on animism (and its companion concept, perspectivism) is potentially productive, not only in revising and expanding the present understanding of indigenous cosmologies and religion in Southeast Asia but also in challenging the current standard notion of animism itself. The present volume is an effort in this direction.

Its purpose is thus both theoretical and empirical. By presenting a series of case studies of what is broadly known as animism in the regional literature, the volume attempts to bring the ongoing theoretical and comparative conversation on animism to bear on a largely unexplored body of ethnography from mainland and insular Southeast Asia. In so doing, we hope to enrich the debate on non-modern ontologies in general and deepen and possibly reconfigure the regional discussion on indigenous cosmology and religion in Southeast Asia.

This and the following chapter outline the broader theoretical and ethnographic context framing the ensuing case studies. In this chapter, I first provide a review of current thinking on animism in anthropology and then, in the later part of the chapter, take a close and critical look at relevant regional literature on the topic – what I take to be the regional doxa on animism in Southeast Asia. In the next chapter, Guido Sprenger explores some analytical dimensions of animism in Southeast Asia designed to enable the systematic comparison of the case studies.

On the basis of the review of theoretical and regional discourses on animism in this chapter, I draw a general conclusion that will be developed in the following pages: that the predominant form of animism in Southeast Asia (the prototype) differs in significant respects from the current standard concept and therefore suggests an alternative to the standard notion – a broader concept of animism, understood as a continuum of phenomenal forms, ranging from an egalitarian or horizontal form (the standard notion) to a hierarchical or vertical type – what I refer to as hierarchical animism.[4]

The former, egalitarian type is the rare exception in Southeast Asia, here exemplified by the Chewong case (Howell, this volume), while the latter, hierarchical form is the prototype, exemplified by the majority of cases in the volume. As a phenomenal type, hierarchical animism does itself vary with increasing socio-political hierarchization – from moderately ranked societies ('hill tribes') to strongly hierarchical societies (principalities and kingdoms). The bulk of this introductory chapter will be devoted to substantiating this contention.

Animism: New and Old

Purged of its evolutionist content, the new animism concept has retained part of what we may call Tylor's phenomenological concept of animism, understood as a propensity among indigenous peoples worldwide to anthropomorphize non-human beings and things – i.e., the notion that not only human beings have soul (consciousness, will, intentions) but also animals, plants and a whole host of other objects and phenomena. As such, to Tylor, animism was a particular reality-posit – what he called a systematic 'philosophy of nature' (Tylor 1903: 169).

It seems to me that, in this largely sound characterization of a significant feature of indigenous cosmologies worldwide, there was an abortive intuition of a distinctive non-modern ontology which Tylor was unable to bring to fruition because of his grossly evolutionist stance. He thus attempted to explain the origin and development of religion with a speculative scenario, later known as his 'soul theory' of animism: the idea that the human soul – the awareness of an immaterial self or person derived from dreams and visionary experiences – was transposed onto non-human beings and things. According to this scenario, the generic idea of non-human souls (animism) with time evolved into the notion of personalized spirits and deities (polytheism) and, eventually, into monotheism.

Although Tylor's account of animism soon came under criticism for being psychological and excessively speculative, it was nevertheless immensely influential in anthropology and the study of religion well into the twentieth century. It deserves mentioning here because two of its features, which are lost to the new animism concept, are, I think, worth holding on to: first, Tylor's phenomenal account of animism was broad and inclusive, comprehending both the idea of a 'philosophy of nature' and the notion of elementary religion, and, secondly, it assumed a connection between the generic idea of the anthropomorphization of nature ('animate nature') and the conceptualization of spirits as autonomous subjects or agents – the stuff from which ('high') religion evolved.

I will return to the relevance of these two features of Tylor's intuition below; let me here only anticipate my argument by saying that the current standard notion of animism not only is a thoroughly revised version of Tylor's original intuition but also a considerably downscaled concept of animism – one that has severed the link with 'religion' or left it largely un-problematized.

*

In place of Tylor's evolutionist and speculative theory of animism, the refigured concept formulates animism as a distinctive ontology – a monistic alternative to naturalism. It dissolves the naturalistic distinction between nature and culture, things and persons, and posits the possibility of sentient nature – 'ensouled' plants, animals and natural objects. Animist cosmologies assume a 'social' cosmos populated by human and non-human persons (animals and plants), communicating and interacting with each other as autonomous subjects in an intersubjective field of relations.

In this cosmic society, subjectivity and intentional agency constitute the ultimate ground for being and order. However, animism also admits physical or 'natural' causation in the form of a naïve physics (Bloch 2012: 61), understood as an expression or epiphenomenon of the cosmic order which itself is intentionally constituted.

This qualification needs to be stressed: the anthropomorphic subjectivity of non-human beings and things is not a given or constant condition in the animist world; it is an emergent quality in particular situations and in specific human-environment relations (as developed by Sprenger in Chapter 2, this volume). Indeed, as various contributions in this volume argue, humanity itself is an emergent condition, not restricted to biological humans; it is a universal but contextual and relational condition. By the same token, humanity as a conditional quality may be lost or removed by ritual means: human enemies and strangers, just as animals, may, for example, be ritually dehumanized or desubjectified in order to be killed and/or consumed (Chapter 14, this volume; Fausto 2007; Praet 2014).

Animism, then, is an ontology very different from naturalism with which Western moderns are familiar – and yet it is an ontology which (a) assumes a notion of 'natural' order which in many of its pragmatic manifestations is consonant with the naturalistic worldview, (b) is perfectly consistent and coherent in terms of its own basic premises, and (c) in several respects offers an alternative view of human-environment relations which may potentially better account for fundamental features of the world than the currently reigning paradigm(s) of natural science (Hornborg 2006; Ingold 2000, 2011).

New Animism: Two Lines of Thought

In significant respects, the current understanding of animism was anticipated by Irving Hallowell in the 1960s. In a seminal paper on Ojibwa ontology (Hallowell 1960), he observed that the Ojibwa live in a thoroughly personalized cosmos. In their ontology there is no concept of physical laws of nature apart from intentional action and personalized agency. Nor is there a place for impersonal 'supernatural' forces, allegedly 'magically' influencing the events of the world, for the simple reason that there is no concept of 'nature' in the Western, naturalistic sense of the term (ibid.: 43–5). In this depiction of Ojibwa ontology, and though he did not use the term, Hallowell provided the main building blocks of the new animism concept.

The term itself, explicitly used in the new and refigured sense, resurged in the 1990s from two theoretical sources and developed along parallel lines of thought which, despite their differences, nevertheless converged on a largely similar phenomenal formulation of animism – what I refer to as the current standard notion. One line of thought, notably represented by Philippe Descola and Eduardo Viveiros de Castro, may be labeled structural; the other, represented here by Tim Ingold and Nurit Bird-David, I refer to as phenomenological.

Perspectivism and the Structural Approach

It is almost ironic that it was Philippe Descola, intellectual heir of Lévi-Strauss, who resurrected the term animism and thus reopened a theoretical debate which Lévi-Strauss had declared closed in his celebrated essay on totemism (Lévi-Strauss 1962), almost contemporary with Hallowell's Ojibwa paper. In a sequence of influential papers, Descola (notably 1992, 1996) recovered the term animism to characterize a cosmological type widespread in Amazonia and native America at large.

Initially Descola defined animism as the symmetrical inverse of totemism: a mode of conceptualizing nature in terms of the elementary categories of society. Thus, if totemism models society after nature, then animism models nature after society. However, Descola notes, there is a fundamental difference between the two modes of constructing the human-environment relationship: while totemism presupposes a metaphorical relation and, thus, a discontinuity between nature and culture, animism implies a metonymical continuity between the two orders. As opposed to totemism which, on Lévi-Strauss's account, treats natural species as signs, animism assumes animals and plants to be real 'persons': it endows natural beings with human dispositions and, thus, incorporates nature into the social domain. Animic cosmologies, says Descola, are in effect sociologies of nature.

This notion of animism as 'humanized nature' was developed in an original direction by Viveiros de Castro in his highly influential paper on Amazonian perspectivism (Viveiros de Castro 1998; cf. also Århem 1993). By perspectivism, Viveiros de Castro means a variety of animism, characteristic of many Amazonian indigenous groups, which not only posits the human-like subjectivity of animals (and other natural kinds) but develops the idea of a universalized subjectivity to the point of depicting a distinctive 'objective world' from the perspective of every significant living kind.

Very briefly, the defining features of perspectivism, as rendered by Viveiros de Castro, are: (1) humanity is regarded as the universal condition of being; all living beings and certain things are 'human' in the sense that they are subjects with a point of view (soul). (2) What differentiates humans from animals (and plants, etc.) and what distinguishes one kind of animal from another is its body – understood in the broad sense of a distinctive bodily form with distinctive capacities, habits and affects. The body defines the point of view to the effect that it determines what is seen (the identity of the objects perceived). Consequently, Viveiros de Castro identifies perspectivism as the somatic complement to animism.

Since the subjectivity (soul) of every kind of being is formally the same, (3) each being 'sees' the same world, structured in the same way as the human life world. But the identity of the beings and objects it sees differs, since the perceiver's perspective varies with its bodily form and affects: a prey animal perceives a human hunter as a jaguar or predatory spirit while a jaguar or spirit sees a human being as prey or 'food'. By the same token, what humans see as blood, jaguars perceive as manioc bread – the human staple food – and so on. Put differently, *the way* all beings see the world (and themselves) is the same, but *what* they see differs from species to species. (4) The point of view thus defines both self and other, subject and object.

Perspectivism, Viveiros de Castro emphasizes, is relational, not relativistic. Indeed, perspectivism differs from naturalism in precisely the sense that, while naturalism defines culture as particular (relative) and nature as general (universal), perspectivism posits the opposite: culture (soul, spirit) is universal and nature (body) is relative (varying with perspective and subject position). Thus, in a now famous formulation, Viveiros de Castro argues that while naturalism is multicultural, perspectivism is multinatural – it assumes one culture and multiple natures.

Descola's Typology

Little more than a decade after his initial reformulation of the notion of animism, Descola published his monumental study, *Beyond Nature and Culture* (Descola 2013 [2005]), in which he presents a fourfold typology of generic ontological types – animism, totemism, analogism and naturalism – under which he subsumes all historically and ethnographically known cosmologies. His point of departure is what he takes to be a universal cognitive dichotomy between 'interiority' and 'physicality' – self-reflexive inwardness, on the one hand, and the bodily endowments and dispositions enabling physical action, on the other.

Starting from this premise, there are four logically possible ways in which a hypothetical subject (self) may identify an Other in terms of similarity or difference: (1) shared interiority but different physicality (animism); (2) shared physicality but different interiority (naturalism); (3) shared interiority and physicality (totemism); and (4) different interiority and physicality (analogism).[5]

In this scheme, animism and naturalism are each other's mirror opposites and logical complements. Descola here rectifies his earlier formulation of animism as the conceptualization of nature in terms of social relations. In his new formulation, animism parallels (and comprehends) perspectivism as an ontology wherein humans and non-humans have the same kind of interiority but are differentiated by the bodies they inhabit. Naturalism, by contrast, posits a unifying nature (objective physical reality) and a multiplicity of subjectivities (culture-specific representations of nature); what differentiates is the mind, interiority or culture.

We may also note in passing that totemism here is characterized rather in line with its classical pre-structuralist rendering as a form of mystical 'participation' in nature. Explicitly distancing himself from Lévi-Strauss, Descola now defines totemism as the sharing of essence and substance, interiority and physicality, among the human and non-human members of a totemic class (or collective). I will return to analogism below since it bears significantly on the topic of the present volume. First, however, we need to briefly examine the cognitive premise of Descola's theoretical edifice.

*

In *Beyond Nature and Culture*, Descola not only formulates the definitive structural definition of animism which, in broad strokes, he shares with Viveiros de Castro, but also develops an epistemological position – one where he possibly parts company with Viveiros de Castro – on the basis of which he constructs his grand vision of a universal and timeless grammar of cosmologies.

Descola's project is to develop a theoretical framework that allows an objective understanding of other subjectivities, thus avoiding the pitfalls of the post-enlightenment nature/culture dualism. To this end, Descola turns to the psychological concept of cognitive schemas. Schemas – deep-seated and abstract schematizations of experience through which people perceive and interpret reality – are, he affirms, sufficiently general and abstract to allow a variety of specific cultural expressions and institutional forms. They are structural rather than cultural models.

The schemas that interest Descola are those that he calls integrating schemas: non-reflective, collective and internalized cognitive structures that constitute 'principal means of constructing shared cultural meanings' (Descola 2013: 103). He distinguishes two kinds of integrating schemas which he calls 'identification' and 'relations' (ibid.: 112). These two generic modes generate the 'grammar of cosmologies' he is looking for.

By mode of identification Descola means the ontological schemas constituting the four ontological types outlined above – the 'terms' by which reality is constituted. By mode of relations he means 'sociological schemas' specifying the relations between the 'terms' – the sociological expressions of a given ontological type (ibid.: 114). While the mode of identification (the ontological schemas) are at the forefront in Descola's study, he also discerns six possible modes of relations (sociological schemas) – giving, taking, exchanging and producing, protecting, transmitting – which may articulate the constituent entities of his four ontologies. Any single ontology can be combined with a variety of sociological schemas. What mode of relations goes with what type of ontology is a matter of empirical investigation.

The premise for Descola's entire theoretical edifice is that ontology logically precedes sociology (ibid.: 112, 124). He thus turns the Durkheimian sociological tradition – from Mauss to Mary Douglas – on its head. Descola posits that 'sociological realities (stabilized relational systems) are analytically subordinate to ontological realities (the system of properties attributed to existing beings)' since 'a relational system can never be independent from the terms that it brings together, if by 'terms' we mean entities endowed from the start with specific properties that render them either able or unable to forge links between one another [...]' (ibid.: 124). On this epistemological premise, Descola formulates his 'syntax for the composition of the world, from which the various institutional regimes of human existence all stem' (ibid.: 125).

Relational Epistemology and the Phenomenological Approach

From very different epistemological premises Tim Ingold and Nurit Bird-David have developed a concept of hunter-and-gatherer perception of the environment which, in phenomenal terms, is very similar to the notion of animism proposed by Descola. While Ingold has consistently been cautious about using the term animism for what he specifically refers to as the hunting-gathering mode of perceiving the environment (and, more generally, the 'dwelling mode'), Bird-David has explicitly adopted the term for the same idea – what she alternatively refers to as 'relational epistemology' (Bird-David 1999). Both of them have contributed significantly to shape the current concept of animism and the discourse surrounding it. I will refer to their closely related views as the phenomenological approach to animism.

Ingold's project involves a sustained critique of the dominant anthropological notion of cognition and of culturalist and constructivist tendencies in the discipline. The combined legacies of symbolic and ecological anthropology, Ingold argues, tend to reify the Western dichotomy between nature/culture and are, thus, singularly ill-suited to make sense of non-Western ways of life and thought. Hunter-gatherers, he asserts, do not perceive their environment via or through cultural images or conceptual constructs. There is no cultural or mental model intervening in their perception and cognition of the world; perception is cognition. Cosmology, he maintains, is a construct of Western modernity.

Therefore, to compare Western and non-Western cosmologies is wrong from the start. What should be compared are different ways of perceiving or apprehending the world. In Western tradition, a detached mode of apprehending the environment has crystallised into a dualist 'ontology of detachment', which is systematised as a cosmology or cultural representation of reality. Hunters and gatherers, by contrast, perceive their environment in the course of their active, practical engagement with it. Theirs is a monistic understanding of reality. This engaged mode of apprehending the world – which he, inspired by Heidegger, calls the 'dwelling perspective' – is tantamount to an 'ontology of engagement'; it does not amount to a view, or representation, *of* the world, but to take up a view *in* it (ibid.: 42, 216).

On Ingold's account, the Western nature/culture dichotomy is replaced by the person-environment dyad. The mind, he writes, subsists in the very involvement of persons in the world; it is never detached from it. Hunter-gatherers know the world through participating in it. Ingold seems to imply that an ontology of engagement, the world apprehended in a dwelling perspective, does in fact better describe the nature of reality than the Western dualist ontology of detachment. However, this active engagement with the environment yields not propositional but experiential and deeply personal – intuitive – knowledge. The person-environment relation is mutually constitutive. By contrast to conventional ecological thinking, the environment is not given or inert but alive and responsive. Hunter-gatherer ecology is a 'sentient ecology' (ibid.: 25).

As opposed to the Western ontological dualism between nature and culture, hunters-gatherers apprehend the word as unitary: humans, animals, plants and inanimate things all exist on a single ontological plane. They are ontological equals – persons. As such, animals and plants have will, intelligence and agency. Human personhood is only one of many (outward) forms of personhood. Thus, the relationship between human and non-human persons is one of inter-subjectivity or rather, says Ingold, one of interagentivity, since persons are not mere minds but whole beings (mind-and-bodies). The convergence between Ingold's phenomenology and Descola's animism is evident. But instead of Descola's 'society of nature', Ingold posits 'sociology as ecology' (ibid.: 60).

For hunters and gatherers, the person-environment relationship is not symbolic or metaphoric; it is not *modelled* on human sociality. It is inter-agentive because animals and plants are, in fact, *perceived* – not conceptually constructed – as persons. 'The constitutive quality of intimate relations with non-human and human components of the environment is one and the same' (ibid.: 47). The hunter-gatherer concept of the person is relational. Human and non-human persons are mutually constituted in the life process.

*

Ingold's understanding of hunter-gatherer perception/cognition and its relevance for the reconceptualization of animism is made lucidly explicit in Nurit Bird-David's influential paper on animism among the South Indian Nayaka (Bird-David 1999, cf. also her 1993 article). Animism, she argues, is *not* a strange religious belief system – the belief in nature spirits or animate nature – but a relational mode of knowing the world.

Drawing on her Nayaka ethnography, Bird-David makes several important points. Personhood, she asserts, is a relational and emergent quality of particular relationships. In Nayaka society, sharing is the basic organizing principle. It not only governs their social relationships but also their relationship with the environment and constitutes their concept of personhood: a person is one whom one shares with. Consequently, as Nayaka relate to animals and plants 'in a sharing mode' they actively constitute them as persons. It is *not* that non-human beings and objects are classified or categorically represented as persons and therefore treated as such. Rather, it is the other way round: as, when and because humans engage with particular animals, plants or inanimate objects in a sharing mode, they constitute them as persons.

She concretizes this affirmation by an illuminating discussion of the notion of spirits. In the Nayaka context, animals and things – elephants, stones and hills – are situationally perceived and treated as spirits. In their daily chores, Nayaka continuously attend to their environment, and when they perceive what is interpreted as a responsive sign from particular beings or objects, such objects are perceived as spirits. Spirits, then, are objects in their person-aspect; they objectify particular and personalized relationships with the environment.

In conclusion, she proposes that animism is best understood as relational epistemology – a specific way of knowing the world through relating to it. The responsive engagement with non-human beings and things as persons sharpen attention to, and increases knowledge about, the environment. On this account, animism makes people aware of the connectedness of the self and the environment.

Bird-David's condensed paper on animism powerfully concretises Ingold's dwelling perspective – his claim that hunters-gatherers universally affirm an 'openness to the world' whose contours and properties are emergent rather than given, relationally constituted in active engagement with a world in 'continuous birth' (Ingold 2011: 69). This fundamentally indeterminate and relational concept of cognition, which Ingold sees as characteristic of animism, is developed in his end comment to this volume.[6]

Divergences and Convergences: A Summing Up

In almost every respect, Ingold's (and Bird-David's) theoretical position would seem to contrast with that of Descola. The latter's whole project in *Beyond Nature and Culture* is premised on the logical primacy of ontology over sociology. The nature of the terms (the ontological properties of existing beings) determines the range of relational modalities that obtain between them. The phenomenological and radically relational view of Ingold and Bird-David seems to imply the opposite. In his end comment to the present volume, Ingold prefers to speak of animism not as a ready-formed ontology but rather as an ontogeny – a stance that is open to a world that is itself continuously in the process of becoming (see also Janowski, Remme, both this volume). In Ingold's relational world, nothing is given or preformed. If anything, relations would seem to logically precede the terms they constitute.

While Ingold's ecological-phenomenological understanding of the world privileges relations over form, process over product, becoming over being, Descola's cognitive-structural approach privileges form over process and terms over relations. On this view, ontological rather than ontogenic, ideas and patterns of behaviour are understood as the output of cognitive schemas and cultural models. The contrast with Ingold's relational ontogeny could not be greater.

And yet they converge on the phenomenal account of animism in terms of a world inhabited by human and non-human persons in intersubjective and inter-agentive communication with one another. In this perspective, the difference between the two views becomes one of figure and ground: what is figure to Descola is ground to Ingold – and vice versa.

Given that both Ingold and Descola – and the phenomenological and structural approaches they represent – define animism in terms of universalized subjectivity (what I take to be the *phenomenal* standard notion), their different views on animism boil down to a question of the ontological status of personhood: is personhood (human and non-human) ontologically given or is it an emergent, relational property of an undetermined world, ever in the process of formation?

New Animism and its Residue

The current concept of animism implies a significant reduction in scope of Tylor's original notion of animism as both 'philosophy of nature' and 'elementary religion'. On the one hand, there is a strong venatic slant to the standard concept (cf. Viveiros de Castro 1998) which is consistent with an assumption that animism posits an ontological equality between human and non-human beings/persons. The anthropomorphization of wild animals and the perception of animal alters as immanent subjects is diagnostic of the current concept. It is no wonder, then, that animism is associated predominantly with hunter-gatherers and horticultural societies where hunting plays a prominent role.

On the other hand, the emphasis on the body as cosmological differentiator seems to make any superior and transcendent subject – spirit or divinity – superfluous in the new animist cosmos. There is little elaboration of the human-spirit relation – what Viveiros de Castro (ibid.: 483) refers to as Supernature. The animist universe is understood as an egalitarian cosmic society of the segmentary type in which each living kind constitutes a tribe of human-like subjects – what Descola refers to as 'tribe-species'.

This horizontal and venatic notion of animism excludes vast swathes of the ethnographic world – including indigenous Southeast Asia – where human-animal relations are of minor cosmological concern while human-spirit relations are at the forefront of metaphysical reflection. Thus, a large range of societies that Sahlins (1968) has referred to as tribal societies fall outside the socio-political segment to which the current standard notion of animism applies. It excludes tribal societies of mixed farmers where agriculture and livestock husbandry dominate economy and motivate cultural imagination, societies which tend to be associated with the presence of modest rank distinctions and incipient hierarchy – in short, the range of societal forms located midway between the egalitarian and the hierarchical extremes of Sahlins' tribal continuum.

In other words, the new animism concept leaves a huge residue of non-modern cosmologies associated with tribal societies which, on Tylor's broad phenomenological characterization, were originally part of the animist universe and which early ethnologists treated as exemplary cases of animism.

Analogism

A considerable virtue of Descola's ontological typology is that he breaks away from the dualist mold by which most thinkers have formulated their ideas about animism and its conceptual cognates (primitive mentality, savage mind, participation, ontologies of engagement and the like) – all in opposition to naturalism or its equivalents. In Descola's rendering, however, animism is not naturalism's sole ontological other. Instead, he introduces three non-naturalistic ontologies, of which analogism is the broadest and possibly most controversial type. Under this label, Descola subsumes the large residue of tribal cosmologies falling outside the narrow concept of new animism – those associated with segmentary tribal societies on Sahlins' definition, notably in West and Central Africa and, as I will discuss in the following, Southeast Asia. A brief review of the concept of analogism is, therefore, pertinent.

To this end we need to unpack Descola's cryptic and empirically vacant definition of analogism – different interiority, different physicality – and picture a world where all existing beings are different from one another in both essence and substance, held together only by the postulated similarities and symbolic associations between them. Analogism assumes a cosmos whose constituents are divided up into a 'multiplicity of essences, forms and substances separated by small distinctions and sometimes arranged on a graduated scale' that links them 'into a dense network of analogies' (Descola 2013: 201). The doctrine of correspondences in ancient China and the 'great chain of being' of medieval Europe are paradigmatic cases in point.

The fact that every existing being is distinct from every other is totally at odds with the animist premise of a universalized subjectivity shared by human and non-human beings (ibid.: 213). On the same account, the prototypical animist image of the person as constituted by a constant inner being and a variable outer physical covering does not apply to the analogical ontology. Rather, beings and things – including human persons – are inconstant combinations of both essence and substance, each forming a unique alloy of multiple material and immaterial components (ibid.: 224). In fact, this distinctive analogical notion of being would seem to challenge the very basis of Descola's ontological typology – that of the universality of the dichotomy between interiority and physicality on which his entire theoretical edifice is erected.

There is 'nothing anthropomorphic about analogical systems', writes Descola, because 'the diversity of the parts that compose the systems is so great and their structure so complex that one single creature could not possibly constitute an overall model' (ibid.: 218).[7] Nevertheless, 'humans constitute a privileged cohort, for their persons offer a reduced and, therefore, manageable model of the relations and processes that govern the *mechanics of the world*' (ibid.: 226; my italics). And, by virtue of their privilege of imposing order and bringing meaning into the world, humans occupy a preponderant position in the analogical cosmos, superior to that of non-human creatures in the hierarchy of being (ibid.: 298). As opposed to the ontological equivalence between existing beings in animism, ontological hierarchy is constitutive of analogism.

For the same reason, the working of the analogical cosmos is typically made comprehensible and manageable by an impersonal and unintentional dynamics – analogical mechanics or 'symbolic physics' of sort – which Descola contrasts with the interpersonal intimacy and intersubjective relatedness of the animistic cosmos (ibid.: 323–5). Although Descola does not state as much, it seems to me that analogism operates on the principles of magic – Frazer's laws of sympathetic (homeopathic) and contagious magic respectively. The analogical ontology in Descola's scheme would seem to be one where naturalism's physical causality and animism's intentional causality are replaced by a 'magical' causality predicated on metaphorical and metonymical associations.

Yet, subjectivities or intentionalities – Descola's terms for souls and spirits – proliferate in the analogical universe, but they are fragmented and dispersed, refracted in a sundry of beings and objects. There is thus in analogism a 'universalism of diffused subjectivities that animate all things' (ibid.: 300) that, on Descola's account, is entirely different from the universalized subjectivity of animism. Hypostasized as personalized spirits, this diffused subjectivity inhabits the most diverse collection of beings and things (stones, trees, human persons ...), and reified as power, potency or vitality it reveals itself by its effects (witchcraft, sorcery, fertility, health and wealth ...).

Hierarchy is the fundamental structuring principle in analogical systems. On Descola's account, hierarchy is an 'expedient way of managing' the extraordinary proliferation and flux of singularities constituting the analogical cosmos (ibid.: 227). In this cosmos, the predominant relational schemes are those that presuppose asymmetry (non-equivalence) between terms – notably those referred to by Descola as relations of production, transmission and protection. Accordingly, the typical form of the analogical collective, the pre-modern state or chiefdom, is hierarchically organized according to the logic of segmentary nesting by which humans not only are hierarchically ordered among themselves (in castes or classes) but also connected to other beings from the infra-world to the heavens.

This ontological hierarchy and its political expression in the analogical polity is motivated and legitimized by the idea of an 'exceptional singularity' – a Supreme

Being, Mythical Ancestor or Divine Ruler – who hypostasizes the world collective and ensures the social and cosmic order (ibid.: 301). In the form of a Supreme Divinity, the exceptional singularity emerges as a Transcendent Subject – the absolute and totalizing subject missing among the mortal beings of the analogical universe. As such, the Supreme Being is the source of the diffuse and dispersed subjectivities that animates the analogical world, the generative source of life and vitality that suffuses the cosmos.

Analogical Institutions

On Descola's account, the analogical ontology is empirically identifiable by a distinctive complex of related ideas and institutions which include: a proliferation of mantic practices – divinatory modalities, sign-reading and elaborate ritual calendars; a diversity of ritual specialists including priests, oracles, mediums, geomancers and star-gazers/astrologists; an inordinate attention to the dead and the afterlife; ancestor worship, spirit possession and, above all, the institution of sacrifice. All of these features serve to 'cement together a world rendered fragile by the multiplicity of its parts' (ibid.: 227).

Similarly, Descola argues, sacrifice forges a relationship of contiguity between initially separate entities which need to be linked (referring here to an idea formulated by Lévi-Strauss (1966: 225). Just as ancestor worship, sacrifice expresses the hierarchical structure of the cosmos and the relation of protective dominance of spirits over living humans. It establishes the indispensable connection with the supreme subject (spirit and/or divine ruler) who ensures cosmic order and the reproduction of all life.

Descola here also advances his own theory of sacrifice: given that the killing of a sacrificial animal establishes a link with a transcendent power, the effectiveness of the sacrificial act 'stems from the fact that the victim [the sacrificial animal] is presented [to the deity] as a composite package of diverse properties some of which are identical to those of the sacrificant', while other properties are identical to those of the deity (Descola 2013: 230). It is precisely 'this decomposition of the victim's attributes, against the background of a general splitting of existing beings into a mass of components', Descola suggests, 'that allows it to serve as a link thanks to each actor in the rite identifying with at least one of its properties' (ibid.). Sacrifice, he implies, can thus be understood as an institution developed in the context of an analogical ontology (ibid.: 231).

*

Southeast Asian ethnography challenges Descola's typology on several scores. Perhaps the greatest challenge is that the majority of indigenous cosmologies in Southeast Asia share some features with both animism and analogism (as defined by Descola) while, at the same time, differing from both in other respects. Thus, the prototypical cosmology in indigenous Southeast Asia features an elementary form of the institutional complex that Descola holds to be diagnostic of analogism – ancestor worship, spirit possession, priesthood and sacrifice – but lacks the system of formal features constitutive of the analogical ontology – the idea of a fractured world reflected in a fragmented and unstable subject and held together by a dense web of stipulated analogies. Instead, Southeast Asian cosmologies tend to posit a universalized subjectivity, differentiated by degree and linking the existing beings in an asymmetric, hierarchical field of intersubjectivity which I, following Sahlins (2014), refer to as hierarchical animism.

On the basis of a review of Southeast Asian cosmologies, and drawing on contributions in the present volume, I propose a broadening of the current standard concept of animism. On this view, animism emerges as a phenomenal continuum ranging from its egalitarian standard form to a hierarchical type common in Southeast Asia (and possibly Africa). Concomitantly, I propose a narrowing of Descola's overly broad and inclusive category of analogism, reserving the term for its paradigmatic and codified form, functionally linked to pre-modern state formations.

The Challenge of Southeast Asian Ethnography

Indigenous Southeast Asia comprises a staggering diversity of ethno-linguistic groups (five super-stocks), ecosystems and livelihood adaptations, religions (including the five world religions) and social organization. Indigenous societal types range from mobile hunting-gathering bands and segmentary tribal communities to chiefdoms and autochthonous state formations. Cosmologies vary accordingly – from venatic animism of the standard format through various modalities of hierarchical animism to something close to the analogical type in Descola's scheme.

And yet, there are evident cultural and cosmological commonalities across this vast ethnographic region, suggesting a common and deep-seated cosmological base structure underlying the cultural diversity, and perhaps most clearly, manifest among the village-centered, rice-cultivating, and livestock-raising communities constituting the majority of indigenous societies in Southeast Asia.

A convenient starting point for reviewing the diverse cosmologies in the region is to identify their major modalities and map them onto the spectrum of societal types – from the hunting-and-gathering groups at the egalitarian end of the spectrum to the indigenous proto-states (such as the Bugis and Toraja polities in Sulawesi) at the hierarchical end of the spectrum whose inhabitants long since profess to one of the world religions – Buddhism, Islam, Hinduism or Christianity.

The venatic animism at the egalitarian end of the continuum is the rare exception in the Southeast Asian context. At the opposite extreme we find hierarchical animism in its most developed form – a type with several features in common with Descola's analogism. For reasons I hope to make clear in the following, I will alternatively refer to the two basic modalities of animism as immanent and transcendent animism respectively.[8]

Between these two extreme cosmological types there is an intermediate type which is best characterized as an elementary or generic form of hierarchical animism – the Southeast Asian base model or indigenous prototype associated with the moderately ranked segmentary societies that make up the majority of indigenous societies in the region (explored more fully in Chapter 14). A brief review of these cosmological modalities serves to substantiate my argument.

A Spectrum of Cosmologies

The Chewong (Howell, this volume), hunters and gatherers of Peninsular Malaysia, are prototypical animists according to the conventional definition; indeed, their cosmology is of the perspectivist variety characteristic of Amerindians. In the Chewong case, the perspectival elaboration is objectified in their notion that all beings with 'soul' have species-specific 'eyes' which literally define their vision of the world and distinguish each 'species' – human and non-human – from every other. As such, it is subtly apposite in so far as the eyes of a person objectify the interface between soul (inner being) and body (outer form).

In the manner of standard animism, the Chewong world is populated by different kinds of 'people' (subjects or 'personages' in Howell's vocabulary), distinguished by their species-specific bodies but identical in terms of soul (interiority) across the whole range of embodied subjects (and, in so far as spirits also have 'eyes', they also have bodies). Accordingly, animals are said to live in houses and settlements, subsist by hunting and gathering and have their proper ritual specialists. This generalized anthropomorphization of non-human beings assumes ontological equality between all living beings. The perception of animal alters as immanent subjects is the constitutive feature of this ontological type – hence immanent animism in my terminology.

In this horizontal cosmos of ontological equals, shamans and spirits stand out as exceptionally powerful persons, epitomized by their singular capacity of 'double vision'. Thus, while common persons only see the exterior form (bodily cloak) of existing beings, shamans and spirits also see the interior form – the human-like inner being. With this perceptive capacity comes the ability to metamorphose – to change body: shamans (who seem to be equated with spirits) can freely don the bodily cloak of other kinds of beings and see the world from the others' point of view. Bodily metamorphosis, then, is the shamanic way of knowing, attuned to an animist ontology where the body defines the identity of both subject and object in a perspectival world.

Upon death, powerful shamans are said to turn into tigers. In fact, Chewong hold that a shaman never dies; he only changes his bodily cloak and becomes a human tiger – a were-tiger.[9] When, by contrast, an ordinary human dies, he is buried in a simple grave with little ceremony, reminiscent of the way the dead in many parts of Amazonia are actively forgotten (see Chapter 14). A common idea in animist societies of the venatic variety is that as the body disintegrates, so does the person (soul). Between the living and the dead there is no social or metaphysical connection; the rupture is total.

*

The venatic or immanent animism of the Chewong contrasts with the cosmological type at the hierarchical end of the societal spectrum. Highly stratified Austronesian societies, such as the Bugis and Toraja in Sulawesi, are divided into ranked, hereditary classes of nobles, commoners and slaves. The Islamicized Bugis are organized in centralized polities comparable to the sultanates of the Malay Peninsula (Errington 1983). The rank structure is predicated on a notion of graded potency (*sumange'*): the higher the birth rank, the higher the degree of potency or life force.[10] The high rank of nobles is said to be physically manifested in their 'white blood' inherited from ancestor spirits and believed to be pure and intrinsically potent (ibid.: 559).

Because high-ranking people are intrinsically powerful, their very presence is assumed to have a protective and benevolent influence. But they may also be dangerous. Too close or inappropriate contact with a high-ranking person may inflict harm on a lower-ranking individual and vice versa. A person must know his/her appropriate place in society and act accordingly. Else, affliction may come from above as well as from below (ibid.: 568). Errington stresses that rank is the overriding structural principle in Bugis social universe, over-determining all other structuring templates and distinctions, including gender (ibid.: 569).

The neighboring Sa'dan Toraja are similarly stratified into three caste-like (endogamous and hereditary) classes: nobles, commoners and slaves. According to Tsintjilonis (2004), these classes are perceived as different 'natural kinds' of people; their creations or origins are different, their bodies differently constituted, and their bodily habits and appurtenances distinctive (ibid.: 441): the nobles were mythically created out of gold, the commoners from iron, and slaves from sugar-palm hearts. These intrinsic, 'naturalized' bodily attributes are understood as manifestations of the different degrees of potency (*sumanga'*) constitutive of each class, thus also legitimizing the social hierarchy. Classes of people are *essentially* different – different in spirit and, therefore, different in body.

Comparing the venatic (and perspectival) animism of the Chewong with the hierarchical cosmologies of the Bugis and Toraja, the horizontal segmentation of the former into different 'peoples' (tribes-species) is replaced in the latter case by a vertical grading of the human *socius* into ranked classes (or castes) – that is, different kinds of humans. Rank, in societies such as Toraja and Bugis, is thus naturalized in the sense that members of the same class are identified in terms of 'same spirit, same body' but sharply differentiated from members of other classes – as if they were different natural kinds.[11] The overriding ontological principle accounting for the hierarchical ordering of society and the cosmos seems to be 'different degrees of spirit/potency, different bodies'.

At the top of the traditional hierarchy is the Ruler (Bugis) or Sovereign (Toraja) embodying the supreme spirit. The Ruler of the domain (in the case of the Bugis) was not regarded as human; he was the supreme spirit incarnated (Errington 1983: 564). His role was to protect the entire realm 'which consisted of people (his followers) who served the Ruler in order to enjoy the benefits of fertility and prosperity that the *sumange'*, lodged in the Ruler, effected in all that surrounded it' (ibid.: 568). The passage appositely captures the underlying idea of the centralized

Austronesian polity: at the center of the realm was the Ruler whose divine power radiated outwards, blessing and protecting the people and the land. The Ruler was the life-giving 'soul' of the realm, the people and the land his 'body'.

The Cosmological Prototype

In between the polar types of the cosmological spectrum, there is the generic form of hierarchical animism characteristic of the broad category of sedentary and village-based mixed farmers. In Southeast Asia, the typical society in this category is the rice-growing and livestock-rearing community in which domestic animals have replaced wild game in terms of social, economic and ritual significance.[12] The cosmological type that goes with it represents the majority of upland and inland peoples on mainland and insular Southeast Asia and also predominates among the cases described in this volume (Rmeet, Katu, Ifugao, Kelabit and Bentian). It is commonly referred to as 'hill-tribe cosmology' (cf. Kirsch 1973). A brief summary of its main features permits us to flesh out the notion of hierarchical animism.

An outstanding feature of hill-tribe cosmology is the proliferation of spirits – nature spirits, ancestors and ghosts of all kinds (see, for example, the detailed account of spirits among the Bentian; Sillander, this volume). The universe of spirits tends to be hierarchically ordered with a Supreme Being – a transcendent subject – at the apex. It is typically part of a more comprehensive ontological hierarchy comprising also living physical beings and things, including humans, inserted between the spirits of the Upper World and the beings of Below (the dead, ghosts and spirits of wild animals and plants …).

This hierarchy is articulated in the idiom of sacrificing: humans sacrifice livestock (and in the past human heads and/or blood) to ancestors and superior spirits including the Owners of Land, Forest and Water. Wild animals, on their part, are often themselves regarded as the 'domestic animals' of the forest spirits (personified as Master and/or Keepers of Animals). Among the Katu, for example (Chapter 5), the successful hunt culminates in a communal ritual where the slain animal is presented as a sacrificial gift to the hunter's village which, in turn, ceremoniously offers the animal up to the village spirit. The hunt, then, is construed as a (double) sacrifice.

Sacrifice, then, is the central religious act in Southeast Asian societies. It expresses human dependence on, and submission to, the spirits but also a trust in their benevolence and the expectation of their blessings. In contrast to the symmetric intersubjectivity of human-animal relations in venatic animism, ontological intersubjectivity in the sacrificial animism of indigenous Southeast Asia is fundamentally asymmetric and centered on human-spirit relations.

With this goes a particular Southeast Asian form of perspectivism: the exchange of perspective between humans and spirits as opposed to the human-animal exchange in Amerindian and Siberian perspectivism. This perspectival exchange elaborates the different but homologous points of view of spirits and humans: to spirits, humans are contextually prey or livestock – i.e., spirit food – while, to humans, the superior spirits are variably either protective masters or ruthless predators.

The culturally integrated complex of livestock rearing and animal sacrificing is also the driving force in the 'ritual economy' of hill-tribe societies (Kirsch 1973; Friedman 1975). The possession of livestock, abundant crops and ritual valuables – large porcelain jars, gongs, bronze drums and woven, decorated textiles – confers on the owner power and distinction. Such ritual wealth is regarded as objectivized spirit power – an indication that the owner is blessed and protected by powerful spirits. Spirit power also manifests itself in good health and a large family.

The blessings of the spirits are gained by proper conduct – keeping to the precepts of the cosmologically underpinned social and moral order – and, above all, by continuously hosting animal sacrifices, the so-called 'feasts of merit'. Wealth, sacrifice and spiritual blessing are thus linked in an endless positive feed-back circuit. The implied reification of spiritual potency in the form of wealth, rank and worldly power – its acquisition and accumulation as well as its loss – is central to Southeast Asian cosmology and politics.

Ancestors play an exceedingly important role in upland Southeast Asian society and cosmology; little or nothing of importance is done without their consent (cf. Couderc and Sillander 2012). Ancestors – generally treated as an anonymous collectivity – are the collective subject to whom the living turn for support, guidance and protection. As sublimated and superior 'selves', the ancestors are said to live a life parallel to the living, in houses and communities of their own, tilling their own fields and hunting and fishing in the same forests and streams as their living descendants – invisible but tangibly influencing the affairs of the living. In this respect, the communities of ancestor spirits in the hierarchical cosmologies of Southeast Asia are reminiscent of the human-like societies of animal alters in the venatic animism of the Chewong (and indigenous America and Siberia).

It goes without saying that death is the object of profound and sustained intellectual reflection in Southeast Asian cosmology as well as the occasion for elaborate public rituals and ostentatious feasting. The funerary sequence, often involving secondary burial, is a major event literally bringing about the transformation of dead into ancestors. As such, it ensures the continuity between the living and the dead and the reproduction of society and life at large.

Another feature in Southeast Asian society, congruent with the salience of spirits and ancestors in indigenous cosmology, is the institution of spirit possession (discussed in some detail in Chapter 14). Suffice here to note that, in Southeast Asia, publicly recognized spirit mediums, serving as vehicles of ancestors and alien spirits, take over many of the functions of the typical Amerindian and Siberian shaman (cf. also the Chewong shaman). However, in spirit possession, the agency is shifted, as it were, from powerful humans (shamans) temporarily embodying animal spirits to the powerful spirits themselves, momentarily possessing their human vehicles (mediums and/or mediumistic healers).[13]

To round up this summary account of the basic features of transcendent animism in upland societies of Southeast Asia, the defunct practice of headhunting should be mentioned (see Chapter 14). The rationale for this formerly widespread form of institutionalized violence – a form of ontological predation analogous to war anthropophagy in Amazonia – was to capture the souls of strangers and enemy people and ritually incorporate them in the killers' community. The ritually incorporated soul of the victim, lodged in the head, was then offered on behalf of the killers' village to the superior spirits (the village spirit and/or the Supreme Being) to secure for the victorious villagers the blessings of the spirits.

It is significant that in Amazonian war anthropophagy, instead of the victim's soul being offered up to the divinities, his body was ritually consumed in the killer's village to empower its inhabitants. The different forms of ontological predation in Amazonia and Southeast Asia reflect the essential contrast between the prototypical forms of animism they represent: the immanent form of animism in Amazonia and the transcendent modality in Southeast Asia.

The Austronesian Doxa

If, as is evident, the cosmological prototype of indigenous Southeast Asia deviates in several respects from the current convention on animism, it is equally evident that Descola's concept of analogism is highly relevant for an understanding of cosmology and religion in the region. This is particularly so in light of the scholarly works on Austronesian cosmology and religion over the past thirty years or so. I refer to this body of work, which is impressively consistent in its treatment of the topic, as the regional doxa.

Southeast Asian ethnography contains several classical works on animism (in the broad Tylorian tradition) written in the early decades of the twentieth century. They include Skeat's (1900) standard work on Malay magic and Kruyt's (1906) volume on animism in Insular Southeast Asia as well as later works by Cuisinier (1926, 1951), Adriani and Kruyt (1950–51) and Winstedt (1961), which have served as sources for more recent writers such as Endicott (1970), Benjamin (1979) and Fox (1987), to mention only a few.[14]

In all this work, the notion of spiritual potency or life force emerges as a shared idea that connects upland and lowland, mainland and insular Southeast Asia. Endicott's comprehensive analysis of Malay folk religion (Endicott 1970) focuses on the fundamental Malay concept of *semangat* as the key to Austronesian traditional religion and worldview at large. He shows that the notion of *semangat* refers to an all-pervading and impersonal vital force or energy. This vital force animates the entire universe – beings and things, natural objects and phenomena as well as artefacts.

In its most inclusive sense, *semangat* thus imbues everything that exists with life, potency and agency. However, this inclusive concept is contextually differentiated into at least three distinct (and increasingly specific) notions corresponding to three semantic levels of the generic concept. At the first level, the term distinguishes between embodied soul (*semangat*) and what Endicott refers to as 'free spirits' *hantu* – disembodied spirits which may inhabit or take up their abode in physical objects and beings.

This dichotomy between soul and 'free spirit' indicates an ontological distinction between, on the one hand, the world of visible, material beings and objects (which have soul) and, on the other, the immaterial and invisible realm of 'pure essence' (which includes both souls and free spirits in essential form). Endicott stresses that the material world of objects and the essential world of souls and spirits constitute aspects of the same reality. Every object has a spirit aspect (soul) while free spirits (*hantu*) have a capacity – indeed, propensity – to manifest themselves in and through material objects and phenomena. These two contrastive realms can be envisioned as two parallel planes of existence whose beings – embodied souls and bodiless (free) spirits – form distinct but complementary aspects of the generic notion of *semangat* (cf. Benjamin 1979; also Janowski, this volume).

At a second level of differentiation, 'ensouled' beings and objects are subdivided into what we would classify as animate beings ('with breath') and inanimate objects (that 'lack breath') – except that the latter category, apart from rocks and stones also comprises plants and 'lower animals'. Death is conceived of as the 'loss of breath'. It is this objectified aspect of the generic soul – 'breath' or *nyawa* – that turns into ghost at death. At a third level of differentiation, human beings are set apart from all other living and breathing beings in that they alone have *rôh* (consciousness, self-awareness), which distinguishes men from animals.

Depending on context, Endicott concludes, one or the other aspect of *semangat* may be emphasized to either separate man from the rest of creation or unite him with it. The differentiation of the concept corresponds to 'successive stages in the differentiation of the soul material of man' (ibid.: 79). At the most inclusive level, the idea of life force unites all beings and things. As such it constitutes, in Endicott's words, 'a single unitary essence that is diffused throughout creation […] more or less individualized in the myriad of visible things and forms of life' (ibid.: 45).

*

Later works paint a similar picture of traditional Austronesian religion and cosmology, sustaining the same fundamental idea of an impersonal vital force or creative energy animating the entire cosmos. In a widely cited review of traditional religion in insular Southeast Asia, Fox (1987) formulates this idea in terms of the 'immanence of life' which can be said to articulate the doxic view on Austronesian animism. By this notion he means that life is present and manifest in all physical forms and phenomena: 'There is a plurality of beings and, at the same time, a recognition of the oneness of the individual with the whole in the community of life' (ibid.: 524).

The scholarly understanding of traditional Austronesian cosmology – expressed by the idea of 'the immanence of life' – is thus one which stresses cosmological continuity across the whole spectrum of societal and cultural types from the mobile hunter-gatherer bands to the complex and stratified traditional kingdoms and sultanates. But hardly life in the biological sense; rather it is a notion of animacy in the classic animistic sense of anthropomorphic consciousness, subjectivity and agency – but one that is much broader than the current standard concept and, in Fox's words (ibid.: 526), ultimately amounts to 'a celebration of spiritual differentiation'.

Thus, the spectrum of Southeast Asian cosmologies outlined above, Fox's differentiated immanence of life, and Endicott's analysis of the Malay concept of *semangat* that sets 'man' apart from and above all other beings of the cosmos, suggest a differentiated and hierarchical notion of soul/spirit – a 'differentiation of the soul material of man' (Endicott, op. cit.) – which points in the direction of Descola's analogical type.

Hill-Tribe Cosmology on the Mainland

According to Kirsch's (1973) seminal, though now somewhat dated, comparative analysis of hill-tribe cosmologies in Mainland Southeast Asia, these are similarly predicated on a fundamental notion of potency/fertility. Following Leach (1964), Kirsch notes that hill-tribe societies range between two socio-political extremes – a 'democratic' and an 'autocratic' type.[15] In the former, status differentiation between households and lineages tends to be limited, and competition between them intense. In the latter, status and ritual privileges are increasingly concentrated to particular lineages, and status differentiation is marked. Accordingly, status tends to become hereditary in particular lineages.

Kirsch takes the democratic version of the system to be the basic model of hill-tribe cosmology, the autocratic type being an extreme development of it. Contrary to Leach, he does not locate the source of the political dynamic in hill-tribe society in a universal notion of power but in a specific cultural and religious notion of potency/fertility common to the upland groups. More recently, Durrenberger and Tannenbaum (1989) have argued that the pursuit of spiritual potency and protection also unifies village-based upland groups and the Buddhist Shan principalities in the lowland.[16]

What is more, the similarities between Kirsch's account of hill-tribe cosmology centered on potency/fertility and Fox's characterization of traditional Austronesian religion in terms of 'immanence of life' are striking. They also echo Benedict Anderson's classic formulation of the Javanese idea of power as 'that intangible, mysterious, and divine energy which animates the universe' and is 'manifested in every aspect of the natural world, in stones, trees, clouds, and fire, but [...] quintessentially in the central mystery of life, the process of generation and regeneration' (Anderson 1990: 22). And just as the notion of potency unifies the upland societies of the Mainland and link them to the valley principalities, so Fox's 'immanence of life' underpins all traditional Austronesian cosmologies, and the Javanese concept of power, in Andersons's rendering, 'provides the basic link between the 'animism' of the Javanese villages, and the high metaphysical pantheism of the urban centers' (ibid.: 22).

The relevance of these observations to the present argument is that Kachin and Shan correspond to different cosmological modalities along what I take to be an animism-analogism continuum – from hierarchical animism in its two hill-tribe modalities roughly corresponding to Leach's rendering of Kachin *gumlao-gumsa* types – to the analogism associated with pre-modern state formations such as the Shan principalities and the Javanese kingdom, with the Bugis-Toraja examples positioned in between.

*

Kirsch's probing analysis, furthermore, provides some highly relevant details on hill-tribe notions of potency/fertility (which I can only summarize here). At one level, he demonstrates, potency can be interpreted as a contextual rendering of 'soul', or an aspect of the soul, intrinsic to a being/object – similar to the notion of *semangat*. As such it is a defining attribute or quality of the being/object, but one that may be weaker or stronger along a graded scale of potency. At another level, it represents an attribute originating from outside the person or object associated with it, acquired from an external source and usually perceived as a spirit – a personalized hypostasis of the attribute in question: courage, ambition, cunning, strength of will, hardness and so on.

Now, both as an aspect of soul (interiority, subjectivity, personhood ...) and as an attribute deriving from an external source and identified with a spirit, the notion of potency tends to be reified as something concrete or substantial – essence, soul material, force, energy – which is detachable from the subject/object with which it is associated. This substantive quality of potency is conducive to its differentiation or 'quantification' in terms of a graded scale of power. Thus, Kirsch speaks of the hill-tribe notion of personhood as a *'theory of unequal souls'*. This hierarchical differentiation of subjectivity/power – which, I propose, is characteristic of hierarchical animism in Southeast Asia as a whole – is carried to its extreme in stratified polities such as those of the Bugis and Toraja where *sumange'/a'* (power/vitality/soul) is objectivized ('naturalized') as innate bodily form and affects.

Potency – both in its intrinsic and acquired form – is regarded to have effects which are caused by intentional as well as impersonal (magical) agency. If, as Anderson (1990: 79) suggests, notions of power essentially are metaphors for causality answering the question 'why things happen as they do', then the hill-tribe notion of potency, the Austronesian *semangat* or 'immanence of life' and Javanese power all express the idea of social or intentional causation (characteristic of animism) *and* the notion of magical and impersonal causation (typical of analogism).

The 'theory of unequal souls' not only sets humans apart and above other beings but also, as we have seen, allows the grading of humans into ranked categories (nobles, commoners and slaves). This graded concept of human personhood would also seem to imply a particular 'theory of unequal bodies': On the hill-tribe assumption that the degree of potency is manifested in a man's wealth and prosperity, this wealth and prosperity can be regarded as an external, socially achieved 'body' – the bodily cover of the inner person – in analogy with the ranked natural body in hierarchical societies such as the Bugis and Toraja. But whereas the ranked body among the latter is assumed to be fixed and innate (natural), the external (social) body of hill-tribe persons – their wealth – is ephemeral and changeable, varying with the fluctuations of luck, blessing and inner potency.

In this perspective, the entire hill-tribe ritual economy can be interpreted as a means of constituting complete persons in a metaphysical environment of graded personhood – a progressive construction *not* of the body (as in Amazonian cosmology) but of the differentiated 'soul' as both the basis for the spiritual matrix of bodily constitution and the ritually acquired external body manifest as wealth and prosperity.[17] Along the continuum from segmentary hill-tribes to centralized valley kingdoms and principalities, rank is increasingly naturalized and internalized. Potency as rank becomes innate and hereditary, objectified not only in wealth and privileges but also in the physical being.

Hierarchical Animism

The proposition that animates this volume and justifies its title is that the majority of indigenous groups of Southeast Asia represent a particular variety of animism. I call this variety hierarchical animism. Like standard animism, hierarchical animism posits a universalized subjectivity – but one that is graded along a vertical scale rather than segmented along a horizontal plane. While, in standard animism, beings are integrated by a principle of symmetric intersubjectivity between ontologically equivalent beings and differentiated along a somatic axis on the formula 'same spirit (interiority), different body (physicality)', in hierarchical animism beings are integrated by a principle of asymmetric intersubjectivity between 'unequal souls' and differentiated according to the formula 'different degrees of spirit/potency, different body'.

The two modalities can be seen as contrastive permutations of each other. The focus on the body and bodily differentiation in the standard form is shifted to a focus on spirit and spiritual differentiation (contextually reified as potency) in the hierarchical form. Concomitantly, the salience of shamanism and bodily metamorphosis in the former is replaced by spirit possession and mediumship in the latter. The probing attention to the living environment– wild animals and plants – in venatic animism is shifted to a consuming concern with ancestors and the afterworld; hence, my alternative rendering of hierarchical animism as transcendent animism to distinguish it from the immanent or somatic bent of the standard notion.

Instead of death implying a rupture with deceased relatives, as in immanent animism, the continuity between the living and the dead is a fundamental structuring template in transcendent animism. And instead of the ritual concern with prey animals in venatic animism, domestic animals take pride of place in transcendent animism as sacrificial gifts to the spirits, signaling the difference between a venatic ontology predicated on predation and a sacrificial one centered on transcendent subjects. In all these respects, the prototypical cosmology of indigenous Southeast Asia represents a transcendent permutation of immanent animism – a shift towards transcendent subjects and an asymmetric relational matrix of dominance and submission epitomized by the institution of sacrifice.

In sum, where standard animism posits a horizontal, egalitarian and symmetric cosmos, Southeast Asian cosmologies assume a vertical, ranked and graded cosmos in which objects contextually present themselves as subjects and vice versa but where all subject-objects, human and non-human, are graded in terms of degree of power and agency. Spirit, personified as subject or reified as power, is here the integrator but also the differentiator – by degree rather than kind. The 'body', in hierarchical animism extended to include livestock and other forms of wealth, is also a manifestation of difference – but only as an objectification and material expression of the differentiated spirit.

*

No doubt Descola would refer to hill-tribe cosmology in its elementary, 'democratic' form as a stabilized hybrid between animism and analogism and to its extreme, 'autocratic' form as incipient, or even typical, analogism. However, apart from a certain reluctance to adopt the unwieldy concept of analogism (and the awkward notion of hybridity), it seems to me, for reasons already given, that the notion of hierarchical or transcendent animism is a more apt term in the present context – not least since it is uncommitted to any of the two grand theoretical projects that energize the new animism debate. The concept of hierarchical animism expands the standard concept which, in my view, is unnecessary narrow, and captures what they have in common – the universalization of subjectivity or personhood – as well as what distinguishes them – the hierarchical grading of subjectivity or personhood in the hierarchical form.[18]

Having said this, and as implied by the foregoing, I find it provisionally useful to retain Descola's notion of analogism in a considerably trimmed-down version to refer to an ontological type displaying its distinctive features – a hierarchical cosmos fractioned into innumerable constituent parts, linked only by a symbolic physics of postulated analogies – but reserving it for the type associated with mature pre-modern state societies. As such, the analogical cosmology emerges as a codification of associative thinking into a systematic conceptual construct which bears the imprint of a class of ritual specialists in a complex and, perhaps, partly literate society.

However, I don't go as far as Sahlins in his recent commentary to Descola's ontological typology. On Sahlins' (2014) account, the notion of hierarchical animism encompasses or replaces Descola's concept of analogism. His argument for a broadening of the notion of animism is similar to the one I have forwarded here, namely that the ethnographic record of a number of 'analogical' cosmologies suggests that they are better understood in terms of a universalized subjectivity or generic anthropomorphization of the world. But just as I limit Descola's notion of analogism, I reduce Sahlins' concept of hierarchical animism – reserving it for the 'tribal' segment in his 1968 typology of socio-political formations.[19]

If nothing else, the continuum model of animism that I propose – expanding the standard concept while reducing Sahlins' very broad notion – has a pedagogical and heuristic value in so far as it may be correlated to Sahlins' typology of socio-political forms. Superimposing my formulation of the animism-analogism continuum on this still very useful developmental typology, animism would correspond to the broad but analytically bounded segment encompassing hunting-and-gathering and segmentary tribal societies while passing into analogism at the point where tribal chiefdoms turn into pre-modern state formations.

Notes

1. I have benefitted greatly from Guido Sprenger's comments on earlier versions of this chapter. If it were not for his tough but necessary pruning of the text, the chapter would have been even longer.
2. The recent animism debate has had significant impact on science and technology studies, political economy/ecology and material culture studies; e.g., Henare et al. (2007); Hornborg (2006, 2014 and 2015); Latour (2009, 2010).
3. Notably works by Descola, Viveiros de Castro and Fausto, and contributions in Pedersen et al. (2007); Brightman et al. (2012); and Harvey (2013) (see References).
4. Hugh-Jones (1996) proposed the terms horizontal and vertical shamanism to make a rather different point in relation to the phenomenology of Amazonian shamanism. My use of the terms in the present context will become clear in the course of this chapter. The term hierarchical animism I borrow from Sahlins (2014) but use in rather more strict sense, as is explained in the latter part of this chapter.
5. Descola's matrix is a perfect analogue to Lévi-Strauss' table of permutations by which he defines totemism as a particular combination of relations between two series of terms – one natural, the other cultural (Lévi-Strauss 1962: 17).
6. In a recent work, Istvan Praet (2014) develops a basically phenomenological view of animism in a new and original direction. While retaining a relational notion of life and personhood, he claims an analytical space for culture and cultural meaning in the analysis of animism that is underplayed in Ingold's approach.
7. See also Descola's (2014) refutation of Sahlins' (2014) argument that the totalizing subject typical of analogical thought is best understood as a magnified anthropomorphic subject.
8. My use of the term transcendent animism is quite different from Holbraad and Willerslev's (2007) notion of transcendent perspectivism referring to Siberian/Mongolian cosmologies.
9. As will be discussed in Chapter 14, the notion of were-tigers also occurs in hierarchical animism but, I argue, in a different institutional and semantic context.
10. Errington alternatively translates *sumange'* as energizing life-spirit or vital energy.
11. The relation between members of the same class is one of totemic identity in Descola's (2013) sense which brings to mind Lévi-Strauss' (1966) earlier analogy between totemism and the caste system – the latter an analogical structure in Descola's typology.
12. Nevertheless, hunting may also be of considerable social and ritual importance in livestock rearing societies as evidenced in various chapters in this volume (particularly Chapters 4 and 5).
13. The term shaman is also frequently used for mediumistic healers in Southeast Asia although the latter operate according to a logic different from that of the metamorphosing shaman in Amazonia (as discussed in Chapter 14, this volume).
14. For additional references to early works on animism in Southeast Asia, see Chapter 2.
15. Kirsch also assumes, like Leach, the historical oscillation between the two types – an assumption that today is controversial but irrelevant for the present discussion.
16. I owe this observation to Sprenger (pers. comm.).
17. This specifically Southeast Asian notion of personhood is the conceptual premise for animal sacrifice: livestock are vicarious persons, "the self as body". This notion, as pointed out to me by Guido Sprenger (pers. comm.) also fits well with the "house societies" of Eastern Indonesia, where heirloom valuables embody the rank of the house (Waterson 1995).
18. This contention provides an alternative perspective on the transformation of the human-animal relationship implied by the transition from hunting to animal husbandry (see Ingold 2000: 75; Naveh and Bird-David 2014).
19. Sahlins' (2014) broad notion of animism comprises also totemism under the category "segmentary animism".

References

Adriani, N. and Kruyt, A. C. (1950–1) *De Bare'e Sprekende Toradjas van Midden-Celebes*, I–III, Verhandelingen der Koninklijke Nederlandse Akademie van Wetenschappen, Amsterdam. (Also available in English translation in *Human Relations Area Files* [1968], Yale University).
Allerton, C. (2009) 'Spiritual Landscapes of Southeast Asia', Special Issue, *Anthropological Forum*, 19(3).
Anderson, B. (1990) *Language and Power: Exploring Political Cultures in Indonesia*, Ithaca, NY: Cornell University Press.
Aragon, L.V. (2000) *Fields of the Lord: Animism, Christian minorities and state development in Indonesia*, Honolulu, HI: University of Hawai'i Press.
Århem, K. (1993) 'Ecosofia makuna', in F. Correa (ed.) *La selva humanizada: ecología alternativa en el trópico húmedo colombiano*, Bogota: ICAN.
Benjamin, G. (1979) 'Indigenous Religions of the Malayan Peninsula', in Becker and A. Yengoyan (eds.) *The Imagination of Reality: Essays in Southeast Asian Coherence Systems*, 9–27.
Bird-David, N. (1993) 'Tribal metaphorization of human-nature relatedness', in K. Milton (ed.) *Environmentalism: The View from Anthropology*, London: Routledge.
———. (1999) '"Animism" Revisited. Personhood, Environment, and Relational Epistemology', *Current Anthropology*, 40 (supplement): 67–91.
Bloch, M. (2012) *Anthropology and the Cognitive Challenge*, Cambridge: Cambridge University Press.
Bovensiepen, J. (2014) '*Lulik*: taboo, animism, or transgressive sacred? An exploration of identity, morality and power in Timor-Leste', *Oceania*, 84(2): 121–37.
Brightman, M., Grotti, V.E., and Ulturgasheva, O. (eds.) (2012) *Animism in Rainforest and Tundra: Personhood, Animals, Plants and Things in Contemporary Amazonia and Siberia*, New York, NY: Berghahn Books.
Couderc, P., and Sillander, K. (eds.) (2012) *Ancestors in Borneo Societies: Death, Transformation, and Social Immortality,* Copenhagen: NIAS Press.
Cuisinier, J. (1951) *Sumangat: l'ame et son culte en Indochine et en Indonésie*. Paris: Gallimard.
Descola, P. (1992) 'Societies of nature and the nature of society', in A. Kuper (ed.) *Conceptualizing Society*, London: Routledge.
———. (1996) 'Constructing natures: symbolic ecology and social practice', in P. Descola and G. Pálsson (eds.) *Nature and Society: Anthropological Perspectives*, London: Routledge.
———. (2013) *Beyond Nature and Culture*, Chicago: The University of Chicago Press.
———. (2014) 'The grid and the tree: reply to Marshall Sahlins' comment', *HAU: Journal of Ethnographic Theory*, 4(1): 295–300.
Durrenberger, E.P., and Tannenbaum, N. (1989) 'Continuities of Highland and Lowland Religions of Thailand', *Journal of the Siam Society*, 77(1): 83–90.
Endicott, K. (1970) *An Analysis of Malay Magic*, Singapore: Oxford University Press.
Endres, K., and Lauser, A. (eds.) (2012) *Engaging the Spirit World: Popular Beliefs and Practices in Modern Southeast Asia*, Oxford and New York, NY: Berghahn.
Errington, S. (1983) 'Embodied *sumange*' in Luwu', *Journal of Asian Studies*, 42(3): 545–70.
Fausto, C. (2007) 'Feasting on people. Eating animals and humans in Amazonia', *Current Anthropology,* 48(4): 497–530.

Fox, J. (1987) 'Southeast Asian Religions: Insular Cultures', in M. Eliade (ed.) *The Encyclopedia of Religion, Vol. 13*, New York, NY: Macmillan Publishing Company, 520–30.

Friedman, J. (1975) 'Religion as economy and economy as religion', *Ethnos*, 40(1–4): 46–63.

Hallowell, A.I. (1960) 'Ojibwa ontology, behavior, and world view', in S. Diamond (ed.) *Culture in History: Essays in Honor of Paul Radin*, New York, NY: Columbia University Press.

Harvey, G. (ed.) (2013) *The Handbook of Contemporary Animism*, Acumen Publishing Ltd.

Henare, A., Holbraad, M., and Wastell, S. (eds.) (2007) *Thinking Through Things: Theorising Artefacts Ethnographically*, London: Routledge.

Holbraad, M., and Willerslev, R. (2007) 'Transcendental perspectivism: anonymous viwpoints from Inner Asia', *Inner Asia*, 9: 329–45.

Hornborg, A. (2006) 'Animism, fetishism, and objectivism as strategies for knowing (or not knowing) the world', *Ethnos*, 7(1): 21–32.

———. (2014) 'Technology as fetish: Marx, Latour, and the cultural foundations of capitalism', *Theory, Culture and Society*, 31(4): 810–23.

———. (2015) (forthcoming) 'Artefacts, agency and global magic: how Amazonian 'ontologies' can illuminate human-object relations in Industrial Modernity', *HAU: Journal of Ethnographic Theory*.

Hugh-Jones, S. (1996) 'Shamans, prophets, priests and pastors', in N. Thomas and C. Humphrey (eds) *Shamanism, History and the State*, Ann Arbor, MI: The University of Michigan Press.

Ingold, T. (2000) *The Perception of the Environment: Essays on Livelihood, Dwelling, and Skill*, London: Routledge.

———. (2011) *Being Alive: Essays on Movement, Knowledge and Description*, London: Routledge.

Johnson, A. (2014) *Ghosts of the New City. Spirits, urbanity, and the ruins of progress in Chiang Mai*, Honolulu, HI: University of Hawai'i Press.

Kirsch, A.T. (1973) *Feasting and social oscillation: Religion and society in Upland Southeast Asia*, Ithaca, NY: Cornell University Press.

Kruyt, A.C. (1906) *Het Animisme in den Indischen Archipel*, den Haag: Martinus Nijhoff.

Latour, B. (2009) 'Perspectivism: 'type' or 'bomb''? *Anthropology Today*, 25(2): 1–2.

———. (2010) [2009] *On the Modern Cult of the Factish Gods*, Durham, NC: Duke University Press.

Leach, E. (1964) [1954] *Political Systems of Highland Burma: A study of Kachin social structure*, London: G. Bell and Sons, Ltd.

Lévi-Strauss, C. (1962) *Totemism*, London: Merlin Press.

———. (1966) *The Savage Mind*, The University of Chicago Press.

Naveh, D., and Bird-David, N. (2014) 'How persons become things: economic and epistemological changes among Nayaka hunter-gatherers', *Journal of the Royal Anthropological Institute*, 20: 74–92.

Ong, A. (1988) 'The Production of Possession: Spirits and the Multinational Corporation in Malaysia', *American Ethnologist*, 15(1): 28–42.

Pedersen, M., Empson, R., and Humphrey, C. (eds.) (2007) 'Inner Asian Perspectivism', *Inner Asia*, 9 (Special Issue).

Praet, I. (2014) *Animism and the Question of Life*, London: Routledge.

Sahlins, M.D. (1968) *Tribesmen*, New Jersey, NJ: Prentice-Hall, Inc.

———. (2014) 'On the ontological scheme of *Beyond Nature and Culture*', *HAU: Journal of Ethnographic Theory*, 4(1): 281–90.

Skeat, W.W. (1900) *Malay Magic: An Introduction to the Folklore and Popular Religion of the Malay Peninsula*, London: Macmillan and Co., Ltd.

Tsintjilonis, D. (2004) 'The flow of life in Buntao: Southeast Asian animism reconsidered', *Bijdragen tot de Taal-, Land- en Volkenkunde*, 160(4): 425–55.

Tylor, E.B. (1903) *Primitive Culture* (Vol. II), London: John Murray.

Viveirosde Castro, E. (1992) *From the Enemy's Point of View: Humanity and Divinity in an Amazonian Society*, Chicago, IL: University of Chicago Press.

———. (1998) 'Cosmological deixis and Amerindian perspectivism', *Journal of the Royal Anthropological Institute*, 4: 469–88.

Waterson, R. (1995) 'Houses and hierarchies in Island Southeast Asia', in J. Carsten and S. Hugh-Jones (eds.) *About the House: Lévi-Strauss and Beyond*, Cambridge: Cambridge University Press.

Winstedt, R.O. (1961) *The Malay Magician: Being Shaman, Saiva and Sufi*, London: Routledge and Kegan Paul.

2 Dimensions of animism in Southeast Asia

Guido Sprenger

Generalizing about animism in Southeast Asia is a difficult enterprise,[1] given the notorious diversity of cultural representations and social institutions in the region. However, the islands and the mainland areas which were shaped by external, mostly maritime trade, oscillating power centres and overlapping waves of religious influence are markedly different from the stateless societies of Melanesia and Australia, the expansive apparatus of the Chinese empire and the Hinduist sphere of India. Therefore, looking for commonalities uniting the region might be a fertile undertaking. In the first part of this introduction, Kaj Århem proposes a continuum of general features of Southeast Asian animism, setting it within a global comparative framework of cosmologies and ontologies. I will, in the second part, undertake a complementary effort. I will try to turn diversity into an asset by approaching Southeast Asian sociality as being based on the dynamic production of alterities. Within this dynamic, certain dimensions stand out which are correlated with each other and might allow a comparative description of case studies in the region. I am thus proposing a toolkit of analytical terms which might help to systematize the differences defining the region.

A few remarks on the history of the term should lead up to this effort. On several levels, the original concept of animism was informed by the Western distinction of mind and matter. Edward Burnett Tylor, defining religion as 'belief in spiritual beings', initially conceived animism as the foundational concept of all religion, the principle which separated it from materialism (Tylor 1958: 86; Stringer 2013: 65). This stress on spirit and matter as hallmarks of an ontological divide is reproduced by Tylor's intellectualist approach which considers the evolution of religion mostly as a result of observation and thought. This suggested a separation of animism as philosophy of nature and religion, which was elaborated by Cornelius Peter Tiele (1873). Tiele taught at Leiden University and had an immediate influence on Georg A. Wilken, who held the chair for studies of the 'Indian Archipelago' and authored the first comprehensive volume on animism in (Dutch) Southeast Asia (Wilken 1884–1885). The mind-body distinction also shaped Albert C. Kruijt's subsequent account on the same topic (1906), and Tylor's intellectualism lived on in Anton Nieuwenhuis' proposition, based on Dayak data, that 'soul' was merely a place holder for an unresolved problem, comparable to the 'black boxes' of the natural sciences (Nieuwenhuis 1918: 65). It is curious how the current debate on animism seems to mirror these earlier approaches, by focusing on practice instead of thought, and on body instead of soul (Descola 2011; Ingold 2006, this volume; Viveiros de Castro 2007). This seeming reversal indicates the difficulties of dealing with ontologies which do away with the mind-body distinction[2] altogether.

If animism is not informed by the mind-body dichotomy, the question arises, which other distinctions are pertinent for its Southeast Asian forms? Animism denotes a field of alterity which concerns social relations between living human beings and specific others like spirits and life forces. This field of alterity is situated within a multitude of other types of alterity that make up Southeast Asian diversity, like states, ethnicities, livelihoods, languages, centres and peripheries and, most notably in this context, religion. Religion most prominently appears in the form of so-called world religions, or rather, transcultural religions, that have been variously localized in Southeast Asia. Theravada Buddhism, Chinese cosmologies, Islam, Christianity and certain forms of Hinduism all claim to be majority religions in certain areas in the region.

Everywhere, however, these dominant ideologies coexist with systems of animist relationships. This occurs in two forms: first, as groups who do not identify with transcultural religions at all, in particular in the highlands of the mainland, in inner Borneo, Eastern Indonesia, and upland Philippines; second, as a concern with life forces and spirits which runs below, or besides, or within the seemingly dominant world religion in place. The question how these two fields, world religion and animism, are interrelated, has produced a massive literature, concurrent with the debate in Southeast Asia itself. Forms of this coexistence range from unreflected complementary practices to strongly debated discourses about proper cosmology and ritual (e.g., Endres and Lauser 2011; Horstmann and Reuter 2013; Gottowik 2014). In regard to the second form, the term *animism* survived, albeit with little theoretical amibition, in Southeast Asian studies well into modern and even postmodern anthropology (e.g., Condominas 1975: 257, Geertz 1964, Ong 1988: 30, Spiro 1967: 241–42). This makes the limited engagement of Southeast Asianists in the current debate, as mentioned by Århem above, all the more surprising.

However, as animism is mostly practical, its coexistence with world religions is not by necessity a contradiction. Animism is not a belief system separate from the hands-on practices of everyday life, nor different from knowledge (Fox 1987: 524). Animism covers doubt as much as belief, guesswork and experimentation, as much as tradition and convention. I take the term animism, therefore, as shorthand for animist relationships, which contingently crystallize into more-or-less stable cosmologies.

Animism has thus proven to be tenacious, as the relationships cultivated in animist rituals and discourses are often constitutive of sociality as such. This is true for conspicuously modern contexts as well. While states and cities do not figure prominently in the present volume, spirits and potencies play a crucial role in these settings (e.g., Chambert-Loir and Reid 2002; Platenkamp 2010; Holt 2009; Van Esterik 1982). While urban spaces are replete with spiritual agencies (Goh 2011; Johnson 2012, 2014), even in rural areas, important local spirits are said to originate in faraway historical kingdoms (Rhum 1994; Tsing 1993).

Such alterities at the core of sociality – of spirits and humans, locals and foreigners – are also present in the concepts of heterogeneous origin held by many Southeast Asian communities, which define themselves as composed of autochthonous and immigrant people (Sahlins 2008). This accommodates 'multicosmological' societies, in which cultural difference itself produces spirits (Long 2010). Constitutive alterity also specifies the conditions for the adoption of extrinsic cosmological concepts, like transcultural religions, as Benjamin has argued for Malay Islam (Benjamin 1979; see also Aragon 2000; MacDonald 1992).

Other types of alterity, like classes, or centres and peripheries, equally provide the context for animist relationships. In a unified cosmos, these various alterities intersect or serve as models for each other. This produces considerable variation even within groups or categories of people, while at the same time certain ideas and practices – most notably notions of potency and spirits – spread across boundaries, thus enabling communication. Therefore, animism – which is usually thought to be mostly local in nature – provides linkages between conventional intra-regional distinctions like upland and lowland or insular and mainland Southeast Asia (e.g., Benjamin 1979; Durrenberger and Tannenbaum 1989; Endicott 1979: 26–27, O'Connor 2003; Platenkamp 2007). Therefore, the use of ethnonyms or country names in the following remarks does not ascribe exclusive or even defining representations to these groups, but rather indicates the conditions under which data were collected.

Analytical dimensions which outline the productive principles of animist relations would, therefore, enable us to address various scales of analysis: events, actors, communities, ethnically or locally defined groups, as well as transcultural or region-wide practices and ideas. I propose to analyze such ways of reproducing and relating alterities by three dimensions, which help to grasp their local variations: exchange, accessibility to the senses, and hierarchy.

Exchange

As the ethnography of Southeast Asia, including numerous contributions to this volume, demonstrates, the notion of exchange has been crucial for understanding the region (Barraud and Platenkamp 1990; Fox 1980; Errington 1989; Josselin de Jong 1983). Most conspicuously, societies with asymmetric marriage alliance, ranging from Myanmar and northeast India (Leach 2001) down the Annamese Cordillera to Eastern Indonesia (van Wouden 1968) highlight the dominant role of exchange in the reproduction of socio-cosmic orders. In societies like Tanebar Evav and Laboya in Eastern Indonesia (Barraud 1990b; Geirnaert 2002) or Rmeet and Katu on the mainland (Århem, Sprenger, both this volume), matrimonial exchange is indissolubly connected to exchange relations with ancestors and spirits. Thus, for these societies, stopping to venerate the ancestors would equal stopping to marry. The 'flow of life' characteristic for Southeast Asian animism is generated through such kinship relations (Fox 1980, 1987). As exchange is possible only between actors who are different, exchanging often creates these differences even between nominally equal or similar groups – for example, by defining them as (superior) givers or (inferior) receivers of brides or valuables. It thus constitutes asymmetries and alterities as the base of social life.

However, I argue that an exchange paradigm of sociality does not only apply to societies of what Errington (1989) has called the 'exchange archipelago' or similar ones on the mainland. Exchange here is understood in an encompassing sense, not just as reciprocity, where two parties exchange gifts and recognize them as returns, but as the circulation of material and immaterial items and services that create and sustain particular socio-cosmic relationships (Barraud 1994; Gregory 1980; Mauss 1974). Gift giving, ceremonial exchange, mutual sharing and trade all are differentiated, but related types of relationships reproducing alterities. Indeed, the classical Maussian notion of the gift as creating social wholes would not work if exchange was restricted to reciprocity. The imbalance of gifts is actually favourable to the integration of such wholes, as Lévi-Strauss' (1967) understanding of asymmetric alliance has demonstrated. But while Lévi-Strauss still focuses on the contractual aspects of Mauss' model, more recent approaches have stressed the uncertainty of each act of giving, without losing sight of its constitutive social character (e.g., Caillé 2000; Därmann 2010). Such openness and risk account for the non-reciprocal elements of sharing, including them into the notion of exchange (*pace* Willerslev 2007: 45–6).

The inclusion of non-humans into exchange networks allows us to address the conspicuous difference in the role of animals in hunting and sacrifice. As Århem has observed in the first part of this introduction, while the new animism debate has mostly focused on relations between hunters and prey, many Southeast Asians see themselves as agriculturalists which raise animals for sacrifice. As Descola (2011: Chapter 15) has pointed out, venatic animism and sacrifice are based on different notions of transfer. In venatic animism, human beings take animal lives, and (the spirits of) animals take human lives in return. Human illness and death are seen as counter-predation or counter-sharing. Sacrifice, however, is usually understood differently. Spirits attempt to take human lives, but what they receive instead are the lives of domesticated animals. Thus, while animals appear as humans in hunting animism because they see each other as human beings (Viveiros de Castro 1998), sacrificial victims are like humans because they can replace them in the confrontation with spirits. The principle of replacement thus separates sacrifice from hunting, implying a hierarchy between humans and animals mostly absent from hunting animism (see also Lévi-Strauss 1973: Chapter 8). The primacy of domestic animals in sacrifice might be a major reason why classifications and ritual rules concerning wild animals are modelled upon those for domestic ones (Tambiah 1985). Many sacrificial rituals thus assume the form of more or less asymmetrical exchange (Howell 1996: 21).

This correlation of hunting on the one hand and agriculture and animal husbandry on the other with distinct forms of relations with non-human beings could easily lead to the conclusion that the differences in cosmological ideas arise from differences in livelihood. For two reasons, I argue against such a materialist determinism. First, many societies practicing venatic animism also cultivate plants, including the Amazonian Achuar (Descola 1996a). However, the Achuar conceive of their relationships with manioc in terms of mutual predation. Human beings feed upon manioc, while the plants draw blood from humans. Hunting animism thus encompasses relationships with plants, while in contrast, in many Southeast Asian societies, sacrificial animism encompasses hunting (e.g., Ellen 1996). The notion of replacement seems even present in societies without domestic animals, as, for example, among Malaysian Orang Asli who sacrifice their own blood to appease the thunder god (Endicott 1979: 156–159; Needham 1963; see also Valeri 1994). It is thus a matter of how a particular society defines its own constitutive relationships, more than how they produce their livelihood in material terms.

This leads to the second, more pertinent argument regarding exchange. Much of classical economic anthropology – and economic theory in general – separates the production of goods from their distribution and exchange, taking the first as a condition for the latter. This distinction implies that production is a relation between persons and things (i.e., resources) while exchange is a relation among persons. However, in many subsistence-based societies in Southeast Asia, what seems to be production is in fact understood as a kind of gift exchange or circulation. Humans socially engage with the – sometimes ancestral – spirit owners of the rice, the ground or the forest animals, in order to safely acquire food. In particular, the production of stable crops hinges upon successful relations with the spirits (Walker 1994; in particular Terwiel 1994; Sprenger 2006a). Even gathering – an important subsidy of diet among many agriculturalists – involves entering the domains of harmful spirits, which force people into exchange relationships that might demand a sacrifice. Small amounts of food, tobacco, libations, which are constantly left for the spirits, bear testimony to the pervasive and everyday character of such exchanges.

However, I do not propose some kind of strict cultural determinism either. The material qualities of the non-human beings involved do shape relations with them as well (see Latour 2000). Thus, it seems, while hunters like the Chewong (Howell, 1984, this volume), on the one hand, differentiate between relations among humans and those between humans and non-humans by applying 'cosmo-rules' to the cooking of food, self-identified agriculturalists, on the other hand, tend to express their human-to-non-human sociality in terms of place and space, in particular through the fertility of the land (Kammerer and Tannenbaum 2003; Allerton 2009).

Looking at livelihoods from the point of view of exchange reveals how humans and non-humans are involved in a unified, but internally differentiated social cosmos. As relations between non-human and human beings become part of an encompassing reproduction of life, it becomes decisive how relationships are valorized in relation to each other and which relations are used as models for others. For example, hunting relations might be shaped in terms of sacrifice (Sprenger, this volume) or in those of affinity (K. Århem, this volume).

This also pertains to productive relationships other than subsistence. Southeast Asian societies have been involved in trade and relations with political centres for many centuries. Markets, states and money have fed into the ways non-human agency has been managed. In the present volume, both Kenneth Sillander and Timo Kaartinen point out how the relations of alterity that link people with foreigners, like traders, and with spirits, match and thus reinforce each other on a conceptual level (see also Gibson 1986: 194–200). Market and trade are often characterized as a field of cultural alterity which corresponds with the alterity of the spirits, for example in the presence of spirit markets (Sprenger 2014). As Dove (2011: 92) has argued for Borneo, rituals and their spiritual addressees shift together with shifts in the economy, from a livelihood based on collecting to one based on cash crops. Spyer has demonstrated how the exchange relations with the spiritual 'sea wives' of the pearl divers on the Aru Islands in eastern Indonesia enable exchange with the traders for whom the pearls are collected (Spyer 2000: 137, 143–5). Urban prosperity cults articulate another way of giving shape to relations with spirits via consumer goods and market success (Endres 2011). Trade is thus located within the field of exchanges among humans and between humans and non-humans as linked modes of alterity. It is, therefore, fitting that the ritual language used to address spirits is often identified as the language of ethnic others or heavily relies on loanwords (Sillander, this volume).

The presence of trade is also hinted at in the asymmetry of value in exchange with spirits. In the eastern Indonesian myths analyzed by David Hicks (this volume), human beings frequently enter into reciprocal relationships with spirits. However, the gifts transferred are usually not properly recognized. The human heroes of these stories receive unassuming everyday items for their services in the spirit world, which turn into valuables like gold and buffaloes only after their return to the human world. Part of the plausibility of these myths, I suggest, originates from the asymmetry of valorization experienced in trade, where inconspicuous local products can be exchanged with outsiders for money and other valuables. As Dove (2011: 249–50) and others have observed, some of the most desired trade goods in Southeast Asia, like rubber, spices and pepper, were not used by their producers. This parallels the ritual gifts for spirits which are often old, broken or miniature specimens of valuables or everyday items (e.g., Erb 1996: 31).

Two principles of exchange emerge from this, the sacrificial principle of replacement already mentioned, and the asymmetry of the gifts exchanged between wife-givers and wife-takers. The latter is often couched in terms of relations between autochthonous and foreign people and enabled through trade goods as bridewealth. Thus, the exchange relations that connect human beings with each other are based on alterity, similar to their relations with spirits, which humans need for their livelihood. Exchange is thus the means by which alterity is constantly produced as the base of sociality (see Därmann 2010; Moebius 2009). Southeast Asian exchanges thus comprise an open system, as they relate potentially infinite chains of differences to local systems of reproduction, in the form of just so many asymmetries. The alterity of the spirits is merely one version of this process, to which diverse relations might become attached, spanning kinship, trade and animals (see Viveiros de Castro 2007).

Therefore, when analyzing animism in Southeast Asia, we should direct our attention to the dimension of exchange and query: What is the specific alterity on which it is based? How is it articulated through what is given and what is received? Is the relationship supposed to be durable or temporary? Does it aim at complementation, for example, in order to produce life, or separation, which protects life from being drawn away?

But such a grammar of exchange is not only a language of relating, but at the same time a language of being. At this point, the question who is exchanging and how these beings are constituted through their relationships becomes crucial.

Personhood and the Accessibility to the Senses

Being is often a matter of sensing, and in Southeast Asia, spirits are usually defined by the way they are being detected. The following section explores their accessibility to the senses, as the second dimension of analysis. Before doing so, I need to address two related issues, personhood and the question why some Southeast Asian concepts sometimes designate impersonal life forces and sometimes persons, an issue mentioned by Århem above. The range thus runs from the concepts which Anderson (1972) has discussed as 'power' or Fox (1987) as 'immanence of life', to rather concrete, even physical beings. Examples of such concepts are *semangat* among Malay (Cuisinier 1951, Endicott 1970), *ruwai* among Chewong (Howell, this volume), *lulik* on Timor (Bovensiepen 2014) and *lennawa* among Ilongot (Remme, this volume) – all terms denoting impersonal life forces, personal souls or personalized spirits in different contexts.

As Benjamin (1979) has shown in a brilliant comparative article, the fixedness of souls and the dangerous and sacred unboundedness of spirits provides the central axis by which animist relationships can be analyzed within and across cultural boundaries in Southeast Asia. The distribution of traits of personhood, like bodies, agency, visibility, etc., and the stability of the relationships between these traits is a central concern in these cosmologies. As such, it has drawn the attention of numerous previous scholars. Albert C. Kruijt, in his early account (1906) shaped by his own protestant background, misleadingly assumed a deep conceptual gap between the impersonal life force ('soul stuff') and the personalized soul which emerges after death (see also Aragon 2000: 163–5). Endicott (1970) has argued that the classification as well as the degree of boundedness of spirits corresponds with the features of a more general classification system. A less bounded category, therefore, is represented by a less clearly defined spirit. While the idea that the boundedness of categories follows particular rules across a classification system is plausible, the assumption that a taxonomy of spirits and a classification of other categories simply match is less so. Endicott, after all, assumes that souls, spirits and potencies are representations or metaphors (ibid.: 75). However, for Malay and other Southeast Asians, spirits and life forces are beings in their own right, defined by their own rules and relationships. Therefore, there is no clear correspondence between spirit taxonomies and other classifications, even though relationship models move from one domain to another, as Sillander (this volume) has demonstrated.

Tsintjilonis (2004) attempts at solving the seeming contradiction between the processual nature of spiritual forces and their stable emergent forms by describing Toraja cosmology as a complementation of animic and totemic elements. While life as a process is animic in Ingold's (2000) sense – all beings emerge from interactions with each other, based on a flow of life – its hypostatized forms are totemic in the sense of early Descola (1996b). The essential differences of the bodies of people of different class are associated with other beings and thus form ontologically separate totemic classes which emerge from a differentiated distribution of life force (see above). However, as Kaartinen (this volume) argues, the differentiation is not so much one of beings but of human-spirit relationships. Consequently, I will add, the question of the boundedness, concreteness and accessibility to the senses of a non-human being is primarily a matter of relationships, and not so much of essence (see Bird-David 1999). How, then, can we analyse the processes which shape these relationships?

The issue of sacrificial replacement already touched upon the relation between personhood and exchange. Considering personhood from the angle of exchange has produced important insights into how social action and its subjects are understood in Southeast Asia (e.g., Barraud 1990a; Platenkamp 2010). In this view, the various aspects or components of personhood are constituted by exchange and circulation between humans and non-humans (Marriott 1976; Strathern 1988). The word *aspect* describes the constitution of Southeast Asian personhood perhaps better than *component*, as it suggests various sides of a person, like faces of a crystal, which come into being because they are directed to something other than the person – a relationship that creates the respective aspect. As Sillander (this volume) observes, for the Bentian, the concept of the person corresponds with the multiplicity of relations. Human beings thus appear as temporary hypostases of cycles of reproduction which outlast human lifespans.

This becomes particularly obvious in mortuary rites, which are of central importance for many Southeast Asian societies. Often, these rituals stress the disassembling of persons through exchanges, secondary funerals and so on. A typical case is the Laboya of Sumba, where the dead differentiate into a name, which sustains its social group, and liquid matter, which turns into fertilizing rain, life-giving but undifferentiated in terms of personhood (Geirnaert 2002). Substances, objects, powers travel along particular relationships within a sociocosmic space and temporarily coagulate to form human persons.

The relational character of personhood helps understanding the diverse appearances of spirits and non-human forces in Southeast Asia. If exchanges are seen as risky and systems as tentative, then the persons and forces which emerge as actors in the course of the exchanges will show various degrees of agency and boundedness, ranging from concrete person to abstract force. This is what I call graded personhood (Sprenger, this volume). The question which relationships are possible with spirits and which form these beings assume are therefore immediately related. One way to approach this issue is by looking at the manner spirits and spiritual forces are experienced, that is, how they are accessible to the senses.

The Southeast Asian ethnography suggests that visibility is the main feature that differentiates spirits and humans. Spirits, as many Southeast Asians are reported saying, are invisible, and some societies even tell stories how humans and spirits separated after living together before (Schefold 1990: 291; Tooker 2012: 100).

However, scanning the ethnographic material reveals that this is only partially true. Rather, the sensual accessibility of spirits is selective and often depends on their own agency. The popular Thai story about Nang Nak tells about a young man returning from war who does not realize that his wife has died during his absence, as she keeps performing all the tasks of a housewife (McDaniel 2011). Stories like those analyzed by Hicks (this volume) tell about humans touching, healing and marrying spirits. Spirits might also appear as shadows or reflections (Kaartinen, this volume) or reveal themselves in dreams and during trances. Ominous events like the birdsong omens described by Janowski or Amster (both this volume) are forms of selective sensual communication by spirits.

Visibility is thus merely the dominant indicator of accessibility to the senses. It is not a stable ontological given but a mode of relating, sometimes symmetric, sometimes asymmetric. Platenkamp, in an important analysis of visibility in Southeast Asia, observes that 'to be *visually acknowledged* by other people and spiritual beings is a precondition of human existence and a fundamental dimension of social life' (2006: 80, original italics). Spirits are not only invisible, 'what – or how – they *see* is not identical to what people see' (Sillander, this volume). As Howell elaborates in her chapter, for the Chewong a particular quality of the eyes determines how the beings of the world appear to the beholder. Stories about human beings marrying non-humans also demonstrate that vision is the sense that determines the relationship. In the Pura myth collected by Rodemeier (2009) and analyzed by Hicks (this volume), a young woman destined to marry a fish spirit is able to see the smoke from the spirits' swiddens, that is, she realizes that spirits socialize space in the forest like humans do. Later, the girl and her husband produce a fish-like child. But the affinal relationship with the spirit world is terminated when the girl's mother, of all things, plucks out one of her grandchild's eyes.

The last example suggests that differentiated accessibility to the senses indicates social distance. McKinley (1976) argues that tribal Southeast Asians imagine their cosmology as continuous, connecting the spirit realms with those of humans. Therefore, even distant human neighbours tend to be seen as spirits, ordered in a gradual transition from humanity to non-humanity. Such differences are systematically acknowledged when people who define themselves as farmers see both markets (Sprenger 2014) and hunter-gatherers as close to the spirit domain. Agriculturalists of Thailand and Laos called the hunting and gathering Mrabri 'spirits of the yellow leaves' (Bernatzik 1941, Trier 2008). Not only are Mrabri, like spirits, rarely seen, their practices of producing persons might be quite incompatible with what their neighbours accept as sociality (see Praet 2014).

Thus, material and sensual qualities are not essential givens preceding communication, but emerge in relationships. In Ingold's terms, perception is a movement out into the environment, towards immediate interaction with other beings (Ingold 2000: 18). The sensual accessibility of spirits is thus a function of the relationship they establish with their human counterparts. Among Tobelo in Halmahera, for example, someone seeing or otherwise perceiving a spirit enters into a special relationship with it, often leading to illness and death (Platenkamp 2006: 83; see also Formoso 1998).

In those cases where amorphous life forces and the concrete personification of spirits coexist within the same conceptual framework, we can think of the flow of life as a potential of hypostasis or crystallization, similar to conceptions of space which encompass boundedness as well as diffusion (Endicott 1970: 33–35; Tooker 2012). The relationship between humans and spirits thus also conditions the material, or rather, sensual qualities of things, as in the differing appearance of the gifts from spirits, mentioned above. What is more, human actors often provide sensual forms to non-humans in order to facilitate communication with them: shrines and bodies of wood, clay, stone (Cederroth, this volume) or other materials, to be addressed or fed during ritual. Communicative devices like artefacts and sacrifices not only materialize relationships with spirits, but usually result from the prospering of the flow of life themselves, in particular crops and animals, but also trade. Thus, they evidence a process by which spirits and life forces become increasingly material, bounded and differentiated. For addressing the spirits, the abundance of rice is transformed into portions, often clearly differentiated on an offering tray into separate little heaps. Offerings are named or additional, specific ingredients are added. Sacrificial victims are cut up, their body parts differentially valorized and distributed to different actors (Howell 1996).

Thereby, a language of things and gifts often provides shapeless, disembodied spirits with concrete forms (Ladwig 2011, 2012). The gifts themselves embody the principle of differentiation, and thereby involve the recipients in the same process. This implies that the concrete form of the beings involved emerges from the process of relating them to each other.

This communication thus might operate on different levels with the same effect: It channels amorphous life force, personalizes a spirit, or opens up a spirit towards human sociality. This is highlighted by Howell (this volume). Differentiation is the condition for a cosmology of humans and non-humans to exist in the first place (see Bovensiepen 2014). After the offering, after the ritual, the non-human agents might dissolve again, waiting for receiving concreteness and differentiation in the next interaction. At the same time, both the asymmetry of the exchange principle and sensual differentiation enable the elaboration of hierarchies. It is not just the intensity of communication, which determines concreteness. Communication is also shaped by hierarchical relations.

Hierarchy

As Århem has argued above, hierarchy is a constitutive feature of animism in Southeast Asia. Other than most regions that the current animism debate focuses on, Southeast Asia has a long history of political centres, endowed with military might, cultural splendour and trade connections outside of the region. Within and around these centres, hierarchies of power and status took shape, which are articulated through emboxed spirit cults (Tambiah 1985; Tanabe 1988). These hierarchical relations shaped the lives and identities even of hunters and gatherers (Benjamin 1985). As Nikolas Århem's chapter makes clear, the state also plays into the way spirit relationships are recognized (see also Jonsson 2012; Kwon 2008).

But the presence of states is not simply the model or condition for the importance of hierarchy. While political centres were notoriously unstable, the differentiation between centre and periphery provided another common idiom of hierarchization, be it as upland and lowland in the mainland, or coast and hinterland in insular Southeast Asia, but also as society and wilderness in general (Tooker 1996, Sprenger 2008a). In addition, stratification is not alien to societies with little centralization or urbanization, like Tanimbar in the Moluccas (McKinnon 1995), 'Maloh' in Borneo (King 1985: 83) or Bugis and Toraja (Tsintjilonis 2004).

This type of hierarchy is transitive and has absolute tops and bottoms. But besides it, there are intransitive and relative hierarchies, in which each position is subordinate and superior to specific others at the same time. The classical example is the superiority of wife-givers over wife-takers in a system of asymmetric marriage alliance (Parkin 1990; Sprenger 2010; K. Århem, Chapter 5, this volume). In such systems, wife-givers appear as givers of life, health, the fertility of the fields and the households. The definition of their power as either economic, ritual or political is a matter of emphasis, as Leach (2001) or Kirsch (1973) have demonstrated. Such systems are often circular.

This highlights that many hierarchies, including those of political power, are, first of all, hierarchies of value, which motivate actions, create priorities or legitimize judgements (Dumont 1986, Iteanu 2009). Even societies with strong egalitarian values profess a worldview structured by hierarchy. The Buid of Mindoro, whose central social value derives from the equality of husband and wife, are 'obsessed with hierarchy', as Gibson (1986: 185–8) notes, referring to relations with animals, spirits and neighbouring groups. This consideration of outsiders and non-humans renders Southeast Asian cosmologies hierarchical. Relationships are based on asymmetric values, which inevitably results in hierarchies, even without recognizable political or economic dimensions stabilizing them. Indeed, many value hierarchies are reversible according to context. Thus it seems that equality is the balancing of hierarchies and a peculiar human achievement within a hierarchical universe.

This sheds additional light on the shifting status of spirits and non-human forces, addressed above. One somewhat atypical case might serve as a model. The Ma'Betisék of the Malay Peninsula recognize two value levels in relation to non-humans, in particular animals and plants. In the context of *tulah*, animals and plants are food, while in the context of *kemali* – mostly during healing rituals – they are persons and addressees of ritual gifts. *Tulah* denotes the curses which human beings have put on potential food, thus keeping it from shape-shifting and reversing its lot by predating upon humans. However, plants and animals sometimes overcome their cursed state and cause illness among humans. In these cases, they need to be addressed as persons in the *kemali* context (Jahan-Karim 2004 [1981]: 8–10, 196).

The case is atypical, as the non-human actors are visible beings like in Amerindian animisms. But it is still helpful for making my point, as the hierarchy in question is not modelled upon hierarchies among humans, which are absent. The status of plants and animals as food results from their subordination through superior ritual techniques. The hierarchy thus created is not permanent, but reversible. 'Object status', in this system, can be described as the disregard of the agency of a being, even when its recognition would be an option (Sillander, this volume).

This type of hierarchy is more stabilized in relationships between householders and domestic animals in their defining context, sacrifice. Animals are part of households, sometimes under the protection of a house spirit or a localized spiritual force. They can represent the householders in their relations with spirits or vice versa (e.g., Forth 1998: 25–6; Sprenger 2006b), but as they are defined as edible in the context of sacrifice, and householders as eaters, they do not stand on equal terms with their human owners. The hierarchical principle enables householders to use animals as sacrifice without running the danger of ritual auto-cannibalism (see Fausto 2007).

As Remme (this volume) argues, such shifts between person and object status are a necessity for animist ontologies, as the productive and the destructive aspects of non-human agency need to be negotiated properly. The graded personhood of non-human beings, in particular souls and spirits, partially reveals degrees of hierarchization. Some non-human beings in Southeast Asia are not non-persons because they lack the ontological potential to be persons, but rather because their situation does not allow them to talk back. Human beings recognize hierarchies by treating others more person-like or less so, but they also recreate these hierarchies by reformulating them through ritual. Ritual thus often serves the – temporary – stabilization of ontological and communicative statuses.

This also addresses the case of the spirit owners of game, which can be seen as the hypostasis of an entire category. As Tsintjilonis (2004: 437) has observed in regard to the Toraja, the ancestors of rice, the animals, etc., have intentionality and a biography, but the individual plants and animals do not. The latter only have life-force, which assigns them to a lower order of the hierarchy, where they are subordinate to the human beings handling them. Only as a category do they achieve the degree of complexity in their relation with human beings which constitutes their status as persons (see also Sillander, this volume).

Hierarchy thus implies that the recognition of personhood is often a matter of degree, and not so much of an absolute threshold. The origin stories of totemic clans among Rmeet (Sprenger 2008b) and Khmu (Lindell 1984: 127–33) in Laos tell of a reversal of the normal relationship between a forest creature and a human being. A man handling a bush knife is startled by the call of a forktail and kills himself; a civet saves the life of a boy who is chased by his dead girlfriend. Their descendants become the clans of forktail and civet, respectively. These mythic animals are usually not personalized, nor are their present-day specimens, but they still had a decisive influence on life and death. Therefore, they have shifted their hierarchical position in relation to humans which usually assert their superiority by hunting and eating animals. The mythic animals became like ancestors, while the present-day specimens, like humans, cannot be consumed.

The focus on hierarchy also offers an approach to the relationship between local animistic relations and transcultural religions, like Buddhism or Islam, a central theme in Southeast Asian scholarship. As Spiro has noted, professed doubt in spirits is no uncommon stance among Buddhist Burmese. What this statement expresses, however, is not always disbelief in their existence, but rather in their power to affect the speaker. Both these attitudes exist and are argued for with the superiority of Buddhism. Fewer men express belief in spirits than women, who are less protected by Buddhism and therefore more vulnerable to spirit attack (Spiro 1967: 56–9). Belief in spirits is thus not an attitude regarding their absolute ontological status, but the recognition of potential relationships with them. What seems like a shift in ontology, from 'animism' to 'world religion', is often enough a shift in the hierarchical order of the cosmos (see also Kammerer 1990; Platenkamp 2007; Tooker 1992; Janowski, Amster, both this volume). This only becomes a contradiction when animist practices are identified as religious and therefore in competition with doctrinal religions. Thus, reformist and modern versions of world religions may actively curtail communication with spirits. In so far personhood depends on the recognition of the ability to communicate, spirits might become less stabilized and gradually diminish in this cosmology – in the long run.

In summary, as Århem has already argued above, Southeast Asian ethnography in general does not support the suggestion of several scholars (Descola 2011, Chapter 13; Pedersen 2001; Sillander, this volume) that animism goes along with egalitarian social values.

Toward Comparison within Southeast Asia

I refrain to set up a comparative model of animism in Southeast Asia by defining large contrastive categories or subregions of societies. Instead, I argue that three major factors will help to analyse the varieties of animistic relationships in Southeast Asia in any specific case. All provide form to the production and reproduction of alterities. The asymmetry of exchange is a major means to establish communication and define alterities, both social and cosmological. Accessibility to the senses is a horizon of the intensity of communication. Hierarchy is the dimension that orients communication in terms of values. Both the accessibility to the senses and hierarchy establish, in different ways, the recognition of actors. All three factors contribute to the creation and dissolution of human and non-human beings in Southeast Asia, which shift in and out of personhood.

The brevity of this introduction does not allow me to consider in more detail a number of contexts in which animist relationship are prominently situated – animism in cities (Johnson 2014), in politics (e.g., Bubandt 2009; Ong 1988) and in its relation to transcultural religions, possession cults and mortuary rituals. However, the three dimensions established above help to determine variations in the production of animist relationships. Exchange, accessibility to the senses and hierarchy are first of all types of difference in a processual view. These differences integrate social roles and corporeality, existence on both sides of the life/death boundary, humans and non-humans. While the differences are usually ordered and, to a degree, ranked, the complexity of the multitudinous factors which produce these differences makes it difficult to stabilize and constrain this order. Thus, constant debate and variation characterize animist discourses. Members of the same community provide different accounts of the nature, number and function of the cosmological forces and persons, and even single individuals produce diverging information according to context (e.g., Bovensiepen 2014; Endicott 1979: 198–214). Current local debates about proper ritual and belief also emerge from this process.

Anthropologists trying to derive stable models of local ontological discourses from such complex data sometimes run the risk to perform as – foreign and unrecognized – theologians. Therefore, the necessity of stable models in the communication of knowledge – not at least in modern academia – should not divert from the insight that animist relationships emerge from permanent becoming and improvisation. Animism is the ever unfinishable project of socializing humans and non-humans in the project of life-producing difference. If this does not necessarily result in a stable cosmology, the question is: Which types of difference do Southeast Asians use to assemble their relations with non-humans, types which make such relationships comparable across events, myths and rituals, across villages, cities, strata, institutions, networks, ethnic categories and regions? My proposal is to employ the analytical dimensions I have suggested as tools for the analysis of contingent cases without classifying them.

The Chapters

In Signe Howell's chapter, the production of socio-cosmic difference is at the center of the analysis of the hunting and gathering Chewong of Malaysia. While the Chewong are treated as prime examples of a monist universe in the current animism debate, Howell points out how human and non-human agency are kept separate through the observation of 'cosmo-rules' regarding food preparation. Thus, relationships within communities of living Chewong are separated from relationships between Chewong and non-humans in an idiom of food and the body.

The chapter by Guido Sprenger is also concerned with hunting, but this time from the perspective of an agricultural society, the Rmeet of Laos. He demonstrates how personhood is constructed and acknowledged gradually through ritual. In this framework, wild animals are like domestic animals from the point of view of their spirit owners. As sacrifice is the encompassing idiom for relationships with domestic animals, hunting needs to establish game as non-sacrificial animals in order to be successful.

Kaj Århem's chapter deals with comparable practices in a similar society, the Katu on the Vietnam-Laos border. However, subtle differences in myth and ritual show how the relationship between hunters and game is construed entirely different from the Rmeet, as the idiom of alterity is not so much derived from sacrifice but from affinity and the imagery of the asymmetric exchange. Game appears as bridewealth provided by a forest spirit who relates to the Katu as a wife-taker.

Nikolas Århem's complementary chapter on the Katu adds relationships with the state to the set of alterities. Both the state and the spirits were involved in the decision to move a village in a highly selective way. The two were seen as mutually exclusive and a tense relation pertains between them. Still, the relationality and the practical character of animism were maintained. Similar to Burmese Buddhists (see above), some Katu's disbelief in spirits had less to do with their assumed non-existence but with the denial of their influence on modern subjects.

Jon Remme, in his chapter on the Ifugao of the Philippines, analyses a paradigmatic case of human-non-human relationships as a continuous phenomenal process. Ifugao constantly heed a host of spirits, which emerge as various appearances of the life force/soul *lennawa*. In a way comparable to Howell, Remme stresses differentiation. He argues that the omnipresent potential of non-humans to become persons asks for a highly selective actualization of personhood. Otherwise, the distinction between the beneficial and the destructive potentials of human-spirit relationships could not be managed. Thus, in animism, sociality needs to be proportionate.

In his chapter on the Bentian of Borneo, Kenneth Sillander points out that integration and alterity are not mutually exclusive. The same types of relationships apply to relations among humans and between humans and spirits. However, many of the latter are characteristic for relations with humans which are socially distant – trade, tribute or mutual predation, for example. The social universe thus appears not so much differentiated into spirits and humans, but into Bentian and non-Bentian.

In her comparative chapter on Sarawak, Monica Janowski observes marked differences between the hunting and foraging relations of the Penan on the one hand, and agricultural relations, as exemplified by the Kelabit, on the other. Clearing plots in the forest amounts to an act of domestication that separates the attention people pay to the beings within the human sphere from that paid to those in the forest. The types of relationships thus shape their respective 'education of attention' (Ingold, this volume). Janowski places the adoption of Christianity within the framework of differentiated spirit power. For the Kelabit, the Christian God now appears as an extension of the more generalizing end of the continuum of manifestations of potency.

Matthew Amster, in his chapter, significantly complements this argument. For Christian Kelabit, the relationship with Jesus Christ encompasses and subordinates all the relations with competing spirits, who are thus not non-existent but rather muted, the Good News drowning out the call of the omen birds. At the same time, Christianity opens up the local system of relationships to transnational networks also on the level of non-humans. However, as relationships with spirits remain important, Amster proposes that animism should be considered as a mode of thought or identification rather than a religion in any exclusivist definition.

A similar coexistence of transcultural religion and animist concepts is subject of the following two chapters. Timo Kaartinen's chapter provides a general outlook on relations of alterity in Eastern Indonesia, substantially referring, among others, to his research on Muslim Bandanese. He stresses that, contrary to the standard model of animism, the principle of differentiating humans and non-humans is less connected to different bodies, but to an inversion of humanity. This alterity is represented by ethnic others, in particular traders. The effort to maintain humanity, as indicative of animism, is thus shaped rather by what we might conventionally call cultural diversity.

Sven Cederroth's chapter equally speaks about Indonesian Muslims, this time on Lombok, and their parallel animist practices. The area stands out as the only one in this volume that featured a pre-modern state. Adherents of Wetu Telu identify the Muslim God with the supreme being of a local cosmology populated with numerous other types of spirits: ancestors, locality spirits, capricious ghosts. As in Janowski's account, animist potency appears in a distinctively physical form, here as stones. This concreteness is also represented by the relation between spirits and territoriality.

In the final ethnographic chapter, David Hicks provides an analysis of a set of myths from Eastern Indonesia, most of them connected through the motif of a lost fishhook and water as the medium between the human and the spirit world. Once again, alterity and integration appear as necessarily related, as both domains reproduce themselves through mutual exchanges. As in perspectival animism, the spirit world resembles the world of living humans, but is marked off by a different visuality.

All contributions suggest the recurrence of certain ideas – monist cosmologies which integrate human and non-human agencies, structured by the differentiated and graded nature of personhood and sociality, the cultivation of differences and alterities, and – often ambiguous – hierarchical orders.

Notes

1. Earlier versions of this chapter were presented at the 7th EuroSEAS Conference, Lisbon, and at the universities of Zurich, Hamburg, Freiburg, Marburg, Berlin and Heidelberg. I profited greatly from discussions there and particularly thank Kaj Århem, Annette Hornbacher, William Sax and Susanne Rodemeier.
2. The absence of the mind-body distinction is most prominent in Ingold's (2000) writings on non-Western ontologies but even Descola (2011), whose interiority-physicality distinction echoes the mind-body distinction, points out that the latter is only one version of the former.

References

Allerton, C. (2009) (ed.) 'Spiritual Landscapes of Southeast Asia. Special Issue', *Anthropological Forum*, 19 (3).

Anderson, B.R.O'G. (1972) 'The Idea of Power in Javanese Culture' in C. Holt (ed.) *Culture and Politics in Indonesia*. Ithaca, NY and London: Cornell University Press, 1–69.

Aragon, L.V. (2000) *Fields of the Lord: animism, Christian minorities and state development in Indonesia*, Honolulu, HI: University of Hawai'i Press.

Barraud, C. (1990a) 'Kei society and the person: An approach through childbirth and funerary rituals', *Ethnos*, 3–4: 214–31.

——— (1990b) 'Wife-Givers as ancestors and ultimate values in the Kei Islands', *Bjidragen tot de Tal-, Land- en Volkenkunde*, 146: 193–225.

Barraud, C., de Coppet, D., Itéanu, A., and Jamous, R. (1994) *Of relations and the dead: four societies viewed from the angle of their exchanges.* Oxford and Providence, RI: Berg.

Barraud, C., and Platenkamp, J.D.M. (1990) 'Rituals and the Comparison of Societies', in C. Barraud and J.D.M Platenkamp. (eds) *Rituals and Socio-Cosmic Order in Eastern Indonesian Societies, Part II: Maluku*, Special Anthropological Issue. *Bijdragen tot de Taal-, Land- en Volkenkunde*, 146(1): 103–23.

Benjamin, G. (1979) 'Indigenous Religions of the Malayan Peninsula', in Becker and A. Yengoyan, (eds.) *The Imagination of Reality : Essays in Southeast Asian Coherence Systems*, 9–27.

——— (1985) 'In the long term: three themes in Malayan cultural ecology' in K. Hutterer, (eds.) *Cultural values and human ecology in Southeast Asia*, 219–78. Ann Arbor, MI: Center for South and Southeast Asian Studies, University of Michigan (Michigan Papers on South and SoutheastAsia; 27).

Bernatzik, H.A. (1941) [1937] *Die Geister der gelben Blätter: Forschungsreisen in Hinterindien*, Leipzig.

Bird-David, N. (1999) '"Animism" Revisited. Personhood, Environment, and Relational Epistemology.' *Current Anthropology*, (40, supplement): 67–91.

Bovensiepen, J. (2014) '*Lulik*: taboo, animism, or transgressive sacred? An exploration of identity, morality and power in Timor-Leste', *Oceania*, 84(2): 121–37.

Bubandt, N. (2009) 'Interview with an ancestor: spirits as informants and the politics of possession in North Maluku', *Ethnography*, 10(3): 291–316.

Caillé, A. (2008) [2000] *Anthropologie der Gabe*, Frankfurt am Main: Campus. (first: *Anthropologie du don.*).

Chambert-Loir, H. and Reid, A. (eds.) (2002) *The Potent Dead: Ancestors, saints and heroes in contemporary Indonesia*, Honolulu, HI: University of Hawai'i Press.

Condominas, G. (1975) 'Phi Ban cults in rural Laos', William Skinner, G. and Thomas Kirsch, A. (eds.) *Change and persistence in Thai Society*, Ithaca, NY and London: Cornell University Press, 252–73.

Cuisinier, J. (1951) *Sumangat: l'ame et son culte en Indochine et en Indonésie*. Paris: Gallimard.

Därmann, I. (2010) *Theorien der Gabe: zur Einführung*, Hamburg: Junius.

Descola, P. (1996a) *Leben und Sterben in Amazonien.* Stuttgart: Klett-Cotta. (first: *Les Lances du Crépuscule*. Paris: Plon, 1993).

——— (1996b) 'Constructing natures: symbolic ecology and social practice', in: P. Descola/G. Pálsson (eds.) *Nature and Society: Anthropological Perspectives.* London: Routledge, 83–102.

——— (2011) [2005] *Jenseits von Natur und Kultur*, Frankfurt am Main: Suhrkamp (first: *Par-delà nature et culture*. Paris: Gallimard.

Dove, M. (2011) *The Banana Tree at the Gate: A history of marginal peoples and global markets in Borneo*, New Haven, CT and London: Yale University Press.

Dumont, L. (1986) *Essays on individualism: modern ideology in anthropological perspective,* Chicago, IL: University of Chicago Press.

Durrenberger, E.P., and Tannenbaum, N. (1989) 'Continuities of Highland and Lowland Religions of Thailand', *Journal of the Siam Society*, 77(1): 83–90.

Ellen, R.F. (1996) 'Cuscus and cockerels: Killing rituals and ritual killing amongst the Nuaulu of Seram', in: S. Howell (ed.) *For the sake of our future: Sacrificing in eastern Indonesia*, Leiden: Research School CNWS, 263–81.

Endicott, K. (1970) *An Analysis of Malay Magic*, Singapore: Oxford University Press.

——— (1979) *Batek Negrito Religion: The World-View and Rituals of a Hunting and Gathering People of Peninsular Malaysia*, Oxford: Clarendon.

Endres, K. (2011) *Performing the divine: Mediums, markets and modernity in urban, Vietnam.* Copenhagen: NIAS.

Endres, K., and Lauser, A. (2011) (eds) *Engaging the Spirit World: Popular Beliefs and Practices in Modern Southeast Asia*, Oxford and New York, NY: Berghahn.

Erb, M. (1996) 'Talking and eating: sacrificial ritual among the Rembong', in S. Howell (ed.) *For the sake of our future: Sacrificing in eastern Indonesia*, Leiden: Research School CNWS, 27–42.

Errington, S. (1989) *Meaning and Power in a Southeast Asian Realm*, Princeton, NJ: Princeton University Press.

Van Esterik, P. (1982) 'Interpreting a Cosmology: Guardian Spirits in Thai Buddhism', *Anthropos*, 77(1): 1–15.

Fausto, C. (2007) 'Feasting on people. Eating animals and humans in Amazonia' *Current Anthropology*, 48(4): 497–530.

Formoso, B. (1998) 'Bad Death and Malevolent Spirits among the Tai Peoples.' *Anthropos*, 93: 3–17.

Forth, G. (1998) *Beneath the Volcano: Religion, cosmology and spirit classification among the Nage of eastern Indonesia*, Leiden: KITLV Press.

Fox, J. (ed.) (1980) *The Flow of Life: Essays on Eastern Indonesia*, Cambridge: Cambridge University Press.

—— (1987) 'Southeast Asian Religions: Insular Cultures', in M. Eliade (ed.) *The Encyclopedia of Religion, Vol. 13*, New York: Macmillan Publishing Company, 520–30.

Geertz, C. (1964) [1960] *The Religion of Java*, London: MacMillan.

Geirnaert, D.C. (2002) 'Witnessing the Creation of Ancestors in Laboya (West Sumba, Eastern Indonesia)', in H. Chambert-Loir and A. Reid (eds) *The Potent Dead: Ancestors, saints and heroes in contemporary Indonesia*. Honolulu, HI: University of Hawai'i Press (e.a.), 32–47.

Gibson, T. (1986) *Sacrifice and Sharing in the Philippine Highlands: Religion and Society among the Buid of Mindoro*, London and Dover: Athlone.

Goh, B.-L. (2011) 'Spirits Cults and Construction Sites: Trans-Ethnic Popular Religion and Keramat symbolism in Contemporary Malaysia', in A. Lauser and K.W. Endres (eds.) *Engaging the Spirit World: Popular Beliefs and Practices in Modern Southeast Asia*, New York, NY and Oxford: Berghahn, 144–62.

Holt, J. (2009) *Spirits of the Place: Buddhism and Lao Religious Culture*, Honolulu, HI: University of Hawaii Press.

Horstmann, A., and Reuter, T. (2013) (eds) *Faith in the Future: Understanding the Revitalization of Religions and Cultural Traditions in Asia*, Leiden: Brill.

Howell, S. (1984) *Society and Cosmos: Chewong of Peninsular Malaysia*. Singapore: Oxford University Press.

—— (1996) 'Introduction', in S. Howell (ed.) *For the sake of our future: Sacrificing in eastern Indonesia*, Leiden: Research School CNWS, 1–26.

Ingold, T. (2000) *The Perception of the Environment: Essays on Livelihood, Dwelling, and Skill*, London: Routledge.

—— (2006) 'Rethinking the animate, re-animating thought', *Ethnos*, 71(1): 9–20.

Itéanu, A. (2009) 'Hierarchy and Power: a comparative attempt under asymmetrical lines', in K.M. Rio and O.H. Smedal (eds) *Hierarchy: Persistence and Transformation in Social Formations*, New York, NY and Oxford: Berghahn, 331–48.

Johnson, A. (2012) 'Naming chaos: accident, precariousness, and the spirits of wildness in urban Thai spirit cults', *American Ethnologist*, 39(4): 766–78.

—— (2014) *Ghosts of the new city. Spirits, urbanity, and the ruins of progress in Chiang Mai*, Honolulu, HI: University of Hawai'i Press.

Jonsson, H. (2012) 'Paths to freedom: Political Prospecting in the Ethnographic Record', *Critique of Anthropology*, 32(2): 158–72.
Josselin de Jong, J.P.B. de (1983) [1935] 'The Malay Archipelago as a Field of Ethnological Study', in: P. E. de Josselin de Jong (ed.) *Structural Anthropology in the Netherlands*, Dordrecht: Foris, 164–82.
Kammerer, C.A. (1990) 'Customs and Christian conversion among Akha highlanders of Burma and Thailand', *American Ethnologist*, 17: 277–91.
Kammerer, C.A., and Tannenbaum, N. (2003) (eds.) *Founders' Cults in Southeast Asia: Ancestors, Polity, and Identity*, New Haven, CT: Monograph 52, Yale University Southeast Asia Program.
Karim, W.-J. (2004) [1981] *Ma'Betisék Concepts of Living Things*, Oxford and New York, NY: Berg.
King, V.T. (1985) *The Maloh of West Kalimantan*, Dordrecht: Foris.
Kirsch, A.T. (1973) *Feasting and social oscillation: religion and society in Upland Southeast Asia*, Ithaca, NY: Cornell University Press.
Kruijt, A.C. (1906) *Het Animisme in den Indischen Archipel*, 's-Gravenhage: Nijhoff.
Kwon, H. (2008) *Ghosts of war in Vietnam*, Cambridge: Cambridge University Press.
Ladwig, P. (2011) 'Can Things Reach the Dead? The Ontological status of Objects and the Study of Lao Buddhist Rituals for the Spirits of the Deceased', in K. Endres and A. Lauser (eds) *Engaging the Spirit World: Popular Beliefs and Practices in Modern Southeast Asia*, Oxford and New York, NY: Berghahn, 19–41.
—— (2012) 'Visitors from hell: transformative hospitality to ghosts in a Lao Buddhist festival', *Journal of the Royal Anthropological Institute*, 18: 90–102.
Latour, B. (2000) *Pandora's Hope: Essays on the Reality of Science Studies*, Cambridge, MA.: Harvard University Press.
Leach, E. (2001) [1954] *Political systems of Highland Burma: A study of Kachin social structure*, London and New York, NY: Continuum.
Lévi-Strauss, C. (1967) *The elementary structures of kinship*, Boston, MA: Beacon.
—— (1973) *Das wilde Denken*, Frankfurt am Main: Suhrkamp. (First *La pensée sauvage*. Paris: Plon.)
Lindell, K., Swahn, J.Ö., and Tayanin, D. (1984) *Folktales from Kammu III: Pearls of Kammu literature*, London and Malmö: Curzon.
Long, N.J. (2010) 'Haunting Malayness: the multicultural uncanny in a new Indonesian province', *Journal of the Royal Anthropological Institute*, 16(4): 874–91.
Macdonald, C. (1992) 'Protestant Missionaries and Palawan Natives: Dialogue, Conflict or Misunderstanding?', *Journal of the Anthropological Society of Oxford*, 23(2): 127–37.
Marriott, Mc.K. (1976) 'Hindu Transactions: Diversity without Dualism', in B. Kapferer (ed.) *Transaction and Meaning: Directions in the Anthropology of Exchange and Symbolic Behavior*, Philadelphia, PA: Institute for the Study of Human Issues, 109–42.
Mauss, M. (1974) *The Gift: forms and functions of exchange in archaic societies*, London: Routledge and Kegan Paul.
McDaniel, J. (2011) *The Lovelorn Ghost and the Magic Monk: Practicing Buddhism in Modern Thailand*, New York, NY: Columbia University Press.
McKinley, R. (1976) 'Human and proud of it! A structural treatment of headhunting rites and the social definition of enemies', in G. N. Appell (ed.) *Studies in Borneo Societies: Social Process and Anthropological Explanation*, Center for Southeast Asian Studies, Northern Illinois University. Special Report; 12, 92–126.

McKinnon, S. (1995) 'Houses and Hierarchy: the view from a South Moluccan society' in J. Carsten and S. Hugh-Jones (eds) *About the House: Lévi-Strauss and beyond*, Cambridge: Cambridge University Press, 170–88.

Moebius, S. (2009) 'Die elementaren (Fremd-)Erfahrungen der Gabe: Sozialtheoretische Implikationen von Marcel Mauss' Kultursoziologie der Besessenheit und des "radikalen Durkheimismus" des College de Sociologie', *Berliner Journal für Soziologie*, 19: 104–26.

Needham, R. (1963) 'Blood, thunder and the mockery of animals', *Sociologus*, 14(2): 136–49.

Nieuwenhuis, A.W. (1918) Die Wurzeln des Animismus: eine Studie über die Anfänge der naiven Religion, nach den unter primitiven Malaien beobachteten Erscheinungen'. *Internationales Archiv für Ethnographie*, 24, Suppl.: 1–87.

Ong, A. (1988) 'The Production of Possession: Spirits and the Multinational Corporation in Malaysia', *American Ethnologist*, 15(1): 28–42.

Parkin, R.J. (1990) 'Ladders and Circles: Affinal Alliance and the Problem of Hierarchy', *Man*, 25: 472–88.

Pedersen, M.A. (2001) 'Totemism, animism, and north Asian indigenous ontologies', *Journal of the Royal Anthropological Institute*, 7: 411–27.

Platenkamp, J.D.M. (2006) 'Visibility and Objectification in Tobelo Ritual', in P. Crawford and M. Postma (eds.) *Reflecting Visual Ethnography - using the camera in anthropological fieldwork*, Aarhus: Intervention Press & Leiden: CNWS Press, 78–102.

—— (2007) 'Spirit representations in Southeast Asia: a comparative view', in F. Laugrand and J. G. Oosten (eds.) *Nature des esprits et esprits de la nature dans les cosmologies autochtones / Nature of spirits and spirits of nature in aboriginal cosmologies*, Quebec: Les Presses de l'Université Laval, 99–129.

—— (2010) 'Political change and ritual tenacity: The New Year's ritual of Luang Prabang, Laos', in A. Iteanu (ed.) *La coherence des societies: Mélanges en hommage à Daniel de Coppet*. Paris: Maison des Sciences de l'Homme, 193–233.

Praet, I. (2014) *Animism and the question of life*, London: Routledge.

Rodemeier, S. (2009) 'Bui Hangi – the Deity's Human Wife', *Anthropos*, 104: 469–82.

Rhum, M.R. (1994) '*The ancestral lords: gender, descent, and spirits in a Northern Thai village'*, DeKalb, IL: Center for Southeast Asian Studies, Northern Illinois University.

Sahlins, M. (2008) 'The Stranger King, or Elementary Forms of the Politics of Life', *Indonesia and the Malay World*, 36/105: 177–99.

Schefold, R. (1990) 'Natur und Kultur im Weltbild indonesischer Stammesgesellschaften', in W. Böhm and M. Lindauer (eds.) *Viertes Symposium der Universität Würzburg, Woher, wozu, wohin? Fragen nach dem menschlichen Leben*, Stuttgart: Klett, 285–336.

Spiro, M. (1967) *Burmese Supernaturalism: A Study in the Explanation and Reduction of Suffering*, Englewood Cliffs, NJ: Prentice Hall.

Sprenger, G. (2005) 'The way of the buffaloes: Trade and sacrifice in Northern Laos', *Ethnology*, 44(4): 291–312.

—— (2006a) 'Out of the ashes: Swidden cultivation in Highland Laos', *Anthropology Today*, 22(4): 9–13.

—— (2006b) 'Bone transfers: Incomplete replacement in Rmeet ritual exchange', *Taiwan Journal of Anthropology*, 4(1): 79–111.

—— (2008a) 'The problem of wholeness: Upland Southeast Asian cosmologies in transition', *Zeitschrift für Ethnologie*, 133(1): 75–94.

—— (2008b) 'Do the Rmeet have clans?', in M. Lorrillard and Y. Goudineau (eds.) *Recherches nouvelles sur le Laos*, Paris: Ècole française de l'Extrême-Orient, 559–78.

—— (2010) 'From power to value: ranked titles in an egalitarian society, Laos', *Journal of Asian Studies*, 69(2): 403–25.

—— (2014) 'Where the dead go to the market: market and ritual as social systems in upland Southeast Asia', in V. Gottowik (ed.) *Dynamics of Religion in Southeast Asia: Magic and Modernity*, Amsterdam: Amsterdam University Press, 75–90.

Spyer, P. (2000) *The memory of trade: Modernity's entanglements on an eastern Indonesian island*, Durham, NC and London: Duke University Press.

Strathern, M. (1988) *The gender of the gift: problems with women and problems with society in Melanesia*, Berkeley, CA: University of California Press.

Stringer, M.D. (2013) 'Building on belief: Animism in Tylor and contemporary society', in G. Harvey (ed.) *The Handbook of Contemporary Animism*, Durham, NC: Acumen, 63–72.

Tanabe, S. (1988) 'Spirits and ideological discourse: The Tai Lü guardian cults in Yunnan', *Sojourn*, 3(1): 1–25.

Tambiah, S. (1985) 'Animals are good to think and good to prohibit', in: S. Tambiah: *Culture, Thought and Social Action*, Cambridge: Cambridge University Press, 169–211.

Terwiel, B.J. (1994) 'Rice legends in mainland Southeast Asia: history and ethnography in the study of myths of origin' *Contributions to Southeast Asian Ethnography*, 10: 5–36.

Tiele, C. P. (1873) *De plaats van de godesdiensten der natuurvolken in die godsdienstgeschiedenis*. Amsterdam. https://download.digitale-sammlungen.de/pdf/1393848068bsb11158874.pdf Access 3. 3. 2014.

Tooker, D. (1992) 'Identity systems of Highland Burma: 'Belief', Akhazang, and a critique of interiorized notions of ethno-religious identity', *Man*, 27: 799–819.

—— (1996) 'Putting the Mandala in its place: a practice-based approach to the spatialization of power on the Southeast Asian 'periphery' - the case of the Akha', *Journal of Asian Studies*, 55(2): 323–58.

—— (2012) *Space and the production of cultural difference among the Akha prior to globalization: Channeling the flow of life*, Amsterdam: Amsterdam University Press.

Tsing, A.L. (1993) *In the realm of the diamond queen : marginality in an out-of-the-way place*, Princeton, NJ: Princeton University Press.

Tsintjilonis, D. (2004) 'The flow of life in Buntao: Southeast Asian animism reconsidered', *Bijdragen tot de Taal-, Land- en Volkenkunde*, 160(4): 425–55.

Tylor, E.B. (1958) [1873] *Religion in Primitive Culture*, Vol. 2. New York, NY: Harper & Row.

Valeri, V. (1994) 'Wild Victims: Hunting as Sacrifice and Sacrifice as Hunting in Huaulu', *History of Religions*, 34(2): 101–31.

Viveiros de Castro, E. (1998) 'Cosmological deixis and Amerindian perspectivism', *Journal of the Royal Anthropological Institute*, 4: 469–88.

—— (2007) 'The Crystal Forest: Notes on the Ontology of Amazonian Spirits', *Inner Asia*, 9(2): 153–72.

Walker, A. (1994) (ed.) *Rice in Southeast Asian myth and ritual*. Contributions to Southeast Asian ethnography 10, special issue.

Wilken, G.A. (1884–85) 'Het animisme bij de Volken van den Indischen Archipel', *De Indische Gids*, 6(1): 925–1000; 6(2): 19–100; 7(1): 191–242.

Willerslev, R. (2007) *Soul Hunters: Hunting, Animism and Personhood among the Siberian Yukagirs*, Berkeley, CA: Berkeley University Press.

Van Wouden, F.A. (1968) *Types of Social Structure in Eastern Indonesia*, The Hague: Nijhoff.

Part II

Case studies – Mainland and the Philippines

3 Seeing and knowing

Metamorphosis and the fragility of species in Chewong animistic ontology

Signe Howell

The relationship between physicality and interiority – between body and consciousness – as this affects identity, has dogged the anthropological study of animism from the time of Tylor (1871) until the present. In this chapter, I seek to shed some light on this relationship by drawing on ethnographic material from the Chewong, a hunting, gathering and shifting cultivating group of people in the Malaysian rainforest.[1] Chewong ontology and cosmology conflate with a comprehensive understanding of causal processes in 'nature' in which every object and being is a potential subject. I shall argue that the forest in which the Chewong live is animated in the sense that it is home to numerous non-human animate and conscious beings whose personhood and lives mirror those of the Chewong, but who have, nevertheless, a unique identity that maintains their separateness as a species. This identity is a question of the particular physicality – interiority relationship in each case which is species-specific and which is manifested by the eye through which each perceives reality. I suggest that the Chewong do not divide the world into human versus the rest of nature, but that they make a distinction between those species who have *ruwai* (consciousness, subjectivity or 'soul') and those who do not.

The relationship that the Chewong entertains with their animated environment is based on a number of prescriptions and proscriptions. These I call cosmo-rules because they are predicated upon ancestral knowledge communicated through myths and shamanistic songs. Cosmo-rules guide most daily activities, keeping the awareness of the wider world constantly at the forefront of attention and, as such, may usefully be thought of as onto-praxis (see Remme this volume). Human action is not excluded from 'nature', rather it is integral to the conditions at any given time of the environment in which they live – animate as well as inanimate. We can, I suggest, gain an enhanced understanding of animism by studying some implications of Chewong ideas and practices. I shall consider my interpretation of Chewong animism with reference to some recent contributions to the topic, in particular those made by Descola and Viveiros de Castro and discuss whether what we are faced with can be solved by characterizing it 'a continuity of souls and a discontinuity of bodies' (Descola 2006: 141).

I start by recounting an abbreviated version of a myth about elephants told by Chewong. According to Chewong understanding, elephants have consciousness (*ruwai*), a quality which makes them people and subjects. When they are in their own land, which is in the jungle and, in principle, identical to the Chewong human world but invisible to the ordinary human eye, they abandon their elephant 'cloaks' and appear to each other in human shape and behave in a recognizable human rational-emotional manner. Formally speaking, from a Chewong point of view, elephants are *people* on a par with themselves, but there is, nevertheless, a unique elephant quality which renders them elephants and people at the same time. My discussion of their understandings of the animate environment will be anchored in Chewong ontology and cosmology and the understanding of personhood that springs out of this.

Bongso and the Elephants

A man, Bongso [this name indicates that he has shamanistic abilities and, as such, that he has cool eyes and can see through all layers of reality and through all deceptions invisible to ordinary humans who have hot eyes] threw his spear at an elephant who came to eat his bananas. The spear stuck in the elephant's flank as he ran off. Bongso did not want to lose his spear so he followed after him. He followed a bloody trail for three days and three nights until he arrived at Elephant Village. Here the elephants were all without their elephant cloaks and appeared in human form. Thinking he was one of them, they gave Bongso food and told him about an old man who had suddenly taken very ill. No-one knew what the matter with him was. Bongso went to have a look. He saw his own spear sticking out of a wound in the man's side and knew it for what it was. He said a few spells and extracted the infection from the wound. Then he went into the jungle and cut a long tube of bamboo which he placed over the spear and pulled it out so that nobody could see it. They all had hot eyes and could not see the spear and did not know what Bongso was doing. The old man recovered and gave Bongso his two daughters as wives. After a while Bongso got homesick and set off to his mother's settlement with his wives. They were wearing elephant cloaks outside their village. When they were close to his mother's settlement, they took off their elephant cloaks, but they became frightened and wanted to return to the Elephant village. They put their elephant cloaks back on again and left. Some time later Bongso missed them and returned to the Elephant village and settled down with his wives. He was given an elephant cloak to wear whenever he went into the jungle. From now on he lived as an elephant and had become an elephant-person. But he was still shaman and, as such, had cool eyes. "If we meet an elephant who is not frightened by us and who does not attack us," Chewong told me, "that is Bongso'". (For fuller versions, see Howell 1982, 1984, 1989).

This is only one of a great number of myths in which the boundaries between the human world and the many animate non-human worlds of conscious beings (plants and animals, and in some cases inanimate objects) of the forest are far from absolute. In what follows, I am going to draw on other Chewong myths, and

I will use Chewong cosmo-rules as sources for my interpretation of the relationship between humans and non-human conscious beings in their environment – a relationship that is predicated upon Chewong ontology and cosmology and which constitutes practice. I treat myths and cosmo-rules as a narrative discourse. Narrative discourses carry cultural meanings and constitute interpretations that guide perception, interaction and action. Narrative discourse organizes life – social relations, interpretations of the past and plans for the future (cf. Bruner 2002). Telling stories, particularly in non-literate societies, influences how people perceive their world, confirms the basic principles for living, provide explanations for events, and guide behavior.

The myth about the elephants is a good example of Chewong narrative tradition as it confirms what they already know about the world in which they live and hint at correct behaviour. It clearly shows how the various worlds exist side by side, invisible to all but those with cool eyes. This means that Chewong environment – or landscape – may not be what it at first appears to be to the outsider, or to the hot-eyed Chewong. It is deceptive to human perception, full of what I call visual fallacies in the sense that one can never take for granted the reality of what one sees. For example, a clump of trees may be an elephant people village; some boulders in a river could be the settlement of frog people. Knowledge of such places and beings are expressed through the agency of Chewong myths, shamanistic songs and associated ritual activities, all of which are central in establishing individuals' understanding of reality: the world in which they live, personhood, relatedness and sociality. Knowing is profoundly linked to doing, and doing may, and does, influence details in narrative discourses, but does not alter them in a structural sense. For example, shamanistic songs describe the shaman's journey into the world of non-humans and provide new details about these worlds and the beings who live in them. Not every animal or plant species in the forest is *people*, but *potentially* they all are. Change in the world of sentient beings is communicated through shamanic narratives; new causal connections between human action and its effect upon the natural world are similarly revealed. Upon learning such details, people have to adjust their behaviour accordingly.

Chewong ontology cuts across familiar dualistic boundaries erected in Western science and folk cosmology between humanity on the one hand, and all other species of natural kinds and inanimate things on the other; between the human habitat and the many non-human ones in the forest – in other words, between any simple distinction between nature and culture.

My Research on Chewong Cosmology

When I submitted my DPhil thesis, entitled *Chewong Modes of Thought* in 1980, animism – understood as a religious belief in the soul of non-human animate and inanimate objects – was a concept that was firmly entrenched in the dark ages of the evolutionism of Tylor, Frazer and others, and had no place in contemporary anthropology at the time. Although my fieldwork with the Chewong brought to mind what I had read about animism, I was advised not to use the term. Instead,

I wrote about person and personhood and speculated about the meaning of consciousness as it was manifested throughout the animated forest environment in which the Chewong lived.

My concern was to understand the relationship between humans and the many non-human people with whom they interrelated; to analyse their cosmology in terms of an overarching argument that there was no existential distinction between society, nature and cosmos, and that the numerous conscious personages – as I called them – of some, but not all, animals, plants and natural objects, such as rocks and celestial phenomena, were essentially *human*, but distinguished by their bodies (cloaks) and their eyes. The latter I called 'relativity in perception'. By this I meant that members of one conscious species see the world around them according to identical criteria as do all others, but what actually constitutes an object or person to members of one species appears to those of another as something very different. I argued that '… Chewong posit a relativistic view of reality. As far as members of a particular species are concerned, the world that they view is the true one … [notwithstanding a] basic belief in the "psychic unity" of all personages … What differs between [them] is their notions as to what constitutes food, weapons and other objects, both cultural and natural.' (Howell 1984: 165) They all have different ways of perceiving reality and this difference is explained in terms of the eyes. The significance of this is further underlined by their notion that eyes are made first of all when a foetus is being developed inside its mother's womb (ibid.: 156).

Thus, all conscious beings in Chewong world share their existential approach to living (same needs, rationality, motives, behaviour, morality, way of life), but are differentiated from each other not just by the body (cf. Descola 1996, Viveiros de Castro 1998), but also the body-*ruwai* interrelationship (see below) and the eyes that mark the uniqueness of that interrelationship.

By the late 1990s, animism had re-emerged as one of the more exciting concepts in the anthropology of religion. The theoretical interest in animism lies in the relations that pertain between humans and conscious non-human natural kinds – and how these are manifested through the body-mind relationship in each case. It is the attempt to analyse the meaning and practice of such relationships that challenges the outside observer. Detailed explications upon such ontologies are vital, but particularly difficult given the metaphysical chasm that exists between observer (anthropologist) and observed (people studied). In an earlier contribution to the debate on how to define and interpret the slippery category of animism, Descola (1996) made a useful distinction between three types of human's interaction with the natural world around them, namely totemism, animism and naturalism. In a more recent re-evaluation of this schema he introduced a fourth type, namely analogism (2006). I return to this toward the end of the chapter. Viveiros de Castro's concept of perspectivism (1992, 1998, 2004), derived from his study of the Arawaté and inspired by Århem's work on the Makuna (2003 [1998]), added new interest in the comparative investigations of animism.

A number of other anthropologists have also entered the animist debate. Bird-David's overview article from 1999 proposed that animism had best be understood as 'relational epistemology', only to be opposed by Viveiros de Castro who suggested that relational ontology be more appropriate (1999: 580). When, more recently, these concepts were brought to Siberia and Inner Asia, a number of very detailed and perceptive publications resulted, refining and expanding their meaning and application (e.g., Pedersen 2001, Willerslev 2007).

The time is ripe to revisit my own early work. Returning to my ethnographic material from Chewong I shall ask to what extent perspectivism and Descola's four-fold schema are helpful analytic concepts in furthering my understanding of Chewong beliefs and practices. Clearly, our attention have been caught by similar features prevalent in the societies we studied. Despite the geographical distance between them, the animistic world of the Amazonian Indians bear a remarkable similarity to the cosmology I demonstrated in my work with the Chewong. Interestingly, our analyses followed a similar path. My concept 'relativity in perception' displayed many similarities to the Amerindian perspectivism Viveiros de Castro characterized as '... cosmologies concerning the way in which humans, animals and spirits see both themselves and one another' (1998: 469), manifesting 'spiritual unity and corporal diversity' (ibid.: 470). But there are also some differences, the most important of which is the idea of metamorphosis that is central to Chewong cosmology because, ultimately, it implies bounded species.

The term metamorphosis has been used by others in their discussion of animism (e.g., Viveiros de Castro, Willerslev), but the concept has been employed more loosely than I would wish to, and the implications have not been sufficiently theorized. Although I noted in my early work that metamorphosis was an integral part of Chewong animistic thought, I had not, until recently, appreciated its pivotal significance. In light of Chewong species-specific perception of the world around them, I shall examine in some detail what Chewong understanding of metamorphosis entails and ask how this affects personhood and sociality. Apparently unlike Amerindian ontologies, that of the Chewong opens for both temporary and permanent inhabitation of the body of another species. Moreover, both humans and other species of conscious beings may take on the body of others. I shall suggest that this throws a somewhat different light on the relationship between physicality and consciousness and the meaning of perspectivism and relational ontology.[2]

Connectedness and Separation: Chewong Notions of Consciousness, 'Speciesness', Relatedness and Vision

A seeming paradox characterizes Chewong cosmology and ontology. While everything is connected in an existential and, indeed, life-giving, manner, different beings, domains and objects of significance must be kept separate. Chewong relations with each other and with the multifarious forest environment are predicated upon these two principles of connectedness and separation which, I suggest, constitute the semantics of sociality. The notion of connectedness runs parallel to an idea of discontinuity, in the sense that domains and things are to be kept separate. As I discuss later when considering the significance of metamorphosis, how relations between humans and non-humans are conceptualised rests fundamentally on these two ontological principles.

By performing the cosmo-rules correctly, Chewong individuals ensure continuous reproduction in its broadest sense – of people, other species, society, cosmos. This is expressed most persistently in the numerous myths that elaborate the cosmo-rules of correct practice in matters of food and sex. Correct practice invariable concerns not mixing that which should be kept apart; be this in marriage and/or sexual relations – between human Chewong themselves[3] or between humans and species of conscious non-humans; or in the preparation and consuming different kinds of food. Failure to observe the cosmologically founded prescriptions and proscriptions (cosmo-rules) that orchestrate the maintenance of separation, invariably leads to mishap of some kind; indeed to potential destruction. Chewong causal explanation for the flow of life and its disruptions – for desirable or undesirable events – hinges on the possession and application of relevant knowledge, i.e., knowledge that is integral to their metaphysics: what is the nature of reality; and to their ontology: what types of things exist in the world and how they relate to each other (Howell 2012). The cosmo-rules implicitly express moral values integral to their concept of personhood and define the subjectivity of self and the non-human conscious beings with whom they interact. Cosmo-rules orchestrate the relations between humans and the natural environment.

To live in accordance with the cosmo-rules as guides for daily action, however seemingly banal to the outsider, is best understood, I suggest, as ritual acts. They bring the humans and non-human conscious beings into a continuous, but prescribed, relationship of mutuality, rendering the cosmo-rules 'techniques for life-saving' (cf. Hocart 1970 [1936]: 33–34; see also Kaj Århem's notion of ritual as 'techniques of survival'; Chapter 5, this volume). As Chewong sociality extends beyond humans into the wider worlds of consciousness, practice is never neutral, but embedded in and constituted upon ontological and cosmological understanding that emphasize the mutuality of relations (cf. Remme's discussion of onto-praxis, this volume). While social life in general is predicated upon two rules (*punén* and *maró*) that demand that everything harvested in the forest must be shared and that to 'eat alone' is *the* heinous transgression, the continuity of society is further predicated upon those cosmo-rules that demand separation of unlike elements. In what follows I shall explore some ramifications of cosmo-rules that manifest the principle of separation of categories, for it is here, I suggest, we may find some clues to Chewong animism.

For these claims to make sense I need to elaborate a little further upon the principles and values that constitute the Chewong social world – a social world that is co-extensive with their cosmos (Howell 1984, 1989, 1996) and what I mean by consciousness, people and personage in the Chewong context. These terms all spring out of the indigenous concept *ruwai* – a concept that dogged the whole eighteen months of my first fieldwork. Concepts that deal with metaphysical matters in alien cultural traditions are notoriously difficult to translate. I resolved the problem of how to interpret *ruwai* by splitting it into three separate meanings – interlinked, but independent, and each brought to bear contextually. This, I caution, was a heuristic device, and I do not claim to have caught the full Chewong understanding of it. I stated: 'firstly [*ruwai*] may broadly be understood as "vital principle". Secondly, it may be translated as "personage", by which I mean the manifestation of consciousness as rationality, present in certain animals and plants and inanimate objects as well as in all humans and the immortal superhuman beings. Thirdly, *ruwai* refers both to a spirit-guide and to the possession of one such' (Howell 1984: 125). It is the tantalising challenges of the second interpretation that I shall pursue in this chapter.

All beings and things with *ruwai* in the sense of consciousness (rationality, intentionality, emotionality) are also people (*beri*). As conscious, sentient, beings they are people – regardless of their exterior form; be this human, leaf-monkey, frog, lemongrass or whatever, but, when they are in 'their own land', they appear to each other in human form – but not to people of other species, viz. the elephant myth above. Interaction between all sentient species is non-hierarchical, mirroring the profoundly egalitarian basis for all Chewong relationships (Howell 1984, 1985, 2010). The acid test of sentience is the possession of *ruwai*. The *ruwai* is at the same time universal in its qualities and species-bound in the manifestation of these qualities. Conscious species distinguish themselves from each other through species-specific bodies – the cloak – and, most importantly through the eyes. Each species has its own special body by which it may be recognized, and the *ruwai* of each – despite its universal characteristics – is nevertheless constituted in and through the body. In other words, it is not a matter of indifference which *ruwai* inhabits which body at any given time. Moreover, as stated above, the eyes of each species perceive the surroundings in a somewhat different way from the rest, *but with the same intention.* What I want to argue is that Chewong animism distinguishes itself somewhat from those described by others by insisting on a necessary interconnected relationship between cloak, eyes and *ruwai,* which means that together these constitute the identity of each species. Prolonged inhabitation of *ruwai* in an alien body leads to metamorphosis of identity (see below).

To take the analysis of this body-*ruwai* interrelationship one step further, I draw on the notion of embodied understanding first developed by Johnson (1987). Johnson alerted us to some important aspects of the construction of knowledge which may also be helpful in the interpretation of the construction of experiencing of identity. He urges us in our study of rationality and knowledge to 'put the body back in the mind'. He reminds us that human beings have bodies and that '... human bodily movements, manipulations of objects, and perceptual interactions involve recurring patterns without which our experience would be chaotic and incomprehensible' (op. cit.: xix). To this I wish to add that these patterns are not self-generated, they are those deemed significant in the particular social contexts in which individuals operate and learn and, in the context of animistic ontologies, to the particular species in each case. According to Toren, '[...] for a model of mind that is anthropologically, biologically and phenomenologically sound it has to be based on the recognition that mind is embodied' (1993: 462). Yes indeed, but again I wish to add that for humans (and in the Chewong case, all sentient species) the reverse also pertains, namely, to coin a phrase, 'bodies are minded' (Howell unpublished manuscript). This mutuality of body and mind, I suggest is highly pertinent in Chewong ontology as it highlights both the continuity and separation of conscious beings.

Shamanic Qualities and Power

According to Chewong understanding some individuals in every species possess special abilities that enable them, interalia, to travel between the different species-bound worlds, usually during healing ceremonies, but also at other times such as in dreams, or as in the case of the elephant myth above, by entering another when walking in the forest. They are shamans (*putao*). Some form of shamanistic practice is a common corollary to an animistic cosmology.[4] As already explained, there are a number of villages and houses in the forest that are the home to the different species of conscious beings. To ordinary *hot*, human eyes they are just clusters of trees or leaves; to the species themselves they are houses and fields just like human houses and fields. Because shamans have cool eyes, like Bongso in the elephant myth, they can see the true nature of these worlds; that is, they can see beyond the trees, stones, and so on to a settlement on par with a Chewong settlement. Shamans are also able to take on and off their cloaks and don that of other species whose land they are visiting. This deception is not apparent to people and they are accepted as *bona fide*. Human shamans can also discern imposters from other species who enter their own world clad in human cloak.[5] Ordinary individual personages have hot eyes and must be content with the appearances, not the reality. Chewong mythology is full of stories that narrate the encounter between members of different species – between those with hot, unknowing, eyes and those with cool – that is, knowing – eyes. Often those with cool eyes deceive and play tricks on those with hot eyes, whether for purposes of retrieving the stolen *ruwai* of a sick individual or just for fun.

Perception being species-bound is profoundly important in distinguishing one species from another. In one sense all species see the same world, and have the same intentions and needs; only what makes up the material objects in each world differs (see below for elaborations on this). For example, human eyes see a wild pig as edible animal; potential meat. A gibbon sees certain leaves as the staple manioc. A *bas* (group of potentially harmful spirits that are activated to perform a harmful act upon humans following a breach of a cosmo-rule) sees human *ruwai* as meat. In other words, they all see the world in the same way, only what makes up the various things are perceived differently by different species (Howell 1984). While they are in 'their own land', the well-being of all conscious species is dependent upon the observation of cosmo-rules, which specify the same prescriptions and proscriptions like those of the Chewong; but again, what actually constitutes the offence – and the effect – is species dependent. Below I will give some examples taken from myths which exemplify situations when things go wrong and metamorphoses take place.

I have argued (e.g., 1982, 1984, 1996) that Chewong understanding of the animated world in which they live may be thought of as anthropomorphic, or more precisely, Chewongmorphic. At the same time, each different species of sentient beings not only has a distinctive body; they also live according to the specificity of their own interpretation of the material world as this is perceived through the species-specific quality of the eyes. Chewong adhere to a psychic and cognitive unity of all species of people, at the same time as they maintain the disjuncture between each species. Chewong know how the natives' points of view differ from each other. Intentions and values are identical, actual material details that make up the world in each case are different. From this perspective the animated world around them is a composite world that, arguably, may be characterized as consisting of many natures but only one culture (cf. Viveiros de Castro 1998). However, as I shall argue, Chewong ontological understanding is not quite as straightforward as this celebrated formula seems to imply.

Importantly, those with shamanic abilities who have established a permanent relationship with a spirit-guide (*ruwai*) can send their consciousness (*ruwai*) on a journey into space during a healing séance. On such journeys they meet the various immortal spirits as well as the shamans of other species. This experience is a continuous source of ontological knowledge. Chewong animated universe is not static, it is a social world in constant flux. During shamanic journeys some species previously not thought of as people, may reveal themselves as such. Any being or object may appear as a conscious being. For example, one shamanistic song refers to the *ruwai* of Japanese airplanes that was encountered during World War 2 by a shaman as the planes flew over the forest. His songs are still sung by his grandson. Others that are not encountered for some time may be forgotten. There is thus no *a priori* separation between animate and inanimate, human and non-human; the potential for movement between them is ever-present. Knowledge about who is what is carried forward through myths and shamanic songs and is added to by contemporary shamanic revelations. Although all species of conscious beings view their world from their own perspective, they are all unified through a Chewongmorphic construction of reality. According to Chewong, the fact that there are many significant others being like us provides a basis for mutual sociality to be performed and for shamans from different species to communicate when they meet.

Animism is often associated with hunting societies. It has been suggested that the practice of hunting, killing and eating animals in one's environment which are attributed with human-like spirit qualities and with whom one engages in prescribed relationships, gives rise to the hunter's dilemma (Pedersen 2001: 422). Århem (Chapter 5, this volume) similarly argues that the fact that animals are a kind of 'people', presents animistic people with 'an existential dilemma: how to avoid metaphysical "warfare" with the "animal people"'. There is little evidence to support such a dilemma as far Chewong are concerned. Hunting does not give rise to moral qualms; questions of subjectivity only arise in specific contexts, and hunting is not one of them. For example, when out hunting, the hunter does not see the monkey that he shoots with his blow-pipe as a subject, only as legitimate food. Any notion of cannibalism or cannibalistic predation – as reported from the Amazon (Viveiros de Castro 2004: 480) – is not present in Chewong ontological schema. Unlike many Inuit or Siberian hunter-gatherers (cf. Willerslev 2007), Chewong do not adhere to beliefs in rebirth in any sense – of either humans or other conscious beings – nor do they believe that hunters are responsible for the rebirth of their prey. They do, however, acknowledge a responsibility toward the fecundity of species that they kill in order to eat, and this is performed by singeing the fur of animals before butchering them. The smell of the burnt hair goes to the land of the animal in question manifesting itself as food for the beings who live there. They perceive the smoke as meat. This is an expression of an exchange relationship that pertains between Chewong and their prey, but in the context of the hunt and the meal it is irrelevant if the hunted belongs to a species known to be people or not. It is important to remind ourselves that not all animals and plants, whether edible or not, are people, but that edible and inedible animals, plants and also natural objects may be so.

The use of nicknames (*cho punén*, lit. *punén*[6] name) for a range of plants and useful things collected in the forest (e.g., bamboo for baking manioc bread in) that are important in some way or other – primarily as food, but not necessarily – is a practice that shows that the Chewong de-subjectify them before use. The true name of these natural kinds should not be spoken while out in the forest; this is 'to speak badly', especially if one is in search of them. Rather, its nickname must be used. For example, the tree from which they extract dart poison is called *dog*. The preparation of the poison is subjected to a number of prescribed actions and the poison has *ruwai* and is people – the poison maidens. When a man is going into the forest to collect the red sap from the tree, he refers to it as *ai le eg* (the image of blood). Bamboo spear traps (also people) erected along the edges of manioc fields in order to catch wild pigs are called *bladen*, but when building them they must be called *ai taloden* (image of snakes). When going to fetch water (*ta'm*) in a distant river, the water must be called *ai haredj* (image of sweat). A kind of edible leaf vegetable with long stems is called 'the image of the long ones' (*ai gisogn*). Tigers (*kle*) are not eaten, but they are greatly feared and frequently feature in myths and songs (see below). The tiger's true name is never spoken except in whispers, and the animal is usually referred to by clutching the right hand into a claw. By not taking care in their speech on such occasions, Chewong render themselves vulnerable to attack by a tiger, a snake, a bear, or a spider – whether by the actual animal or its *ruwai*.

Through the use of nicknames, they acknowledge the importance of certain animal and plant personages and their connectedness to themselves while, at the same time as they are being de-subjectified, rendering them edible or usable.[7] The practice may be linked to the analogous use of nick-names for individual persons. This is prevalent among the Chewong (Howell 1984: 187–89). A name taboo exists between opposite sex parents and children in-law. However, nicknames are never told to outsiders; their employment is confined to significant relations – just as are the *punén* names of natural kinds.

Separation and Metamorphosis

Chewong conceptions of being and consciousness are thus central to an interpretation of their social world beyond that of the Chewong themselves. Regardless of species, the principle of separation emphasises the important principle that each person, species, entity or element contains its own existence, its own domain and its own premises for social life which should not be disturbed or contaminated by interference from other worlds. This principle of discontinuity between domains manifests itself most commonly in narratives when a representative of one species crosses the boundary and enters that of another.

Seeing and knowing 65

In practical daily life this is expressed most clearly in the classification and treatment of food. The most commonly performed principle of separation springs out of the cosmo-rules that demand the keeping of different categories of food separate. As such, cosmology is kept at the forefront of people's minds. Different food stuffs must not be mixed. They must be carried and placed apart, cooked over separate fires, and they may not be eaten at the same meal. Several myths recount the unfortunate result of putting different species of game in the same basket, or an animal together with wild fruit, or of cooking one kind of meat on the same fireplace where another kind of meat has previously been cooked. Chewong settlements display a number of fireplaces; e.g., one inside the house for the cooking of staple manioc and rice, fish and monkeys (these may be cooked in the same fireplace), separate fireplaces on the ground outside for wild pig, for monitor lizards, porcupines and so on, and for different kinds of wild fruit or vegetable. Failure to adhere to this activates harmful species, (*bas*), and allows them to attack the transgressor – body or *ruwai,* either is equally vulnerable - which they now see as meat or staple that they may legitimately hunt and eat. Similarly, to eat fruit shortly after having eaten meat leads to terrible stomach upset caused by some other *bas*. Theory of health and illness is thus integral to their relationship with other beings in the environment and one major source of illness is expressed through the medium of food.[8] As stated above, Chewong shamanism, unlike that of the Amerindians, does not entertain the notion that it is possible to eat *ruwai* – although their own *ruwai* may be eaten by non-human species. Neither do they think that the act of eating a specific animal or plant leads to revenge. Once killed, an animal is inanimate meat. When harvested, wild fruits and vegetables are just food.

The overriding rule, then, is to keep that which is different apart. The maintenance of boundaries between unlike elements ensures socio-cosmic order. This is highly apposite in the relationship between the different species of conscious beings. The relevant *ruwai* must in normal circumstances be in the relevant body. If not, metamorphosis may occur. However, humans and members of non-human conscious species who possess cool eyes, may mix socially in each others' lands within prescribed constraints and for short periods of time. This may involve the donning of the other's cloak. Commonly, this occurs during healing séances when shamans go into trance and move around in the worlds of non-human personages in search of the lost *ruwai* of the sick. The drumming keeps the path back home open, because if s/he stays away too long, s/he may not find his/her way home to the body and be lost for ever. Songs describe his journey and the people they meet.

Various kinds of other cross-species encounters are described in myths. They follow a set pattern which involves the main character shedding his/her species-bound cloak and replacing it temporarily with that of another species. This may go both directions – from humans to animal or plant, or from animal or plant to human. In all cases, the performers are individuals with cool eyes. For example, a man or woman from a non-human sentient species (e.g., spider, dog, frog, rambutan fruit) moves into the Chewong human world and exchanges their original cloak with that of a human cloak and pretends to be human. Usually they meet a human of the opposite sex and marry him or her and live as a Chewong. But they keep their original cloak somewhere out of harm's way and put it on from time to time to return to their original world. However, the deceit is invariably discovered.

At such moments two options are available. A non-human interloper whose spouse discovers the deception may choose to return to its own world. The human spouse may follow, usually with their children, thereby abandoning their Chewong status for ever. They are metamorphosed into the relevant species. Alternatively, the Chewong spouse may get hold of the cloak before the imposter has time to put it on and disappear and destroy it by fire, thereby preventing the imposter from returning to his/her true nature and the world to which he/she truly belongs. From that moment onwards, the person becomes a proper human Chewong unable to resume his former nature, and henceforth perceives reality according to human perception. Similarly, a human individual may pretend to be the member of a non-human species, marry someone there and, upon discovery, the same scenario follows. Invariably, the deceiver becomes metamorphosed, unable to resume her original cloak, eyes and life. An interesting variant on this theme is the story about the woman who had put on a squirrel cloak and was shot by a human hunter who thought she was a real squirrel. In death she reverted to her human form and the hunter found a human body, not a squirrel.

Another scenario is for a human person to don a non-human cloak and pretend to be a member of that species. Again the myths exemplify. The deceiver marries a woman or man who thinks that they have a spider or frog, or whatever, spouse, until they discover that the spouse takes off the alien cloak in order to bathe, or eat human food in secret, hunt with the blowpipe or perform some other activity for which it is necessary to be in human form. When the non-human spouse discovers this, she burns the cloak and the spouse is henceforth doomed to remain in the non-human cloak. He/she becomes metamorphosed.

In all these cases, until he or she is found out, the person who has exchanged his or her cloak continues to see according to the vision of their original species and observe the cosmo-rules of that world while, at the same time, they know what they are doing and refrain from transgressing the lines of proper behaviour in the world that they pretend to belong to. There is thus a kind of double vision at work here, which demands a fine balancing act by the imposter concerned and which they do not always manage to control. If an imposter fails to practice the demands of his original species this leads to metamorphoses, i.e., their identity (cloak and *ruwai* together) changes permanently.[9] For example, prolonged behaviour of the assumed species that goes against acceptable human behaviour can lead to permanent loss of humanity. One myth tells of a Chewong man who pretended to be a dog person and married a dog-woman. She did not know his true identity. Together with his dog brothers-in-law, he ate the stomach content and licked the blood of killed animals. This meant that he had abandoned his human perception of reality to such a serious degree that he became a dog, unable to return to the world of humans.

The story of the man who carried a leaf-monkey and *howaw* fruit (unacceptable mixing) in his basket during 'hot rain' – that is, rain and sunshine at the same time, another unacceptable mixing, this time of meteorological conditions which indicates that harmful and uncontrollable spirits are around – led to serious repercussions.[10] This double transgression of boundaries meant that the man turned into a tiger – the ultimate human opposite – and went in pursuit of his brother-in-law. The latter managed to wound the tiger with his spear and asked him why he pursued him, 'I only see you as meat', replied the tiger. These two examples demonstrate the interconnectedness between body, *ruwai* and eyes. At a certain point these fuse and stand forth as unequivocally one identity. They also demonstrate the fragility of boundaries and the uncertainty about the reality of others.

Temporary inhabitation of the body of another sentient species does not result in metamorphosis, but prolonged overstepping invariably leads to permanent transformation; to metamorphosis. The eye is the pivotal bodily attribute that marks the metamorphosis. It is when an individual sees the world around her/him from the point of view of another species that s/he has become metamorphosed. Then the borrowed cloak and the *ruwai* associated with it fuse and replace the human cloak and *ruwai*. The previous human has acquired the doggishness or elephantness of those whose behaviour he or she had copied. Similarly, the previous elephant or frog who has been a guest in a human body and started to behave in a human manner, will acquire humanity. I am not suggesting that these stories are taken as true and accurate depiction of what goes on in the Chewong forest, that elephants and frogs that one meets while walking actually are people in a cloak and that proper care must be taken in one's interaction with them. Even though all Chewong know the myths about frog people, or spider people or whatever people, this does not affect their reactions to them in daily life. It is when cosmo-rules are invoked in particular contexts of tabooed behaviour, or when illness or mishap occurs that the narrative discourse of the animated environment is made relevant. Having said that, I repeat that that this knowledge is not metaphorical. The observation of food taboos amply demonstrates this.

The death rituals of powerful shamans illustrate this in a different way. The boundary between humans and animals may be legitimately crossed in the case of great shamans and tigers. The ultimate Chewong spirit-guide is the tiger. Very few shamans are able to contract such a relationship as it is regarded as highly dangerous, but once established, renders the shaman tremendous powers. Such shamans occupy a liminal – or perhaps pivotal – position between ordinary humans and the immortal beings. This is marked by not burying their corpse, but by placing it on a specially constructed platform in the forest. Those who dare check the site after a couple of days invariably discover the body to be missing. It has metamorphosed into a tiger; in fact, it has fused with the shaman's tiger spirit-guide and has become an immortal were-tiger. The case of Cheii, a powerful shaman who died in 2004 or 2005, shows that this sequence is not questioned even today. I was told how his relatives were terrified of touching the corpse. They built a platform but, instead of preparing the corpse in the prescribed manner and solemnly placing it on it, they grabbed him by his arms and legs and flung him onto the platform and ran away. No-one dared return to check what happened to the corpse, but it was generally assumed that he had turned into a were-tiger. In fact, although there was some disagreement about this, it seems that the tiger spirit-guides of living shamans, are in fact such a deceased shaman.

Analysis

Chewong, like many other Southeast Asian people discussed in this volume, share their personhood with many (but not all) animals, plants and other seemingly inanimate features of their environment. Most anthropologists who today work in societies that may loosely be characterized as animistic eschew any distinction between nature and culture – or nature and humanity. Rather, we seek alternative ways to understand and interpret the reality that we encounter during our fieldwork: the ontology, morality and metaphysics of the people we study are placed at the centre of analysis, not the preoccupations of our own. But we are as much caught in the constraints of our own language and concepts as they are in theirs. These are the challenges that anthropologists such as myself, Descola, Viveiros de Castro and others, including the contributors to this book, are grappling with and, in conclusion, I shall assess in what ways some recent interpretations coincide with my own.

Viveiros de Castro introduces the notion of perspectivism, based on Amazonian cosmologies, and this concept has subsequently been applied elsewhere by others. It corresponds closely, I believe, to what I referred to as 'relativity in perception' in my early work (Howell 1984: Chapter 7). In this respect, the cosmologies of Amazonian societies appear to be quite similar to that of the Chewong. But I wish to suggest that the particular Chewong ontological understanding of personhood as a mutually constitutive relationship between body, *ruwai* and vision, and the associated phenomenon of metamorphosis – linked to the argument about simultaneous contiguity and separation between that which is dissimilar – demands further analysis, and can enhance our understanding of perspectivism in practice.

Animism raises the perennial question of the relationship between thought and action, and between physicality and interiority. From Chewong epistemological point of view, action is informed by thought and thought informs action. Similarly, for them, bodies cannot exist without a mind, and minds cannot exist without a body; the two constitute the identity of a person. According to Chewong thinking, both bodies and minds are species-specific. Species-specific *ruwai* need to be in the relevant species-specific body (cloak); body and *ruwai* are mutually constitutive. While they may separate at times and, in the case of shamanic trance journeys, the *ruwai* may travel on its own into the worlds of other conscious species, the separation must be short-lived lest the *ruwai* loses its way back to its body and the person dies.

As is amply shown by myths and other narrative discourses, when someone dons the body of another species and pretends to be one of them, this must be of temporary duration. During such short-lived occasions the shamans employ a double vision; that of their true nature and that of the species whose cloak they temporarily inhabit. However, as also shown, extended habitation within another species' cloak leads, necessarily, to metamorphosis. Once the performance of practices integral to other species are experienced as normal, the intruder's eyes view the world as would a member of that species and the intruder's *ruwai* and body are permanently metamorphosed into those of the other. When an individual perceives the world around him in the same manner as those whose body he is wearing, then metamorphosis has occurred. This amply demonstrates how action

Seeing and knowing 69

influences mental processes and the consequent need for maintaining boundaries between species identity.

To recapitulate: the forest world in which Chewong live is made up of a number of other species of conscious beings whose essence is formally identical to that of the Chewong. Such an ontological understanding links the environment and the people in a highly intimate, but also fragile, manner. Potentially everything may turn out to be imbued with consciousness, you never fully know what's what. However, the cosmo-rules enable individuals to live in a meaningful relationship with their animated environment, providing them with a sense of control. In this sense, I suggest that it is through action that reality is brought into being by each category of sentient being. Moreover, relevant actions are always relational. The direct cause-effect sequences that are expressed in the cosmo-rules and that characterize the relationship between the human and non-human worlds are an integral part of Chewong animism (Howell 2012). Therefore, statements and narratives about the world in which they live are, for the Chewong, not symbolic or metaphoric, they are descriptions of reality. This apparent paradox may be likened to Marx analyses of capitalism and fetishism of value: the commodity is a fetish which is 'mystical' and yet also real in its effects; it has real power by virtue of people's beliefs (McNeill 1988). In seeking to explain the value of a commodity Marx writes: 'In a sort of way, it is with man as with commodities. [...] Peter only establishes his own [...] identity as a man by comparing himself with Paul as being of like kind. And thereby Paul, just as he stands in his Pauline personality, becomes to Peter the type of the genus homo' (Capital I: 59 footnote).

This analogy is rather similar to the sort of Hegelian approach which Marx rejects in his early writings. But I find it rather enlightening – as applied to the Chewong. Thus, using 'fruit' as an example Marx writes:

> 'The speculative philosopher argues somewhat as follows [...] "*the* fruit" is not dead, undifferentiated, motionless, but a living, self-differentiating, moving essence.[...] The different ordinary fruits are different manifestations of the life of the "*one* Fruit"; they are crystallisations of "*the* Fruit" itself. [...] (Thus,) "*the* Fruit" presents itself as a pear, "*the* Fruit" presents itself as an apple, "*the* Fruit" presents itself as an almond; and the differences which distinguish apples, pears and almonds from one another are the self-differentiations of "*the* Fruit" and make the particular fruits different members of the life-process of "*the* Fruit". Thus "*the* Fruit" is no longer an empty undifferentiated unity; it is oneness as *allness*, as "totality" of fruits, which constitute an *organically linked series of members*'. (*The Holy Family*, In *Coll. Works 4*: 57–9. Original emphasis.)

I posit the idea that Chewong *ruwai* may be analogous to 'the Fruit' in so far as *Ruwai* (capital R) presents itself variously as elephant, leaf-monkey, rambutan fruit. The differences which distinguish one species from another are the differentiations of *Ruwai* that make the different conscious beings different members of the life-process of *Ruwai*. *Ruwai* is thus not an empty undifferentiated unity; it is a 'totality of *ruwais*, which constitutes not just 'an organically linked series of members', but a series of members that must be kept separate for *Ruwai* to be a 'living, moving essence'.

Chewong cosmological understanding of self and other results in a composite multifaceted world of equivalences, the parts inexorably linked through mutual dependency for the reproduction of social and individual life to occur. Their categorisation of sentient species indicates both sameness and difference. The cosmorules indicate a fragile relationship between species.

While it would be accurate to state, with regard to the Chewong situation, that 'humanity is the general condition, not man as species' (Descola 2006: 141),[11] I would – at least as regards the Chewong – question Descola's other suggestion that animism is 'a continuity of souls and discontinuity of bodies'. Although *ruwai* are, formally, identical regardless of body, but, as the elephant myth shows, so are also bodies: sentient species look like human bodies to each other when they are in their own land. Moreover, *ruwai* may don and discard own and others' bodies but, when the chips are down, there is a necessary one-to-oneness of the two within each species which demonstrates that they are part and parcel of each other and, ultimately, better understood as one and not identical across species.

The particular phenomenon of irrevocable metamorphosis[12] that I describe in this chapter requires, I suggest, a reconsideration of the concept of animism. The particularity of Chewong animistic metaphysics may be regarded as yet another variant upon a common, and exceedingly complex, theme.

Notes

1. The original fieldwork consisted of eighteen months from September 1977 to April 1979. At the time, Chewong lived deep inside the rainforest and had little contact with the outside world. My discussion of Chewong animism is based on my findings from that time. Since that time, Chewong have been pulled into the outside world through logging, trading, more or less forcible resettlement on the new edge of the forest, and the establishment of an elephant sanctuary nearby. Had I started my fieldwork today, I very much doubt if the world I describe here would have been accessible to me. Although the main principles of what I learned then are still valid, their structuring force have diminished and young children today do not constitute their being in the world on the same narrative discourses as people did thirty years ago. Cosmological and ontological knowledge of that time is clearly on the wane: practice is explained by a multitude of references from a range of cultural sources (Howell 2011).
2. In an article from 2004, Viveiros de Castro addressed the difference between what he calls transformation and metamorphosis. By transformation he (confusingly perhaps) means something close to what I call metamorphosis. He states that if non-shamans 'happens to see a non-human (an animal, a dead human, a spirit) in human form, he or she runs the risk of being overpowered by the non-human subjectivity, of passing over to its side and being transformed into an animal, a dead human, a spirit' (2004: 468). This is, however, a different process from the one I describe as metamorphosis among the Chewong, when a person has donned the cloak of another species and fails to behave according to the norms of his or her own species. Viveiros de Castro terms a temporary move into the body of another species metamorphosis.
3. Chewong principles of kin relations are a simple version of cognatic bilateral kinship. Marriage rules are negative: marriage between siblings and parents and children is forbidden. Cousin marriage is preferred, especially that between children of sisters,

while that between children of brothers is discouraged although not forbidden by a cosmo-rule. Mishaps may be attributed to such marriages.
4. As is clear from several chapters in this book, animistic beliefs and practices may occur in societies where shamanism is not present. However, an all-encompassing animistic ontology is most commonly found in shamanistic societies.
5. One must assume that there was no person with shamanistic qualities in the elephant village that Bongso visited who could have revealed his identity.
6. *Punén* is one of the most important cosmo-rules and usually refers to failure of sharing, and to the experience of unfulfilled desire (mainly for food). To call nicknames for *punén* names indicates the seriousness of the offence of speaking badly in these cases.
7. By giving significant natural kinds nicknames, they can be said to acknowledge their special status in their lives.
8. The cosmo-rule *punén* states that all food must be shared equally between all present. Failure to do so – to eat alone – similarly allows a *bas* to attack. In this case, it is not the offender who is attacked, but the person(s) offended against. *Punén* is thus a cosmo-rule that emphasizes connectedness – that between all Chewong.
9. A similar notion may be found among the Katu. When a man has donned a tiger body and begins to eat raw meat, he will not be able to return to his humanity, but must remain a tiger (Århem, personal communication).
10. For rain and sunshine to occur at the same time is regarded as abnormal mixing. It occurs outside Chewong control and is, as such, dangerous, indicating stronger powers at work.
11. 'Humanity' here must be seen as Chewong humanity.
12. Chewong metamorphosis differs from transformation as described by Viveiros de Castro in so far as it occurs through overstepping the boundaries between self and other and starting to *behave* as the other – not just through seeing the other as human. As this metamorphosis is described in the myths there is an element of choice on the part of the person who is metamorphosed – whether from Chewong to some animal or plant or from some animal or plant to Chewong (see Howell 2012).

References

Århem, K. (2003) [1998] *Makuna: Portrait of an Amazonian People*, Washington, DC: Smithsonian Institute.
Bird-David, N. (1999) 'Animism revisited: Personhood, environment and relational epistemology', *Current Anthropology*, 40: 67–91.
Bruner, J. (2002) *Making Stories: Law, Literature, Life*, Cambridge, MA: Harvard University Press.
Descola. P. (1996) 'Constructing natures: Symbolic ecology and social practice', in P. Descola and G. Pálsson (eds.) *Nature and Society: Anthropological Perspectives*, London: Routledge.
———— (2006) 'Beyond nature and culture', *Proceedings of the British Academy*, 139:137–55.
Hocart, A.M. (1970) [1936] *The Life-Giving Myth and Other Essays*, London: Methuen.
Ingold, T. (2000) *The Perception of the Environment: Essays in Livelihood, Dwelling and Skill*, London: Routledge.
Howell, S. (1982) *Chewong Myths and Legends, Royal Asiatic Society*, Malaysian Branch: Monograph no 11.
———— (1984) *Society and Cosmos: Chewong of Peninsular Malaysia*, Oxford University Press. Re-issued 1989 in paperback edition by University of Chicago Press.
———— (1985) 'Equality and Hierarchy in Chewong Classification', in R.H. Barnes and D. De Coppet (eds.) *Context and Levels*, Oxford: JASO Monograph no. 4.

―― (1994) 'The socioemotional construction of embodied knowledge', unpublished manuscript.

―― (1996) 'Nature in Culture or Culture in Nature? Chewong ideas of "humans" and other species', in P. Descola and G. Pálsson (eds). *Nature and Society: Anthropological perspectives*, London: Routledge.

―― (2010) 'Sources of Sociality in a Cosmological Frame: Chewong, Peninsular Malaysia', in T. Gibson and K. Sillander (eds.) *Anarchic Solidarity: Autonomy, Equality, and Fellowship in Southeast Asia*, New Haven, CT: Yale University Press.

―― (2012) 'Knowledge, Causality and Morality in a "Luckless" Society: the case of the Chewong in the Malaysian rainforest', in G. da Col and C. Humphrey (eds.) *Economies of Fortune, Special Issue: Social Analysis*, 56(1): 133–147.

Johnson, M. (1987) *The Body in the Mind: the Bodily Basis of Meaning, Imagination and Reason*, Chicago, IL: University of Chicago Press.

Marx. K. and Engels F. (1975) *Collected Works, Vol I*. Moscow: Progress.

McNeill, D. (1988) Fetishism and the Value Form: Towards a general theory of value. PhD thesis submitted to University College London, London University, (also available at: http://www.lulu.com/product/file-download/fetishism-and-the-value-form-towards-a-general-theory-of-value).

Pedersen, M. (2001) 'Totemism, Animism and North Asian Indigenous Ontologies', *Journal of the Royal Anthropological Institute*, 7(3): 411–27.

Stocking, G.W. (1987) *Victorian Anthropology*, New York, NY: Free Press.

Toren, C. (1993) 'Making History: The Significance of Childhood Cognition for a Comparative Anthropology of Mind', *Man*, 28(3), 461–78.

Tylor, E.B. (1871) *Primitive Culture*, London: Methuen.

Viveiros de Castro, E. (1992) *From the Enemies' Point of View: Humanity and Divinity in an Amazonian Society*, Chicago, IL: University of Chicago Press.

―― (1998) 'Cosmological Deixis and Amerindian Perspectivism', *Journal of the Royal Anthropological Institute*, 4: 469–88.

―― (1999) 'Comment to Bird-David', *Current Anthropology*, 40, Supplement: 79–80.

―― (2004) 'Exchanging Perspectives: the transformation of objects into subjects in Amerindian ontologies', *Common Knowledge*, 10: 3.

Willerslev, R. (2007) *Soul Hunters: Hunting, Animism and Personhood among the Siberian Yukaghirs*, Berkeley, CA: University of California Press.

4 Graded personhood

Human and non-human actors in the Southeast Asian uplands

Guido Sprenger

Among the many misconceptions about animism is the idea that, in an animist cosmology, 'everything has a soul'. This is obviously untrue. Certainly, animist cosmologies differ from modern naturalist cosmologies by ascribing person-like features to entities that appear as mere objects in the latter (Hallowell 1960). However, the ascription of personhood, intentionality and agency to non-human entities is highly selective and subject to particular conditions. The question thus arises, what are the conditions for an entity to gain person-like traits? The analysis of animist cosmologies thus has to determine the point at which a non-human being becomes classified in a category that modern observers might translate as 'spirit' or 'soul'.

The following analysis of rituals and value-ideas of the Rmeet of upland Laos attempts to determine some of these conditions. The point of departure is their relationship with animals. Two categories of animals are relevant: domestic animals, which are used as sacrifices for spirits; and game animals, which are also subject to ritual treatment. I argue that the difference between raising domestic animals and hunting wild ones cannot be properly understood in terms of 'production', that is, as a relationship between human actors and objectified resources. The different relations with animals can be accounted for more precisely in terms of exchange processes that constitute different domains of the social. These exchanges organize not just Rmeet village society, but also relationships with animals, with the forest and with other ethnicities. All human and non-human entities involved in these exchanges might acquire person-like traits according to their position in and relevance to the (re-)production of the exchange network. Personhood emerges at the point of friction between exchanging and being exchanged. It appears not as an essential feature of particular classes of beings but is indicated and construed by communication.

Animism in the Uplands

The Rmeet number about 20,000 persons who mostly live in the northern provinces of Laos, Luang Nam Tha, Bokeo and Udomxai.[1] Their villages typically depend on swidden farming, and Rmeet society has no indigenous centres larger than these villages. They speak a Mon-Khmer language and thus belong to a category of ethnicities preceding the Tai-speaking Buddhist kingdoms of the lowlands. Their identity is clearly distinct from lowlanders, but has developed in interaction with them over many generations.

The Rmeet recognize three constitutive components or aspects of persons: *to*, the body; *pääm*, the living movement distinct to humans, animals, and plants, indicated by growth and breath, but also meaning character or mood; and *klpu*, the 'soul', that occurs only among humans, buffaloes, and, according to earlier usage, rice. Human *klpu* is one conduct of communication with the spirits (*phi*), as it often sees the world from their vantage point in dreams and turns into a spirit after death. The integration of *klpu* and body is crucial for a person's well-being, as their separation leads to illness and death. The stability of their relation in turn depends on relations with other persons: People need to be involved with ancestors, affines and spirits in order to remain healthy (Sprenger 2006a, 2009). The spirits of the ancestors are located on the graveyard in the forest, but a conglomerate of the patrilineal forebears of a particular household forms that house's house spirit. This spirit is, like the village spirit, protective, but relations with it should be regularly reinforced by sacrifices. Not all spirits are former people, though. The earth and the sky are home to a variety of non-human beings which interact with humans, usually in a harmful way.

Rmeet conceive of different ways how animals and objects might be like persons or otherwise bound up with Rmeet sociality. Sacrificial animals are like persons in so far they can be exchanged for a component of persons – *klpu* – which has been removed through interaction with spirits. Spirits are like persons because they can own or control other beings and enter into exchange relations with humans. As I will argue, objects like bronze drums or money might acquire person-like features by the same notions of agency and replacement.

The background of such emerging personhood is a field of high cultural diversification in mainland Southeast Asia, a region conventionally characterised by its contrast between Buddhist lowland centres and a 'shatterzone' of animist (and sometimes Christian) uplanders. At the end of this chapter, I will show that the differential distribution of person-like features addresses interethnic relations as well, for in upland Southeast Asia, exosociality is an integral part of social structure.

Exosociality[2] denotes those relationships that connect to domains beyond shared values, spaces and identities and in the present case has two aspects. One of them is cosmological, and for animist uplanders, it concerns the realms outside their villages, forests, mountains, the sky and, to a degree, the graveyards. This is the exosociality of spirits, and the recent developments in the theory of animism, as advanced by Descola (2011), Bird-David (1999), Ingold (2006), Viveiros de Castro (1998) and others mostly refer to this domain – although with qualifications, as we will see.

The other aspect could be called ethnic exosociality. Since Leach's classic work (Leach 1960, 1964), research in upland Southeast Asia is best known for its contributions to the theory of ethnicity. This scholarship has demonstrated how ritual and social systems develop in relationship to other, neighbouring systems (for Rmeet, see Sprenger 2010a). Thus, this type of exosociality does not relate to different species or spirits but to different ethnicities.

This chapter seeks to draw these two fields of exosociality together, by focusing on exchange. Thereby, cosmological and ethnic exosociality appear as aspects of the same encompassing system. The questioning of the ontological status of humans which this argument ensues in turn demands a different understanding of ethnicity, which has been mostly considered as a form of political action, from Leach's classics towards James Scott's recent (2009) book. For these scholars, the cultivation of cultural difference was mainly an effect of the strategic acting of human persons or groups in relation to each other. From this secularist perspective, rituals articulate or negotiate power relations, and relationships with game animals, livestock, forests and land appear in terms of political economy (but see Kirsch 1973; Jonsson 2012). They were first of all relations of humans with objects – resources – that helped these humans shaping their relationships with others of their kind. In these studies, the question of the distribution of agency is a political one: Do the uplanders have agency, or are they passively sinicized, tai-ized and dominated?

However, this is not at all the way many Southeast Asians seem to consider these matters, and the Rmeet are just one of many examples; therefore, I am asking the same question in an ontological framework. From the perspective of uplanders, the domain of activity that modern economic discourse identifies as production is primarily a form of exchange. It is not about relating to things which provide the material base for the relations with people. 'Production' itself is a process based on relating to persons, although non-human ones. The spirits of the earth need to be propitiated so that humans are able to make rice fields, the spirit of rice equally demands to be fed and lured into the field hut in order for the rice to be plentiful. Similar procedures apply to hunting, as I will demonstrate below. Thus, from the point of view of Rmeet subsistence, production is exchange, and exchange is the base of any engagement with human and non-human actors. In regard to the reproduction of life and society, there is no separation between an engagement of persons with material 'resources' ('production') and of persons with persons ('exchange'). The model that shapes these relationships encompasses both endosociality and exosociality, and the relationships with spirits and with foreigners are modelled by the same semantic resources (Sillander, this volume, Gibson 1986: 194–200). This does not mean that there are no differences between spirits and foreigners. But the distinctions between the various types of exosocial relationships emerge from identical principles. The classes of beings are different, but the boundaries separating and linking them to endosocial reproduction form a series of transformations. Within this series of boundaries, certain communicative practices and modes of relating form dominant models from which other relationships are being deducted. But first of all, I will try to determine the types of relationships Rmeet cultivate between themselves, animals, and spirits.

What Kind of Animists are the Rmeet?

The Amerindian perspectivism of Viveiros de Castro (1998) and the new animism of Descola (2011) both stress the difference between Amerindian and European conceptions of nature. In their scheme, animals situate human sociality in two respects: First, they constitute alternative societies whose distinguishing variable is the different physicality of their bodies. An animal has social relationships with humans, objects and other animals just as humans have, only the choice of the entity that fills in a particular position in that social universe differs according to the physical layout of the animal: A jaguar's beer is blood in human perspective, and what appears as game animals to him are humans in human eyes.

The second aspect, which is closely related to this, is the perspective implied by these different and yet similar socialities of humans and animals. The equation of blood and beer, human and wild pig is not just a metaphorical explanation of how animals socialize; it is a description of the way they perceive the world.

I want to situate the Rmeet case in relation with this approach by pointing out two significant differences: First, animals play a comparatively subordinate role in upland Southeast Asian cosmologies. While both Latin and Northern American mythology and art provide a plethora of animal images, Southeast Asian representations are often dominated by the human figure – gods, religious characters like the Buddha, and ancestors (but see Howell, this volume). This is particularly true for less centralized and upland societies, where the paradigmatic cosmological others are spirits, in particular those of the dead. As I will show, these spirits are attributed with a perspective, like Amerindian animals.

The second point concerns the dominant model of human-animal relationships in both areas. While the model of the relevant Amerindian cases is that of a relation between hunter and prey (Viveiros de Castro 1996: 194), the model concerning us here is predominantly one of animal husbandry as a complement to agriculture. Upland societies like the Rmeet, Khmu, Akha, Karen or Hmong primarily see themselves as agriculturalists. The paradigmatic human-animal relationships of these societies are with domestic animals like buffaloes, pigs, chicken and dogs. These relationships belong to a human socialized space – the village – which contrasts with the domain of the forest. The latter is seen alternatively as non-social or representing a different sociality, depending on perspective and definition. Most of the domestic animals are not tended as sources of food but predominantly as sacrifices.

Sacrifices

Both in Amerindian societies and in upland Southeast Asia, animals are to a certain degree like humans. However, the likeness is conceived in two different ways. In the Amerindian model, animals are like humans because they have a similar sociality – they relate to each other and to the world like humans do, although their bodies provide them with a different perspective. In the Southeast Asian uplands, domestic animals inhabit the same domain as humans, and they are like them in regard to their relationship with spirits. This is, they can act as surrogates for humans in sacrifices which are conceived as exchanges with spirits. They are not so much replicas than replacements for humans, and their sociality is not separated from but integrated into human sociality. Thus, their person-like features are defined and distributed in a different manner, in congruence with their relationships with humans.

The most conspicuous example among Rmeet is buffaloes. Buffaloes are sacrificed to the house spirit when people are severely ill, during funerals and annual village rituals and on a few other occasions. In the past, annual propitiations of ancestors and weddings provided even more opportunities for such sacrifices (Izikowitz 1979). According to a number of interlocutors, buffaloes have *klpu* and, when they are sacrificed, their *klpu* become the buffaloes of the dead. *Klpu* embodies a particular relational potential of buffaloes, as they can stand in for a human in his or her relationship with spirits. Illness is often seen as an exchange of aspects of persons: A spirit captures the *klpu* of a living human being and at the same time enters his body. This replacement is conceived as a single event, with no separation of 'taking away' and 'entering'. The entities being exchanged are not objects but persons: a soul and a spirit. There is thus no clear separation between the giving actor and the entity given, an argument that will become more important below. The spirit is a relationship imbued with agency.

The disturbed relationship with spirits, which illness represents, can be rectified by sacrificing an animal, the most important being a buffalo, pigs and chicken being lesser victims. Buffaloes are also the most human-like animals in regard to their integration into the house, which is at once difficult and ritually enforced. Being a complete and healthy person in Rmeet sociality implies being integrated into a family house (*ña*) under the protection of the house spirit (*phi ña*). Buffaloes are at once integrated in and peripheral to houses. When bought, they are fed some salt that has been rubbed on the hearth, the steaming pot and the kitchen door – all places animated by a kitchen spirit, which will keep the buffalo from running away.

Feeding salt solution to buffaloes is the most important way of keeping these animals close to the house and their owners. They are not used as draft animals but roam in the forest where their owners often search for them. Searching and caring for a buffalo is a typical male activity which might take up entire days. If a buffalo roams too far, a particular ritual may be performed upon his return, involving a chicken sacrifice and the tying of strings around the animal's horns – ritual acts explicitly modelled upon *dondii*, the wrist-tying and blood-smearing for humans whose *klpu* is in danger (see Izikowitz 1941). Both rituals have the same effect of binding the life of the addressee, human or buffalo, to the house. The word for the buffalo ritual is the same as the one for the ritual that integrates a new born into the household.

However, buffaloes are not humans, and their personhood is subordinate to human personhood. Their potential for replacing human *klpu* captured by spirits is a major function of this. Buffaloes do not possess the differentiated relations with ancestors and affines which humans depend upon for their completeness as persons. When humans are ill, relating to the dead or the wife-givers offers opportunities to heal them by reinforcing their constitutive relationships. No such opportunities are available to buffaloes. Thus, they are less well defined, less complex than human persons. The similarity between them, however, is suggested by ideas about the perspectives of spirits, in particular the spirits of the dead. In their view, which is revealed to humans in dreams, the world is reversed – as dreams are the *klpu*'s perspective. Day is night and night is day, as everyone who experiences daytime while dreaming at night might know. Everyday objects put in a grave for the dead person's convenience are broken, as spirits see only broken things as complete. But the spirits of the dead also conflate orders of being: They do not seem to perceive a difference between humans and buffaloes. In stories, they talk about humans as the buffaloes which they might kill. When confronting the spirits of the dead in rituals, people draw stripes of red colour from their nostrils to their ears – these, as one interlocutor told me, look like the ropes tied around buffaloes' heads and signal to the spirit that 'this buffalo already has an owner', so that the spirit will not take the human person (his *klpu*) away. The hierarchical relationship characteristic for humans and buffaloes is hierarchical both in the sense of social superiority and ownership and in a conceptual sense, in which the owner is a more complete model of a person than the owned.

The harmful spirits of the wilderness, however, reverse the relationship with humans along a code fitting their environment. They often perceive humans as game animals like deer or wild pigs, ready to be hunted. In all cases, the spirits appear to themselves as complete persons while the humans they perceive are not. Human-spirit relationships thus can be conceived as a competition about whose perspective is more valid, about who is prey and who is hunter, who is the owner and who is the sacrifice (cf. Lima 1999).

The diminishing of the complexity of personhood concerns other sacrificial animals as well. Just as buffaloes are lesser versions of humans, pigs are lesser versions of buffaloes. They also serve as sacrifices, but usually only after some bargaining of the shaman with a spirit who demands a buffalo. They do not possess *klpu* according to most accounts, however a wooden object called 'the pig's soul' (*klpu liik*) is used during the ritual as a replacement. Chicken and eggs are even lesser gifts to spirits. Thus, in relation to the spirits, personhood (see Howell 1996) is not an absolute quality of human beings, but graded and differentially distributed, according to the ranking of sacrifice:

Humans > buffaloes > pigs > chicken > eggs

I found no context in which eggs are attributed qualities of personhood. However, their non-personhood is established by their position in a graded sequence, not by some 'natural' quality. This gradation of personhood indicates potentials of exchange, or rather: exchangeability and the position in an exchange system constitute various degrees or types of personhood. As Nadasdy (2007: 28) has pointed out, understanding exchange is crucial for the analysis of human-animal relations. This also corresponds with the insights of both Luhmann's autopoietic systems theory and actor-network theory, both of which assume that actors are constituted by communication and their positioning in a social system. Persons thus 'condense as a side effect' of the operation of social systems (Luhmann 1995: 149, my translation). Exchange in particular is a major way to constitute persons (Strathern 1988).

Following this reasoning, recognizing that the other has a similar perspective on the world as oneself means to attribute a complex type of personhood to this other. In so far communication is shaped by expectations regarding the other, the other's specific view of things is not taken into account when addressing lesser persons. Therefore, Rmeet do not attribute perspective to domestic animals but to those others with whom exchange relationships constituting the socio-cosmic order have to be maintained. This corresponds to those animist hunting societies which conceive of the relationship between prey and hunter as one of exchange often aligned with that to affines (Århem, K. 1996 and this volume; Howell 1996; Lima 1999; Nadasdy 2007; Viveiros de Castro 2001).[3]

Buffaloes have attributes of personhood because they are aligned with humans on their side of the human-spirit divide, the leading difference structuring the cosmos. But they are not attributed a specific perspective. Spirits have a perspective because they are on the other side of the divide. It is the major exchange partners who are recognized as having a society and a perspective, because this indicates the type and the degree of relatedness that qualifies them as exchange partners in the first place. Along a series of positions ranging from entities that are being exchanged to those who do the exchange, entities acquire a perspective that is being taken into account, that is being treated as information, 'difference that makes a difference' (Bateson 1972: 453) for the communication of those addressing them.

Hunting as Non-Sacrifice

How does this articulate with hunting? Is the field of hunting for Rmeet ontologically separate from their relations with sacrificial animals and the spirits they engage with in sacrifice? I will argue that in the Rmeet ritual system, the hunter-prey relationship is to a large degree informed by the relationship with domestic animals, and that the latter provides the position from which the hunting relationship is conceptualized.

In rural areas, hunting is a common activity for men, the most common larger game being deer and wild pigs. These are shot with rifles and more rarely trapped. Birds and rodents like bamboo rats are also trapped. While hunters regularly experience success, there are clear indications of overhunting, as several species are hardly found any more or have entirely disappeared. The most conspicuous of them is the gaur (*Bos gaurus*), the largest species of wild cattle, which occupies a special role in hunting, presumably due to its similarity with buffaloes (see below).

I did not come across the idea that game animals have a perspective or inhabit a social world that they perceive in a similar way as humans perceive theirs. There is a lord of the animals called *yaa gemeai*, 'Grandmother Widow'. She cares for the forest animals – the word *cheo* is used both for caring for domestic animals and raising children – and makes them available to hunters by releasing them.

Thus, the relationship between her and forest animals resembles the one between a living Rmeet and his domestic animals. Otherwise, there is an amazing range of incompatible – and occasionally openly disputed – statements about the nature of the Widow. Some interlocutors classified her with the sky spirits, others with those of the earth and the trees (all dangerous). Some identified her with the spirit of hunting (see below), while a majority clearly separated the two. Some assumed her to be a single spirit, while for others there where many of them, and a minority claimed the Widow to be male. This variance suggests that it is only the fact that the Widow cares for and then abandons forest animals which appears on the horizon of human sociality and therefore becomes common knowledge. The factors less relevant for human relations with her are less defined and, in the non-doctrinal manner typical for upland cosmologies, tend to diversify along several lines of imagination, interpreted experience and tradition. In so far the existence of spirits is relational, only those aspects of their personhood which are continually and conventionally reproduced – by ritual – are stabilized (see also Remme, this volume).

What is, however, significant is the designation of the spirit as a widow. Widows occupy a somewhat marginal position in Rmeet social structure and their sociality is reduced in comparison to the full persons who own sacrificial animals. The word for widow, *nee gemeai*, is pejorative and should not be used in the presence of a widow. Widows often are the only kind of persons who live in a house alone, in case the children have moved out. This is a somewhat ambiguous position, as it implies a community with the house spirit of her deceased husband, even though she is not a descendant of his line. As the house spirit, who is a conglomerate of lineal ancestors with their wives, now includes her husband's spirit, the situation is ambivalent in regard to kinship and dangerous for her. In some cases, this conundrum is solved by the widow moving into a small bamboo hut and joining her children for meals.

What is more, although the house spirit is a relationship ('the spirit of mother and father'), it can only be addressed by men of the 'father's' line. If a widow living in her husband's house needs to perform a sacrifice, she must call male agnates of her deceased spouse for this task. Thus, although the Widow-spirit in the forest owns the forest animals, the relationship is less complex than the one between a householder and his animals. A householder has a relationship with his house spirit who also protects the domestic animals and who can be addressed by sacrificing one of them. For this reason, I presume, the fact that the forest spirit is a widow implies that she cannot use her animals for sacrifice, as these rituals require male performers. Therefore, she can care for the forest animals, but she is outside the field of relations maintained through sacrifice.

The condition for a successful hunt is that the widow chases away, literally 'releases' (*mbläh*) an animal, for example for misbehaviour. When a hunter has killed the animal, people say, he puts up its left ear on a stick at a crossing for the Widow to see. Thereby she will know that the animal is dead and return home. The prey is then brought into the village. Thus, when the Widow releases an animal, this is by no means like a sacrifice. In a way, this is a reversal of the Katu case (K. Århem, this volume) where the hunting ritual is a mirror image of the sacrifice of the animal given by the Animal Masters. When I stress that hunting is a non-sacrifice, this is due to the fact that Rmeet see the Animal Master as a single woman, while the Katu see theirs as a couple.

However, it is not the Widow who is the main addressee of the hunting rituals, but the spirit of hunting, *phi phrean*, which is usually separated from the Widow and considered to be male.[4] He is the force that ensures hunting success, and failure to perform the ritual will result in failure to obtain prey. The first step of the rituals is performed after the dead animal has been brought into a *cuong*, a type of ground-floor building outside the authority of house spirits. A *cuong* is either 'big', being the community house where the village spirit is located, or 'small', belonging to a private house as a kind of workshop.

Before cutting up the body, the hunter places the rifle used for the killing on top of the dead animal, pointing at its tail. He puts a raw egg into the animal's ear and some cones made of rolled-up banana leaves on the rifle and then pours liquor on these objects. Several gift items – replicas of woven fans and buffaloes made of bamboo and so on – are placed on a little rack under the roof of the *cuong*. All of these are offerings to the hunting spirit.

Next, the head, tail and right ear of the animal are placed on a gift bowl together with the banana leaf cones and liquor and then presented to the hunting spirit. After part of the meat has been distributed to the villagers and the remains are cooked, the skull is fixed at the same spot, together with the rifle, and smeared with blood and raw meat. The hunter proceeds to smear the raw egg on the skull. The egg is then fried in a container made of banana leaf and used for another smearing. This act of feeding the spirit enables further hunting success. The ritual verse pronounced on this occasion is addressed to the spirit of hunting: 'plug ears with cotton, blind eyes with rags' – the animal should be made unaware of the approaching hunter. This is the only moment during the ritual procedures when the agency of the animal is acknowledged, although it does not express its specific perspective.

The bits of the meal which both skull and rifle receive before everyone starts eating indicate a reordering of the entities involved in the ritual: During the hunt, hunter and rifle formed one side of the encounter, opposed to the prey animal. Now, skull and meat of the animal are separated and form two different entities. Cooking has turned the meat into a representation of the hunter's sociality, and giving it to both the rifle and the skull establishes the identity of the latter two items, united as *phi phrean*. This identity is important, since all the skulls in the *cuong* should be placed in the same place, thus creating a shared space for them that localizes the spirit. In the past, skulls were fixed under the section of the workshop's roof pointing in the direction where the animal had been killed, in order to catch more animals in the same place (Izikowitz 1979: 196–97). Thus, the ritual consolidates the relationships connecting the hunter, the skulls of the game animals inside the village, the site of their successful killing and of presumed future successes in the forest, and the rifle. Indeed, the spirit of hunting actually consists of this relationship between agentive objects, past and future events. The hunter, by the ritual, transforms the relationship into a durable object, the skull and the ritual gifts and objects, all together called *phrean*. The *phi phrean* is thus the spirit of these objects.

Like for any other spirit, the food-giving rituals addressed to *phi phrean* are called 'making the spirit' (*plo phi*). The steps of the ritual employ the same elements and semantics as other exchanges. On any occasion, gift bowls are presented to both human recipients and spirits. They are a sign of respect and submission, usually constituting the spirits who receive them as helpful and protective, like house and village spirits. They also make the male spirits of the earth and the fields less inclined to attack people.

In this respect, the hunting spirits are similar to the female spirit of rice in that they are less well-defined and more fleeting than most other spirits who belong to particular places or families. Also, like the spirit of rice, they do not actively harm people but only withdraw their support when insulted. As the rice spirit provides people with their most important food stable, which is also a trade good, she occupies a major position in the reproduction of society via exchange. She is also a function of the ongoing negotiation of people with forces outside the village, as the success of rice growing depends on sacrificial relations with the dangerous male spirits who own the swidden. The hunting spirit, on the other hand, represents the rice spirit's male counterpart in relation to hunting and the forest. It is a personalized relationship of luck in hunting. A hunter might have or not have *phi phrean*, implying that this person is involved in an exchange relationship rather than being possessed and owned. An aging hunter might even transfer his hunting spirit to a younger man – his son, for example – when the latter offers a gift tray to the older person. The 'making' of *phi phrean* after a hunt is an occasion for such transfers to occur.

The meat of a game animal is distributed along lines similar to domestic animals sacrificed for the house spirit. Neck and behind go to lineage members ('brothers', *yuu ääk*). Certain parts, like the skin, are distributed to anyone who likes to receive them. In addition, each ritual distribution of meat recognizes relations more specific to the occasion. The hind leg of a game animal goes to the village headman, who is in charge of the relations with the state, another exosocial category. Those who helped carrying the carcass into the village receive the front leg. Thus, hunting is implicated in the language of sacrifice, with the prey being transformed into a gift to the hunting spirit, like other animals killed for spirits. However, this is the sacrifice of the hunter, while the spirit owner of the animal, the Widow, is disengaged from the sacrificial process.

The embodiment of spirits by objects is equally common. In particular, the illness-inducing sky or earth spirits are given temporary bodies of clay that serve as physical recipients of food gifts. A revealing parallel is provided by the village spirit. This spirit emerges from the community of house spirits during the founding and initial growth of a village. It is not a ritually socialized spirit of the locality. During annual rituals dedicated to him, he both receives parts of the sacrificial buffalo or pig and is represented by them. The head of the buffalo, together with other ritual objects, is placed inside the village *cuong* and receives gifts of food made from the animal's other body parts. The skull remains there as the site where the village spirit is concentrated – or rather 'being made' – during rituals. Thus, the skulls of sacrifices for the village spirit and the skulls of prey animals representing the hunting spirit coexist in the space of the village *cuong*. Both represent the relationship between gifts and their receivers, which actually brings the receivers into existence, 'personalizes' them and secures the ongoing existence of the human givers as healthy, complete persons.

This last point raises the question, what kind of relationship exists between the village spirit and the hunting spirit, if they occupy the same space? When Rmeet simply claim that the village spirit is 'bigger', I suggest that this is because the village spirit establishes the inside-outside relationship which the hunting spirit needs in order to be addressed in the first place. Village spirits have an internal and an external aspect. The internal one is located in the village *cuong* at the centre of each village, the external one just outside the village boundaries, usually in a particular tree. In some villages, the skulls of the sacrificial animals are placed at the latter, looking away from the village. In at least one village, the external aspect is called 'gaur person' (*he ii ketiing*). Thus, the village spirit embodies the internal cohesion of the village as well as its relation with the outside. The association of the village spirit with the forest and a buffalo-like wild animal establishes a relation with the external domain that is vital for the existence of the village and, in turn, for the performance of hunting rituals. Therefore, the production of (relations with) the hunting spirit depends on the village/forest divide, and the relation with the village spirit, as manifest in the physical structure of the *cuong*, encompasses that with the hunting spirit.

These transformations of inside-outside relations ascribe a peculiar role to the gaur, the double of the buffalo in the forest. Izikowitz notes that the village was closed when a gaur was killed, allegedly out of fear of the vengeful spirit of the animal (Izikowitz 1979: 197–99). Thus, gaurs were special in having a *klpu* like buffaloes, an individualized spirit which does not exist in other game animals, a 'big spirit' (*phi läh*), as Rmeet say. In addition, the proscription to enter or leave the village during the feast is characteristic of village sacrifices and, in the 1930s, used to be enforced during private buffalo sacrifices as well (ibid.: 327). The ten day prohibition on trespassing the village boundaries following the killing of a gaur equals that for buffalo sacrifices to the village spirit.

This special role was corroborated by one interlocutor in his seventies, the only person I spoke to who prided himself of having killed a gaur in his lifetime. Because the gaur has a spirit, his killing made a sacrifice for the house spirit necessary. My interlocutor slaughtered two buffaloes, and still, he said, his father died the following year. Other interlocutors provided similar stories, claiming that killing a gaur demands a wrist-binding ritual, a health-inducing sacrifice for the hunter. They, too, had stories to tell about hunters who, in spite of this measure, died within a year after the gaur hunt, proving the power of the animal's spirit. The gaurs have a male spirit master (*jao,* Lao: lord) and thus are not under the tutelage of the Widow, or at least not under the same Widow as the other game animals – although in some accounts it is typically unclear if the lord and the spirit of the gaur are separate entities. The lord of the gaurs is the reason why they are not found any more in the forests. 'He has left to another country', my interlocutor said, 'to care for the gaurs in a place where there are no people.'

Thus, in many respects gaurs are similar to people. However, I suggest, they gain these qualities not so much because they are exchange partners in the forest realm, but because of their similarity to the major sacrificial animal, the buffalo. The designation of the external aspect of the village spirit as 'gaur person' highlights this. Just as the spirit in its internal version at the *cuong* at the centre of the village is embodied by buffalo sacrifices, its external or peripheral aspect is associated with the buffalo's undomesticated counterpart.

As in the case of the Widow, hunting is part of a system of exchange which is dominated by the idea of the sacrifice. The focal type of relationships in this system is that between the human keepers of animals who are sacrifiers and full persons, domestic animals which are partial persons in so far they can replace humans in sacrifice, and spirit recipients of sacrifices who are also full persons, endowed with a point of view in which humans appear as buffaloes or prey. Hunting is also a transfer, but it is a non-sacrifice by the terms of sacrifice: The spirit owner cannot sacrifice her animals to the hunters because she is a widow. Person-like entities emerge in the interaction between hunters, successful hunting events, objects and gifts of food.

Expanding the Network

Animals of the forest and of the village are implicated in the exchange networks between socio-cosmic persons in a system of sacrifice. The sacrifice here is a gift that represents the giver, not just in a metaphorical way, but as a quality of the giver's relational being (Descola 2011, Chapter 15; Mauss 1990 [1924]). If some non-Western ideologies conceive of persons only as emergent from their relationships, as Melanesianists have argued (de Coppet 1995, Strathern 1988), then the gift objects which share some of these relationships gain qualities of personhood as well. They might not be complete persons, but the difference between person and non-person is, after all, graded and even situational. A complete human person among Rmeet needs to have relations with his patrilineal ancestors as well as with his wife-givers, and buffaloes do not possess these relatives. Still, they do possess *klpu* as a function of their exchangeability with human *klpu* in healing rituals or as bridewealth. But the emergence of personhood through exchange is not restricted to humans and animals. It also applies to other non-human entities involved in exchange, like money or bronze drums (Sprenger 2007, for the neighbouring Khmu see Lundström and Tayanin 1981). Bronze drums, major items of exchange and status in the past, do have a spirit, and there is also a spirit of money leading a somewhat unobtrusive existence.

Objects and animals are persons to the degree that they are involved in the same exchange networks that humans or spirits are. By being involved in the relationships which constitute humans as persons they, almost by necessity, acquire degrees of personhood. A relation that constitutes a person and does so by involving a non-human entity ascribes personhood to that entity as well, as otherwise the relation could not produce personhood in the first place. The condition for this is the superiority of relations between persons over relations between persons and things (see Dumont 1977).

In this respect, the network of human and non-human actors (Callon 1986; Latour 2000, 2008) encompasses not only humans, animals, and spirits, but also things and, as I will argue, other ethnicities. The latter might seem obvious, but when personhood is a function of exchange and less of a naturalistic ontology, the status of other ethnic groups is not self-evident. I expand upon Howell's argument that the distinction between persons and non-persons might be superior in the ideological organization to the one between human beings and animals (Howell 1996: 136, see also this volume). I argue that the distinction between people and spirits subordinates the human-animal distinction. Like the Chewong of Malaysia, as analyzed by Howell, Rmeet have terms for the particular features that classify the exchange potential of entities in this network – these are the related notions of *klpu* (soul) and *phi* (spirit). While *phi* are primarily external to the sociality of living humans, the *klpu* of the living turns into *phi* after death, thus establishing the homology that forms the base of the exchange potential in persons.

The strongest push towards personhood is accomplished by items that are replacements for persons. Although buffaloes never affect humans like spirits do, they do possess *klpu* and may become recipients of sacrifices (as in the ritual strengthening their bond with their owner's house). This is by virtue of their possible identification or rather, complementary identity with humans – both in sacrifices and as obligatory parts of bridewealth, that is, the exchange of a human being for valuables. Bronze drums used to be important parts of bridewealth as well. Consequently, the drums are endowed with spirits that might become dangerous, thus actively affecting humans and their houses (Izikowitz 1979: 100–2, 117). The spirit's relational person needs to be redefined, complemented and manipulated by gifts which themselves represent qualities of relationships.

In this network of more or less person-like exchange nodes, one major structuring distinction is the one between Rmeet and other ethnicities. Several of them feature prominently in their mythology and cosmology. Most distinctive are the lowland polities, the Lao kingdom of Luang Prabang and the Northern Thai kingdom of Lan Na. Terms associated with statehood and royalty are often derived from these polities and applied to cosmological relations. The word the gaur hunter above used for their lord, *jao*, is the lowland word for ruler and king. Major myths are concerned with the origin of the upland-lowland distinction (Sprenger 2006b). Thus, these lowland polities are integrated into the cosmology, as are other ethnicities. The aforementioned animate bronze drums, for example, originate from the Karen in Thailand (Izikowitz 1979: 102; Cooler 1995).

The integration of ethnic others suggests a certain ambivalence about the status of their personhood (see also McKinley 1976; Turton 2000: 17; Praet 2014). If people are created by a set of specific exchange relations, and we see human beings walk around who might not have a complete set of these, how human are they really? Do they fulfil the ontological criteria of being human? The Rmeet do not explicitly doubt the humanity of ethnic others, although the potential is there. When the first Americans appeared in the mountain villages during the Second Indochina War, they were thought to be spirits. For similar reasons, lowlanders share some structural qualities with spirits. In the lowland markets where you meet them, Rmeet argue, you might run into your dead grandfather trying to sell his coffin (Sprenger 2014). In dreams, lightning spirits appear as Hmong, and dangerous earth spirits as soldiers (both of the latter leave pain-inducing objects in people's bodies), and people who have just decided where to clear the forest for the year's rice fields, heed such dreams – they indicate the presence of dangerous spirits, and the farmer will therefore choose a different plot. Big cities in dreams are what people awake see as graveyards (Sprenger 2010b). Dreams, after all, reveal qualities of relationships from the point of view of the *klpu* and the spirits. Just as *klpu* relates to a graveyard, a living human Rmeet relates to political centres. Just as a man who has decided where to clear his next rice field relates to the spirits of his chosen plot, living Rmeet relate to invading soldiers. It is revealing that the Lao loanword *phi* has replaced the Rmeet term *mbroong* for spirits within the last eighty years.

Thus, other ethnic groups provide categories in which to speak about spirits. This view is reciprocated by lowlanders who identify the uplands as a domain of dangerous spirits (e.g., Moppert 1981: 47). For Rmeet, spirits and lowlanders as major categories of others are separate, as they occupy differential positions in the exchange system. While the relations with spirits are structured by one of the most important exchange types, the destruction of life for gifts, the relations with ethnic others work by other types, predominantly the state government and market exchange. As these exchange types are mutually dependent within the exchange network, not least because buffaloes are rather bought than raised, the persons involved in them seem translatable into each other, along the axis between spirits and humans, as marked by the perspectives of the sleeping and the waking eye.

The distinction between different polities or ethnicities thus gains cosmological dimensions. The Rmeet ritual system conceives local communities and the state to be in a relation of mutual dependency, as they occupy different positions in an overarching exchange system which includes spirits as well. The distinction between Rmeet on the one hand and state-building Lao or Thai on the other complements the spirit-human distinction in the definition of differentiated personhood. These exchange types need to be maintained as different. As one interlocutor, who had worked in Thailand for a while, poignantly explained in negative terms: 'In Thailand, you have to be afraid of robbers; among Rmeet, you have to be afraid of spirits'. If one excludes the other, you have to maintain both of these domains of exchange.

Conclusion

In the philosophical biology of Jakob von Uexküll, there are no objects. Seen from any subject position, there are only bearers of meaning and utilizers of meaning, bound up in a relationship that is not so much determined by inexorable laws of nature but by asymmetric, often non-consensual communication (von Uexküll 1940). Thus, agents and patients are more apt terms to describe the relationship between two beings in any specific interaction or communication. The status of object or person is a function of the communicative process. If the recipient of the communication is rather like an 'object' or rather like a 'person' – both terms used conditionally here – depends on the follow-up communications, that is, on the connectivity of the initial interaction (see Luhmann 1984). If no resistance and no counter-communication, no response that alters the conditions of the follow-up communications is recognized by the agent, the patient will more likely tend towards a category of 'object' (or something similar). If the follow-up communications show transformation, resistance and a degree of uncontrollable (self?)determination of the patient, the patient might be recognized for having person-like features. The more the ongoing communication depends on the acknowledgment of the patient's conditioning of the communication, the more person-like the patient becomes for the agent. Or, to make use once more of von Uexküll's terms: Every patient is part of an agent's environment. However, ongoing communication with the patient might elucidate to the agent the conditions of the patient's way of responding and communicating. This leads the agent to recognize that the patient also has an environment to which the agent belongs. The agent needs to understand what kind of world the patient lives in, in order to communicate with him. It is at this point, that the patient might acquire even more traits of a person and be recognized to have a 'perspective'.

In the socio-cosmic system of the Rmeet, exchange is a crucial factor for creating and identifying relationships and attributing features of personhood. Exchange recognizes chains of communication in various ways. The most distinctive types concern the well-being of persons, households and villages. Life and fertility as well as illness and death are seen as results of positive and negative exchanges – communications altogether – between human and non-human actors. Beings that are being exchanged are less complete persons than those who do the exchanging. Beings that are exchanged but stand in for complete persons have more agency than other non-humans – they might possess souls or spirits.

Ultimately the most important exchanges are with those beings which the Rmeet recognize to have their own environments, their own perspective on the world. These include non-human entities like spirits who see the world differently than humans do. This perspective, however, is accessible to humans by their own *klpu*. *Klpu* sees the world as spirits do, in dreams and shamanic states of consciousness. Animals are subordinated to these exchange partners and, other than in societies where hunting defines relationships with animals, do not have a perspective. Their personhood is a function of their exchangeability, which is primarily defined by sacrifice. Sacrificial rituals provide the model by which hunter-game relations are constructed.

The personhood of ethnic others is part of this system of assigning personhood to exchange partners. Thus, innovation and the adoption of features of other ethnic groups or the state, be it in form of goods, behaviour or the recognition of relations like employment for labour, schooling and so on, can be considered as the recognition and adoption of the perspectives of others. It is conceivable that, from the Rmeet ritual system's point of view, the Rmeet become 'modern' and 'developed' in the same way that a Chewong might ultimately turn into an elephant (Howell, this volume) or a Juruna might ultimately turn into a wild pig (Lima 1999: 110–11). The politics of interethnic relationships are cosmological.

Notes

1. Research was conducted from 2000 to 2001 and in 2002 for altogether eighteen months with funding from the German Research Council and for six months in 2005 and 2007 with funding from the Academia Sinica, Taipei, and the Frobenius Institute, Frankfurt am Main, Germany.
2. With exosociality and endosociality, I use terms introduced by Friedman (1997) and Friedman/Ekholm-Friedman (1995) in a slightly different definition: not as characteristic features of particular communities, but as complementary aspects of any society or community.
3. This corresponds with Lévi-Strauss' classical thesis that affines are the paradigmatic exchange partners (Lévi-Strauss 1967).
4. Izikowitz' description of hunting rituals in the 1930s seems to focus exclusively on this spirit, alternatively identified as *mbrong pran*, 'spirit of the forest', and *phi pran*, the spirit watching over wild animals (Izikowitz 1979: 194–98), *mbrong* being the old Rmeet word for the Lao *phi*. *Pran* is a different pronunciation of *phrean* and does not mean 'forest' but the arrangement of objects resulting from the ritual. Izikowitz's account suggests that the two are identical or at least less distinct than the Widow and the 'hunting spirit' of most of my interlocutors.

References

Århem, K. (1996) 'The cosmic food web', in P. Descola and G. Pálsson (eds.) *Nature and Society: Anthropological Perspectives*, London: Routledge, 185–204.

Bateson, G. (1972) *Steps to an Ecology of the Mind*, New York, NY: Ballantine.

Bird-David, N. (1999) 'Animism' revisited: on personhood, environment and relational epistemology', *Current Anthropology*, 40: 67–91.

Callon, M. (1986) 'Some elements of a sociology of translation: Domestication of the scallops and the fishermen of St. Brieuc Bay', in J. Law (ed.) *Power, Action and Belief: A New Sociology of Knowledge?*, London: Routledge, 196–233.

Cooler, R.M. (1995) The Karen bronze drums of Burma: Types, iconography, manufacture and use', Leiden: Brill.

de Coppet, D. (1995) ''Are'are society: A Melanesian socio-cosmic point of view - How are Big Men the servants of society and cosmos?', in D. de Coppet and A. Itéanu (eds.) *Cosmos and Society in Oceania*, Oxford and Washington, DC, 235–74.

Descola, P. (2011) [2005] *Jenseits von Natur und Kultur*, Frankfurt am Main: Suhrkamp. (original: *Par-dela nature et culture*. Paris: Gallimard).

Dumont, L. (1977) *From Mandeville to Marx: The Genesis and Triumph of Economic Ideology*, Chicago, IL: The University of Chicago Press.

Friedman, J. (1997) 'Simplifying somplexity', in F. Olwig and K. Hastrup (eds.) *Siting Culture: The Shifting Anthropological Subject*, London: Routledge.

Friedman, J. and Ekholm-Friedman, K. (1995) 'Global complexity and the simplicity of everyday life', in D. Miller (ed.) *Worlds Apart: Modernity Through the Prism of the Local*, London: Routledge.

Gibson, T. (1986) *Sacrifice and Sharing in the Philippine Highlands: Religion and Society among the Buid of Mindoro*, London and Dover: Athlone.

Hallowell, I. (1960) 'Ojibwa ontology, behaviour and world view', in S. Diamond (ed.) *Culture in History: Essays in Honor of Paul Radin*, New York, NY: Columbia University Press, 19–52.

Howell, S. (1996) 'Nature in culture or culture in nature? Chewong ideas of 'humans' and other species', in P. Descola and G. Pálsson (eds.) *Nature and Society: Anthropological Perspectives*, London: Routledge, 127–44.

Ingold, T. (2006) 'Rethinking the animate, re-animating thought', *Ethnos*, 71, 1: 9–20.

Izikowitz, K.G. (1941) Fastening the soul: some religious traits among the Lamet, French Indochina, Gothenborg: *Göteborgs Högskolas Arsskrift* 47/14.

—— (1979) [1951] *Lamet: Hill Peasants in French Indochina*, New York, NY: AMS Press.

Jonsson, H. (2012) 'Paths to freedom: political prospecting in the ethnographic record', *Critique of Anthropology*, 32(2): 158–72.

Kirsch, A.T. (1973) *Feasting and social oscillation: religion and society in Upland Southeast Asia*, Ithaca, NY: Cornell University, Dept. of Asian Studies.

Latour, B. (2000) [1999] Die Hoffnung der Pandora: Untersuchungen zur Wirklichkeit der Wissenschaft. Trans. Gustav Roßler. Frankfurt am Main: Suhrkamp.

—— (2008) [1991] Wir sind nie modern gewesen: Versuch einer symmetrischen Anthropologie. Trans. Gustav Roßler. Frankfurt am Main: Suhrkamp.

Leach, E. (1960) 'The Frontiers of Burma', *Comparative Studies in History and Society*, 3: 49–68.

—— (1964) [1954] *Political Systems of Highland Burma*, London: Bell.

Lévi-Strauss, C. (1967) *The elementary structures of kinship*, Boston, MA: Beacon.

Lima, T. S. (1999) 'The two and its many: reflections on perspectivism in a Tupi cosmology', *Ethnos*, 64(1): 107–31.

Luhmann, N. (1984) *Soziale Systeme: Grundriß einer allgemeinen Theorie*, Frankfurt am Main: Suhrkamp.

—— (1995) *Soziologische Aufklärung 6: Die Soziologie und der Mensch*, Opladen: Westdeutscher Verlag.

Lundström, H. and Tayanin D. (1981) 'Kammu gongs and drums 1: The kettle gong, gongs and cymbals', *Asian Folklore Studies*, 40(1): 65–86.

Mauss, M. (1990) [1924] Die Gabe: Form und Funktion des Austauschs in archaischen Gesellschaften, Frankfurt am Main: Suhrkamp [first as Essai sur le don, in: L'année sociologique N.S. 1: 30–186].

McKinley, R. (1976) 'Human and proud of it! A structural treatment of headhunting rites and the social definition of enemies', in G.N. Appell (ed.) Studies in Borneo Societies: Social Process and Anthropological Explanation, Center for Southeast Asian Studies, Northern Illinois University, 92–126.

Moppert, F. (1981) 'La révolte des Bolovens (1901 – 1936)', in P. Brocheux (ed.) *Histoire de l'Asie du Sud-Est: révoltes, réformes et révolutions*, Lille: Presses Universitaires de Lille, 47–62.

Nadasdy, P. (2007) 'The gift in the animal: the ontology of hunting and human-animal sociality', *American Ethnologist*, 34(1): 24–43.

Praet, I. (2014) *Animism and the question of life*, London: Routledge.

Sprenger, G. (2006a) *Die Männer, die den Geldbaum fällten: Konzepte von Austausch und Gesellschaft bei den Rmeet von Takheung*, Laos, Berlin: LitVerlag.

—— (2006b) 'Political periphery, cosmological center: the reproduction of Rmeet socio-cosmic order and the Laos-Thailand border', in A. Horstmann and R. Wadley (eds.) *Centering the margin: Agency and Narrative in Southeast Asian borderlands*, New York, NY and Oxford: Berghahn, 67–84.

—— (2007) 'From kettledrums to coins: social transformation and the flow of valuables in Northern Laos', in F. Robinne and M. Sadan (eds.) *Social Dynamics in the*

Highlands of Southeast Asia: Reconsidering "Political Systems of Highland Burma" by E.R. Leach, Leiden: Brill, 161–86.

―――― (2009) 'Die Pflege der Dissoziation: Die Ideologie der Moderne und die Schamanen der Rmeet, Laos', *Curare*, 32(1): 64–77.

―――― (2010a) 'From power to value: ranked titles in an egalitarian society, Laos', *Journal of Asian Studies*, 69(2): 403–25.

―――― (2010b) 'Sharing dreams: involvement in the Other's cosmology', in A.S. Grønseth and D.L. Davis (eds.) *Mutuality and Empathy: Self and Other in the Ethnographic Encounter, Oxon*: Sean Kingston, 49–68.

―――― (2014) 'Where the dead go to the market: market and ritual as social systems in upland Southeast Asia', in V. Gottowik (ed.) *Dynamics of Religion in Southeast Asia: Magic and Modernity*, Amsterdam: Amsterdam University Press, 75–90.

Scott, J.C. (2009) *The Art of not being governed: An anarchist history of upland Southeast Asia*, New Haven, CT and London: Yale University Press.

Strathern, M. (1988) *The gender of the gift: problems with women and problems with society in Melanesia*, Berkeley, CA: University of California Press.

Turton, A. (2000) 'Introduction', in A. Turton (ed.) *Civility and Savagery. Social identity in Tai states*, Richmond: Surrey, 3–31.

Uexküll, J. von (1940) *Bedeutungslehre*, Leipzig: Barth.

Viveiros de Castro, E. (1996) 'Images of nature and society in Amazonian ethnography', *Annual Review of Anthropology*, 25: 179–200.

―――― (1998) 'Cosmological deixis and Amerindian perspectivism', *Journal of the Royal Anthropological Institute*, 4: 469–88.

―――― (2001) 'GUT feelings about Amazonia: potential affinity and the construction of sociality', in L.M. Rival and N.L. Whitehead (eds.) *Beyond the Visible and the Material: The Amerindianization in the Work of Peter Rivière*, Oxford: Oxford University Press, 19–44.

5 Animism and the hunter's dilemma

Hunting, sacrifice and asymmetric exchange among the Katu of Vietnam

Kaj Århem

This chapter examines certain features of the animist cosmology of the Katu people living in the upland forests of central Vietnam. In many ways the Katu exemplify the classical concept of animism: they conceive of the world as populated by a plurality of spirits – ancestors, ghosts and 'nature spirits' – which continuously influence and ultimately determine human life and well-being as well as the working of the cosmos at large. In the Katu cosmos, the spirits are omnipresent, and men and women do nothing of importance without consulting them, appeasing them with sacrifices and food offerings, requesting their help or asking for their compassion.[1]

The recent rethinking of the notion of animism has radically revised the classical – evolutionist and largely obsolete – account of the phenomenon to which the concept refers. Animism is no longer understood as a primitive form of religion based on ignorance of the laws of nature but as a subtly developed ontological stance, articulating a holistic (systemic) understanding of person-environment relatedness associated with peoples living in close engagement with their natural surroundings.[2]

As such, animism presents itself as the conceptual opposite to naturalism, the reigning ontology of modernity. Its defining feature, in a nutshell, is a radical propensity towards the subjectification of reality – of perceiving beings and things first and foremost as subjects and only residually as objects. In animism, subjectivity, not physicality, is the common ground of existence. Instead of physical laws there are intersubjectivity and person-to-person relations. Instead of nature there is society transcending the human/non-human divide, a sentient ecology positing a universe of communicating and interacting subjects.

One implication of such a relational and intersubjective ontology is that non-human animals (and plants) tend to be attributed with human-like capacities and sensibilities; they are conceived of as other-than-human persons (Hallowell 1960). Humanity is only one form of subjectivity among many. In a number of animistic societies, people literally speak of, and relate to, wild animals (and certain plants) as 'people' (cf. Howell, this volume; Ingold 1986; Sahlins 2008; Willerslev 2007). The hunter communicates with his prey as a social other, and the relationship between them is understood as a morally charged social relationship. In many Amazonian societies, for example, the word for human beings ('people') is also used for animals and plants; there are different classes of mammal people, fish people, tree people and so on (Århem, K. 1996, 2003; Descola 1996; Viveiros de Castro 1998).

In such societies, where animals are culturally construed as humanlike subjects, everyday hunting and fishing and the daily consumption of animal food is commonly experienced as a dangerous and potentially violent engagement with powerful others. The spirit of the killed animal may strike back on the human hunter, causing illness and even death. In many parts of Amazonia, the consumption of game and fish is therefore considered a major source of spirit-induced illness. Even cooked and otherwise prepared animal food is believed to retain the predatory agency of the animal subject and, thus, its capacity to reverse the hunter-prey relationship. Therefore, Amazonian Indians subject animal food to shamanic treatment: by means of 'magical' blowing and silent chanting, the hunter removes the potentially harmful agency lingering in the animal's body, thus turning it into harmless and vitalizing substance (food).[3]

This notion that animals are other-than-human persons presents animistic societies and ontologies with a profound dilemma: how to avoid metaphysical 'warfare' with the 'animal people' and how to avert its possibly lethal consequences (cf. Fausto 2007)? How to turn hunting for food into a harmless and everyday subsistence activity – in other words, how to avoid the risk of deadly retaliation and counter-predation? This is a very real dilemma for indigenous peoples around the world, and one which is inherent – tacitly or explicitly – in animistic cosmologies. Much of what in older ethnographical literature is referred to as hunting magic is precisely dedicated to solve this metaphysical problem. I refer to this distinctively animist predicament as the 'hunter's dilemma'.

On this account, the way different animist peoples conceptualize their relationship with animals in general and game animals in particular becomes significant for understanding their specific varieties of animistic cosmology. I suggest that the notion of hunting, understood in the conventional sense of pursuing and killing wild animals for food, may serve as a diagnostic template for the comparative study of animism: how do different societies conceptualize and institutionalize hunting and other forms of killing animals for food? How do they legitimize hunting as a human form of predation and how do they mitigate its potentially lethal consequences? In short, how do they deal with the hunter's dilemma?

In the present chapter, I explore the ways in which the Katu in the uplands of central Vietnam tackle – and resolve – this predicament. I do so by way of a contextual analysis of their central hunting ritual.[4] It will become apparent that the Katu notion of hunting can only be understood in the light of the institutions of animal sacrifice and asymmetric marriage, both equally important for the working of Katu society. Indeed, I will argue that the principle of asymmetric (or generalized) exchange shapes their entire understanding of reality. Their relational cosmology – and thus their variety of animism – is 'asymmetric'. In the concluding section I make some comparative reflections on what I call symmetric and asymmetric forms of animism, based on my own successive fieldworks in Amazonia and Southeast Asia.[5]

The Katu

The Katu people are one of a dozen or so Mon-Khmer speaking groups of swidden cultivators inhabiting the Central Annamite Cordillera on both sides of the border between Laos and Vietnam.[6] In many respects they are typical of indigenous upland peoples in Southeast Asia: settlements are small, kinship-based and organized around a large communal house (*guöl*) which serves as the public, ritual centre of the village. In the past, villages were semi-mobile and located to hill tops and forested ridges; the settlements shifted location according to the requirements of their rotational cultivation system and the contingencies of resource fluctuations, epidemics and feuding (Århem, K. 2010; Århem, N. 2009; Le Pichon 1938).

Today, the population is increasingly concentrated in permanent villages near roads and market towns. Shifting cultivation, supplemented by hunting and fishing, remains the basis for subsistence.[7] Upland rice is the staple. In cultural terms, rice cultivation and hunting – and accompanying rituals – define the social identities of women and men respectively. Domestic animals, principally pigs, cattle and buffalo, are kept as sacrificial beasts and constitute a principal form of wealth, circulated between houses, lineages and villages in complex networks of ritual exchange. The relationship between men, livestock and game animals, and the way these beings are positioned in the cosmic scheme of things, defines the topic of the ensuing analysis.

The institutions of patrilineal descent and asymmetric alliance are the foundations of the indigenous social order, and continue to structure local communities (Århem, K. 2010). The local patrilineage constitutes the basic social unit, serving as an extended domestic unit as well as the minimal exchange unit in the marriage system. While the clan system mainly operates as a classificatory grid and nominal system of social identification, the marriage system connects lineages and villages into wide networks of exchange which, in the past, formed the basis for the Katu polity and which are still at the center of Katu sociality. Asymmetric alliance (or generalized exchange) is an institution widespread in Southeast Asia. In Katu society, it is a total social fact in the Maussian sense with profound cosmological resonances. As such, it also underpins the Katu notion of hunting.

In line with the prototypical model of generalized-exchange systems (Lévi-Strauss 1969), the Katu social universe is divided – from the point of view of any individual – into three sharply distinguished conceptual categories: an 'ego category' (one's own local lineage) within which marriage is prohibited, the 'wife-givers' comprising the groups providing wives for the men of ego's group, and the 'wife-takers' – the groups which marry ('take') women from ego's group. Wife-givers and wife-takers are referred to in Katu as 'parents-in-law' (*cha-chui*) and 'sons-in-law' (*sa sao*) respectively, pointing to the intrinsically hierarchical relationship between them. These distinctions are absolute; accordingly, a group cannot provide wives to the same group from which it takes wives. Direct exchange – as in sister-exchange marriage, which is characteristic of symmetric alliance systems – is prohibited, even unthinkable. If at all occurring, it is believed to bring metaphysical disaster on the intermarrying parties.

Marriage is ostentatiously celebrated. The wedding involves a public exchange of gifts between the two parties of the alliance. The obligatory exchange objects, prescribed in kind but not in quantity, include domestic animals (buffalo, cows and pigs), porcelain jars, gongs and traditional, decorated textile. In the past, large amounts of cooked game meat and fish also formed part of the exchange. The exchange follows an invariant code: the groom's family gives domestic animals, jars and gongs – the bridewealth – to the bride's family; the latter, on their part, give cloth, mats and pillows, all fabricated by women, to the groom's family. The objects composing the bridewealth are regarded as 'male' while the dowry is composed of 'female' objects.[8] The same gender connotations apply to the game-fish exchange: (male) game go with the bridewealth, (female) fish accompany the dowry.

Thus – summarizing what is in reality a very complex exchange – women and cloth move in one direction, domestic animals, jars and gongs in the other. The bride is transferred to the groom's house, eventually to become part of his lineage. For the bridewealth received at his daughter's marriage, the father can obtain a wife for his son (or himself). This is the material logic of the Katu marriage system.[9] The alliance relationship is perpetual and ideally continued over generations. It is maintained by endless reciprocal gift-giving between the two parties, governed by the same asymmetric exchange code: 'male' objects moving one way, 'female' objects the other. This continuous gift-giving between affines very much constitutes and reproduces the Katu social fabric.

The hierarchical relationship between wife-givers and wife-takers is a structural feature of all asymmetric marriage systems.[10] Among the Katu, and in Southeast Asia generally, wife-givers are regarded as superior to their wife-takers. By supplying wives, the wife-givers enable their wife-takers to reproduce and multiply; in effect, wife-givers are apprehended as 'life givers' (cf. Fox 1981). As a result, wife-takers stand in a perpetual debt relation to their life/wife-givers – a debt they can only partially repay through the bridewealth given away at marriage and the ensuing series of gift-giving rituals during which wife-takers are expected to continuously supply their wife-givers with pigs, game meat, jars and gongs. These affinal gifts can be understood as instalments on the original debt incurred through the marriage and the 'gift of life' received by the wife-taking lineage.

Ultimately, this hierarchical – asymmetrical – relationship between wife-takers and wife-givers derives its force and legitimacy from cosmology; it is metaphysically grounded in the relationship between humans and spirits. The Sky, Pleng, is the ultimate life-giver to which humans owe their existence, their life and fertility. Accordingly, humans stand in eternal debt to the spirits for the gift of life – a gift for which they must continually make up in the form of unceasing animal sacrifices and, eventually, with their death and sublimation as ancestor spirits. The marriage system is a social expression – a manifestation at the level of human society – of the very principle structuring the whole of the Katu cosmos.

Living with the Spirits

A brief overview of the basic features of Katu cosmology helps us to unpack the above assertion and to understand the connection between the marriage system and the Katu understanding of hunting.

The Village and the Forest

Very schematically, the Katu reality is divided into two separate, opposed but interdependent, conceptual domains: the village (*buöl*) and the forest (*krung*). The two domains are inhabited by different living kinds and distinct classes of spirits. The village is the domain of humans and the benevolent ancestors, the *yang*, or *abo yang*. The ancestors are also referred to as 'house spirits', *yang doong*. The forest, on the other hand, is the realm of wild animals, ghosts and a panoply of dangerous and powerful spirit beings, generically referred to as *abhuy* or *abhuy krung*, literally 'forest spirits'.

All spirits are said to feed on the vital essence – epitomized by the blood – of living beings, but while the familiar *yang* are content with the blood and meat from the poultry and domestic animals that villagers regularly offer up to them (along with rice, wine and other foods) in sacrificial rituals, the *abhuy* may at any moment attack the villagers and their livestock to satisfy their craving for blood, and thereby causing illness and death. For the Katu, life and existence is very much perceived as a protracted cosmic struggle between the benevolent beings of the village and the dangerous spirits of the forest.

The *abhuy mörieng* – literally 'rainbow spirits' – is a particularly sinister class of spirits, transcending the village/forest divide. Feeding exclusively on fresh blood, the *mörieng* typify the predatory nature of the *abhuy* spirits. They are said to roam the forest in the shape of certain animals (particularly the muntjak) but also have a predilection for invading the village space and take up their abode in domestic livestock. Such animals, possessed by the *mörieng* spirit, are called *töräh* animals and are considered a principal source of illness in humans. Particularly cattle tend to become hosts to *mörieng* spirits. Were it not for the protection of the house spirits, villagers say, the *mörieng* spirits would attack people and eat their souls. Even the village, then, is not exempt from the cosmic struggle between the predatory *abhuy* and the protective *yang* spirits; the battle is taken all the way up to the doorstep of the human dwelling – the very epitome of peace and safety in Katu cosmology.

Good and Bad Death

Like so many other Southeast Asian peoples, the Katu distinguish between good and bad death where the latter notion refers to violent, unexpected and accidental death, particularly death involving profuse bloodshed. The young fertile woman who dies in childbirth is the epitome of bad death. The mode of death and the post-mortem treatment of the human soul (*rövai*) produce the two prototypes of the protective and predatory spirits in the Katu cosmos, the *abo yang* and the *abhuy mörieng*.

The protracted funerary sequence in the case of good death – involving, in turn, burial in a simple forest grave, the subsequent disinterment of the bones, and their final placement in a family tomb or lineage ossuary (*ping*) in the village cemetery – transforms the ghost of the dead into a benevolent ancestor spirit (*yang*).[11] This spiritual transformation, spatially and physically expressed in a movement from the individual graves in the forest to the communal tomb in the village cemetery, also implies a parallel metaphysical movement from the forest to the village – and ultimately into the house of the living. The ancestors are henceforth said to 'dwell' in the lineage wealth – the jars kept on the altar shelf in the house.

The destiny of the soul of a person dying a bad death is utterly different. The dead is rapidly buried in the forest; there is no secondary funeral. In the Katu view, bad death is synonymous with being killed and eaten by *mörieng* spirits. The unhappy soul is thus itself turned into a *mörieng* spirit, denied the community of ancestors and forever removed from its living human relatives. Deprived of a proper funeral and a proper 'home', the bad-death ghosts are doomed to wander the forest, possessing animals and haunting the living, constantly on the hunt for human souls to increase their ranks. Their liminal and asocial state of predation is made permanent. The living do anything to avoid them and keep them at a distance.

Sky and Earth

Above and beyond the dichotomy between forest and village stands Pleng (literally 'Sky'), the supreme power in the Katu cosmos. Distant and powerful, Pleng is the ultimate source of life and fertility but also the master of death and misfortune. As the source of life-giving rain, light and heat, Pleng is beseeched for blessings and prosperity; as thunder and lightning and the final cause of death and disease, he is feared and placated.[12] Arbitrator of life and death, he commands the legions of spirits populating the earth – the benevolent ancestors and house spirits as well as the dangerous spirits of the forest, including the deadly *mörieng* spirits. As the mightiest of spirits, and comprehending them all, Pleng is usually invoked first at every act of worship, followed by the whole array of other spirits in the Katu pantheon.

Pleng is usually called upon in conjunction with Katiec (literally 'Earth'). Pleng-Katiec, Sky-Earth, constitute an invocational formula – as if the two were aspects of a single whole, a dual and androgynous deity appearing in human perception as Sky and Earth. It is near at hand to see the Earth as the visible and tangible counterpart to the ethereal and insubstantial Sky, thus constituting the Sky-and-Earth, Pleng-Katiec, as a divine personification of the cosmos – a 'natural symbol' of the wholeness and unity of being, spirit-and-matter, soul-and-body.

A Spirit Hierarchy

There is an evident but indeterminate hierarchical order in the Katu spirit pantheon, at the apex of which is Pleng, the Sky. The multiple nature spirits, *abhuy*, diversified and ranked among themselves, are regarded as more powerful than the benevolent ancestors and house spirits; indeed, the *yang* are described as mediators between villagers and the forest spirits surrounding the village. Nevertheless, and despite their different 'natures', the *abhuy* and the *yang* are often lumped together in a single class of spirits – *abhuy yang* – owing to their superiority in relations to humans; they are all attributed with the power to dominate and inflict harm on humans and livestock.

At the bottom of the hierarchy are a sundry of lesser spirits which are not included in, and explicitly distinguished from, the class of powerful *abhuy yang*; this diverse group of spirits include the mainly harmless but nevertheless ritually important rice spirit (colloquially referred to as Ayech) and the male and female guardians of game animals (Avua and Komorbarr respectively). These spirit beings, which in the Katu view do not really qualify as spirits at all, are rather regarded as respected non-human familiars; significantly, the 'names' Ayech and Avua are relationship terms literally meaning 'grandmother' and 'great grandparent(s)' respectively. It is not coincidental that these harmless and benevolent beings at the bottom of the power hierarchy are identified with the quintessential human foods: rice and game animals.

The Katu explicitly compare this spirit hierarchy to the army and the state administration – the two powerful agencies today increasingly replacing the spirits as the masters of their world (cf. Århem, N., this volume). However, the distinction between 'higher' and 'lower' spirits is most clearly expressed in ritual practice: thus, humans offer bloody animal sacrifices to the *abhuy yang* but not to the spirit guardians of rice and game animals; the latter are simply treated with 'ordinary' food- and wine offerings – much as respected visitors and relatives are treated. When, in the following, I refer to spirits without specification, I have the Supreme Being, Pleng and the powerful *abhuy yang* spirits in mind.

Animal Sacrifice

Making a living in this spiritually charged cosmos is precarious and largely a matter of enlisting the support of the *yang* spirits against the predatory *abhuy* spirits and, thus, maintaining a propitious balance between the powers of the village and the forces of the forest. In the view of the Katu, survival therefore requires the collaboration of the spirits – including the lesser spirit familiars of rice and game animals. As in all animist societies, rituals form an essential part of the Katu 'technology' of survival and, among the diverse ritual works they carry out, the animal sacrifice is supreme; it is the paradigm for all religious acts in Katu society.

Livestock, along with the ritual property (jars, gongs and traditional cloth), constitutes a principal form of wealth. In cosmological terms, domestic animals are the preferred food of the spirits; they are kept as sacrificial beasts to feed the spirits. Significantly, people consume the meat of livestock only in connection with sacrificial rituals, and only after it has first been offered to the spirits.[13] The spirits consume the immaterial essence of the food they are offered; they 'eat the smell' of the sacrificial food, say the Katu. What is left of the animal (the flesh) is consumed by the human participants during the ensuing feast. Thus transformed into 'food for humans', the meat is always and necessarily communally shared; meat is public – social – food and has strong male connotations (as opposed to rice which is 'female' and largely private food, shared within the house).

Men sacrifice livestock to sustain the spirits; this is the human mission and fundamental purpose in life. Virtuous living and unceasing sacrificing is the Katu religious and moral imperative. Sacrifices, small and large, accompany every significant event in Katu households and communities. The spirits have to be fed in connection with wedding and funeral, planting and harvest, the building of a new house and the clearing of a new field. To sacrifice is a basic necessity of life. By pleasing the spirits, the Katu maintain the cosmic order – avert misfortune, expiate wrongdoings and restore social and moral order. In the Katu view, humans are fundamentally sacrificers.[14]

If neglected or offended, the spirits are angered. When the spirits (including the benevolent ancestors) are angered, they turn 'hungry' – voracious and predatory. The Katu say that hungry spirits 'eat' human beings, capturing their souls and inflicting illness and death. To the spirits, all beings are potentially food; they prey on the souls of the living, on life itself. Predatory spirits are the ultimate source of illness and misfortune – and, eventually, death. The angered spirit capturing and consuming a human soul (which from the spirit's point of view is solid food) is the supreme image of predation; the prowling tiger – appropriately referred to as a mighty forest spirit (*abhuy*) – is its earthly manifestation. Spirit predation is the ... of religious neglect and moral transgression, of disregarding or negating the ... of Katu culture and morality.

*

Needless to say, there is an intimate relationship between domestic animals and humans. The close relationship between a man and his buffaloes is vividly expressed in the context of the sacrificial act. Not only is the sacrificial beast asked forbearance before being killed and lamented after its death; it is effectively identified with its human owner. This symbolic identification between man and buffalo is most clearly expressed when, at the death of a wealthy and respected man, his corpse is united by a string to the buffalo (or cattle) which is consecrated and killed in his name during the mortuary rites. The two belong together as if they were aspects of a single being. The buffalo is a man's animal 'double'. The culturally and linguistically close Rmeet people in Laos hold that the spirits of the dead confound living humans with livestock; to the spirits, humans are livestock (Sprenger, this volume).

Considering the close relationship between humans and domestic stock and the role that livestock play in Katu religious life, I think we are justified in assuming that, in the context of the sacrificial act, the consecrated animal substitutes for its human owner and sacrifier (donor). Thus, when a man sacrifices a buffalo, he (metaphorically) gives up a vital part of his individual and/or social self – his person, household, lineage or village, depending on the purpose and the context of the sacrifice. Indeed, the logic of Katu sacrificing suggests that livestock are vicarious humans. The animal offered to the spirits represents the vital force of the human sacrifier. It is also in this symbolic capacity, as vital signs of social selves, that livestock circulate as a supreme value in the Katu system of ritual exchange.

The Metaphysics of Hunting

Though principally rice cultivators (and livestock keepers), Katu men are also avid and passionate hunters.[15] In their hunting efforts, Katu men combine a prodigious practical knowledge of game animals with a distinctively religious attitude toward the killed prey. Thus, on the one hand, when hunting, men display a pragmatic and matter-of-fact attitude towards the forest and its animals; on the other, hunting is a practice of profound spiritual concern, and the body of a slain animal is treated with great ritual care reminiscent of the treatment afforded a consecrated, sacrificial beast and, indeed, a deceased human relative.

From a practical point of view, Katu hunting is mainly based on the use of an impressive range of ingenious traps.[16] A single dedicated hunter can set and regularly visit several hundred traps of many different kinds in a year. The Katu catch wild boar, deer, muntjak, serow, rodents of all sorts and diverse species of birds (cf. Luu Hung 2007). However, in their own view, the hunter's success ultimately depends on his skillful deployment of hunting 'medicine' (*yeneu*), and the respectful treatment of the carcass – particularly the head. In the words of a Katu master hunter: 'there are two things that help the hunter – animal skulls (*aco*) and magical leaves (*yeneu*).'

The hunting medicine consists of the leaves of various (unidentified) plants, planted and tended in secret gardens in the forest, known only to the owner-hunter himself. These plants are attributed with specific spirit qualities, said to attract the game animals to the hunter and confer on him the power to control his prey. The skull of a slain game animal is regarded as the repository of the animal spirit; after the kill, the spirit is believed to remain attached to the skull which is ritually placed among other skulls in a special gallery at the back of the communal house (*guöl*). Such a gallery may contain a hundred or more skulls featuring the entire range of game animals pursued by Katu hunters.[17]

Guided by his dreams and aided by his magical leaves and the spirits of previously killed animals, the hunter trusts that game will be forthcoming and, thus, that the forest will yield up its wealth to the villagers.[18] At the core of this local understanding of hunting is the relationship between the human hunter and the female guardian spirit of the game animals.

Komorbarr and Avua – The Dual Figure of the Animal Master

Komorbarr is the female guardian of forest animals. 'She looks after the game animals', say the Katu, 'as women look after their herds of pigs'. The game animals are perceived as the livestock of the forest. As a benevolent female spirit being, Komorbarr is best understood, I believe, as a hypostasis of the souls of killed game animals. Just as humans are ritually transformed into protective ancestors at death, the slain game animals turn into benign spirit allies when treated with the proper ritual care and respect. Komorbarr is the personification of this spirit collectivity of slain game animals. Her name literally means 'two maidens' (*komorr*, 'maiden'; *barr*, 'two'). Sometimes she is likened to a young beautiful woman, sometimes to an old woman with a protruding sexual organ and small breasts, reminiscent, Katu informants insist, of the udders of a sow.

Komorbarr is closely associated with the male spirit being known as Avua, portrayed as an old, hairy man with a huge penis compared to a log.[19] The name literally means 'great grandparent' – it is a sexually unmarked relationship term. In fact, Komorbarr is also contextually referred to by the same term; in an extended sense *avua* means 'old and respected person'. Often described as a couple, Komorbarr-Avua are said to inhabit old-growth forest, the principal breeding habitat of large game and the prime hunting ground of the village hunters.

Komorbarr and Avua together control the game animals in the village territory, but it is Komorbarr who has the direct care of the animals (see myth below). It is mainly with her that the hunter communicates in the context of hunting – before the actual hunt (in the form of premonitory dreams) and after a successful kill (during the obligatory hunting feast). It is also Komorbarr that 'gives' the hunter his prey; she conveys the animals to the hunter out of 'affection' or 'compassion' for the villagers in her domain.[20] Avua, her male consort or counterpart, however, plays little role in the ritual practices surrounding hunting. Thus, while Komorbarr, as principal protagonist in the hunting feast, is invited into the center of the communal house, Avua must sit by the door, guarding the entrance to the house.

Avua and Komorbarr should be understood, I believe, as personifications of different aspects of animal subjectivity: Komorbarr is the benevolent, compassionate form of the animal subject, the guest of honor during the hunting feast; Avua, by contrast, is rendered as a sinister, even dangerous being – treated with reserve and considered too dangerous to be allowed into the *guöl* during the ritual. While Komorbarr is close to humans, Avua is distant and indifferent – representing, as it were, the 'otherness' of the forest and its beings. He is the Owner and true Master of the forest animals, Komorbarr their caring Keeper and Guardian, mediator between village and forest. Thus, in the Katu case, the figure of the Animal Master emerges as an ambivalent and composite being, appearing in both male (Owner) and female (Keeper) form, each associated with a distinctive role and a specific set of intrinsic qualities and dispositions towards humans (Fig. 5.1).

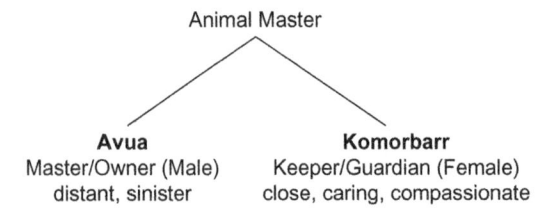

```
                    Animal Master
                    /          \
                   /            \
                  /              \
               Avua            Komorbarr
        Master/Owner (Male)   Keeper/Guardian (Female)
          distant, sinister    close, caring, compassionate
```

Figure 5.1 The dual figure of the Katu Animal Master.

The Hunting Ritual

The communal ritual (*buoih adah*) following every successful hunt expresses and reinforces the villagers' allegiance to the Animal Master, particularly in its female aspect. The central purpose of the feast is thus to affirm the bond to Komorbarr and ensure the villagers a continuous supply of game. The following is an account of such a ritual in Arek village (A'vuong commune) in April 2011, following the kill (in a trap) of a wild boar near the village. The proceedings were similar to other hunting rituals that I had previously observed (cf. Århem, K. 2008).

1. *Bringing the slain animal into the village:* The hunter called out loudly to his fellow villagers, signaling his catch. Several young men run to his assistance, helping him carrying the carcass to the village. When the party enters the village, they are welcomed with gong and drum beat. The carcass is brought into the communal house (*guöl*) and placed on the floor at the centre of the building. (At an earlier occasion in another village, when the animal – a serow – had been killed and cut up in the forest and brought to the village, the pieces of the dismembered carcass were laid out on the floor and carefully reassembled so as to recompose the complete animal, the head pointing towards the back-wall of the house [ibid.]). A woman's cloth is suspended from a roof rafter at the back of the building where the skulls of previous game are displayed. Necklaces and other women's jewelry are attached to the cloth; two men's belts and a hunting basket – part of the dowry customary given to the wife-takers – are placed below it. A live chicken is tied and placed next to the head of the carcass before being killed for the regular chicken-feet augury. Rice grains are thrown towards the suspended woman's cloth (Komorbarr) and toward the door (Avua). A group of men dance around the body, playing drums and gongs.

2. *The first offering (buoih hat)*: Immediately after the chicken augury, the carcass is singed and gutted by a group of young men who proceed to cut up the carcass. The officiant (the ritual master leading the procedures) prepares an offering tray with food for the spirits – uncooked rice and chicken, raw pieces of liver and the heart from the slain animal and a bottle of wine – and places it in front of the suspended cloth marking the 'altar' space during the ritual. The severed and still uncooked head of the animal is placed next to the offering tray. A bunch of green banana – the favorite food of Komorbarr – is stuck in the roof above the offerings. The officiant and a group of elders perform the regular praying ritual; bamboo flowers are thrown onto the cloth while the men invoke the spirits – principally Komorbarr but also the Sky, the village ancestors and the spirits of the magical leaves: 'we have put the cloth up for you, we have decorated it with necklaces and jewelry to make it beautiful for you ... We will cook the food you have given us; please come and join us in our feast. Don't be angry with us; we want you to be happy ...' This is the initial offering, announcing the pending feast and inviting the spirits to join the men of the village. As the prayer is finished, the officiant takes down the cloth, puts the food tray aside and removes the ritual regalia.

3 *Distribution of raw meat:* While this happens, the group of young men portions out pieces of raw meat from the slain animal to each and every household in the village. Each portion is placed on a fresh piece of banana leaf; forty-four portions are neatly laid out on the bamboo floor inside the community house, and children from every house come to fetch their allotted portion. After this unceremonial distribution, the rest of the meat, along with the head and entrails of the animal, are put into a huge cooking pot on a specially prepared fireplace in the *guöl*. The women of each household contribute some uncooked rice to the repast; the meat, entrails and rice are then cooked together into a thick gruel.

4 *Distribution of rice gruel:* When the gruel is cooked and ready, the men extract the head and the pieces of meat from the pot. The head is again placed, now cooked, under the skull gallery at the back of the building. It remains here until the culminating rite later in the evening. A second round of village-wide food distribution now follows; the gruel – the entrails cooked with the rice – is portioned out on banana leaves, one portion for each household, on the same principle as the raw meat earlier. The men in the *guöl* beat the drums and gongs, and women and children from every household come running to fetch their portions which they bring back to their houses.

5 *Cleaning and painting the skull:* At dusk – around seven p.m. – the second stage of the ritual is announced with drum and gong beats, calling both men and spirits back to the *guöl*. Pieces of cooked meat are now portioned out to the participants – all men – for the ensuing meal. The men are sitting in groups in the spacious central hall of the *guöl*, each group centered on a tray with meat and a bottle of wine. Meanwhile, the officiant fills a bamboo tube with the pieces of meat, liver and heart, retrieved from the offering tray (2), and buries the tube in the ashes of the fireplace. Another man carefully removes the meat from the head of the slain animal, after which he paints the cleaned skull with lines, crosses and circles, using soot from the hearth and blood from the animal. He then hands the painted skull over to the ritual master. The meat of the head, supplemented by other pieces of meat, is portioned out to the eating groups.

6 *'Placing the skull' (dahuol):* It is now around 9 pm. The *guöl* again resounds with gong and drum beat announcing the climax of the evening's events. The drum and gong players slowly and rhythmically walk in circle around the central pillar in the dark interior of the building. The officiant receives the painted skull and carefully places it alongside the other skulls in the roof. He then picks up the bamboo tube with grilled meat from the fire place and, as thick smoke emanates from the tube, he moves it back and forth in front of the newly placed skull and addresses the whole gallery of animal skulls: 'Komorbarr (here representing the entire spirit collectivity of slain game animals), please stay in the *guöl* tonight and enjoy the food and drink we offer you. We always try to feed you, let many animals be caught in our traps so that we can feed our families ...' This is the culminating act of the ritual. The name of this act, *dahuol,* refers to the act of placing the skull – literally 'introducing' the new animal spirit to the other spirits present in the *guöl* (cf. Århem, N. 2009: 156).

7 *Divination:* The evening sequence closes with an act of divination: the bamboo tube with grilled meat is split open and the content is distributed among the village elders. The split tube is then thrown on the floor and, depending on how the two parts of the tube fall, the officiant divines the future hunting luck of the village. After this, the eating and drinking start in earnest and continue throughout the night.

8 *Sending back the animal spirits:* At dawn the next day, the sound of drum and gong beats announces the final stage of the ritual. The animal spirits, which at the inception of the proceedings were called from the forest to join the feast, are now sent back to the forest to help the hunters catching more game animals in the future. As he sends the spirits away, the ritual master intones: 'Let us catch many animals, from black to red animals, because wild pigs (black) eat the roots of our cassava and the muntjak (red) eat the leaves of the cassava plant ...'. (At another occasion, the officiant bade the departing animal spirits farewell with the following words: 'You [animals] that are already dead, please help us kill many animals in the future ...').

9 *Closure and the distribution of the cooked meat:* Following this appeal for assistance from the spirits of the 'already dead animals', the remaining cooked meat is now distributed to all the households in the village according to the same procedure as before. The ritual and the communal feast are over.

Hunting, Sacrifice and Alliance: An Interpretation

The most conspicuous feature of the hunting rite is its communal, village-wide character. The ritual takes place in the communal house, situated at the social and ritual centre of the village and symbolizing the village as a social and political community. During the ritual, the meat of the killed animal is (re)distributed in no less than three separate instalments to all households in the village. At the climax of the ritual, when the dried and painted skull has been placed among the other skulls in roof, the men – and only the men – partake of the brain and meaty parts of the animal head. This meal carries all the connotations of a sacred meal, a communion between men and spirts, in which the village elders partake of the animal spirit – the head being its locus – and literally incorporating it in the village body.

Another striking feature of the ritual is that it displays the structure of a full-scale sacrifice. The slain game animal, consecrated after the fact as it were by the small offering ceremony at the side of the carcass, is offered up to the spirits in the opening scene (2) of the ritual drama. At the climax of the ritual sequence (5–6), the skull of the animal is given particular ritual care, the purpose of which is to secure the blessings of the spirits. This culminating act is followed, as in every sacrifice, by a communal feast (7) – the sharing of meat among men and the subsequent allocation of the remaining meat to every household in the village, thus making sure that the blessings accrue to the whole village.

The presence of the basic elements of a typical sacrifice leaves us in no doubt that the hunting ritual is a kind of sacrifice – except for the fact that the sacrificial beast is a game animal rather than a domestic animal and, consequently, that the sacrifier (donor) is not the human hunter, or a member of the village, but the 'spirit owner' of the game animals, the Animal Master. In other words, in the hunt-as-sacrifice, the hunter is merely the immolator of the sacrificial animal supplied by the Animal Master (Avua) and his compassionate consort, Komorbarr.[21]

In this light, the opening of the ritual sequence – the display and consecration of the complete carcass in front of the altar, its subsequent dismemberment, and the placing of the severed head on the altar along with other food offerings – is a re-enactment of the 'real' sacrifice which already took place in the forest when the hunter (or his extension, the trap) killed the animal and thereby executed the act of immolation. On this interpretation, the *guöl* – the scene of the ritual drama – is made to represent the forest where the real sacrifice is taking place. Significantly, the Animal Master, in its dual manifestation as Avua and Komorbarr, acts as both host and guest during the ritual: in the manifest drama played out in the *guöl*, Komorbarr appears as an honored guest in the village; metaphysically, however, Avua is the host and sacrifier in his own forest realm.

The culminating and concluding parts of the ritual (5–9) are concerned with the consummation of the sacrifice and the appropriation of its blessings. In the *dahuol* ceremony (6), the ritual master calls forth the animal spirits and palpably brings them to life – now coming into existence as a personalized spirit being, Komorbarr. By moving the bamboo tube containing the pieces of grilled meat from the slain animal in front of the skull, producing a thick smoke, the ritual master literally resurrects the killed animal as a complete spirit being. In this way, the newcomer spirit is integrated into the community of animal spirits, now present in the *guöl*. According to my Katu interlocutors, this is the high point of the ritual. The soul of the animal, released through its immolation, is now transformed into a protective, compassionate spirit helper. Given a 'home' in the *guöl*, Komorbarr is forever tied to the village and its inhabitants.

Evidently, the hunting ritual – just as the regular sacrifice – has the reinvigorating and regenerative connotations of a fertility ritual. In the *dahuol* ceremony just described, and in the concluding ceremony, when the ritual master sends the animal spirits back to the forest, the vital force released by the killing is channeled back to the herds of game animals under the protection of the Animal Master. The ritual process – from the moment of immolation to the post-mortem treatment of the carcass – enables the forest animals to reproduce and multiply. 'For every animal killed', one hunter said, 'two or three new animals are born in the forest'.

*

When talking to Katu elders about the meaning and purpose of the hunting feast, they invariably stress that the rite is performed to 'tie' the spirits of game animals to the villagers; to make the animals stay in the village territory and let themselves be caught; to make sure that the animals do not run away from the hunter or stray into another territory. In other words, the hunting ritual serves to attach the game animals to the people of the village and, thus, to ensure the continuous supply of wild animal food.

Katu interlocutors also say that, by performing the hunting ritual, the villagers pay due respect to the spirits of the slain animals and make Komorbarr feel compassion for the people in the village; that the ritual makes Komorbarr happy and reaffirms her allegiance to the village so that she will continue to 'release' animals to the human hunters. By performing the ritual in the proper manner, the villagers enlist the spirits of all the animals they have killed to help them in future hunting endeavors. The animal spirit, they say, is the hunter's ally and helper. The hunter's quarry is a gift from Komorbarr and, ultimately, from the forest itself (personified by Avua; see note 19, this chapter).

It appears, then, that the hunting ritual transforms the spirit of the slain game animal from a potentially vengeful foe into a spirit ally and helper. The analogy with the funerary process in the case of a 'good death' is readily apparent.[22] By killing his prey and conducting the correct post-mortem ritual, the hunter permits his prey a 'good death' and its subsequent conversion into 'animal ancestor' (Avua-Komorbarr). By contrast, the slow demise of a mortally wounded animal that escapes the hunter, or the successful kill which is not followed by the proper 'funerary' treatment of the carcass, amounts to a 'bad death' for the animal. In both cases, the animal soul turns into an animal *mörieng*.[23] The bad death of the animal precludes the flow of vitality and generative power from the spirits to the villagers, and from the spirits via the ritual work of men to the Animal Master, thus implying a barren, infertile death.

There is, however, another way of reading the ritual: as an affinal exchange between village and forest. On this reading the hunting ritual takes on the features of a wedding ritual which, among the A'vuong Katu, is hosted by the groom's family and centered on a major animal (ideally buffalo) sacrifice and the subsequent exchange of ritual objects between wife-givers and wife-takers (described above). The sacrificial animal is itself a major part of the bridewealth given by the groom's family to the wife's father. Significantly, it is the bride's father (or his representative) who performs the sacrifice by ritually stabbing the animal to death and appropriating its meat on behalf of his lineage. However, the skull ('soul') is returned to the groom's family – 'to enable it [the groom's family] to sustain and increase its livestock herds'.

Here, then, is the paradigm for the full hunting ritual. Hunter and Animal Master – representing the village and the forest – appear as affinal exchange partners. The hunting feast takes the form of a wedding celebration hosted by the Animal Master who, supplying the 'consecrated' animal, acts as groom (wife-taker) while the hunter and village elders executing its immolation and post-mortem treatment represent the bride's party (wife-givers). As recipients of the sacrificial animal, the villagers become vicarious sacrifiers (performing the sacrifice on behalf of the Animal Master) and 'owners' of its meat which they share within the village. However, the decorated skull is placed in the *guöl*, itself representing the 'forest' in the village, and, at the end of the ritual, the spirit of the slain animal is sent back to the forest to revitalize the herds of wild animals. In other words, just as in the wedding ritual, the food part of the sacrificial animal pertains to the wife-givers while the soul part returns to the wife-takers – the sponsors and ultimate beneficiaries of the sacrificial act.

This interpretation gains credibility in light of the fact that the wedding ceremony can itself be seen as a permutation of the funerary sequence. In metaphysical terms, the two rituals serve the same purpose and convey the same message: the transformation of dangerous others – whether hostile strangers or predatory ghosts – into close allies. The wedding ceremony actually compresses in a single event a long sequence of ritual exchanges between the groom's and the bride's families which has as its explicit purpose to convert a relationship of potential hostility into one of intimacy and familiarity. In fact, the very term for affines, *kalang tamoi* (literally 'path to/between strangers'), can be translated as 'strangers turned friends' (Århem, K. 2010: 88).[24]

But where is the 'bride' in this account of the hunting ritual? A widespread myth provides the answer.

Myth

The myth, recounted in a variety of local versions, explains the origin of Komorbarr and sheds additional light on the Katu notion of hunting. In one version (from Aro village, recorded by Århem, N. 2009: 159):

> Two sisters followed their elder brother on a hunting trip into the forest. The brother caught and killed a muntjak [on the top of a hill]. When the two young women saw the animal, they started to laugh since it had a very short tail and a curved back. At that very moment the two girls became stuck to (imprisoned in) a tall *lepaang* tree [unidentified]. Their brother (the hunter) called for help from his village but when the villagers tried to release the girls from the tree by cutting it, the tree started to bleed. So they stopped [...], and the two young maidens died inside the tree. Their laughter can still be heard from inside the tree on full-moon nights. *This is how Komorbarr came to exist.* The name means 'two maidens'.

Another version (from Arek village) tells a similar story while adding some significant details:

> A hunter brought the carcasses of a bear and a monkey (langur) back to the village. Two young village girls started to laugh as they saw the quarry because the (big) bear had a very short tail while the (small) monkey had a very long tail. The girls kept laughing until they suddenly died. As the villagers buried their bodies in the forest, Avua took them as his wives and made them guardians of the forest animals. This is how the two girls (maidens) became Komorbarr. [...] *Therefore [Henceforth], the Katu perform the adah ritual after every successful hunt.*

The mythic narrative in the two versions above breaks down into a common sequence of significant events: (1) a hunter kills forest animal(s); (2) two village maidens (the hunter's sisters) laugh at the killed animal(s) and thereby offend them; (3) the Animal Master (Avua) retaliates by capturing/killing the village maidens and (4) taking them as (spirit) wives; in effect, they become 'keepers' of the forest animals, Komorbarr. (5) Henceforth, the villagers carry out the hunting ritual after every kill (implying that they thereby avoid the deadly revenge of the Animal Master). In other words, the *killing* of the animals and the *disrespect* showed them lead to *retaliation* (counter killing) and eventually *atonement* (marriage) between the antagonistic parties.

The myth thus refigures the successful hunt as an affinal exchange between villagers and the Animal Master. The mythical marriage between Avua and the (spirits of the) two village maidens effectively constitutes the village and the forest as exchange units in a relationship of asymmetric alliance; they literally become related as wife-givers and wife-takers. Thus, an initial situation of mutual predation – a sinister version of symmetric exchange – ends up in a conjugal alliance – a mutually beneficial relationship of asymmetric exchange. 'War' turns into 'alliance' and predation into a kind of sacrifice.

The myth, then, provides the answer to the puzzle of the 'missing bride': she is none other than Komorbarr, the spirit of the two maidens, captured and killed by Avua, the male Animal Master. The hunting ritual re-enacts the mythical alliance between men and animals, village and forest. During the ritual, Komorbarr is brought forth and given up to the Animal Master – as a bride to her groom – to ensure the fertility of the forest and the continuous supply of game for the villagers.

*

To recapitulate: the Katu conception of hunting assumes an alliance between villagers and the Owner of the forest animals. The asymmetric structure of this relationship redefines the killing of prey as an act of immolation, and the hunt as sacrifice. What would otherwise be a bad – barren and inauspicious – death is turned into a good, productive and auspicious death. The relationship of asymmetric alliance between hunter and Animal Master also implies that the latter's gift to the hunter (the prey) must be passed on – given up as sacrificial food – by the hunter to the ultimate givers of life, the Sky Being and his earthly manifestations, the spirits of the village and the forest. The sacrificial connotations of hunting are entailed by the asymmetric relationship between the exchanging parties. The very concept of livestock means 'sacrificial food', food of the spirits. In the asymmetric universe of the Katu, the hunter's prey is thus necessarily passed on as sacrificial food to the spirits to ensure the circulation of vitality and fertility.

Through the hunt, then, vitality from the forest is conveyed to the village, and from the village to the Sky and the powerful *abhuy yang*. At the same time, life-giving powers from the Sky (Pleng) flow back to the living – literally from Sky to Earth – in the form of fertility and regenerative force. In this revitalizing circuit, humans play a fundamental role as sacrificers. Alone among the living, humans have the capacity to sacrifice. In this defining capacity, they mediate between the spirits and the animals in the forest, thus forming a crucial link in the chain of generative exchanges connecting the living beings with the life-giving spirits.

The distinction between the sacrificial relationship to the spirits and the relationship of affinal exchange with the Animal Master is significant. It points to a conceptual fault-line in Katu cosmology – that between immortal spirits on the one hand and living beings on the other. To humans, the spirits are ontological others, powerful superiors; game animals, on the other hand, are posited as ontological equals but 'social' others (where the identification of the figure of the Animal Master as 'wife-taker' points to an incipient social ranking).[25] Sacrificing defines the virtuous relationship with the exalted spirits, affinal exchange the alliance with animal others. Sacrifice, then, is the religious (vertical) mode of asymmetric exchange, affinity its social (horizontal) mode. Both modalities are means of propagating life and renewal; the former taps the divine source of vitality, the latter circulates its vitalizing force among the living.

Concluding Remarks: Symmetric and Asymmetric Worlds

In an animist – intersubjective and relational – cosmos, hunting takes on a metaphysical quality which it does not have in a naturalistic universe. It presents people with a dilemma which I have referred to as the 'hunter's dilemma' – the specter of counter-predation. Prey animals, in their subject- or spirit form, have the capacity to strike back on the human hunter and afflict him with illness – a misfortune commonly imagined as becoming 'consumed' by the animal spirit. As noted in the opening section of this chapter, the ubiquity of food shamanism in native Amazonia is a cultural response to this existential dilemma. Game food, perceived as pregnant with the power and agency of the animal person, must be subjected to elaborate shamanic treatment as a means of removing its predatory power/agency. In effect, the animal person is desubjectified – 'disarmed' – and turned into 'food' safe for human consumption.

Indigenous peoples in the uplands of Mainland Southeast Asia tackle the hunter's dilemma in a quite different way. In the case of the Katu, game animals are construed as the 'livestock' of the forest, and hunting is conceptualized as a generalized exchange between human villagers and the master of the forest animals. The predator-prey relationship is transformed into a relationship of asymmetric alliance between village and forest where game animals are constituted as objects of exchange, the 'bridewealth' paid by the Animal Master to the villagers for their ritual services in connection with the hunting feast.

Now, there is a fundamental difference in social and cosmological order between native Amazonian societies and animist societies in upland Southeast Asia which may account for their different conceptions of hunting and, hence, their different solutions to the hunter's dilemma. Native Amazonian societies are generally organized around the principle of restricted (symmetric) exchange.[26] Marriage operates on the principle of direct reciprocity, expressed in an ideal of sister exchange. The exchanging parties are social equals – and Amazonian societies are, on the whole, fiercely egalitarian. Translated into the idiom of hunting, the logic of symmetric exchange implies the sinister possibility of reciprocal predation; metaphysical warfare with the animal others is a constant threat. Prey animals, in their spirit form, are attributed with the power to violently retaliate their human predators (by causing illness and death). Food shamanism is a means for the hunter to prevent this metaphysical reversal of the predator-prey relation.

In upland Southeast Asia, by contrast, generalized or asymmetric exchange is the rule, operating both as a social and cosmological template. By construing hunting as an asymmetric exchange between humans and the Animal Masters – indeed, as in the case of the Katu, as a mythical marriage alliance – reciprocal predation becomes unthinkable. In effect, humans relate to the animal subjects as superior wife-givers – in fact, as life-giving 'spirits'. The animal subjects are construed as subservient wife-takers, dependent for their continual reproduction on the ritual services rendered by the human villagers; they are bound to incessantly yield their wealth – their 'livestock' – to the human hunters. The very structure of the asymmetric exchange relationship precludes metaphysical counter-predation. Indeed, constituted as 'livestock', game animals are turned into exchange objects, deprived of their proper subjectivity and agency; they become vehicles of the agency of their masters.

*

The prominence of livestock in Southeast Asia societies is closely associated with the prevalence of asymmetric exchange and the religious importance of sacrifice in the region. In Amazonia, by contrast, livestock and sacrifice are absent. In a broad cultural-historical perspective, the possession and husbandry of livestock is suggestive of the shift from an egalitarian societal type (exemplified by Amazonian societies) towards a more complex and hierarchical type, including the intermediate, modestly ranked and fluid social formations (of the 'Kachin type') characteristic of upland Southeast Asia. Significantly, this latter Southeast Asian type is also the prototype for a society structured by asymmetric exchange in which livestock constitute a principal form of wealth.

The domestication of animals necessarily produces profound changes in the conceptualization of wild animals. Thus, compared with the native Amazonian concept of wild animals as powerful persons, the Katu notion of game as the 'livestock of the forest' implies a conceptual transformation – indeed, degradation – of the animals from subjects ('people') to objects ('livestock'). This transformation is congruent with a change in the conceptions of the natural world from one populated by a multiplicity of animal 'tribes' (as in Amazonia and circumboreal North America) to one inhabited by a myriad of 'nature spirits' (as in Southeast Asia). In the Southeast Asian cosmological landscape, non-human subjectivity is imagined in terms of spirits rather than differently embodied 'peoples'.

*

Tim Ingold (1986), in a seminal paper on circumboreal peoples in Northern Eurasia and America, presents a picture of their conceptions of hunting that is remarkably similar to the one I have outlined for the Katu.[27] Building on an impressive amount of ethnographic data, Ingold shows that northern hunters conceptualize wild deer (their main prey) as a gift from the Animal Master, and the killing of their prey as an act of immolation – a sacrifice dedicated to the Supreme Being on behalf of the Animal Master. The gift to the hunter from the Animal Master is conceived of as a token of appreciation for the service of immolation.

This remarkable similarity between the two types of societies, despite their entirely different environmental settings and material conditions of life, is of great comparative interest. The Siberian groups from which Ingold draws most of his data are either both hunters and herders, or hunters who live side by side with reindeer-keeping pastoralists. As in the case of Southeast Asian highlanders, the familiarity with domestic animals and the idea of sacrifice seems to mould their conceptions of hunting and their perception of reality at large.[28] In Amazonia, by contrast, where domestic animals and sacrifice are absent but the notion of the Animal Master very much present, hunting is formulated in terms of an exchange with the Animal Master – often with explicit affinal and sexual overtones – but one that lacks sacrificial connotations.

One more piece of comparative ethnography brings us back to the dichotomy between symmetric and asymmetric exchange. In his grand synthesis of kinship structures, Lévi-Strauss (1969) demonstrates that systems of generalized (asymmetric) exchange are distributed along an axis from northern Burma to northeastern Siberia. He calls it the Burma-Siberia axis of generalized exchange. It forms a structural continuum with the Kachin at one end and the Gilyak at the other displaying almost identical and simple forms of the system – with various hybrid forms in between (including the Naga and the Tungus-Manchu systems). It is not fortuitous, I think, that the sacrificial connotations of hunting, demonstrated by Ingold for Siberian hunters and by my Katu data, largely coincide with the endpoints of this belt of asymmetric exchange. In other words, not only does the 'sacrificial' notion of hunting presume livestock keeping but it also harmonizes with systems of generalized exchange in marriage; both hunting conceptions and marriage practices would seem to be cultural expressions of the same fundamental structure of exchange.

*

In my comparative reflections on the hunter's dilemma, I have been guided by my own research in two vastly different ethnographic fields, Amazonia and upland Southeast Asia, and a brief excursion into Siberia (where I relied on the work by Ingold). I have suggested that the ethnography from these diverse fields represent two different forms of animism associated with two distinct structures of exchange. No doubt this is an oversimplification which, fortunately, is redressed – at least in part – by the detailed analyses in other contributions to this volume. My general argument, however, is that the animistic cosmologies of societies governed by symmetric and asymmetric exchange tend to differ systematically. We are justified, I believe, in distinguishing between symmetric and asymmetric forms of animism – one structured by the principle of restricted (symmetric) exchange, the other by generalized (asymmetric) exchange.

This is so, I argue, because the different exchange regimes are fundamental structural templates, structuring not only society but also perception and cultural imagination; they generate, as it were, different experiential worlds. Symmetric and asymmetric worlds are differently 'curved' cosmologies, to borrow a naturalscience metaphor. Elementary social facts such as exchange, reciprocity and notions of intersubjectivity take fundamentally different shapes in the two worlds. So also the idea of predation and its human form, hunting – with great implications for notions of existential security, illness and curing, and human-animal relations: in a symmetric world, hunting and the consumption of game food carry the threat of counter-predation, a possibility which is ruled out – perhaps inconceivable – in an asymmetric world. However, in both worlds, the conceptualization of the human-animal relationship is diagnostic of their particular forms of animism. And in both, the metaphysics of predation/hunting is predicated on the constitutive principle of socio-cosmic order in each – symmetric exchange in one, asymmetric exchange in the other.

Notes

1. This chapter was drafted for the EuroSEAS conference in 2010 and completed in 2011. It was written as the first of my three contributions to this volume, followed by Chapter 14 and Chapter 1, in this order. In the course of the four years that has passed since I wrote the chapter (Chapter 5), I have become increasingly aware of the fact that the predominant form of animism in Southeast Asia differs in important respects from the standard notion of animism derived mainly from Amerindian and North-Eurasian ethnography. The careful reader will thus notice a significant shift in perspective and theoretical positioning between my first and last text. This change of perspective also reflects the fact that Chapters 5 and 14 were written before reading and fully taking in the implications of Descola's landmark study of elementary ontologies (Descola 2013) while Chapter 1 directly addresses them.
2. See Chapter 1 (this volume) for a review of the new animism concept and the theoretical debate it has generated.
3. See Århem, K. (1996, 1998) on the Makuna for a poignant Amazonian example.
4. My analysis is preliminary and inconclusive – an attempt to make sense of the ethnographic data at my disposal. Thus, my present interpretation differs in several respects from an earlier attempt (Århem, K. 2008, cf. also Chapter 14, this volume).
5. Fieldwork was carried out in Northwest Amazonia 1971–74, 1987 and 1990. In Vietnam I have worked in Katu communities along the middle A'vuong River (Quang Nam province) intermittently since 2003.
6. For an overview of the Katu in Laos, see Goudineau 2008.
7. As a result of government policy and development interventions over the past few decades, local livelihoods are increasingly oriented towards commercial farming and market-oriented agro-forestry production (see Århem, N. 2014).
8. The Katu refer to 'male' exchange objects as 'hard and imperishable', as opposed to 'female' objects which are referred to as 'soft and perishable'.
9. A father with few daughters and many sons may find himself in trouble obtaining sufficient bridewealth for his sons' marriages.
10. This hierarchical relationship does not, however, congeal into institutionalized social stratification. The asymmetry is intransitive and, as such, insufficient as a basis for society-wide political stratification (Lévi-Strauss 1969; Leach 1966).
11. The traditional funerary sequence is now increasingly shortened and simplified as a matter of state policy.

12. Although having indeterminate and ambivalent gender connotations, I refer to Pleng in the masculine form – as manifest in his most powerful apparition, the Sun.
13. The same is true, as we shall see, for game meat.
14. Since women cannot own livestock nor carry out sacrifice, they are said to be dependent on men for spirit protection. A widow or otherwise single woman is thus considered vulnerable to spirit affliction and other kinds of misfortune.
15. When, in the following I speak of hunting, I also imply trapping.
16. Cf. Izikowitz (2001) for a very similar technology; see also Tayanin and Lindell (1991) and Luu Hung (2007).
17. In this chapter I concentrate on the ideas surrounding game spirits and the animal skulls. However, a rounded understanding of Katu hunting conceptions requires an integrated analysis of the significance of both the magical leaves (*yeneu*) and the notion of animal spirits (*abhuy adah*). Nikolas Århem (2009) provides a list of *yeneu* plants and their uses in hunting; a preliminary analysis of the significance of hunting medicine and dreams can be found in Århem, K. (2008).
18. Only in the case of protracted hunting failure do hunters feel compelled to carry out particular offering rituals before visiting the traps or setting out on hunting trips (Århem, K. 2008: 49).
19. In myth, Avua appears as a personification of the old forest itself; the forest animals are described as 'the lice in his hair'.
20. The terms *cörvai* ('love') and *dang* (literally 'to bring a gift') are used when referring to Komorbarr's relationship to the villagers. Every large forest area is divided into 'Komorbarr areas' (*karchal Komorbarr*), each traditionally corresponding to a village territory (cf. Århem, N. 2009: 103).
21. Ingold (1986) has developed a similar argument for the circumboreal hunters in northern Eurasia and America.
22. There are also close parallels with the former Katu practice of 'blood hunting' – a Katu variety of the formerly widespread institution of headhunting in Southeast Asia (see Chapter 14, this volume). On blood hunting, see Århem, N. (2009); Costello (1972); Hickey (1993) and Le Pichon (1938).
23. On animal mörieng, see Århem, N. (2009: 128–9).
24. Significantly, the word *tamoi/tamöi* and its cognates in Katuic languages also connote 'enemies' (Gerald Diffloth, pers. comm.).
25. I qualify this contention in my theoretical discussion of Southeast Asian animism in Chapters 1 and 14 (this volume), proposing Katu cosmology as an example of a hierarchical ontology (hierarchical animism) where animals are posited as inferior or partial subjects.
26. This is crude generalization, and the extent to which symmetric alliance underlies the diversity of kinship systems in Amazonia is debated. Nevertheless, there is no doubt that symmetric alliance is a prominent principle in Amazonian kinship and marriage systems.
27. My interpretation of the Katu hunting ritual is to a considerable extent influences by Ingold's analysis.
28. Ingold's (1986) general argument is that the structure of the sacrificial rite, which is a corollary of domestication, is prefigured in the native conceptions of hunting among the circumboreal peoples.

References

Århem, K. (1996) 'The cosmic food-web: human-nature relatedness in the Northwest Amazon', in P. Descola and G. Pálsson (eds.) *Nature and Society: Anthropological Perspectives*, London: Routledge.
―――― (1998) 'Powers of place: landscape, territory and local belonging in Northwest Amazonia', in N. Lovell (ed.) *Locality and Belonging*, London: Routledge.

—— (2003) [1998] *Makuna: Portrait of an Amazonian People*, Washington, DC: Smithsonian Institution Press.

—— (2008) 'The spiritual significance of Katu hunting', *Vietnamese Studies: Special Issue (Hanoi)*, 1–2 (167–168): 29–66.

—— (2010) The Katu Village: An Interpretive Ethnography of the Avuong Katu in Central Vietnam, Katuic Ethnography Project Report, Papers in Social Anthropology (SANS 11), Gothenburg University.

Århem, N. (2009) In the Sacred Forest: Landscape, Livelihood and Spirit Beliefs among the Katu of Vietnam, Katuic Ethnography Project Report, Papers in Social Anthropology (SANS 10), Gothenburg University.

—— (2014) Forests, Spirits and High Modernist Development: A Study of Cosmology and Change among the Katuic Peoples in the Uplands of Laos and Vietnam, Uppsala: Acta Universitatis Upsaliensis, Uppsala Studies in Cultural Anthropology no. 55.

Costello, N. (1972) 'Socially approved homicide among the Katu', *Southeast Asia: An International Quarterly*, 2(1): 77–87.

Descola, P. (1996) 'Constructing natures: symbolic ecology and social practice', in P. Descola and G. Pálsson (eds.) *Nature and Society: Anthropological Perspectives*, London: Routledge.

—— (2013) *Beyond Nature and Culture*, Chicago: The University of Chicago Press.

Fausto, C. (2007) 'Feasting on people: eating animals and humans in Amazonia', *Current Anthropology*, 48(4): 514.

Fox, J.J. (ed.) (1980) *The Flow of Life: Essays on Eastern Indonesia*, Cambridge, MA: Harvard University Press.

Goudineau, Y. (2008) 'L'anthropologie du Sud-Laos et l'origine de la question Kantou', in Y. Goudineau and M. Lorrilard (eds.) *Recherches nouvelles sur le Laos*, Vientiane – Paris: EFEO.

Hallowell, A.I. (1960) 'Ojibwa ontology, behavior and worldview', in S. Diamond (ed.) *Culture in History: Essays in Honor of Paul Radin*, New York, NY: Columbia University Press.

Hickey, G. (1993) *Shattered World: Adaptation and Survival among Vietnam's Highland People during the Vietnam War*, Philadelphia, PA: University of Pennsylvania Press.

Ingold, T. (1986) 'Hunting, sacrifice and the domestication of animals', in T. Ingold, *The appropriation of nature: Essays in human ecology and social relations*, Manchester: Manchester University Press.

Izikowitz, K. G. (2001) [1951] *Lamet: Hill Peasants in French Indochina*, Bangkok: White Lotus Press.

Leach, E. (1966) 'The structural implications of matrilateral cross-cousin marriage', in E. Leach, *Rethinking Anthropology*, London: The Athlone Press.

LePichon, J. (1938) 'Les chasseurs de sang', *Bulletin des Amis du Vieux Hue*, 25: 357–404.

Lévi-Strauss, C. (1969) [1949] *The Elementary Structures of Kinship*, London: Eyre and Spottiswoode.

Luu Hung, A. (2007) A Contribution to Katu Ethnography, Katuic Ethnography Project Reports, Papers in Social Anthropology (SANS 9), Gothenburg University.

Tayanin, D. and Lindell, K. (1991) *Hunting and fishing in a Kammu village*, London: Curzon Press.

Viveiros de Castro, E. (1998) 'Cosmological deixis and Amerindian perspectivism', J. Roy. Anthropology Institute, 4: 469–88.

Willerslev, R. (2007) *Soul Hunters: Hunting, Animism, and Personhood among the Siberian Yukaghirs*, London: University of California Press.

6 Wrestling with spirits, escaping the state
Animist ecology and settlement policy in the Central Annamite Cordillera

Nikolas Århem

This chapter illustrates, by means of a collage of narratives, how the inhabitants of two Katu communities in the central Annamite Mountains of Vietnam attempt to negotiate their relationship with the spirits of the local landscape and the omnipresent state authorities. The stories explore how two influential village elders, Alang J'rreng of A'urr village and Bling Chen of Dövil village, try to guide their communities, in the course of a series of settlement movements, through the spirit-animated forest landscape while, at the same time, not diverging too far from government policies.

This is no easy task: on the one hand, villagers have to comply with the government's often-strict settlement and land use regulations; on the other hand, they must abide by the age-old taboos (*dieng*) of the landscape, defining where people can and cannot settle, cultivate and/or hunt – depending on the presence or absence of powerful forest spirits, *abhuy*. Thus, the two elders and the communities in which they live are caught between two very different but, to the Katu, equally real and demanding powers, presupposing very different modes of relating to the landscape – the state ('*nhà nước*') and the spirits (*abhuy*).[1]

The chapter demonstrates how concerns for the spirits and commitment to government policies combine to influence land use and settlement dynamics. Bling Chen, the elder of Dövil, meticulously attempts to abide by his tutelary hill spirit, Pöblow, whereas his brother-in-law, elder J'rreng of A'urr – in his attempt to comply with the demands of the state – strays from the unwritten laws of the land. In the case of elder Chen, the relationship between village and tutelary spirit is a balanced and largely auspicious one – the spirits help the villagers but also demand their due. Elder J'rreng, by contrast, challenges the spirits and chooses to settle in a place traditionally considered taboo – unsuitable for settlement. Later, he breaks further taboos pertaining to the place. Eventually, this inconformity with traditions triggers a sequence of ominous events that finally prompts the villagers to abandon the settlement.

Through their stories – about settlement movements, spirits, portent dreams and tragic death – the two elders disclose a highly complex view of reality in which people, spirits and the landscape are closely interconnected. The notion of spirits and the notion of landscape, or 'nature', are intriguingly interlinked; in many ways the local concept of spirits corresponds to, or fuses with, the features of the landscape and its beings. This is so since 'nature', in the Katu view, is not objectified, in a Western, scientific sense but instead imbued with agency and 'mind' (c.f. Bateson 1972). The narratives reveal a convergence in Katu thought between 'morality' and 'ecology', where moral rules and ecological observances always walk hand in hand.[2]

Background

The stories unfold in the forested uplands of northern Quang Nam and southern Thua Thien Hue provinces in central Vietnam at a time when the region is riven by momentous social and economic change. Beginning in the mid-1970s, in the aftermath of the Vietnam-American War, the upland communities of central Vietnam were urged by the authorities to leave their mountain refuges and resettle in more accessible areas under the control of the new socialist administration. This nationwide resettlement program, here referred to as the 'sedentarisation program' (or FCSP), aimed at transforming the marginalised mountain minorities into sedentary, progressive and productive communities in the service of the new socialist state.[3]

The communities figuring in the stories are located in the northernmost portion of what is today A'vuong commune in Tay Giang district, Quang Nam province. I will refer to this area as the Upper Mraang area after the small river, an affluent of the A'vuong River, that waters this part of the A'vuong commune. It is a sparsely populated area of forested hills, narrow valleys and swift-running streams. Though the population in Upper Mraang today (2012) amounts to a mere one hundred souls or so, the pre-war population figure was much higher, perhaps between five hundred and six hundred people distributed between nine traditional villages.

This post-war depopulation of the Upper Mraang area was the direct result of the sedentarisation program implemented in the region in 1975. The entire Upper Mraang population was relocated to a resettlement area in what is today Nam Dong district in the Thua Thien Hue province. Our two interlocutors tell us about this forced exodus and how, after more than a decade of hardships and suffering in the resettlement area, a group of the resettlers eventually returned to their homeland on the Upper Mraang where they soon were to face new challenges in their efforts to secure a stable and secure living in the forests of their forefathers.

*

The recent history of the Upper Mraang reflects the turbulent history of Vietnam at large. During the twilight period of the French colonial project in Indochina, the Katu gained certain notoriety as fierce and indomitable savages – particularly through a published account by Le Pichon (1938). Le Pichon, who was a military officer assigned to pacify the rebellious Katu, titled his account of his experiences among the Katu *Les Chasseurs de Sang* – 'The blood hunters'. The epithet referred to an ancient Katu practice whereby groups of young Katu men from powerful villages occasionally raided distant settlements, killing humans in order to bring blood from the victims back to the perpetrators' village. It was believed that the blood would enhance the fertility of the village's rice fields and the power and prosperity of its inhabitants.

The Katu very early came under communist influence from North Vietnam. Already in the 1940s, when still under the French colonial rule, the communists set up their independent administrative structure in the region and gradually established effective control over the Katu territory. After the North Vietnamese victory over the French at Dien Bien Phu (1954), the numbers of communist cadres multiplied in the Katu territory. These cadres had an enormous impact on the Katu society, introducing Kinh (Vietnamese) language and customs, and familiarising the Katu with the communist cause and Vietnamese society at large. By the late 1950s, Vietminh cadres had almost completely eradicated the 'blood hunting' activities and many other customary practices of the Katu (including traditional taboos and large-scale, public animal sacrifices which the communists found 'wasteful').

The Vietnam-American War constituted a watershed in Katu history. Living along the network of trails and roads known as the Ho Chi Minh Trail, the Katu were severely hit by the war. It is estimated that some 200,000 native people died in the whole of the Central Highland region in Vietnam as a direct consequence of the war (Hickey 1993: 267). We do not know the exact numbers of Katu losses, but they almost certainly amounted to several thousand of a total pre-war Katu population of between 30–40,000 in Vietnam.[4] Apart from the loss of human lives, the incessant bombings and the spread of defoliants caused massive destruction and threw the entire indigenous society into disarray.[5]

After liberation (1975), the new government's sedentarisation policy was implemented with full force. Practically all Katu settlements were affected. Traditional villages, located on hill tops or mountain slopes, were moved to lower areas along roads and near market towns and, whenever possible, to resettlement areas suitable for intensive wet-rice cultivation. Previously scattered, small and mobile settlements were merged into larger, composite and permanent ('fixed') villages. Shifting cultivation was discouraged and, indeed, became illegal. Instead, wet-rice cultivation and cash-crop production was promoted as the basis for the new, future-oriented rural society.

Although the sedentarisation program had a largely disruptive impact on Katu society and culture, uprooting communities from their ancestral lands and unsettling their traditional livelihood patterns, it is only with the high-modernist *doi moi* policy initiated in the late 1980s that the state (supported by international development agencies) has finally penetrated into the Katu heartland and fully converted it into state-space (cf. Scott 1998).[6] The symbolic apotheosis of this program is the completion of the 'Ho Chi Minh Highway' in 2005, confirming the rule of the state and the market in this remote region, and the integration of the Katu into the mainstream society of Vietnam.

A Tale of Three Settlements

In the high areas of the Upper Mraang River, there were in 2004 three Katu settlements: A'urr, Dövil and Galai (Figure 6.1). However, from the point of view of the district government, there was only one administrative village, named after the largest settlement, A'urr. The two other settlements, Dövil and Galai, were officially regarded as satellites, expected (indeed required) to merge with the larger A'urr settlement. While A'urr had a population of some forty-five persons, Galai and Dövil were inhabited by only a few closely related families. Yet, to their inhabitants, these two small outlying settlements were independent settlements – in effect, small villages.

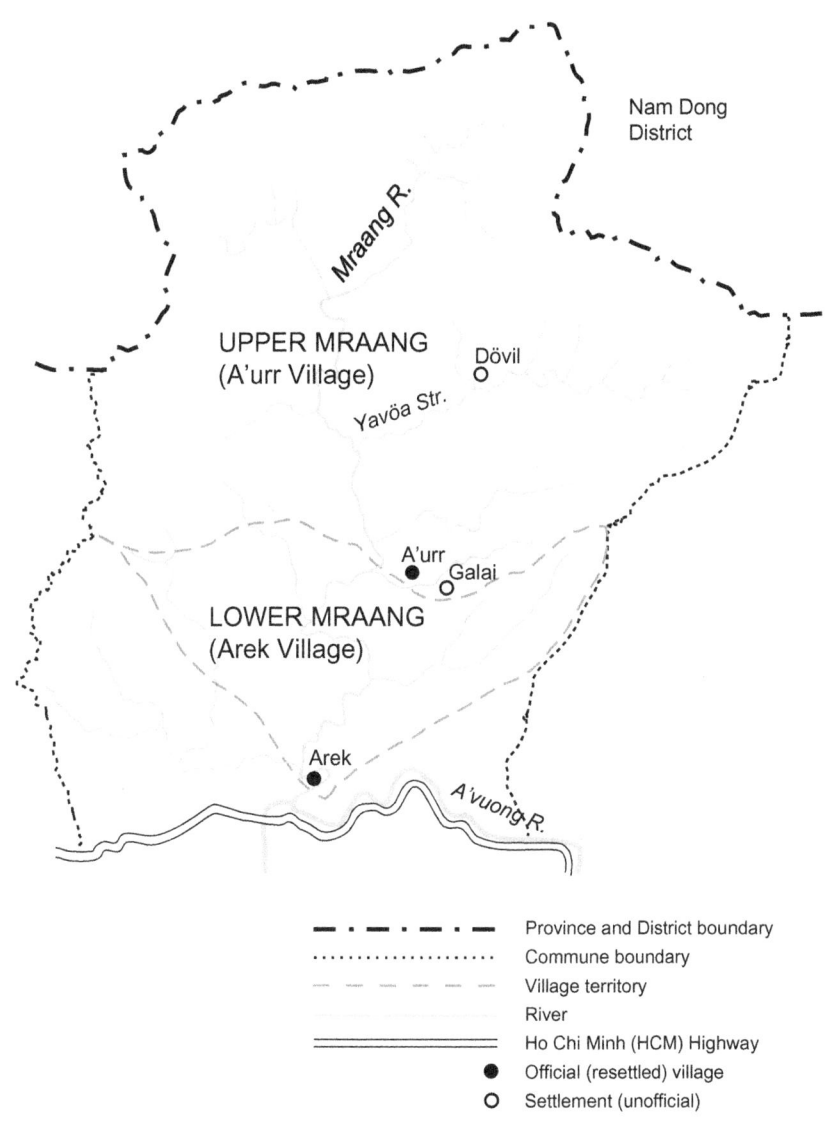

Figure 6.1 The Mraang basin in the northern part of the A'vuong commune (Tay Giang district, Quang Nam province). The map shows villages and settlement in 2004.

All three settlements had distinctive histories, reflecting the internal and external pressures on Katu communities at the time; each of them had chosen to navigate the government- and spirit landscapes differently. A'urr and Dövil had, for over a decade, reluctantly endured resettlement in Nam Dong district in Thua Thien Hue province but finally resolved to return, in several waves between 1984 and 1990, to their homeland on the Upper Mraang. Meanwhile, the inhabitants of Galai never moved. All three settlements were isolated, surrounded by deep, roadless forest. Foot paths connected them to each other and to the new HCM highway some fifteen kilometres away through the forest.

The A'urr settlement had, in fact, only been 'founded' in the previous year, 2003.[7] Though, at the time of my first visit, its houses had just been completed, and had the characteristic metal-sheet roofs provided by the district government, the settlement nonetheless exuded a very traditional atmosphere compared to the roadside villages I had previously visited: the spatial layout of the village – a semi-circle of houses on top of a hill – and its remote location contributed to this atmosphere. The settlement was an amalgamation of families from several of the pre-war villages in the area. Indeed, the present settlement was located on the land of the original, pre-war A'urr village which was dissolved with the wholesale relocation of the Upper Mraang population. Straddling the top of the Perrlah hill, the 'reborn' A'urr settlement contained, in 2004, ten houses of closely related families.

Galai was the oldest and smallest of the three settlements. Here lived the almost one-hundred-year-old Mr Lip and his elderly wife, parents of Alang J'rreng, together with their youngest son, Phot, and his family. In 2006, the old man died. Only months later his son Phot also died; he was then only in his mid-forties, and his death was sudden and unexpected. As a result, the settlement was abandoned; the two widows and Phot's children joined the A'urr settlement the same year.

Dövil was the most remote of the three settlements, located on the lower slopes of Dövil hill about two hours of walking distance from A'urr through leech- and snake-infested forest. The trail was narrow and winding, at some sections cutting into the steep hillsides, at other crossing swift streams, and continuously alternating between almost vertical ascents and precipitous descents. In 2005, a new, broader and more level trail was prepared by the villagers with support from the district government. It was only after the new trail had been completed that 'development' began in earnest in the area: two teachers took up residence in A'urr, and district and commune officers started to arrive on brief visits.

*

Before the Vietnam-American War, each of the nine traditional villages in the Upper Mraang area was associated with a delimited village territory providing the necessary resources to sustain its population – forest for shifting cultivation and hunting, and streams for fishing and the daily water supply (Figure 6.2). The pre-war population of some five hundred people or more suggests an average settlement size of about fifty-five persons (cf. estimates in K. Århem 2010: Appendix 2).[8] The villages were all circular in layout, centred on a traditional community house; they were widely dispersed and mobile – each changing location within its specific territory in accordance with the availability of game and fish and the requirements of their rotational system of shifting cultivation (with ten to twelve years' fallow periods).

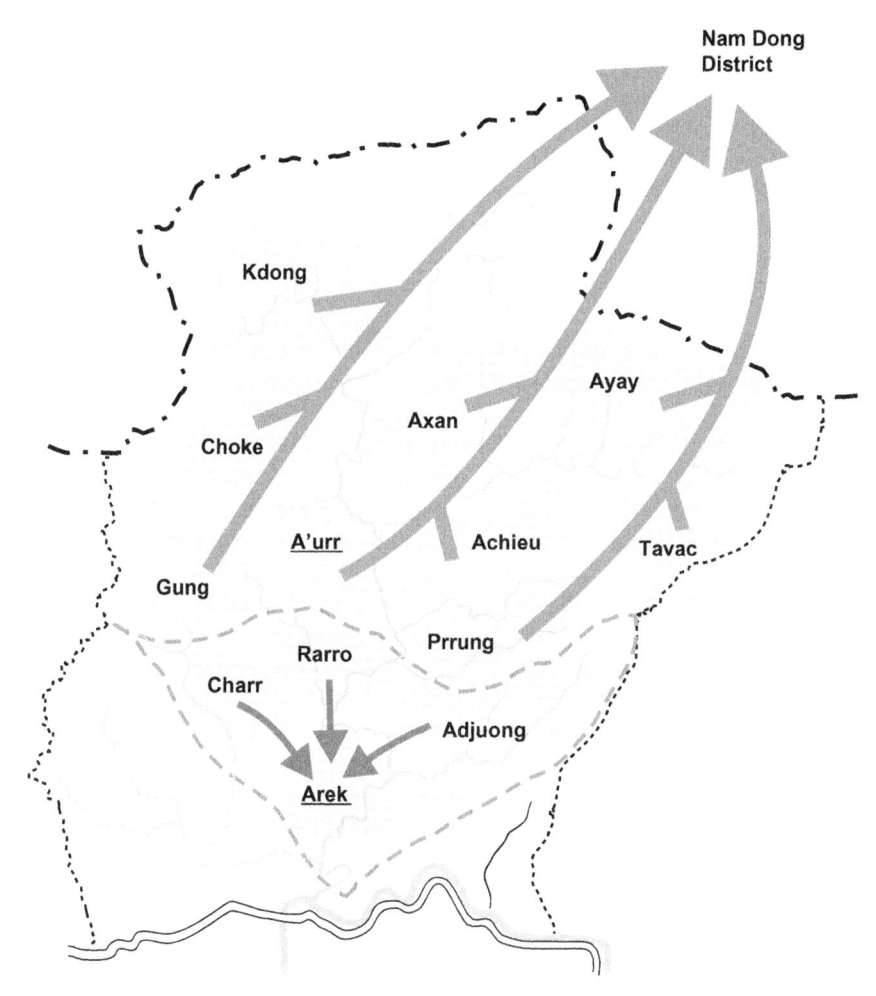

Figure 6.2 The distribution of pre-war village territories in the Mraang basin and the effects of the 1975 resettlement campaign (FCSP) in the area.

Bling Chen recalled that, when he was a teenager, there were plenty of wildlife in the Upper Mraang forests, including bears and gibbons – and even tiger. But about that time, beginning in 1958, the Revolution ('*Cách mạng*') came to the area. Communist cadres brought large quantities of guns to the communities 'to help fight the enemy, but also for hunting'. It is likely that the early cadres arriving in the area were interested in having a share of the game meat procured by local hunters; food supplies were notoriously scarce for the revolutionaries and they generally had to survive on local foods. From then on, there was, according to Chen, a massive increase in hunting – and a concomitant decline in wildlife in the area.

Vattana Pholsena (2008), writing about the encounters between the Vietminh and the Katuic-speaking natives across the border in Laos, describes how the Vietnamese cadres attempted to change the customs of the local people they met:

> '[…] The Vietnamese encouraged young villagers to eat game meat during the field-clearing period, despite this being considered a serious breach of the local customs. The youngsters complied with the wishes of the Vietnamese, and after noticing that none of them had any ominous dreams despite the customary breach, the youngsters decided to abandon the custom altogether.' (ibid.: 629, my translation)

Pholsena cites the document *History of the Revolution in Sekong, 1945–75* which describes how the local customs were progressively transformed:

> '[…] the youngsters stopped filing their teeth and piercing their ears, stopped wearing silver and copper rings around their necks and wrists. The women and girls started wearing skirts and shirts […] and the families [learnt how to] drink and eat in good hygienic conditions.' (ibid.: my translation)

Pholsena's article deals with the Vietnamese cadres active in Sekong (Laos), but the situation would have been very similar across the border in Vietnam. As opposed to the French, the Vietminh did not force villagers to feed them with domestic animals but their presence in the villages was, on the other hand, far more lasting and their impact more pervasive: it was not uncommon for small groups of communist cadres to stay for several months or even years near Katu villages (long before the North Vietnamese Army started moving southward en masse) trying to 'convert' the villagers to the revolutionary cause. As a result, and as the conflict escalated, the local communities would inevitably become more and more entangled in 'the struggle for national liberation'.

According to elder Chen, it was in 1963 that the first South Vietnamese and American soldiers ('*địch*'; literally 'enemies') came to the Upper Mraang area and the war broke out in earnest. Villagers saw themselves forced to disperse in the forest to avoid bombing and enemy attacks. Some Katu joined the North Vietnamese Army in fighting South Vietnamese and American bases in the area, and local losses were heavy. As violence receded, villagers moved back to their previous settlement sites, trying to resume the regular routines of everyday life. The supply of wildlife and fish was severely depleted as a result of the war. Chen does not explicitly mention the effects of defoliants and bombs on the environment, but other informants have done so. Hunting continued throughout the conflict, with both soldiers and locals killing animals in great quantities.

*

In 1974, when the conflict had subsided and the end of the war was near, the sedentarisation program was introduced in the area. The entire Upper Mraang population was urged to move and resettle in a government-sponsored resettlement scheme in Nam Dong (see Figure 6.2). Bling Chen tells:

'Of all the nine villages that used to live in this area, only two people stayed; Mr Lip and his wife on Galai hill. Even Mr Lipp's children moved [except for his youngest son who stayed to take care of his aging parents]. District officials from Nam Dong came here to inform us that we had to move down to the lowland area. The state supplied the rations for the trip to the lowland. The mobilisation [effectuated in 1975] took three or four days to complete. Not a single person was allowed to stay behind.

[Before the relocation] the villagers met to discuss the situation; some were for moving, others were against it. The majority were probably for it; we were told that the government would provide us with everything we needed; there would even be vehicles and houses for us. Those who had 'revolution cards' [proof that they had participated actively in the resistance] would be given money. But to be honest, nobody had any clue about the real conditions awaiting us. If we had known, we would never have gone there. My family did not want to move. We did not like it down there, we just like the forest.

There wasn't any suitable land for cultivation [in the resettlement area]; it was impossible to plant rice there. We had to survive on cassava all year round. Even when the rice grew nicely, the harvests still failed; it was too dry there, there was no water. There were some amenities though [shops, schools ...], but food was a big problem; we just could not figure out how to get food. My father tried to do shifting cultivation but ended up being fined, and he had to cut grass for days on end. He was very tired. In 1984, he decided to return to his homeland (in Achieu).[9]

We stayed there [in Nam Dong] almost fifteen years. Nobody wanted to stay there but the [authorities] did not permit us to return. In the end, the conditions were so difficult that many families decided to risk coming back without permission. Thus, in 1988–90 – some years after my father had left – around thirty more families left. I also decided to leave and rejoin my father. [...] Fifteen of those families came to this area, near their home villages. Most settled at a place called Klunng Mbaang, the settlement was called Saliep. At about the same time, in 1988, my father and his family moved from Achieu to a place on the Dövil stream on Axan land. I joined my father there in 1988 (Figure 6.3).

In 2001, the families in Saliep were ordered to return to Nam Dong, and most did so. My family and a few other families refused to go. In 2003, district cadres came again and urged us to resettle. We made an agreement with them to settle in a permanent village and follow the government policies – but in our own territory. The new village, which was established on A'urr land, was named A'urr after the old village. But most of the inhabitants of the original A'urr village were still settled in Thuong Long (Nam Dong); they did not return to their homeland.'

To recapitulate: by 2003, there existed three small settlements in the Upper Mraang area: A'urr, Dövil and Galai. These settlements – representing only a fraction of the pre-war population in the area – were inhabited by closely related people, native to the area who, defying government dictates, had returned from exile in the neighbouring Thua Thien Hue province. In 2006, the small Galai settlement dissolved as a result of the death of its two male family heads.

The following year, 2007, the Dövil settlement relocated on the upper Yavöa stream where it is found today. In an unexpected move a few years later, in 2010, the inhabitants of A'urr abandoned their settlement on the Perrlah Hill and joined the Dövil settlement on the Yavöa stream. The stories that follow account for these movements in the words of the two narrators: Bling Chen and Alang J'rreng, traditional leaders of Dövil and A'urr settlements. As we shall see, the spirits of the landscape are deeply implicated in these movements.

Chen and the Spirit of Pöblow Hill

To trace the history of Katu settlements is not easy, not least because of their habit to retain the name of the original settlement (which usually refers to the place of founding settlement) regardless of its subsequent movements. So, while Dövil was named after the hill (and stream) on which it was first established, it continued to be called Dövil after its move to the new site on the Yavöa stream. On the same account, A'urr village, established on Perrlah hill in 2003, was named after the original, pre-war village by the same name (Figure 6.2). But now, with the move in 2010 to the (new) Dövil settlement on the Yavöa stream, the story becomes even more confusing since the two settlements – Dövil and A'urr – merge and take the name A'urr.

To help the reader to follow these settlement movements I will add a number to the names of the two settlements/villages at the centre of the narrative, Dövil and A'urr. Thus, A'urr 1 refers to the original, pre-war village of A'urr, named after A'urr hill located west of the Mraang River (Figure 6.2). The small village by the same name established on Perrlah hill 2003, after the return from Nam Dong, is accordingly referred to as A'urr 2, and the current (post-2010) A'urr village on the Yavöa stream, A'urr 3. Likewise, the 1988–2007 location of Dövil village is indicated as Dövil 1 and the present, post-2007 location as Dövil 2. (After 2010, Dövil village merges with A'urr and thus de facto merges with and becomes 'A'urr 3'). The village and settlement moves in the Upper Mraang basin (1988–2010) are shown on Figure 6.3.

Bling Chen returned from his exodus in Nam Dong in 1988. He and his father chose to settle on the now empty Axan land rather than in the territory of their old village, Achieu. The justification for settling on Axan land was probably a matter of preferences: Chen's father – who was the first to return – simply regarded it as the best land in the entire Upper Mraang area. In fact, upon his return, he had 'tested', with the appropriate divinatory procedures, various locations in and around his home village – and the disposition of their respective local spirits. Chen's father chose to settle on the Dövil stream flowing from the nearby hills by the same name.

Wrestling with spirits, escaping the state 123

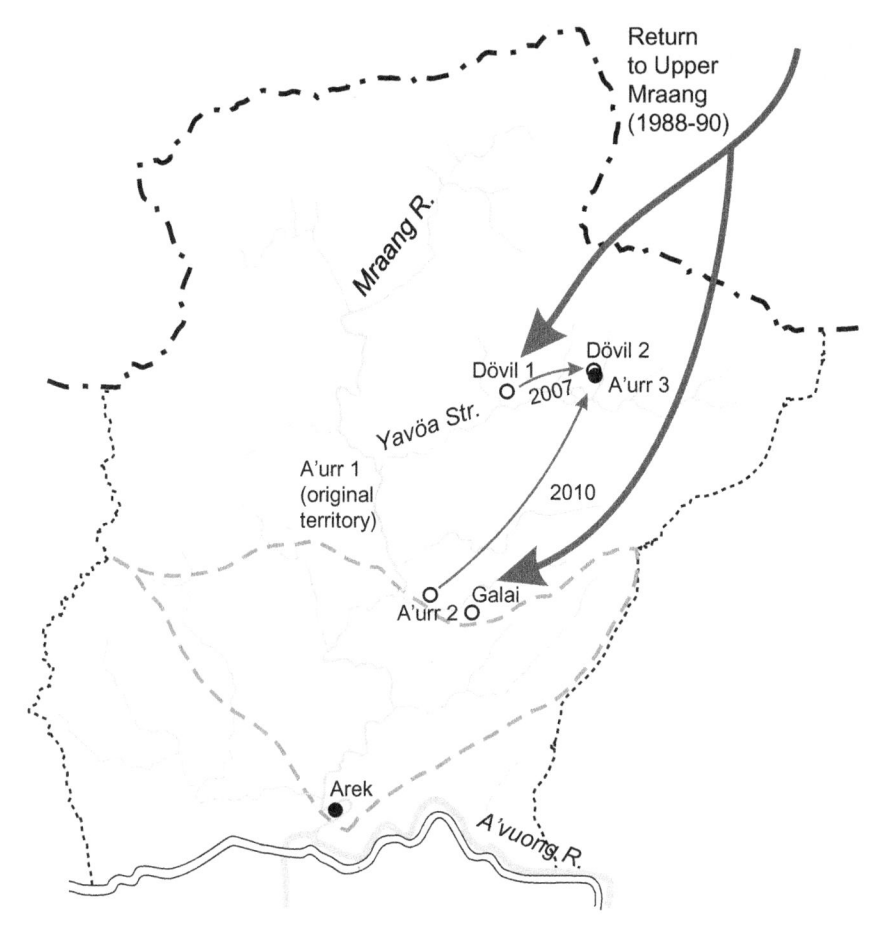

- Current official villages (2010)
- ○ Abandoned settlements:
  Dövil 1 (1988–2007)
  A'urr 2 (2003–2010)

Figure 6.3 The return of the Dövil and A'urr groups to the upper Mraang basin and ensuing settlement moves 1988–2010.

Elder Chen was a man of few words, especially during my first visits to Dövil (Dövil 1), but he could be very straightforward when talking about spirits beliefs. Thus, Chen was the first Katu who explained to me that Katu settlements were guarded by 'spirit hills'; often one hill in particular would take on a 'tutelary' or protecting role *vis-à-vis* the village. He explained that the hill protecting his own settlement was called Pöblow and that its spirit (also called Pöblow) actually *controlled* him and his work ('*quản lý*'). He described how, after he and his father had carried out the correct sacrificial procedure and all the necessary divinations, they had gradually come to know this spirit. The spirit had come to them in dreams and, on a few occasions, it had possessed Chen's father; it had let them know that it was the spirit of Pöblow, that it lived on Pöblow hill, and that it would take care of them. (Pöblow was one of several peaks in the Dövil hills where the stream of the same name had its source).

There were other hills with spirits in the Axan-Ayay area (indeed, it is often said that 'all hills have spirits') but Pöblow was the spirit that had come forth to Chen and his father. As Mr Chen explained:

> 'As far as I know, in this [Upper Mraang] area there are three hills that have *abhuy*: Pöblow on the Dövil stream, Bol Lomooc near the mouth of the Yavöa stream, and also one peak next to the A'urr settlement; the latter spirit is called *abhuy* Kuinn Hook [which is also the name of the peak].'

Chen explained that the relationship between himself (including all residents in the Dövil 1 settlement) and the spirit of Pöblow was similar to that of other villages in the Mraang River basin. Thus, there is a powerful and 'aggressive' spirit on the Konng Dhö hill not far from the large Arek village on the lower reaches of the Mraang River (Figure 6.1). This spirit, Konng Dhö, controls and protects the inhabitants of the Arek village (and, indeed, other, adjacent villages) – but also punishes them if they transgress any of the moral dictates that still govern life in Katu villages. Likewise, the villagers of A'urr 2 had a relationship with the spirit of Kuinn Hook – the tutelary spirit of *that* area. All these tutelary hill spirits are said to share the same characteristics; they take care of the villagers under their control but also demanded their dues ('*quyền lợi*').

Chen did not know whether, before the resettlement in 1975, all the villages on the Upper Mraang had had their own particular spirit hills or not. Perhaps some of them had 'shared' the same hill spirit, he thought, like Konng Dhö hill was shared by several villages around the mouth of the Mraang River. In any case, when he later, in 2007, moved from the Axan land to the Ayay land (Figures 6.3 and 6.2), he was made aware of the fact that he was leaving the jurisdiction of Pöblow and actually entering the territory of another spirit called Palenng:

> 'When I first moved from (old) Dövil to this place [Dövil 2 on Yavöa stream], I dreamt that I saw Pöblow spirit and the spirit of this place [Palenng] arguing with each other. Pöblow insisted that even if I moved into Palenng's area, I still belonged to him, to Pöblow, and that he would continue to take care of me even here in the new area. In the dream there were many people [spirits] present, not only two. The people were divided into two groups, one group represented by Pöblow and the other by Palenng'.

Furthermore, according to Chen's explanation of his dream,

> '[...] just as it is in human society – that one person cannot carry out a lot of different jobs and that work has to be shared among people – so it is among spirits. Both privileges and duties have to be divided among the spirits'.

At this point, Chen paused and asked if there are any *abhuy* in Sweden. I said that their used to be, but now there are not many. Hearing my reply, he said:

> 'There are still *abhuy* here, but they are not as strong as they were before the war; during the war the *abhuy* were scattered (*'phan tan'*) everywhere. The war changed everything'.

Elder Chen on several occasions explained to me that Pöblow was a very kind and friendly spirit, it did not ask for more than he (Chen) could give. On the other hand, Chen told us, the spirit of A'urr village, Kuinn Hook, was very difficult to satisfy: the villagers of A'urr (A'urr 2), he told us, fed Kuinn Hook with 'one or more buffaloes every year' but 'still had had problems with illness and deaths' (we shall see more about this). Chen furthermore explained that A'urr had had all these problems despite their *takah* (elder J'rreng) following many taboos which Chen personally found rather unnecessary and even a bit ridiculous, for example some food taboos which forbade women and children to eat certain kinds of food during certain periods. To Chen, these taboos were just invented by the old men to keep the best meat for themselves! However, despite his open-mindedness about food taboos, Chen was always meticulously careful when it came to his relationship with the 'landscape spirits', particularly his guardian angel, Pöblow.

As we have seen, Chen and his father returned from the overcrowded communes of Nam Dong in the late 1980s without any permission from the authorities. Similarly, Chen's later decision to remain in Dövil (rather than join the other families in the government-sanctioned village of A'urr) was also made without consultation with the district authorities. But, as regards the spirits, *abhuy*, Chen consistently followed the traditionally proscribed procedures.

In 2004, elder Chen – although still settled in Dövil 1 – started cultivating on land that formerly belonged to Ayay village on the upper Yavöa stream, some distance away from his settlement on the Dövil stream. However, before clearing the forest and cultivating in the new area, he had had to carefully inquire into the will of the spirits of the new area. This had to be done through thorough procedures of both divinations and animal sacrifices (to the spirits of the area).

> 'When I came here [to cultivate on Ayay land], I had to make all the appropriate preparations [sacrifices], from small to large, from chicken, to dog, to pig, to goat, to buffalo. I had to sacrifice the animals and ask the *abhuy* here for permission to stay. I did not ask the people from Ayay because when they left for Nam Dong they abandoned this place, they don't manage it any more. I have only asked the *abhuy*, not the authorities of the state (*'chinh quyen'*)'.

In 2007, the small community on the Dövil stream (Dövil 1) moved to the new site, situated on flat and fertile land some two hours walking distance up the clear Yavöa stream (Dövil 2). What began as a swidden and temporary settlement now turned into a fully-fledged and long-term settlement for Chen, his youngest son and his aging and increasingly frail father and their families.

Tension in A'urr and the Move to the Yavöa Stream

Now let us move back from Chen's settlement to the other – slightly more populous – settlement of A'urr (A'urr 2), some four hours closer by trail to 'civilisation'. In early 2010, much to our surprise, despite having constructed an impressive traditional communal house in 2006, and having a village school in operation since 2007, the villagers decided to abandon the site on Perrlah hill and move to Chen's remote outpost on the Yavöa stream – a small and isolated settlement without electricity and no school, quite out of reach to district and commune officers. Why this surprising move?

A'urr 2, by modern Katu standards, was of modest size; most of today's roadside Katu villages have between 250 and 350 inhabitants while A'urr 2 had only forty-five. Moreover, its establishment in forests that had not been cultivated for more than twenty-five years meant that it had ample access to far better swidden land than most Katu villages. And although relatively remote, it was not completely isolated from the amenities of modernity: it had a school and, thanks to its new trail (completed 2005), it was visited by district and commune officers, and its villagers could walk down to the commune shops without too much effort. Dövil (and the former Galai settlement), by contrast, really were disconnected from all these amenities.

We might thus wonder what prompted A'urr villagers to abandon their relative comfort and move to Chen's remoter settlement in 2010 (see Figure 6.3). We might also wonder why Chen never joined his relatives and in-laws in A'urr 2. Most intriguing, however, was perhaps the choice of the old Mr Lip, J'rreng's father, to remain in his small and isolated settlement on Galai hill, thus refusing – as long as he lived – to join the village where most of his children and grandchildren lived. Why did not these three settlements simply merge into the A'urr village – as the district government had wished them to?

When we first visited A'urr 2 in 2004, there was an open conflict between Lip and his eldest son, J'rreng, the traditional leader of A'urr. The father, we were told, accused his son of not adhering to traditions and to 'pretend to be a Kinh' – an ethnic Vietnamese. It even went so far that Lip publicly cut the ritual ties between his own settlement (Galai) and A'urr by refusing to share wild game meat with his relatives in A'urr. Considering that such a break of the ritual ties between close kinsmen and affines is very rare in Katu communities, the whole situation seemed a mystery. Surely, for the old man, life in A'urr – close to his children and grandchildren – would be preferable to remaining isolated on his remote hill top?

These vexing questions would prove to be related and soon find their answers; but the answers were not what they first seemed to be. Thus, when, in 2011, elder J'rreng was asked about the reasons for abandoning the settlement on Perrlah hill, he explained that the villagers had decided to move because there was 'no land for cultivation' in A'urr 2. The answer struck me as odd since only a few years earlier there had been no talk about land shortages. On the contrary, as we have seen, A'urr was unusually well endowed with good forest land. Rather, J'rreng's answer would seem to be a reflection of the increasing government pressure on villagers to abandon swidden cultivation and take up wet-rice cultivation. Hence, although A'urr 2 had in fact an abundance of forest land, it had very little flat and well-watered land suitable for wet-rice farming and gardening.

The new A'urr settlement on Yavöa stream (A'urr 3), by contrast, had plenty of good – flat and well-watered – garden land. In light of the pressure from the government, the relocation of A'urr was thus very reasonable. But there were more complex motives behind the move. As we shall see, the location of the old settlement had long been considered inauspicious, and some of the places in the vicinity of A'urr 2 that *were* potentially suitable for wet-rice cultivation and gardening were considered potent spirit places, *mabhuy*, and thus off-limit for intensive cultivation. The government pressure towards increasing commercial farm production thus started tipping the villagers against the local spirits.

The Death of J'rreng's Wife

In a subsequent conversation with elder J'rreng, he expanded his earlier explanation and acceded that the move to the Yavöa stream (A'urr 3) had not only – nor even mainly – been motivated by a lack of land (although the government had, indeed, stepped up its pressure on the village to give up shifting cultivation in favour of intensive wet- rice and garden cultivation). The principal reason for the move, J'rreng now explained, had to do with Katu traditions – the villagers' relationship to the local spirits.

A'urr 2 – although seemingly traditional in its hill-top location and circular layout – had been established on a site which had until then been considered forbidden (*dieng*). The Perrlah hill, where A'urr 2 was established in 2003, J'rreng said, was an inauspicious place, ridden with malevolent *abhuy*. Although swidden cultivation and hunting were traditionally allowed in the surrounding forest, to settle on the hill had, according to his father and grandfather, been forbidden for centuries. J'rreng's disregard for this age-old taboo when deciding to settle on the hill was, it turned out, also the root cause for his conflict with his father.

J'rreng went on to tell us of the sequence of events that gradually made him realise his mistake and, eventually, abandon the ill-fated site and move to the Yavöa settlement. Chen, in a separate interview, told a similar story about the same events. It all began with the sudden and unexpected death of J'rreng's longtime wife. Her death had served as a kind of wake-up call for J'rreng; it was only after his wife's death in 2009 that he could connect all the signs and omens that had preceded it and understand the true reason for her passing away.

About a year before her death, J'rreng had been clearing trees around a small natural pond, an *abokk,* at the foot of the Perrlah hill. An *abokk* is a pond with no visible inflow or outflow but which is nonetheless perennially filled with water. Perhaps the word 'tarn' is the most suitable English term (cf. Swedish *tjärn*). Near the pond, or tarn, there stood two old *tarr* trees, and J'rreng had resolved to get rid of them so that he could convert the place into a wet-rice field and vegetable garden.[10] He had thus peeled the bark from the base of the two trees with the explicit intention of killing them. He had also cleared some of the undergrowth around the *abokk* and, while doing so, inadvertently cut and killed a black and white snake with his bush knife.

One day several months later, when checking the trees, he found that only one of the trees had died while the other was still alive. He decided to cut down the dead tree. After returning to his house that night, he had an ominous dream. In the dream two people (both of which, he judged, were spirits) warned him: 'If both the trees die, so will your family dry up and die'. Although the two men in the dream were spirits, one looked very much like his dead father, the other like an 'elderly westerner' (with light skin, white hair and beard). The latter appeared to be the *abhuy* of the *tarr* trees. It was however, the other spirit – the one that looked like his father – that had spoken. The pale one remained silent.

Although J'rreng was shaken by the dream, he shrugged it off. Shortly afterwards, however, his wife suddenly died. She was in her mid-fifties, and had always been strong and healthy. J'rreng was devastated. The night after her death, the two spirit persons returned to him in the dream:

> '[The one who] looked like an elderly westerner was deaf-mute ('*diec*'); the other looked like my dead father. They wore loincloths. The one that could talk said that we had to move the village – we must go to live somewhere else, we could not stay in this place [A'urr 2] any longer'.

It was then that J'rreng realised that he had committed a serious offense against the local spirits:

> 'Just before my wife's funeral, my younger sister [the wife of Mr Chen] was possessed by spirits ('*bi ma nhap*') who repeated the same message 'the village has to move, it cannot stay in this place'. It was again the two people, the deaf-mute one and the other one. They insisted that we were not allowed to stay [on Perrlah hill].
>
> We knew this from before; it was nothing new to us. For many generations it had been said that this place should not be inhabited. My grandfather had told my father, my father had told me.
>
> After my wife's death, I sacrificed a pig, a dog, a goat and a buffalo to ask for forgiveness, because I had already cut one of the trees. For several hundred years there has not been a single settlement in this place. People have come to this area to cut trees for their houses and to clear swidden fields, but there has never been a settlement on this hill – not for hundreds of years'.

Realising the consequences of his offense, J'rreng now went to plant a new tree next to the tree that he had cut down. He also carried out a series of animal sacrifices to appease the aggrieved spirits – but to no avail. Soon after his sacrifices, a vine started to grow on the tree he had planted. When J'rreng saw the vine, he cut it, believing it would harm the growth of the planted sapling. However, after doing so, he again dreamt about the same two men: the one that looked like his father asked him 'why did you cut the vine – it is the road for us [the spirits] to climb the tree'.

More portents were to follow. Some time after the death of J'rreng's wife, elder Ating Avi died. Avi was the last really old man alive in the village. In itself, Avi's death would probably not have been regarded as ominous. However, his death was a long and agonizing process, lasting several weeks during which the old man became increasingly paralysed – 'he was like a living dead. He was alive but could not move, or speak…'. Then, at the moment of Avi's death, J'rreng had a violent seizure. Furthermore, after Avi's his funeral, two dogs were observed eating from the tray of funerary food offerings. This is a well-known bad omen for the Katu. Dogs that eat from burial offerings are considered to be possessed by malevolent spirits and must be killed. Some villagers even considered that the (possessed) dogs had caused Avi's death.

But J'rreng saw it as a final warning: the time to heed the spirits' warnings was long overdue. He explained why, for so long, he had been reluctant to acquiesce in the demands of the spirits:

> 'To be honest, we knew that we were not allowed to stay here [on Perrlah hill]. But in 2003, when we decided to settle in this place, we could not find any suitable flat area for the village. We were divided. Chen and his father did not want to stay here and my father chose to remain on Galai. We were all supposed to live here together, but those elders did not want to join the new village. My father also continued, for a long time, to insist that our village should not stay in this place.
>
> From the very beginning we had seen bad signs: first, when we started clearing the place, we were stung by bees – but we still did not believe. Those were not honey bees, they were *arang* bees [a smaller bee without honey or, more probably, a kind of wasp]. Secondly, when we completed the village school we carried out the usual chicken sacrifice and the divination with the chicken's leg – but the sign was bad ['*no bi bam*']. Thirdly, about two weeks after that, a dog chased a muntjac straight into the village and its horns got stuck under a house. We certainly knew – from the old days – that, when a muntjac runs into the village, that is a very bad omen.
>
> *Now* I understand all these signs, and I believe in what the spirits were trying to show us – otherwise I would still be living in that place [A'urr 2][11]. It was difficult to stay there [in the old place]. The government was giving us problems and the spirits too. The problem with the authorities was that there was no place there for growing wet-rice; they really wanted us to cultivate wet-rice and vegetables. The problem with the spirits was that they did not want us to stay there at all. So, we had to move'.

Elder J'rreng Wrestles with the Spirit of the Tarr *Trees*

To understand J'rreng's account, we need to go back to the way the story began, with the clearing of the trees around the *abokk* (the pond) near Aurr 2, and J'rreng's attempt to create a suitable '*ruộng*' (wet-rice field) in the vicinity of the village. During our conversations he had made clear that there was enough land around the settlement for shifting cultivation, even without entering into the 'protected forest' which the government had forbidden the villagers to clear. But, as a matter of policy, the government wanted them to give up shifting cultivation in favour of wet-rice and vegetables.

Since, as J'rreng explained, the spirits of the place had *not* – in the past – forbidden people from cutting trees or even from clearing swidden fields in the forests surrounding the village, the clash with the spirits really came to a head with J'rrengs seemingly insignificant meddling with the *tarr* trees. Even so, the cutting of the trees would probably not have been considered dangerous by itself – were it not for their vicinity to the *abokk*. As I shall show, small forest ponds are (or were, in the past) considered privileged dwellings of powerful *abhuy*. But the longstanding conflict between the community and its 'guardian spirit', Kuinn Hook, also played a role here: the villagers had long been aware of the fact that the settlement was situated in a 'forbidden' place.

In another interview J'rreng talks about his late father, and what his father had taught him:

> 'My father taught me which places [in the forest] I could not clear for cultivation, nor even enter. He also taught me, when I was still young, that I should not marry too quickly; first I should learn to clear and burn the swidden fields, how to make a house, how to get money to buy things for making a living […] He taught me how to look for honey, how to chisel a hole in a tree for bees to nest, how to cut rattan, and how to collect *chay* root. [He also explained to me] how to trade these things in the lowland, because in the past there were no roads or shops like now. One had to walk for five days to go there; that was during the French period, before *Liberation* […] Without a bush hook, without an axe, without salt, without mats, without a loincloth – how was I supposed to marry? But my father only taught me the beginnings, the basics, he didn't teach me everything […]
>
> But most importantly, my grandfather taught my father, and my father me, which places – from the olden days – have spirits, which places are burial grounds, and which places have trees which are kept by the spirits. For example: there are places where there are ponds with an underground water source, where there is no grass [around the pond]; around such [spirit ponds] we find mounds of litter/straw ('*rom rác*'), as if there were an underground cave from which the water comes – near those places we may not set fire […] [And there are] valleys where we can see no water; we cannot burn near such places. If we burn there, they will make us feel pain. We will feel hot in the body, hot in the stomach; as we finish burning [in such a place], we ourselves will feel hot, but not hot as with a fever.
>
> We don't know the spirits that live in those places – they are underground spirits. It is only while dreaming that we know about those spirits, but we cannot see them clearly. It is very rare to see the underground spirits; they are not like the spirits above ground. The *abhuy* under there, we don't know their name nor their signs ('*cu the*') because they do not speak at all. They

are *abhuy blang* [deaf-mute spirits]. Even when we dream we don't know; we just know that when we burn there, we feel pain in our guts.
To be cured, we have to go and cut medicine (*'but thuốc'*). We have to bring them [the spirits] rice grains and a bamboo tube which is black inside [...] and ask them for forgiveness'.

J'rreng then tells us what his father taught him about certain trees and why people cannot cut them:

'We may cut most kinds of big trees, but there are a few kinds that we cannot cut: the first is the fig tree (*'cay da'*; its leaves are like the leaves of the jackfruit tree, and its sap as well). If it is as big as this cupboard we cannot cut it. The second is the *prao* tree; then there is the *chörun* tree [forest mango], then there is the *cheyel* – '*cầm lai*' – tree.[12] When these kinds of trees have grown large, spirits enter them, and don't let us cut them; therefore, we don't dare to cut them or burn them, the spirits keep them. In the 'new' A'urr [A'urr 3] there is a big tree – a '*cầm lai*' – behind elder Chen's house; we do not dare to cut it.

It is just like the story I told you before about my dreams. There is a man – who looks like bearded westerner – who keeps that tree: it is just like when people plant a lot of *mit* trees [durio fruit], we don't mind if buffaloes come and eat from the smaller trees, or if the children come and pick fruits from those small ones – we only really care about the old, big trees. If some of the small trees die, we don't mind. But the big tree – the tree that already has lots of fruits – we want to protect it and we don't let anybody cut it...; well, that's how it is with the trees kept by the spirits.[13]

We don't know the name or shape of that spirit. We just call them all *abhuy*. In this place [A'urr 3] there is only that tree (the tree behind elder Chen's house) that has a spirit. We name the *abhuy* after the particular tree it keeps; if it enters a *chörun* tree, we call it *abhuy chörun*, if it enters a *prao* tree, then we call it *abhuy prao* – just like [we give names to] people. Some time ago I had a dream: I saw the *abhuy* of that tree [the *cheyel* tree behind Chen's house], it wore a loincloth like people and it came down from the tree and said to me 'elder, don't let the children scream around me, its too noisy, my ears are hurting'...'.

*

Bling Chen, in an earlier conversation, shed further light on J'rreng's falling out with the spirit of the *tarr* trees:

'Spirits (*abhuy*) used to stay in those *tarr* trees – in the trees and in the pond. The year before last year, elder J'rreng's wife died because J'rreng peeled the skin off the fig tree and the tree dried up. Then, when he saw it was dry, he cut it. The fig tree is poisonous; it is kept by the spirit. We call it *tarr*.

> When elder J'rreng went to sleep, he dreamt of the *abhuy* telling him 'when the tree dries, then your family will die'.
>
> That was true: when the fig tree dried up, the elder's wife died. There were two trees, he peeled the skin off both, one died but the other survived. After his wife died, he carried out many sacrifices to ask the spirit for forgiveness. Then, one day, when one of his children was taking a buffalo into the forest [for grazing], it suddenly broke loose and ran away. People went looking for it for three days but couldn't find it. Then, elder J'rreng had a dream; *abhuy* told him 'come and pick up your buffalo, I have tied it here to the tree'. When the children went to look there, they saw it next to the tree, like frozen.
>
> Elder J'rreng knew about that place all along, but when he carried out the sacrifices, he still pretended that he didn't know. What I mean is that elder J'rreng *did* believe in the *abhuy* of that place [near the *abokk*], but he didn't *want* to believe; he wanted to erase his own superstitions – his belief in the *abhuy*. But after those events took place, he carried out sacrifices, and pretended he hadn't known'.

Question: Are there any other places like that around A'urr (A'urr 2)?

> 'No, there is only that place, because that is the precise place of the '*ho nho*' [literally 'small lake', referring to the *abokk*]. From the old days, the fortune tellers have said so. In the past there were people that stopped there; then, when they came home, some people felt pain, others died. When they went to see the fortune teller, he told them: 'in those trees there are *abhuy*, you cannot clear there…'; then people let everybody know that the place had *abhuy*'.

Then, Chen enters into a more complex discussion, which leads to the heart of the matter – what it is that makes a place inhabited by spirits:

> 'In this area [the Upper Mraang area], there are a few places that used to have *abokk* but which no longer have it. In Dövil, for example, if you go up to the top of that hill, there used to be an old forest there, so there was an *abokk* there… [In the past] there were fish in that pond. The *abhuy* there is very strong, nobody dared to go there, but it seems that the spirit – I don't know – left that place and went elsewhere. [One day] when we went there to clear the brush, the pool had dried up.
>
> As far as I know, there are three such spirit places around here: the first is Bol Pöblow [the tutelary spirit of Dövil], the second is Bol Lomook and the third is Kuinn Hook, the peak above Old Aurr settlement. [*Bol* in Katu means 'hill' or 'peak'.] But now those pools have disappeared. The water of these places has disappeared. According to me, if there is still water, there is still *abhuy*. The *abhuy* disappeared because the water disappeared. Sometimes I used to hear the sounds of gongs and drums from these hills. At first, I thought that the sound came from other villages, but no, it didn't; it came from those peaks'.

Question: But if the Pöblow spirit has disappeared, how can it still 'control' or manage you and your work (as Chen had explained in an earlier conversation, recounted above)?

> 'According to me, the spirit is still there. The fish that the *abhuy* used to raise in the pond has disappeared; the water has disappeared, but the spirit [of the *abokk*] is still there...[14]
> Every village has an area which the *abhuy* manages [controls, protects]. For example, if we live near a hill, the *abhuy* of that hill will manage us...'.

Chen then repeats his idea (expounded above) that several *abhuy* coordinate their efforts to manage an area, that a single *abhuy* cannot manage a large area (with several settlements):

> 'The tutelary *abhuy* is not in the valley, nor under the water but on the top of the high hill. According to me, it is like this: one man cannot hold several offices ['*kiem nhieu viec*'], work has to be divided in order to be efficient and for some to be able to enjoy relief ['*huong tro cap*'] while others work. Thus, all must receive part of the payment/salary ['*lương bổng*']. Similarly, when the spirits of different places receive "payment" from people [in the form of offerings or sacrifices], they must share the offerings. If, for example, the people in villages A, B and C only pay tribute to the spirit of a single place, say A, then the *abhuy* of the other places would receive nothing'.

*

On several of my earlier trips to A'urr (2004–5), elder J'rreng had denied that there was any tutelary hill spirit in the A'urr area similar to the spirit hill – Konng Dhö – in the Arek territory (mentioned above). It was only later, when he understood that I was genuinely interested in Katu spirit beliefs and realised that I had heard of spirit hills in other villages, that he mentioned the peak of Kuinn Hook and that the villagers of A'urr regularly offered animals to that hill. But he did not mention the *abokk* and the *tarr* trees – not until the tragic death of his wife.

Thus, his account of his wife's death in 2009, and the events which prompted his village to finally move and merge with the Dövil settlement on the Yavöa stream, came as a surprise. It seems to me that his account actually reflects a personal feeling of disorientation and uncertainty which came to a head with his wife's death. Elder J'rreng, I think, was torn between the beliefs of his forefathers and the reality around him – a reality very different from that in which he grew up, and one increasingly imposing itself upon him and his people. His struggle with the spirit of the *tarr* trees was thus, I believe, a struggle with his own beliefs – an effort to come to grips with the changing reality around him.

On one of my first trips to A'urr (2004), J'rreng talked about 'sacred trees' (this topic was apparently not as sensitive as the questions about 'spirit hills'). Some of the things he said then I reported in an earlier publication (N. Århem 2009). He mentioned several kinds of spirit trees but emphasised that some were more dangerous than others. Frequently, he used the word *độc* in Vietnamese (meaning 'poisonous') to convey the kind of danger associated with these spirit trees.[15] The two most poisonous kinds, he said, are the *cheyel* (*Dalbergia*?) and *chölaar* trees. But he also mentioned *prao*, *chörun* ('forest mango'), *bölut*, *rerey*[16] and *lepaang*. He further mentioned the *devönn* (some kind of vine believed to connect the tree with the underworld) and the *chapörr* tree (unidentified) from which dart poison is extracted.

About *prao* trees he said:

> '*Prao* trees are not poisonous in themselves; they become poisonous if a spirit comes to live inside them. Some *prao* can be cut, others not. Tall and big *prao* trees cannot be cut; they have *abhuy*. If a person wants to cut a *prao* he has to check whether it has *abhuy* or not by first clearing the undergrowth around it, then returning home and waiting to see if he feels ill. If he gets sick, it means the tree has a spirit and he cannot cut it. If there are many *prao* trees in an area, the *abhuy* only possess one, and people can cut the others.
>
> Once, my younger brother was clearing an area which had *prao*; he made one cut in the tree and then went home. That night, in his dream, he saw a person [spirit] who told him that if he cut that tree, he [the spirit/person] would not have anywhere to live. My brother decided not to clear on that hill'.

In hindsight, there is one particular remark by J'rreng about the *prao* tree that comes to mind as I now try to make sense of J'rrengs stories about his wife's death and the subsequent events:

> 'If you really want to cut down a *prao* tree, there is a kind of medicine that you can use. You apply it to the tree that you want to cut. Later, after returning home and falling asleep, you will fight with the spirit in your dream. If you lose, the spirit keeps the tree. If you win, the spirit leaves the tree to you ... but you still have to give the spirit a year before cutting it to give the *abhuy* time to settle somewhere else ...'.[17]

I do not know who won or lost the wrestling match with the spirit of the *tarr* trees near the *abokk* in A'urr 2. It would seem that, ultimately, both elder J'rreng and the *abhuy* had to pay a high price for J'rreng's audacity.[18]

*

The narratives I have presented in this chapter speak, I believe, for themselves. Through the voices of our two Katu interlocutors, I have tried to show how reality is perceived and experienced by people living an animistic ontology – or, how an animistic cosmology is actually lived and expressed in everyday life. The chapter highlights the fact that, despite strong pressures from the Vietnamese state for modernisation and cultural integration (in effect, Vietnamisation), the local belief system has still not been asphyxiated – despite its essential incompatibility with state policies. The stories show the great efforts made by Katu villagers to navigate between the two powerful paradigms that govern their lives – that of the forest spirits, and that of the state. But also how state policies increasingly tip the people against their environment – a conflict they perceive as a confrontation with the spirits of the landscape.

At a more general level, the narratives allow us to discern the contours of an indigenous ecology, an animistic understanding of the living dynamics of the landscape. As such, the balance our Katu protagonists seek to achieve in their dealings with the spirits is representative both of a specific cultural ethos, a moral attitude towards 'nature', and a profound practical understanding of the local forest environment.

Notes

1. Since all the interviews with Katu interlocutors were carried out in Vietnamese, I have retained some of the Vietnamese words and expressions they used. To differentiate between Vietnamese and Katu words I will use italics in quotation marks for Vietnamese and italics without quotation marks for Katu.
2. For a summary description of Katu society and culture, see Chapter 5, this volume. For the Katu (Kantu) in Laos, see Goudineau 2008. Fuller accounts of the Katu in Vietnam are given in Århem, K. 2010; Århem, N. 2009, 2014; and Luu Hung 2007.
3. The Fixed Cultivation and Sedentarisation Program (FCSP) – *định canh, định cư* – was officially initiated in North Vietnam in 1968 with the objective of 'reducing poverty, promoting access to education, arresting forest destruction and promoting national security' (Swinkels and Turk 2006). By 1990, this programme had targeted 2.8 million people. Reviewing recent evaluations of the program, Swinkels and Turk conclude that the results of the FCSP are 'mixed at best with [...] only one third of people living happily in their transformed circumstance' (ibid.).
4. Le Pichon (1938: 361) estimates the Katu population to 25,000 while Hickey (1993: 267) gives an estimated population figure of 40,000 for the year 1967.
5. An estimated 85 per cent of all villages in the Central Highlands were destroyed or dislocated by the war (Hickey 1982).
6. *'Doi Moi'* literally means 'New Era' (often translated as 'Renovation') and is the name of a period which set in motion a radically new policy orientation in socialist Vietnam. The period started in 1986 and its goal was – and still is – to create a 'socialist-oriented market economy' in Vietnam.
7. An earlier incarnation of A'urr village, the 'original' A'urr village (A'urr 1), had existed in the pre-war period (Figure 6.2).
8. Some local informants, however, estimated the pre-resettlement population of the Upper Mraang area to between 700 and 900 people.
9. Short-fallow 'shifting cultivation' was apparently permitted in specifically designated areas but did not yield sufficient crops; the soils were too poor. It is thus implied that many people – including Chen's father – tried to carry out shifting cultivation outside the permitted forest areas, but were repeatedly caught and penalised.
10. I have not been able to identify this tree species.
11. At the time when this story was told, J'rreng had already moved to A'urr 3 on the Yavöa stream.
12. The *'cam lai'* tree is probably *Dalbergia oliveri*.

13. Note that although J'rreng compares the spirit tree – i.e., the cheyel – to a durio tree (Katu: *briu*), the *cheyel* tree actually does not have edible fruits.
14. It is unclear whether he is talking about a single fish or several fishes. But, based on other conversations about pools on hill tops, Chen could very well be talking about a single fish.
15. The Katu word used in this context was *mabhuy*; it refers to 'poisonous forest/trees' – but also to dangerous *spirit* places. It is *not* used to refer to other kinds of poison.
16. *Rerey* was also translated as *'cay da'* (strangler fig). Most elderly Katu are not fluent in Vietnamese.
17. I find this sentence particularly interesting; it indicates that the *spirit* can actually relocate if given time, just like a plant can regenerate if given a proper chance to do so. Some comparative observations are pertinent here. Thus, when Howell (1989) discusses the notion of *ruwai* (soul) among the Chewong, (a Mon-Khmer speaking group in peninsular Malaysia; see Howell, this volume), she mentions that her interlocutors explained the meaning of the term by reference to a cassava plant: one can cut the plant itself, but as long as the regenerative capacity of the plant remained intact, its *ruwai* was intact. I think it is useful to look at Elder Chen's statement about what kept a spirit-hill intact in light of the Chewong explanation of the concept of *ruwai*. For a tutelary spirit such as Pöblow or Kuinn Hook to stay in place with a benevolent attitude towards its human protégées, according to Chen, its core areas (the old-growth forest at the hill top, its water pool, etc.) must be left intact.
18. However, in the local view, the price paid by the villagers for their infraction against the *abhuy* was not considered particularly high. In the oral history of the Katu, there are many stories of villages which have been wiped out completely as a consequence of infractions against hill spirits (killing certain animals in the wrong place, clearing forbidden forests, etc.).

References

Århem, K. (2010) *The Katu village: An interpretive ethnography of the Avuong Katu in Central Vietnam*, Papers in Social Anthropology (SANS 11), Gothenburg: University of Gothenburg.

Århem, N. (2009) *In the Sacred Forest: Landscape, Livelihood and Spirit Beliefs among the Katu of Vietnam*, Papers in Social Anthropology (SANS 10), Gothenburg: University of Gothenburg.

––––––– (2014) *Forests, Spirits and High Modernist Development: A Study of Cosmology and Change among Katuic Peoples in the Uplands of Laos and Vietnam*, Acta Univesitatis Upsaliensis: Uppsala Studies in Cultural Anthropology, no. 55.

Bateson, G. (1972) *Steps to an Ecology of Mind*, New York, NY: Ballantine Books.

Goudineau, Yves (2008) 'L'anthropologie du Sud-Laos et l'origine de la question Kantou', in Yves Goudineau and Michel Lorrilard (eds.) *New Research on Laos*, Paris: EFEO.

Hickey, G.C. (1982) *Free in the Forest: Ethnohistory of the Vietnamese Central Highland 1954–1976*, New Haven, CT: Yale University Press.

––––––– (1993) *Shattered World: Adaptation and Survival among Vietnam's Highland People during the Vietnam War*, Philadelphia, PA: University of Pennsylvania Press.

Howell, S. (1989) *Society and Cosmos: Chewong of Peninsular Malaysia*, Oxford: Oxford University Press.

Le Pichon, J. (1938) 'Les chasseurs de sang', *Bulletin des Amis du Vieux Hue*, 25: 357–404.

Luu Hung, A. (2007) *A Contribution to Katu Ethnography: A Highland People of Central Vietnam*, Papers in Social Anthropology (SANS 9), Gothenburg: University of Gothenburg.

Pholsena, V. (2008) 'Entre passé vecu et passe reecrit: Les debuts de la revolution au Sud-Laos (1945–1949)', in Y. Goudineau and M. Lorillard (eds.) *Recherches Nouvelles sur le Laos*, Paris: EFEO.

Scott, J.C. (1998) *Seeing like the State: How Certain Schemes to Improve the Human Condition Have Failed*, New Haven, CT: Yale University Press.

Swinkels, R. and Turk, C. (2006) 'Explaining ethnic minority poverty in Vietnam: a summary of recent trends and current challenges', World Bank, Vietnam. (Background paper for CEM/ MPI meeting on Ethnic Minority Poverty, Hanoi, 28 September 2006).

7 Actualizing spirits

Ifugao animism as onto-praxis

Jon Henrik Ziegler Remme

The world of the Ifugao of Northern Luzon, the Philippines, contains a multitude of various spirits who influence the life of human beings in a most vital way. Despite the apparent coherence of this spiritual world, I demonstrate here that Ifugao animism contains an inherent ontological dynamic. I argue, therefore, that instead of focusing on this spiritual world as a belief system, we gain a better understanding of how Ifugao animism operates by approaching it as a form of onto-praxis (Scott 2007), i.e., practices through which a transformation of the ontological life forms of non-human beings is brought about. This onto-praxis is related to the need for apportioning sociality between humans and non-humans. To this end, I approach Ifugao animism through its practices and demonstrate how these can be understood as actualizations of the potentiality of shared sociality between humans and non-humans. The actualization of non-humans' potential for personhood is characterized by both danger and potential rewards (such as vitality and fertility), and I argue that many of the practices related to encounters between humans and non-humans are concerned with managing the tension created by these two aspects. A totalization of the shared sociality of humans and non-humans would be perilous; therefore, for its life promoting effects to be actualized, the sociality must be kept at the right proportion. The onto-praxis of Ifugao animism is thus concerned with the management of the potential for a shared sociality between humans and non-humans.

The Vagueness of Ifugao Spirits

The Ifugao of whom I speak in this chapter inhabit the village of Batad situated deep inside the precipitous Cordillera Mountains of Northern Luzon.[1] For the most part they are farmers cultivating rice in an extensive system of irrigated rice terraces and, for a majority of them, interaction between humans and spirits represents a core concern of their life. The agricultural yield as well as the health and prosperity of the people are held to depend largely on the goodwill of the spirits. The interaction with the spirits primarily takes place in rituals where the spirits are called by ritual experts, *mumbā'i*, to come to the house where the ritual is held, take part in the feast and receive offerings in the form of betel nuts, spears, clothes, rice wine, chicken and, most importantly, pigs.

The spirits are normally not visible to humans, and although some of the spirits inhabit specific places in and around the village, they exist in a dimension which is both distant and dangerously close. They occasionally show themselves to humans by appearing as human-like characters with a certain abnormality, as for instance a suitor sending wild-pigs instead of domestic pigs to his girl-friend's parents as bride price, or by sending indications of their intentions through birds crossing one's path in a particular manner. Dreaming is also an important arena for interaction with the spirits. In all of these cases, one must take action lest one suffers problems caused by the spirits. It is generally held that encountering spirits is most often a result of distorted relations between humans and spirits. The only way to remedy this is to arrange a ritual where pigs are sacrificed to re-constitute the relation in the right way.

Previous studies of the Ifugao, particularly Barton's '*The Religion of the Ifugos*' (1946), provide a valuable source of insight into Ifugao cosmology. Barton presents it as a widely shared and integrated system of thousands of spirits with particular names, moods and other characteristics, all located in specific domains in a neatly organized cosmological scheme. He groups the spirits into more than forty different classes, and argues that the pantheon he describes is 'given with a fair degree of completeness' (Barton 1946: 7). During my fieldwork in the village, such 'completeness' was hard to find, and even the ritual experts admitted that they no longer knew each and every ritual that their predecessors performed.[2] Others claimed that they knew only the names of some of the spirits and referred to them simply by the generic term for spirits, *bā'i*.

However, although many of the villagers were not particularly concerned with making differentiations between the various spirits inhabiting their world, they were all the more concerned with – and knowledgeable about – how this world works. I will, in the following, elaborate on what I call the operational dynamics of Ifugao animism. I argue that we get a better understanding of Ifugao animism by combining a focus on the ontological system – the entities inhabiting the cosmos and the relations between them – and a focus on the processes through which people engage with these entities, i.e., their ontological practices. By adding a more process-oriented view, the dynamics of how the Ifugao 'put their cosmology into practice' (Århem 1996: 200) are foregrounded and thus better capture the way relations in the human-animal-spirit field operate dynamically.

Hence, instead of studying Ifugao animism as 'a body of context-free, propositional knowledge about spiritual beings, their characteristics and interrelations (…) fully formed inside people's heads, like a "cosmological map" simply waiting to be applied in particular situations of its practical use' (Willerslev 2007: 156), I discuss how relations between humans and spirits are enacted in practice and how they subsist in the flow of activity itself (Ingold 2000: 162, Willerslev 2007: 156). I focus on how these practices are related to the tensions inherent in these relations and argue that the practices have ontological effects in terms of transforming the ontological life forms of spirits. I therefore call these practices onto-praxis (Scott 2007: 20).[3]

In the following I will first show how the idea of a 'shared sociality' between human and non-human agents is a potential that is actualized only in certain situations. A major point here is that spirits fluctuate between two ontological life forms. On the one hand, their existence is imperceptible to humans. On the other hand, they may take on perceptible forms, most often by appearing as animals or by possessing the *mumbā'i*. Secondly, I discuss how the contexts in which these actualizations take place influence the conceptualizations people have of the spiritual world. Thirdly, I describe what I have called the 'perilous potency' of the spirits. By this concept I want to convey that spirits are both a source of danger and a source of life. In the final part of the chapter I show that this characteristic has bearing on the quality of human-spirit relations. If animism can be understood as a continuity of sociality between humans and spirits, Ifugao animistic practices are concerned with keeping this sociality in the right proportions.

Animism Reconsidered

Various contributions to the anthropology of animism (e.g., Descola 2006, 2010;Viveiros de Castro 1998, 2004) emphasize that sociality is not restricted to the human domain, but extends into the domain of non-human beings as well. Descola, for instance, describes animism as an ontology where there is a continuity of sociality between humans and non-humans based on their similarities in terms of having a human-like intentionality. Descola bases his argument on an assumed human disposition to detect qualities among the elements of the world according to a distinction between physicality and interiority or to put it otherwise, body and intentionality. This distinction, Descola points out, generates four major ontologies: animism, totemism, naturalism and analogism. Animism in this perspective is an ontology wherein humans and non-humans have the same kind of interiority but are differentiated by the bodies they inhabit. This ontology gives rise to a particular social formation where all classes of being held to have an interiority similar to that of humans live in collectives that possess the same kind of structures and properties. Due to differences in physicality, however, they live in different collectives, as some sort of 'tribe-species'. These tribe-species establish with other tribe-species relations of sociability, usually of the same type as those that are held to be legitimate within the given human collective. Hence, Descola argues, '[t]he so-called natural and supernatural domains are thus peopled by non-human collectives with which human collectives maintain relations according to norms that are deemed common to all' (Descola 2010: 218).

Viveiros de Castro defines animism as an ontology that postulates the social character of relations between humans and non-humans. Similar to Descola, Viveiros de Castro sees this as related to the common spiritual unity that characterizes humans and non-humans. This spiritual unity is related to the ability to have a point of view and in Viveiros de Castro's notion of perspectivism, having a point of view amounts to being a subject and being a subject is being a human. Animals and other non-humans are therefore subjects, 'not because they are human (humans in disguise); rather, they are human because they are subjects (potential subjects)' (Viveiros de Castro 2004: 467). With this move he is able to argue that humanity is not restricted to humans, but extends into the domain of non-human beings. When animals are understood as humans, there is no projection of substantive human qualities onto these animals. Rather, they are thought to partake in humanity as a condition which all those beings that are considered subjects are members of. What Viveiros de Castro achieves by this definition of animism is, among other things, to locate sociality in the space between nature and society. He thus avoids portraying the sociality of animals and other non-humans as metaphoric as tended to be done in previous understandings of animism (e.g., Descola 1996).

There are other, more fundamental differences between Descola and Viveiros de Castro's conceptualization of animist ontology, but these will not be discussed here.[4] What I want to focus on here is that both of them stress that animistic ontologies are characterized by a continuity of sociality between humans and non-humans. It is also a major point here that this is related to a common feature – a similar kind of interiority in Descola's case and a spiritual unity based on the ability to have a point of view in Viveiros de Castro's case.

As I will show in the following, Ifugao animism features a similar kind of continuity. But this continuity should not be understood as a stable feature of relations between humans and non-humans. I will argue that the continuity of sociality between humans and non-humans rather operates as a potential that can be actualized in certain situations. Willerslev (2007) makes a similar point in his analysis of hunting and animism among the Siberian Yukaghirs. Although they tend to relate to animals as persons, they do not attribute personhood indiscriminately, and neither are they very consistent in their claims about the existence of animals as persons. Willerslev suggests that instead of seeing personhood as an inherent property of people and things, personhood is constituted in and through the relations into which they enter (see also Bird-David 1999). Personhood is thus 'a potentiality of being-in-the-world, which might or might not be realized as a result of their position within a relational field of activity' (Willerslev 2007: 21). In this understanding of the animic ontology, personhood – and I will add the sociality in which personhood is embedded – emerges from relational practices. Personhood and sociality are then, as Ingold states, 'forever on the verge of the actual' (2000: 11–12).

A Potential for Sociality

Knowledge about the spiritual beings is widely and differentially distributed. The ritual experts, known as the *mumbā'i*, have trained for years and have received the authority to perform the *bā'i*, the ritual invocations, by the spirits. These mostly old men have memorized the names of a huge number of spirits and are able to locate them in their different regions of the Skyworld, the Earth, the Underworld, the Upstream and the Downstream. Although most other villagers have a rather rough knowledge of the spiritual world, a shared understanding of a general pattern can be found.

The spirits can be divided into three groups. First, there is the *nun'apuh*, the ancestor spirits. When humans die, their life force, *lennāwa*, continues to live and lurk around the house looking for family members. After a year or so, the corpse will be exhumed from the burial cave, and a ritual is held in which the dead person is told to go to join the ancestors and stop bothering the living human beings. This will make the deceased a proper *nun'apuh*, provided, that is, that the death was natural, which in Ifugao is defined as illness, old age, and sorcery. Further interaction between the *nun'apuh* and the descendants occurs only if the *nun'apuh* contacts them in one way or another or whenever they arrange a sacrificial ritual in which case all the *nun'apuh* of the family will be invoked and asked to attend. The second group of spirits are the *pinādeng* who inhabit large stones, tall trees, river creeks and other particular places in the landscape. These are easily enraged, and especially children are prone to excite them since they have not yet learned to respect the place and might therefore for instance hit them when they throw stones into the river while playing. The third group are the *bā'i*, who are all those spirits associated with specific illnesses, celestial bodies and meteorological phenomena, as well as spirits who control rice production and agricultural yield, the spirit of the rice wine, and an almost unlimited number of others since most things potentially contain a spirit.

Although these spirits inhabit the same world as the living human beings, the two classes of beings exist in different dimensions (cf. Janowski, this volume). Human beings have a body, a physical part, which makes them visible and tangible to each other. The physical body of spirits is invisible to humans. There is a dimensional disjunction between them which is crucial to sustain, and eventual conjunctions must be met by ritual attempts to restore the proper degree of disjunction. I will discuss the importance of this later and turn to a description of an important feature which humans and spirits have in common.

Of vital importance for life in Ifugao is the *lennāwa*, which similarly to the Chewong 'ruwai' (Howell, this volume), has a number of dimensions whose relevance vary contextually. In one sense it refers to a general life force, i.e., what makes everything that lives alive. A living being is alive when the body, *odol*, is conjoined with the *lennāwa*. Together they make up a *tāgu*, a person. For humans this vital conjunction of body and life force can be temporarily disjoined. In dreams, for instance, the *lennāwa* leaves the body and moves around in a dimension where other *lennāwa* can be encountered, both those of the living and those of the dead. In most cases this temporary disjunction of *lennāwa* and body causes no problem, but it is potentially dangerous. The spirits might convince the *lennāwa* to join them, and if the disjunction is prolonged, the body gets ill. Hence, many kinds of illnesses in Ifugao are understood to be caused by the separation of the *lennāwa* from the body, and if the disjunction becomes permanent, the person dies. Such illnesses can only be healed by returning the *lennāwa* to the body. To effectuate this, one arranges a ritual where the spirits involved are invited to come so that they can receive pigs and other offerings in exchange for the *lennāwa* of the patient.

This understanding of *lennāwa* as a life force of the individual human being extends as indicated above to non-humans as well. Everything that is alive – both animals and plants – contains this life force and is subject to the same kind of disjunctional dangers. Killing an animal, as one does in sacrificial rituals, releases its *lennāwa* which then can be taken by the spirits to their domain as an offering. However, although the possession of both *lennāwa* and *odol* makes animals into *tāgu*, persons, human beings do not necessarily relate to them as such. A bird has *lennāwa*, it needs so in order to live, but the type of *odol* it has differentiates it from humans. However, in some cases a bird's *lennāwa* can be taken to be human-like. It can be a manifestation of a spirit, so that the bird's intentionality and rationality is interpreted as belonging to a person. In such cases, the bird is said to have a *lennāwa* in the sense of having personhood. However, mostly the common feature of having a conjoined *lennāwa* and *odol* does not make for much in human-animal interaction. Their potential for shared sociality is mostly not actualized. Only in certain situations does this become relevant, and then they relate to these beings as persons with whom one shares a common sociality.[5]

Hence, almost all animals have the capacity of being persons. When this capacity is actualized, treating the animal as a person is restricted to that individual animal. That, for instance, one particular bird was a person one time does not mean that all birds of that species always are persons. This goes for most animals, but there is an important distinction between wild and domestic animals here.

Much of the anthropological debate on animism is related to interaction with wild animals, and particularly, hunting. The Ifugao, however, are not avid hunters,[6] and most interaction with animals is with domestic dogs, pigs, chickens and water buffaloes. The centrality of domesticated animals in Ifugao animism differentiates it from the forms of animism we've known from the Amazon where much of the discussion revolves around the relation between humans and wild animals. This of course does not mean that wild animals do not play a significant part in Ifugao animism. Rather, the coexistence of wild and domesticated animals implies that human-animal relations take on a greater complexity and variety in terms of modes of interaction (see Sillander this volume and Gibson 1986: 182). Domesticated animals here also have a particular role as mediators between humans and the *bā'i*, and as such the subjectivity of these animals is not a central issue. It is, rather, wild animals, particularly those that traverse the spatial and conceptual differentiations like birds entering into houses and behaving unexpectedly, whose personhood, subjectivity and intentionality become a matter of concern.

The contrast between wild and domestic animals plays, therefore, a significant role in the relations between humans and spirits. In principle, wild animals are owned by the *pinādeng* and cannot be taken from them without their permission. They relate, that is, in the same way to wild animals as humans do to domestic animals. Sacrificing wild pigs would, therefore, have no effect since it would amount to giving the spirits something that is already theirs. Domestic animals, particularly pigs, are suitable for this purpose, but they must then be of the so-called 'native pig' variant. These are pigs that roam around freely in the village and are fed human-like food, like leftovers or sweet potato from the upland swiddens. There is a strong identification between domestic animals and their owners, to the extent that an animal hurt in an accident, for instance, might result in the owner being hurt in the same way unless the animal is given proper treatment. Identification between the person sponsoring a sacrificial ritual and the pigs is also brought about through placing them at particular parts of the house during the ritual.

Of the wild animals, birds are those which most often are treated as persons. For instance, when a bird one evening flew into my room, my host family took it as a sign that the spirits tried to get in contact and made sure that a sacrifice was held to prevent anyone of us from getting ill. Similarly, an old man had walked along the trail on his way to Lamut, a town further south. When he came to a resting spot, he sat down to chew betel nut with some men who were already there. As they sat there, some birds flew over them and twittered in a way which the men interpreted as signifying that these birds were not simply birds, but were spirits trying tell him to turn back and postpone his travel to the day after. The old man thought otherwise, however, and continued his trip towards Lamut. When he arrived, he got ill and later died. He never should have continued, villagers said, since those birds had after all been spirits.

In these and other cases, the birds were understood as spirits appearing in bird bodies. The birds were correspondingly perceived and treated (although post facto) as persons with whom the humans shared a common sociality.[7] Hence, it makes much sense to view Ifugao ontology as characterized by a continuity of sociality between humans and non-humans. In cases where an encounter between a human and an animal results in an understanding that the animal encountered is actually a person, the two parties are held to share a common ground of sociality in which they can interact as persons. Their physical exteriors might be quite different, but the interior element of a personalized *lennāwa* is similar. The parallels to Descola's conceptualization of animism presented earlier are clear. In the confrontation of a human being with an as yet unspecified alter, Descola (2006: 141) argues, a process of identification is set about. The subject detects differences and similarities between himself and the objects in the world by inferring analogies and distinctions of behaviour and appearances, and this is done by means of evaluating similarities and differences of interiority and physicality between oneself and the object encountered. Animism, in Descola's conceptualization, involves an identification between a subject (*ego*) and an object (*alter*), based on a similarity of interiority and difference in physicality (Descola 2006: 140–1).

However, as the above ethnography indicates, the shared sociality between humans, animals and spirits exists in Ifugao as a potential that is not always actualized, but which can be so in certain contexts. Mostly birds are just birds, but they do have the potential to also be spirits. With the actualization of this potential comes also a shared sociality between humans and spirits. In those cases, then, when the animistic potential of Ifugao cosmology is actualized, the subject's identification with the object (cum subject) is the result of a relational process from which the personhood of entities emerges. Inherent in this process of identification is an idea of continuity between them which makes them in principle interchangeable with each other. A human can see the bird as a person with will and intention like himself. There is a potential here for what Pedersen calls 'analogous identification' or a 'continuous substitutions of Same becoming Other, and vice versa' (2001: 416), but this potential is actualized only in certain contexts and is reversible.

The Dynamics of Actualizations

Ingold (2000) presents a theory of animism that emphasizes the importance of lived experience. Animals are perceived and experienced as persons by hunters and gatherers in their direct practical engagement with the environment. Personhood in animals thus comes about as an actualization of the affordances of the environment. In Ingold's understanding it is this kind of direct experience of the environment that produces personhood, and animism can be understood as characterized by a becoming, forever on the verge of the actual. However, in the narration of myths and through the performance of rituals, perceptions and experiences are intellectually elaborated and socially reproduced. Cosmos is made available for personal experience, and the way this is done 'shapes and reshapes [people's] perceptions of reality' (Århem 1996: 200). I will show here, then, that there is a significant dynamic involved between perception and conceptualization that is crucial to appreciate if we want to understand how the actualizations of spirits take place and what specific shapes they take. Although the villagers of Batad were relatively vague on the composition of the Ifugao cosmos, their conceptualizations of it did not run wild, so to speak, but showed a certain degree of consistency. The villagers' conceptualizations of the spirits were not totally idiosyncratic nor were their kept private, but were in fact given shape by being actualized within an interpersonal communicative environment.

While walking along the trails that run through the thick forest and from stone wall to stone wall in the large maze of paths that criss-cross the giant amphitheatre of rice terraces surrounding the village, one is likely to encounter animals of various kinds. Close to the houses, chickens and pigs roam around freely, and in the forest birds, lizards and the occasional snake cross the trail. Usually not much attention is paid to these animals, but in certain cases they might behave in a manner that is unexpected or conspicuous in one way or another. In such cases they suspect the animal to be a so-called *bumāun*, an omen agent or a spirit. In some cases the encounter will not lead to any changed behaviour by the persons encountering the animal. They will simply continue their walk along the trail, and if nothing happens, nothing more than perhaps telling about it to other people is made of the encounter. If things do not go as expected however, as happened with the old man travelling to Lamut mentioned earlier, the animal's status as a *bumāun* is considered. To be sure, however, one needs to consult a *mumbā'i* who can, by various techniques and discussion with the person involved, find out what actually happened and what spirit the *bumāun* actually was.

Hence, perceiving an animal behaving strangely is not enough to include it within a shared sociality. Its status as *bumāun* is most often ascribed to it *post factum*, as a suspicion that the animal encountered must have been a *bumāun* since one has experienced problems after the actual encounter took place.[8] The conclusion eventually comes about through cooperating with the *mumbā'i*. The understanding of the encounter as a human-spirit encounter is, in this way, a product of a collaborative retrospective conceptualization.

Encounters with spirits are a common theme of conversation, and people will often tell stories about these encounters and discuss them further with their family and friends. I suggest that the narratives that come out of these encounters are important for giving shape to the conceptualization of the spirits. Telling the story about one's encounter with the spirit can be understood here as a way of eliciting support for an understanding of what one has experienced (Josephides 2008). The environment in which this meaning negotiation takes place is interpersonal, and the negotiation of relations, both between the teller and the audience, but also between the human beings and the spirits, goes along with the negotiation of meaning (Carrithers 1992: 106). The storytelling is thus born out of experience but also gives shape to it (Ochs and Capps 1996: 19).

In a way, the storytelling about human-spirit encounters can also be seen as an actualization of spirits in itself. Mentioning the names of spirits should be done with caution in Ifugao, and should ideally be accompanied by an offering of at least a chicken. Talking is a powerful practice here, and spirits are known to inflict illness on people by talking to them, and as mentioned earlier, the ritual knowledge possessed by the *mumbā'i* is a collection of memorized verbalized invocations and chants through which the *mumbā'i* make the spirit appear. Demonstrating one's awareness of the spirits by talking about how one has been influenced by their presence can be understood here as having 'the agentive effect of generating relations between the knower and the known' (Chua 2009: 340). The storytelling in this way becomes a performative process of positioning oneself within a field of relations which constitutes a shared sociality between humans and spirits.

In sum, encounters with animals behaving strangely can result in the actualization of the potential of animals to be persons. An important part of this actualization takes place after the actual encounter and by means of collaborating with ritual experts. The retelling of these narratives (re)confirms the actualization and is in itself part of it.

A similar argument can be made about the most common way in which human-spirit encounters take place in Ifugao, namely in sacrificial rituals. These rituals bring to life the spiritual beings, and they provide a controlled, rule-governed context for a relational engagement with them (see Bird-David 1999). They are thus the prime arena for the actualization of spirits.

Most sacrificial rituals begin late at night in the house of the person for whom the ritual is held. Two or more *mumbā'i* are called to perform, and they will sit down on the wooden floor inside the one-roomed house. A series of invocations to various kinds of spirits is performed with short breaks now and again to drink rice wine, chew betel nut and chat. First of all the *liblibāyan* spirits that protect the rice wine have to be invoked. Opening a rice wine jar without their permission can be fatal. The rice wine is also crucial for the ritual's success since the spirits are, just like humans, very fond of the sour, dark, slightly alcoholic drink and would not accept being invoked without being offered it. Next in line follows the *nun'apuh* of the family arranging the ritual, and so it continues with section after section of spirits being asked to come and attend the ritual. At one point in the proceedings, a chicken is killed and cut open so that its bile sac can be inspected. The colour and shape of the bile sac communicate the will of the spirits. An auspicious shape and colour mean that the spirits accept the ritual and that the *mumbā'i* can continue with their invocations. Continuing the ritual after an inauspicious bile sac reading could actually have the opposite of the intended effect of the ritual, and in healing rituals this would mean death. In the case of an auspicious sign, the feathers of the chicken are burned in the hearth in the corner of the room, thus producing a particular smell that the spirits are known to enjoy.

The invocations take hours, and in the early morning visitors from all over the village gather in the yard outside the house. The *mumbā'i* climb down the bamboo ladder from the house and sit down on the stone covered ground immediately beneath the house door and repeat what they did during the night inside the house. Long series of invocations are said and accompanied with more servings of rice wine and now also with gongs playing a rhythm thought to be particularly attractive to the spirits. A couple of red and dark clothes are hung up on a string next to the house as well, also these thought to contribute to the attraction of the spirits to the house. The vocal invocations, the gong playing, the colour of the clothes and the smell of the burned chicken are all conducive to attracting the spirits, leading them from their domain to the house so that they can interact and exchange with the humans.

A crucial part of the ritual is the possession of the *mumbā'i* by the spirits. The possession allows people to talk with the spirits, ask what is wrong and convince them to stop bothering them. The *mumbā'i* calling the spirits to possess them, and eventually one of them will shout out louder and louder, 'come, come, come!' while shaking his body and clinching his hands. He will start to cry and suddenly, in a striking contrast to the extrovert shouting a few seconds earlier, he will talk in a subdued whispering voice. This indicates that the spirit has now entered his body. The audience can then talk to the spirit and usually ask what is wrong and what the spirit wants. The spirit responds, tells them why contact has been made and asks for gift of various sorts. The thing the spirit asks for is put in front of the *mumbā'i*, and in exchange for these gifts the spirit is told to, and actually expected to, stop causing them problems.

With the spirits having first been called to the house, then brought down to the area beneath the house door and made available for direct interaction in the possession rite, the spirits are led further onto the sacrificial animals that are to be given them. In the yard a few meters away from the house, pigs lie on the ground with their feet bound together with a vine. The *mumbā'i* continue with their chanting and at intervals one of them stands up, puts on a feathered headdress and a ceremonial backpack, takes a spear and dances towards the pigs, thus enacting the spirit as a visible, tangible being. This happens a few times, and eventually one of the *mumbā'i* tries to get a rooster to lie still on the back on one of the pigs before dancing over it with a spear. He strikes the rooster lightly with it in order to make it leap away from the pig. The leaping away of the rooster is taken as a communication by the spirits that they accept the pigs offered to them. Then the pigs are killed, after which the carcasses are singed with burning straws and their hair scraped off. The smell that this singeing produces is also thought to be attractive to the spirits, and when the carcasses have been cut up into pieces,[9] some of them are taken up into the house by the *mumbā'i* who tell the spirits to smell the aroma of the pigs and come to eat with them. The spirits then move up again into the house, and from there they eventually depart from the scene, just like the human visitors who leave the yard after having eaten a common meal of rice and pork.

The sacrificial ritual is, I suggest, the prime arena for experiencing spirits as persons one can relate with. The participants in the ritual 'reproduce' the spirits as persons through interacting with them, by taking their needs and wants into consideration, by engaging in conversations and exchange with them. The ritual as an arena for experiencing spirits is, however, not like any other places where spirits are encountered. It is a context that reproduces certain experiences and conceptualizations of the spirits. It evokes an image of a continuous world of shared sociality, of the links existing between them, and of how these relations can be and should be managed. Hence, these human-spirit encounters take place within a context that follows a certain conventionalized performative protocol, associated with an equally codified imagery. Here then, is a source for the certain degree of consistency that the conceptualization of the spirits shows.

Hence, both the narration of human-spirit encounters in non-ritualized contexts and the actual ritual interaction with spirits take place in a wider (meta-)context that is both social and to a certain extent also conventionalized. Both of these contexts involve perception of spirits and a conceptualization of them. In the case of the narratives, there is a dynamic between perception and conceptualization resulting in a process of collaborative retrospective conceptualization, a process that feeds back into the initial perception in a constitutive manner. In the case of the ritual, its conventionality becomes a significant factor in giving shape to the conceptualizations of the spirits. Together, I argue, both narratives and rituals contribute to the development of what Carrithers calls perceptual and conceptual consensibility, i.e., the ability to perceive things in common, to agree upon and to share experiences (1992: 155–6).

From the argument above it follows that actualizations of spirits can occur in human-animal encounters, but also within conventionalized rituals. Furthermore, the actualizations are to a large extent influenced by these contexts. The sociality in the space between human and nature, as Viveiros de Castro describes it, is in Ifugao, therefore, better understood as a potential that may be actualized. In the following I will show that such actualizations have certain common characteristics. They are both risky and potentially fruitful.

Perilous Potency

As in many other parts of Southeast Asia (see other chapters in this volume), spirits are also in Ifugao powerful entities. Their powers are, as most power is, ambiguous. The spirits can be threats to life but can also make sure that life is sustained. Too much contact with the spirits puts humans in danger. So does neglecting their wishes and showing them disrespect. The spirits are, however, also sources of fertility and prosperity and are, if relations with them are good, able to secure life. These two opposing aspects – destruction and creation – characterize Ifugao spirit actualizations to the extent that most practices related to the spirits deal with the

Actualizing spirits 149

tension between them. One needs to keep them in balance.[10] This is a hazardous play with the forces of the cosmos, with outcomes that are productive and potentiating if successful and perilous if not. Let me describe these two aspects more fully.

First, the danger of spirit actualizations: The intimacy produced when spirits are actualized dissolves the disjunction between the spiritual and the human domain. As described earlier, both the *nun'apuh* and the *pinādeng* are infamous for wanting to lure away the *lennāwa* of living humans. Prolonged separation of *lennāwa* and body will result in death. Illnesses are to a large extent caused by such a separation, and situations in which the two domains are conjoined, are particularly prone to result in such separations. Hence, a conjunction of the spiritual and human domain can easily cause problems, and a prolonged continuation of such a conjunction is potentially deadly. A totalization of the shared sociality would actually mean death, so it is imperative that after a conjunction of the two domains, a division is re-established. Sacrificing animals is a way of doing this since this is thought to keep the spirits at bay, although the sacrificial ritual itself is a most tangible conjunction. After the ritual, obtaining the necessary distance to the spirits is ensured by observing taboos – particularly on odours that the spirits find attractive – that re-create the disjunction.

Although I have stated here that the conjunction of the human and the spiritual domain is a potentially perilous situation and that it can result in death, I have not yet specified how this actually operates. The clue here is the connection between death and metamorphosis. I described earlier how at death the *lennāwa* eventually turns into an ancestor, a *nun'apuh*. Death is thus a metamorphosis, a transformation of human into a *nun'apuh*. The *lennāwa* continues to live, first in an ambiguous state of half-living, lurking around the house and trying to get in contact with others, particularly the remaining spouse. Gradually the dead person is transformed into a *nun'apuh* proper and consequently takes on the perspective of the *nun'apuh*. Hence, there is a difference in perspective between humans and *nun'apuh*. Encountering *nun'apuh*, in dreams for instance, is dangerous in the sense that one then runs the risk of 'being overpowered by the non-human subjectivity' (Viveiros de Castro 2004: 468). These encounters carry with them a potential for metamorphosis which, in turn, brings about a change of perspective. If this is not countered, it might lead to this metamorphosis becoming permanent.

As much as the spirits are sources of danger, they are also able to generate and sustain life, to secure good harvest and health. At the various stages of rice cultivation, spirits are propitiated and asked for blessings. During the post-transplanting ritual, *ulpi*, chickens are sacrificed to spirits in the rice terraces, and at harvest time wooden idols of rice spirits are smeared with blood from sacrificed pigs. The rice idols are put into the attic with the newly harvested rice and are thought to protect the rice and even increase the amount of rice stored there. Life is also secured by the ability of spirits to cure people, mainly by them returning the *lennāwa* to the body of the sick person. The spirits have the power to secure people's life and to make the products of their efforts prolific. Humans can make use of this potency, however, only at the risk of exposing themselves to the perilous aspects of the spirits.

I suggest in the following that much of the activities related to the spirits are concerned with the careful balancing that the perilous potency of spirit actualizations demands. This has implications for how Ifugao animism operates in practice, since what this balancing is all about is trying to control the actualizations of the shared sociality between spirits and humans.

Proportional Sociality

The inclusion of non-humans in the sphere of trans-human sociality that Descola and Viveiros de Castro see as a defining feature of animism is, in Ifugao, a process of dynamic and contextual identification. Whether non-humans are identified as persons depends on a number of factors. Many of these factors influence the outcome after the actual encounter, as in the retrospective discussions with the *mumbā'i*. Also in those cases where one suspects an animal to be a spirit, but where nothing unusual happens thereafter, like when a bird flies across your trail twittering in a particular way, but nothing goes wrong when you continue walking, one concludes that one's suspicion was wrong and that the bird was nothing else than just a bird. In those cases where one finds out that a bird actually was a spirit, contact with it needs to be met in the appropriate way lest the conjunction of the spiritual domain and the human domain becomes permanent and total.

This means that, in Ifugao, the space between society and nature which in Viveiros de Castro's argument is social is so only as a potential that can be actualized. There is a potential for totalizing sociality, but this potential is not, and indeed should not be, actualized in full (see also Pedersen 2001). The totalization must then be kept at bay by making sure that the actualizations are met with the appropriate actions. In the case of human-spirit encounters in the forest, the encounters must be met with compliance to the intentions of the spirits – it can be to abort one's travel if a bird crosses your trail or to follow up with a sacrifice if one has experienced problems after such an encounter. This will ensure that the spirits keep their distance and leave people alone. In the case of rituals, the actualizations of spirits must follow a set of conventions that keep the contact with spirits within a controlled environment and must be followed by a series of taboos that subsequently re-establish the disjunction between the two domains.

In both cases, then, the encounter involves practices concerned with keeping the actualization of the potential for a shared sociality in the right proportions. I draw here on Corsín Jiménez's notion of proportional sociality, i.e., the portion of society that one wants to make available to others (2008: 186). Willerslev and Pedersen (2010) have applied this concept on North Asian animism to argue that the interaction with spirits among the Mongolian Darhad and the Siberian Yukaghirs is concerned with keeping the right balance of proximity and distance in the relationship between human and spirits. Joking about the spirits are for them a way of apportioning sociality to these beings in a way that 'allows for an ongoing escape from the always lurking dangers of holistic totalization' (Willerslev and Pedersen 2010: 269). The perilous potency of spirit actualizations in Ifugao leads to, I argue, exactly such practices of keeping sociality in the right proportions.

I should add, however, that this need for controlling the proportion of actualized sociality is not restricted to human/non-human sociality. Sociality is almost always proportional, also in the inter-human domain. Controlling the apportioning of sociality made available to others is after all what is at stake in most rules and regulations regarding marriage, kin relations, and verbal and behavioural restrictions. The sociality between humans and non-human is not qualitatively different from sociality among humans. Sociality in itself is, at least in Ifugao, characterized by what I have termed perilous potency, and I have pointed out here how that feature has consequences for the fluctuations of life forms of spirits in Ifugao animistic ontology.[11]

Animism as Onto-Praxis

The notion of the potential for animals to be persons is a core theme in the animism debate. Indeed, Fausto points out that the fundamental premise of most approaches to animism is that 'intentionality and reflexive consciousness are not exclusive attributes of humanity but *potentially* available to all beings of the cosmos' and that 'animals, plants, gods, and spirits are also *potentially* persons and *can* occupy a subject position in their dealings with humans' (2007: 497, my emphasis). The stress on the potentiality that I marked here is, however, often backgrounded by a focus on the condition where this potential has been actualized. Fausto, for instance, states later on that 'since most edible game *can* act as subjects, they *must* be made into food before being consumed' (2007: 503, my emphasis). I am in no position to disclaim his argument that in Amazonian cosmologies 'the unmarked value for animals is that of the subject' (Fausto 2007: 504), but I have argued for the possibility of an animistic ontology where a key to understanding the modes of relations in the human-animal-spirit field is exactly the tension between potentiality and actuality inherent in it.

I suggest that Ifugao animism operates according to an ontological dynamic where spirits fluctuate between two ontological life forms. One the one hand, they exist as spirits that are imperceptible to humans, and on the other hand, they can take on forms perceptible to humans and thus become actualized. Life is here dependent on this fluctuation, since totalization of either would impede it. People relate to these beings relative to their ontological life forms, and rituals and other kinds of spirit related activities could be understood as a form of onto-praxis, i.e., an engagement by social actors with ontological life forms and their transformation. The practices I have described here have effects in terms of the mode of being – ontological effects – and in this way they can be described as onto-praxis. Hence, spirits and animals can in Ifugao be both subjects and objects, and this indeterminacy requires work of subjectification in order for the potential for subjectivity to become actualized and objectification for them to become objects. Their mode of being emerges from relational practice. It is under negotiation and must be so for life to be sustained.

Notes

1. Fieldwork was conducted in 2003–4 and 2007–8 while I was Visiting Research Affiliate at the Institute of Philippine Culture. Many thanks to Kari Telle, Signe

Howell, Kenneth Sillander, Monica Janowski, Guido Sprenger, Kaj Århem, Christian Sørhaug and Cicilie Fagerlid.
2. This difference might be due to both changes in the way ritual knowledge is managed and views concerning generalization within anthropology.
3. A similar concept, 'cosmonomics', is found in Århem's (1996: 197) description of the protective shaman of the Makuna. The shaman there acts as a cosmic manager who controls the relationships of predation and exchange among humans and non-humans.
4. For more on these differences, see Latour (2009).
5. The ambiguity of *lennāwa* as both life force and a source of individual intentionality closely parallels similar concepts among other Philippine groups. For instance, Novellino describes the concept of *kiaruwa*' among the Batak of Palawan as 'not only the vital principle but the source of individual will and self-assertion' (2003: 177).
6. I emphasize that I mean the Batad Ifugao here since other Ifugao, for instance the Cambulo Ifugao, are much more active hunters.
7. Lambrecht (1957) too points out the close connection between birds and spirits in Ifugao religion. He describes how mythological heroes turn into birds when they descend from the Earth to the Underworld and how the star deities of *Kabunyan* fly home as birds after having visited the Earth.
8. See N. Århem (this volume) for another description of such an encounter.
9. The meat is divided into three parts. One part is boiled and served to visitors in a common meal. A second part is set off for the reciprocation of the small gifts that all visitors bring to the host family. A third part is given by the host family to their relatives. These relatives then divide their meat cuts further and distribute them to their relatives again. I have elsewhere (Remme 2006, 2012) discussed the importance of this practice as a practice of 'kinning' (Howell 2003).
10. See Janowski (this volume) for a similar discussion of the need to control spirit forces.
11. See Remme (2012) for a discussion of how the perilous potency of sociality is found in contexts like kinship, witchcraft and prestige, as well as within the particular sociality produced by the ritual practices of Ifugao Pentecostals.

References

Århem, K. (1996) 'The cosmic food web: human-nature relatedness in the Northwest Amazon', in P. Descola and G. Pálsson (eds.) *Nature and Society: Anthropological Perspectives*, London: Routledge.
Barton, R. F. (1946) 'The religion of the Ifugaos', *American Anthropologist*, 48: 1–211.
Bird-David, N. (1999) '"Animism" revisited: personhood, environment, and relational epistemology', *Current Anthropology*, 40: 67–91.
Carrithers, M. (1992) *Why Humans Have Cultures: Explaining Anthropology and Social Diversity*, Oxford: Oxford University Press.
Chua, L. (2009) 'To know or not to know? Practices of knowledge and ignorance among Bidayuhs in an 'impurely' Christian world', *Journal of the Royal Anthropological Institute*, 15: 332–48.
Corsín Jiménez, A. (2008) 'Well-being in anthropological balance: remarks on proportionality as political imagination', in A. Corsín Jiménez (ed.) *Culture and Well-Being: Anthropological Approaches to Freedom and Political Ethics*, London: Pluto Press.
Descola, P. (1996) 'Constructing natures: symbolic ecology and social practice', in P. Descola and G. Pálsson (eds.) *Nature and Society: Anthropological Perspectives*, London: Routledge.
—— (2006) 'Beyond nature and culture: Radcliffe-Brown lecture in social anthropology', *Proceedings of the British Academy*, 139: 137–55.

—— (2010) 'From wholes to collectives: steps to an ontology of social forms', in N. Bubandt and T. Otto (eds.) *Experiments in Holism: theory and practice in contemporary anthropology*, Chichester: Wiley-Blackwell.

Fausto, C. (2007) 'Feasting on people: eating animals and humans in Amazonia', *Current Anthropology*, 48: 497–530.

Gibson, T. (1986) *Sacrifice and Sharing in the Philippine Highlands: Religion and Society among the Buid of Mindoro*, London: The Athlone Press.

Howell, S. (2003) 'Kinning: the creation of life trajectories in transnational adoptive families', *Journal of the Royal Anthropological Institute*, 9: 465–84.

Ingold, T. (2000) *The Perception of the Environment: Essays on Livelihood, Dwelling and Skill*, London: Routledge.

Josephides, L. (2008) *Melanesian Odysses: Negotiating the Self, Narrative and Modernity*, New York, NY: Berghahn Books.

Lambrecht, F. (1957) 'The missionary as anthropologist: religious belief among the Ifugao', *Philippine Studies*, 5: 271–86.

Latour, B. (2009) 'Perspectivism: 'type' or 'bomb'?', *Anthropology Today*, 25: 1–2.

Novellino, D. (2003) 'Contrasting landscapes, conflicting ontologies: assessing environmental conservation on Palawan Island (The Philippines)', in D. G. Anderson and E. Berglund (eds.) *Ethnographies of Conservation: environmentalism and the distribution of privilege*, London: Berghahn Books.

Ochs, E. and Capps, L. (1996) 'Narrating the self', *Annual Review of Anthropology*, 25: 19–43.

Pedersen, M. A. (2001) 'Totemism, animism and North Asian indigenous ontologies', *The Journal of the Royal Anthropological Institute*, 7: 411–27.

Remme, J. H. Z. (2006) *Significant relations: ritual and person among the Ifugao*, unpublished thesis, University of Oslo.

—— (2012) *Manifesting potentials: animism and Pentecostalism in Ifugao, the Philippines*, unpublished thesis, University of Oslo.

Scott, M.W. (2007) *The Severed Snake: matrilineages, making place, and a Melanesian Christianity in Southeast Solomon Islands*, Durham, NC: Carolina Academic Press.

Viveiros de Castro, E. (1998) 'Cosmological deixis and amerindian perspectivism', *The Journal of the Royal Anthropological Institute*, 4: 469–88.

—— (2004) 'Exchanging perspectives: the transformation of objects into subjects in Amerindian ontologies', *Common Knowledge*, 10: 463–84.

Willerslev, R. (2007) *Soul Hunters: Hunting, Animism, and Personhood among the Siberian Yukaghirs*, Berkeley, CA: University of California Press.

Willerslev, R. and Pedersen, M.A. (2010) 'Proportional holism: joking the cosmos into the right shape in North Asia', in T. Otto and N. Bubandt (eds.) *Experiments in Holism: theory and practice in contemporary anthropology*, Chichester: Wiley-Blackwell.

Part III
Case studies – Insular Southeast Asia

8 Relatedness and alterity in Bentian human-spirit relations

Kenneth Sillander

This chapter explores human-spirit relations among the Bentian, a small group of shifting cultivators of Indonesian Borneo. I will analyze Bentian relations with spirits as expressions of a variety of Southeast Asian animism in light of the new animism literature. It may be seen that human-spirit relations are described in two different ways in this literature. These are most clearly exemplified by Nurit Bird-David and Eduardo Viveiros de Castro, respectively. The first stresses relatedness, integration and sharing between people and spirits, whereas the other emphasizes alterity, perspectivism, and predation. Beyond a shared understanding of human-spirit relations as 'an intersubjective field', wherein 'the other [is] taken as subject' (Viveiros de Castro 1998: 483), these approaches convey very different pictures of relations with non-human beings, characterized by either conjunction or disjunction. While Bird-David portray them as forming a 'network of mutualities', or a 'cosmic economy of sharing', in which otherness is subsumed to an encompassing 'we-ness' (1992: 28; 1999: 73, 78; 2004a: 336), Viveiros de Castro describes relationships of two-way predation in which the crossing of ontological boundaries through the inversion of perspectives is a 'dangerous business' and there is no 'superior metaphysical unity' encompassing difference (1998; 2001: 27; 2004: 468). These contrastive understandings of spirit relations are paralleled by how the authors characterize the social relations between people within human society, and as such notably congruent with two often opposed perspectives in a longstanding debate on Amazonian sociality which Viveiros de Castro labels the 'moral economy of intimacy' and the 'symbolic economy of alterity' (1996: 188–90).

However, rather than being incompatible, and beyond sometimes reflecting different ethnographic realities, and theoretical paradigms, both of these approaches would seem to illuminate important features of relations with spirits which are often *simultaneously* present in many animistic societies around the world, suggesting that there are commonly two sides to these relations. This, at least, holds true for many Southeast Asian societies including the Bentian, whose human-spirit relations exhibit considerable contextual variation and a fundamental ambivalence. Spirits are both alike and unlike, friends and foes, companions and adversaries. Sometimes connection and integration with the spirits is sought, sometimes separation and avoidance. In some contexts, similarity and relatedness is invoked, in others, difference and alterity. Sometimes spirits are perceived to see things as if from a human point of view; sometimes their perspective, and morality, is markedly different. Moreover, the salience of spirits varies markedly. In some contexts an animistic tendency to attribute subjectivity to, and explain events with reference to, unseen agencies in the non-human (or human) environment comes to the fore, whereas in others spirits are ignored while a rather pragmatic and naturalistic attitude to the world and events prevails. However, due to extraordinary frequent rituals, relations with spirits are remarkably salient among the Bentian, and exemplify many qualities identified as central to animism by the new animism theorists. The purpose of this chapter is to discuss these traits and make sense of the two-sidedness of Bentian spirit relations. This entails addressing the question of how animism is predicated upon similarity and difference between human and non-human beings, such as through conceptions of 'humanity as a condition' and 'humanity as a species' (Descola 2006: 141). It involves looking at how Bentian human-spirit relations articulate human society with the non-human world, and organize human experience by mediating various ontological, existential, and social dilemmas of being human and being-in-the-world.

Bentian Society and Religion

The Bentian are a small Dayak group of some 3500 people who live in a thinly populated upriver area in the province of East Kalimantan, close to the border with Central Kalimantan, in which travel until recently was mostly by foot, in a type of area which elsewhere in Borneo was typically inhabited by nomadic hunter-gatherers. Their residence and subsistence pattern promotes a close instrumental and symbolic relationship with the local natural environment, which consists of a mixture of primary rainforest and secondary rainforest in various stages of regrowth.

Most Bentians subsist on the shifting cultivation of rice and a great variety of other food crops complemented by hunting, fishing, gathering, and the rearing of domestic chickens, pigs, and water buffaloes sacrificed during rituals. Cash income is principally obtained from the sale of rattan grown in the swiddens as part of a rotational system since the beginning of the twentieth century, and, to a lesser extent, from the collection of non-timber forest products such as *gaharu* (*Aqularia* sp.) and wage labor for logging and plantation companies, the latter beginning in the 1980s, together with the gradual construction of roads in the area.

Most Bentians practice dual residence in single-family farmhouses and single- or multi-family houses located in small villages in which they begun to gradually settle in the late nineteenth century. Before that, and in some cases until recently, they did not occupy nucleated villages, but lived dispersed in the forest (*sentebar saang laang*), alternating residence between small, impermanent and frequently moved multi-family houses (*lou*) and single-family farmhouses. Residence is still quite dispersed as many people stay for much of the time on their swiddens, which are often located at a distance of several hours walk from the villages. Together with the fact that the forest, including the primary forest, is extensively utilized for hunting and extraction of natural resources, and replete with traces of past human activity, this entails a less strict distinction than in some other shifting-cultivating

Borneo societies between village and forest, and cultural and natural space. Furthermore, it augments a condition of extensive personal and family autonomy, enabled by egalitarianism and the nature of Bentian social organization.

Bentian kinship is bilateral, classificatory and inclusive, and there are no descent groups. The household is the principal economic unit. The social structure is 'open-aggregated' (Gibson and Sillander 2011), entailing flexible association and dissociation of individuals and families with loosely bounded social units, and flexible initiation and termination of interpersonal relationships within and beyond them. Kinship nevertheless provides the basic idiom in which local social relations are couched, and an ethos of solidarity pervades public discourse. In some ways Bentian communities are closely knit. There is a strong tendency for endogamy, and most people are related to most others. Individuals and families engage extensively in visiting, cooperation, and various forms of informal and formal distribution and exchange of resources and services, and families often temporarily pool resources and merge into larger social entities. Yet, social relations are marked by instability. Relatedness is flexibly invoked, and frequently forgotten. Close relations are not and cannot be maintained with all relatives or community members. There are lines of divisions even within small communities, and suspicion and reservation frequently inform attitudes to people beyond those most intimately known. Thus Bentian social life is fundamentally dialectical, marked by oscillation between autonomy and integration, and relatedness and alterity, a pattern replicated in the field of human-spirit relations.

*

Roughly half of the Bentian are Protestants whereas the others identify as Kaharingan, a designation for an indigenous religion accepted as an official religion (*agama*) affiliated with Hinduism in the province of Central Kalimantan since 1980. Kaharingan is most actively practiced in the upriver Bentian villages where I did most of my fieldwork, and it is primarily the spirit relations of Kaharingan followers in these villages that this chapter concerns. Unlike in Central Kalimantan, Kaharingan has not been subjected to rationalization in East Kalimantan, which means that it follows a traditional pattern here. It is essentially based on a tradition of shamanistic rituals (*belian*) in which negotiation with spirits occupies center stage.

According to this ritual tradition and associated beliefs for whose reproduction it is essential, a multitude of widely recognized categories and individual manifestations of unseen agencies populate the local social, natural and cosmic realms. Houses, villages, the forest, the heavens and various natural and cultural objects are perceived to be inhabited by, or associated with, spirits, while people and, to some extent, animals and plants are associated with spirit-like souls (and occasionally by extrinsic agencies in the form of invading spirits). There is thus an unseen dimension of the world in addition to an interrelated one of seen people, animals, plants, landmarks and objects, and the degree to which it is considered animated essentially corresponds to the degree to which it is perceived to be underlain with such a dimension. What this means is that spirits and souls provide the key to Bentian animism, the principle whereby the world is perceived to be alive and confronted in an intersubjective mode. Moreover, it is this unseen world of spirits which Bentian rituals are manifestly about and serve to influence, so as to thereby improve people's living conditions and well-being.

Bentian Spirit Categories

Spirits are relevant to the Bentian in many ways. Spirits, together with souls, not just explain animacy – aliveness and sentience – in the world, they are taken to explain a variety of other social, natural and cosmic conditions as well, and perceived to affect people in various, concrete ways. In Michael Lambek's words, they represent 'local takes on experience and the world', and as such play a central role in the cultural imagination of the world and its workings (1996: 238). They are sources of vitality and potency, of fortune and fate, of illness, misfortune and other adversities. They mediate people's relationships with the natural environment, with other people and peoples, as well as with themselves. Perhaps most importantly, they are a sort of consociates with whom they share their world and maintain relations on a very frequent basis through rituals – almost every week in many villages. Much of what happens, especially major events and challenging enterprises, and untoward experiences and exceptional conditions of most every sort, is interpreted with reference to the spirits and then frequently occasions rituals.

The Bentian recognize a diversity of spirits of which there is a basic and relatively widely shared knowledge which arises from the frequent rituals in which they are invoked and negotiated with. This condition is different from that prevailing in some animistic societies in which spirit knowledge is more limited and generic terms for spirits often indiscriminately applied (cf. Bird-David 2004b: 414; Willerslev 2007: 149; Remme, this volume). The Bentian have, in fact, no generic term for spirits. Spirits are either identified as belonging to one or another *category* of spirits or referred to by individual designations. Boundaries between these categories are sometimes vague, and it is not always clear to what, if any, category a spirit belongs. However, the attributes associated with them represent, to quote Rane Willerslev (2007: 157), 'prototypical notions of what spirits are like' and are as such important in guiding perceptions of them, although apparently in a more differentiated way than their Siberian Yukaghir counterparts described by him, testifying to a basic Bentian assumption that spirits, just like people, are heterogeneous, and need to be addressed in different ways.[1]

Malevolent Spirits, Spirit Helpers, Protecting and Custodian Spirits

Different categories of spirits are important to the Bentian in different, but overlapping, ways. A basic understanding of these ways is provided by a higher-level indigenous categorization which sorts spirits according to the principal roles they play in human-spirit interaction. In discourse and rituals, Bentians often refer to spirits in the capacities as 'malevolent spirits' (*blis*), 'spirit helpers' (*mulung*) 'protecting spirits' (*pengiring*), and 'custodians' (*pengitung*). The last three terms primarily connote distinct ways in which spirits are helpful to people, whereas the first connotes generally harmful behavior, and soul theft in particular. It should be stressed that these terms do not designate specific spirits or spirit categories, but rather, ways in which spirits generally may influence people. Depending on the context, representatives of different spirit categories may occupy several roles. For example, the refined *kelelungan* spirits of the dead are the ritual experts' most important *mulung*, but also important *pengiring* of communities, families and individuals, and they may turn malevolent and steal their souls or disturb them in their dreams. Virtually all spirits typically acting as protecting spirits or spirit helpers may indeed steal souls or exert other malevolent influence, while conversely most spirits commonly featuring as *blis* are occasionally employed as spirit helpers or personal protecting spirits. Although there are important relative differences regarding which spirits do what, the difference is essentially one of degree, and the boundary between good and bad spirits essentially contextual (cf. Wessing 2006).

The designation *blis* is presumably derived from the Malay (and originally Arabic) word *iblis*. There is no specific indigenous term for this generic category, although sometimes the composite term *wok bongai*, which merges the names of the two most commonly contacted spirit categories predominantly acting as *blis*, is used metonymically to denote the *blis* in general. Spirits acting as *blis* are frequently forest spirits associated with deep forest (*alas*), or primary forest groves (*simpung*), and often with special features of the natural environment (e.g., mountain tops, caves, aggregates of stones, puddles, animal wallows, waterfalls, deep pools, river confluences, large trees and trees with special features such as ironwood and strangler figs). However, some are associated with human habitations (e.g., the *wok* with graveyards, *bongai tewinan* with bathing places), and others with the sea and other downstream locations (e.g., *bongai sawa, wok tasik*). Some are also associated with other ethnic groups (e.g., the Benuaq, Pasir, and Kutai and Banjar Malays), while yet others reside in heaven (e.g., some *juata*, to which soul searches are often staged when children fall ill).

Stealing souls is as noted the principal vice of the *blis*. Soul loss makes victims ill so the *blis* are also a principal cause of illness. Besides causing illness through soul capture, the *blis* often do so directly by somehow implanting it in the body. During curing rituals, therefore, the shaman not only tries to return the patient's soul, but usually also remove the illness – commonly described as a pole or sharp object, such as a blowpipe dart of the *bongai* – such as by sucking on the patient's body, or using a shredded banana leaf whisk to extract it. The standard way in which soul loss is remedied is through travel by the shaman's soul and his spirit helpers to the spirit abodes in the invisible realm where a three-staged agenda of paying respect to the spirits (*besemah*), buying back the soul from them (*sentous*), and retrieving it (*berejuus*), is performed. The *blis* may also harm people in other ways than through illness (e.g., by causing accidents, bad luck or bad dreams), but such conditions, like illness, tend to be associated with soul loss (or soul weakness) which indeed forms the paradigmatic state and cause of Bentian ill-being.

The *mulung,* or spirit helpers, are, strictly speaking, spirits employed in rituals as assistants of the shamans (including *belian* and *warah,* life and death ritual shamans). Shamans use *mulung* for most ritual activities, and various special *mulung* are used for numerous specific purposes. The *mulung* are thus much more than spirit guides used for travel in the spirit world. In the somewhat liturgical four to eight day *buntang* family rituals, for instance, *mulung* are employed to assist in most activities, and in many of them *mulung* without importance in other ritual or extra-ritual contexts are used. In some curing rituals – most typically during divination (*preau*) – the *belian* is possessed by the *mulung* although usually the *mulung* work unnoticed with only a few symbolic expressions of their activity in the invisible realm, while the ordinarily calm and composed *belian* describes in lengthy chants the proceedings. The great majority of the *mulung* are used by all shamans although many also have special *mulung* – often foreign – shared only by some or no one else. Generally, shamans employ most available and conceivable spirit helpers rather than just a few.

Many of the *mulung* are *kelelungan* spirits of dead *belian*s and *wara*s, or mythological shamans. Kilip, 'the first and most potent *belian*', Silu, a female *belian* able to resurrect the dead, and Pantak Itak (Grandmother Pantak) are renowned representatives of the latter. Other mythological characters or early ancestors (who never were shamans) are also often employed. Prominent examples include *Luing*, the female spirit of rice who leads negotiations with spirits, Jarung, a former *manti* (leader) called down to oversee the execution of water buffalo sacrifices, and Ayus, a famous mythological trickster nicknamed *tuhan mulung*, 'the lord of the *mulung*'. Although ancestors, mythological or more recent, are the most important *mulung*, various non-ancestral spirits, in other contexts often acting as *blis* or *pengiring*, are also engaged, as are many species of animals and birds.

The word *pengiring*, or the composite term *naiyu timang,* which represents an alternative designation analogous to *wok bongai* designating *blis,* refers to several types of protecting spirits including personal protecting spirits, house and community protecting spirits, and spirit guardians of specific places in nature. Additionally it is sometimes extended to the *pengitung*, or custodian spirits, who exert similar protective influence on a more global level. Etymologically, the word derives from the verb *ngiring*, which means both to accompany and to assist (Payne 2012: 318). As the etymology suggests, the *pengiring* do not just provide protection in a strict sense, but assistance of various sorts, including the positive generation of well-being, and the regulation of social rules and taboos, in which capacity they do not primarily protect particular persons or communities (and may indeed even harm them) but rather *society* in an abstract sense.

The principal way of influencing the *pengiring* and obtaining protection or generalized well-being (symbolically described in terms of 'coolness', *rengin meroe*), is through animal sacrifice in major family and community rituals. The *pengiring* are occasionally contacted and given minor offerings outside ritual, and in minor rituals, but supplication and thanksgiving during major rituals, mediated by blood and cooked meat offerings of the sacrificial animals, provides the principal context of contact with all the *pengiring*, rather like services do for some Christians in respect to God.

The spirit categories most frequently addressed as *pengiring* are the *naiyu, timang, juata, tonoi* and *kelelungan*. Particularly salient and diverse are the *naiyu* which include countless, often zoomorphic, nature spirits; various village-dwelling representatives, often of human origin, associated with ancestral valuables anointed with blood in rituals; and a distinct subgroup of heavenly beings. Being at once major sources of potency, the most important personal and, especially, community protecting spirits, and principal guardians of morality and social rules together with the *pali* and *seniang* custodian spirits, they illustrate the variety of roles which the *pengiring* as a whole perform. The *naiyu* are excessively potent and potentially dangerous helpers, prominently characterized by their appetite for blood. Indeed, potency is so intimately associated with them that the word *naiyu* is used metaphorically to generally designate potency. Expressing this, they are associated with thunder, storms, heavy rains and floods, which are often interpreted as signs of their discontent with human behavior that violates social codes or taboos.

While the terms *pengiring, mulung* and *blis* apply to numerous spirit categories and individual spirits, *pengitung* mainly refers to the celestial and somewhat god-like *seniang* in their capacity as guardians of certain fundamental conditions in the world such as *adat* (tradition, customary law), taboos, fortune, fate, the human life-cycle, the natural cycles, the movements of the celestial bodies, and so on. This collectivity of departmental upperworld deities is normally rather distant and only contacted in major rituals which usually involve water buffalo sacrifice. Like the 'great spirit' of the Kelabit (see Janowski, this volume), they perform a sort of 'higher-level mediating relationship with the environment', although, it would seem, on an even higher level.

The *seniang* do not, unlike some *pengiring*, lend their assistance to socially disjunctive or restrictively individual ends, but act for the common best and promote collective well-being, typically on a global scale. This also goes for the *kelelungan* ancestor spirits (although they may, in response to neglect, steal relatives' souls), who, as *pengiring*, are usually addressed as an anonymous collectivity, and during larger rituals receive cooked food offerings together with the *seniang*. Relations with these agencies, in particular, but also with the protecting spirits in general, negate a common generalization of Bornean spirits as dangerous and onerous (Amster, this volume). They indicate that the spirits are not just adversaries to be kept at a distance, but positive sources of well-being, whose assistance people regularly and actively seek, especially collectively though rituals, but also through personal relationships.

An example of someone who takes obligations to spirits seriously and avidly seeks their assistance is Ma Unsir, a man in his sixties. He is not a *belian*, unlike his father and grandfather who were both known for having many spirit familiars, and as 'crazy *belian*s' (*belian kuto*), inclined to uncontrolled and ostentatious spirit possession, but like them is known for his extensive spirit connections. His son, a practicing *belian* in his late thirties, seems to be following in his footsteps. Besides frequently arranging and overseeing rituals in his capacity as aspiring leader (*manti*) for a house group centred on the multifamily house built by his father, and then inclusively appeasing the lot of the spirits as typical in such rituals, Ma Unsir also maintains personal and more continuous relationships with a number of spirits. These include *biang belau*, a zoomorphic spirit known for its malevolence and dangerousness which is represented in rituals by a wild boar-like effigy made of black areca palm fibers, and Kakah Tuha, an uncategorized human-like spirit familiar of his dead father. During larger rituals I witnessed he was often possessed by these or other spirits, running about in frenzy, eating raw blood from offering trays on display. He and his relatives would also receive advice from his spirits in dreams; Kakah Tuha, for instance, gave instructions about rituals to be held, and suggested that the village, where abnormally many deaths had occurred, should be moved since its present location was afflicted by ill-fate resulting from sorcery conducted by someone in the neighbouring village.

Not everyone maintains equally close contacts with the spirits in equally dramatic ways as Ma Unsir. More commonly, people are quiet about their spirit relations, not showing off them being regarded as the proper etiquette, expressing an idealized self-deferential mode of appropriating unseen powers. For many, the contacts are restricted to occasional dreams and, above all, the rituals, in which they are, for the most part, mediated by the shamans, except during certain collective activities such as blood lustration (*ngulas*) and the tossing of chicken feathers and pig bristles (*mesik merik*) plucked from the sacrificial animals to symbolize the dedication of the sacrifices to the *pengiring*. Most people are nonetheless said to have personal protecting spirits, and an aspiration to maintain contacts with them and other spirits in rituals is quite universally affirmed and regarded as essential for well-being.

This bears out that spirits, and especially the *pengiring* and the *pengitung*, are the principal source of generalized well-being, and as such perceived as a positive phenomenon and a resource, rather than something threatening or debilitating. Clearly, relations with spirits not predominantly regarded as malevolent are intentionally maintained, and ritual, through address of them, is experienced as holding much potential for rectifying things gone wrong, and for safe-guarding positive and safe conditions, and thus relieving people of anxiety in a way which in Borneo studies has often been attributed to Christianity in contrast to traditional religion (e.g., Chua 2011: 9–10; Amster, this volume). People do not live in constant fear of spirits, or under a crippling influence of taboos and omens. Indeed, the Bentian outlook on life, including their relationship with the unseen world, is remarkably pragmatic. While frequent and sometimes costly rituals are demanding and, to an extent, decreases resources for other purposes, and while taboos on eating certain forms of food or doing certain things at certain points of time (travelling, leaving the house, entering other people's houses, failing to share, disobeying elders, etc.) are occasionally constraining, Kaharingan Bentians do not consider religious restrictions overly restricting or appear significantly more encumbered from living ordinary lives or obtaining material welfare than Christians.

Bentian Notions of Soul and Human Spirits

The Bentian concept of soul (*juus*) resembles soul concepts in other Austronesian societies. All living beings are sometimes said to possess a soul (a single one according to most interpretations and dominant shamanistic practice), reflecting a conception of the soul as animating principle. In practice, however, mainly living people, and to some extent larger domestic animals – water buffaloes and pigs – are attributed with a soul. This reflects the fact that the soul not just signifies animation but also subjectivity, and while animals and plants are perceived to be alive (*bolum*), they are not seen, or treated, as conscious, cognizant beings to the same extent as humans. Bentian hunters, for example, maintain a rather instrumental relationship with hunted animals – objectifying them as prey – and no act of desubjectification is performed to render killed game non-human or harmless.

This usually pertains to the use of plants for food as well, although when felling large trees, a brief respectful apology may silently be expressed, which is, however, addressed to the spirit owners of the tree rather than to its soul.[2] The relationship with domestic animals, which are killed only during rituals, is slightly more complicated. They are communicated with in rituals prior to sacrifice, and small portions of rice and lighted cigarettes are then often given to them while it is pointed out that they were once humans and share a common origin. This is presented as involving obligations for them to help humans, as much as it represents an apology by the latter, and most basically serves to prevent the potentially debilitating effects of their death and ensure its intended revitalizing effects by legitimizing their sacrifice by ancestral tradition (*adat*).[3] Rice, the culturally and economically most important plant, which symbolizes humanity, also needs to be treated with special respect, and is sometimes thought to have a soul (*juus*), which may be frightened or weakened, and hardened or fixed through ritual procedures or the storing of charms and stones in granaries. To the extent it is somehow endowed with subjectivity, however, rice is perceived to be animated by the female rice spirit (*Luing*), who was once a human being who transformed into the plant upon being killed. Other cultivated plants are also sometimes said to be animated by *Luing* (e.g., in harvest ritual chants), although not by *Luing* of rice but by *Luing* of their own kind. Thus, in so far as plants, animals, and objects have agency, it generally reflects association with a spirit rather than a soul.

The human soul has the double function of being both animating principle and agency. It may become temporarily lost or weakened, resulting in illness or loss of vitality, and it may travel during sleep, or to spirit abodes during rituals, in the case of the shamans' souls. It is a life force, whose condition – strength and fixity – explains well-being, but also a person-like being, which may experience things (such as affronts, fright, or contentment). In the latter sense it is essentially spirit-like: an unseen agency endowed with consciousness – a 'communicable-with subjectivity', to borrow a term of Geoffrey Benjamin (1994: 45). As such it is perceived as an invisible counterpart of the person that it animates, although it is in rituals also represented as a small object returned to people afflicted with soul loss through an invisible hole (*kerepuru*) at the top of the head above the fontanel (but then symbolizes life force rather than subjectivity). In its aspect as life force, the soul is complemented by some other aspects or counterparts of persons, including 'breath' (*sengat*), the placenta (*juma*, its 'younger sibling'), and cultivated 'plant counterparts' (*samat*). The two latter have invisible manifestations guarded by the *seniang* in heaven (another factor making spirits crucial for human well-being), as has the soul, which has a double (also called *juus*) that resides there, together with its owner's family members' counterparts, in an invisible manifestation of the miniature 'soul house' (*blai juus*) entered by the sponsoring family at the conclusion of *buntang* rituals. Furthermore, the liver (ate) represents a seat of emotions whose condition, like the soul's, expresses emotional states.

One thing that the concept of soul does not do, however, is designate a transmissible, quasi-physical substance or power, which would explain the acquisition of potency and vitality, and their unequal distribution and circulation among beings and in the world, as the notion of 'soul stuff' (Kruyt 1906), or similar concepts like 'cosmic energy' (Anderson 1972), has often done in the regional ethnography. While such an all-pervading animating principle has been identified in many insular Southeast Asian societies – particularly in Java, peninsular Malaysia and Sulawesi, where it has often been associated with the term *semangat* or some cognate, but also among the Kelabit where it is referred to as *lalud* (see Janowski, this volume) – far from all recognize it. Its widely reported presence in Oceania and Southeast Asia was questioned by Roger Keesing (1984) and Rodney Needham (1976), who regarded it as an ethnographic invention, induced by Western folk metaphors of power, and a mechanistic scientific idiom entailing an inclination to postulate an intermediary factor between cause and effect, which Needham argued the 'symbolic thought' of native religious exegesis generally dispensed of.

According to Keesing, only some societies in Oceania had developed such a 'metaphysics of *mana*', and this reflected particular social conditions, more precisely, the emergence of political hierarchy or a class of theologians, while Needham found no evidence of such a principle explaining the acquisition of potency through headhunting in Southeast Asia in the statements of his own and his sources' informants, who instead, like the Bentian, essentially attributed it to the actions of spirits. For the Bentian, in any case, animism does not rest on such a principle, but on a thoroughly anthropomorphic metaphysics more squarely based on Descola's defining principle of the ontology: the extension of interiority to non-humans. In this perception, the distribution of animacy and potency in the world reflects differentiated spiritualization by personified spirit subjects. Discrete spirit-like souls are associated with and explain the animacy of visible life-forms, but the concept of soul, which is indissolubly associated with subjectivity, does not designate potency in the sense of an accumulable, impersonal substance or energy. Potency in the sense of health, vitality and various forms of well-being is sought in rituals, but its acquisition simply reflects, in Keesing's words, 'potentiation by spirits' (1984: 148), the essentially unknowable work of the spirits.

In Bentian conceptions, the permanent dissociation of the soul and body entails death, and the cessation of the existence of the soul as such. In its place, two different spirits of the dead, *liau* and *kelelungan*, come into being when a human being dies, each individual thus giving rise to two different spirits (animals, by contrast, do not turn into *liau* and *kelelungan* upon death). The former is described as bad or unclean (*daat*) and associated with the body, bodily desires, and the detrimental aspects of death antithetical to life, while the latter is regarded as good (*bue*) and clean (*lio*), and associated with the head and so-called higher human capacities.

During the secondary mortuary ritual, which sometimes includes exhumation, *liau* and *kelelungan* are guided to their afterworlds on nearby Mount Lumut and the village of Tenangkai in heaven, respectively. Before that, however, and commonly also after, both may linger in, or temporarily return to, the immanent world of the living. They then often appear in dreams, and in curing rituals as suspects of soul theft, and the *kelelungan* may additionally become a protecting spirit (*pengiring*) and spirit helper (*mulung*), unlike the essentially useless *liau*. This continuing importance of the spirits of the dead is simultaneously desired and undesired: welcomed in *kelelungan*'s case, and unwanted *liau*'s, the dead being subjected to both separation and integration, a condition mirroring the relations with spirits in general.

Reflecting this attitude toward the *kelelungan*, the *kelelungan* of exhumed people may also, along with these people's skulls, be brought to the house to exert a more continuous and proximate protective influence. These highly potent *kelelungan* undergo ritual transformation to become *naiyu* spirits. In the past (including postmythic times), there were also people who upon death metamorphosed into *naiyu* or other spirits directly – without undergoing ritual transformation or prior existence as *kelelungan*. Yet other people are perceived to not have died at all, but to have 'disappeared' (*jawe*), becoming part of the immortal people that continue to live on earth as *gaib* (invisibles).

Integration and Boundaries between Human and Non-Human Beings

Such transformations testify to lack of an absolute boundary between people and spirits, suggesting a condition of latent transformation or ontological permutability on at least some level of existence. Besides through permanent metamorphosis, the boundary between people and spirits can also be temporarily crossed. The shamans, and ordinary people, may be possessed by spirits, something which happens quite frequently, especially during rituals. Then, shamans' souls may also travel to the spirit world, and anybody's soul may encounter spirits in dreams. Spirits also inhabit natural phenomena and cultural objects (e.g., jars, which animals may transform into, and various other ancestral valuables such as gongs and swords) and may shift between different guises, including human (which is how they typically appear in human dreams), animal and their own distinctive spirit form. Additionally, spirits may transform into other kind of spirits (such as *kelelungan* that become *naiyu*, or old python-embodied *naiyu* that become *juata* water dragons).

Metamorphosis, or the crossing of ontological boundaries, is thus a fundamental possibility in Bentian cosmology (although more for spirits than people, and for people today mainly while asleep or after death). Another commonly identified feature of animism which Bentian beliefs about spirits and souls exemplify is perspectivism, suggesting that spirits, and to some extent animals, share with people an underlying commonality in the form of 'humanity as a condition' while appearing different to humans from their point of view, and vice versa. For example, there are notions that spirits, and sometimes animals (e.g., crocodiles), live like humans in their own realms, as demonstrated in rituals when the shaman travels there with his spirit guides. Deep in the woods, under water, and in the heavens, they have villages and houses of their own, and human cultural institutions, such as marriage, kinship, and leadership. Spirits are also talked to as if they were people, and given gifts similar to those appreciated by humans: food and equivalents of human cultural objects (e.g., miniature replicas of water buffaloes, clothes, valuables). Minimally this applies to their masters or leaders (*tuhan*), which are important ritual negotiation partners through whose mediation dealings with other members of their kind are often conducted, and to whom the latter, when unwanted, may be asked to return. Especially for animals, whose individual representatives are usually not, unlike sprits, attributed with interiority, such spirit masters play, as in other animistic societies, the role of 'creating an intersubjective field for human/non-human relations even where empirical non-human species are not spiritualized' (Viveiros de Castro 2004: 473–74).[4]

Yet, what the spirits are given is often not fully identical to what is given to people, because what – or how – they *see* is not identical to what people see. Thus, a coiled liana may represent a gong for the sprits, leaves of different plants their clothes, a species of forest fruit a spirit jungle knife, and small crabs and beetles water buffaloes and chickens. Expressing this, one reason why they steal or hurt people's souls is because of mistaking these for game animals or fish, the human soul appearing to them in distorted form. Consequently, communication with spirits often takes a certain twist. They may be talked to with strange intonation or strange pronunciation of some words, and the language of chants is archaic, replete with loan words from other languages, and special *ritual words* and expressions (*bukun belian*) without meaning in ordinary language – all conditions that sometimes are explained with reference to the spirits' otherness or strangeness. Most spirits are also associated with one or several ritually used miniature spirit houses, which manifestly are very different from human dwellings, even though spirit houses, as described in ritual chants, are basically identical to human houses.[5]

A similar perspectivism applies to the spirits of the dead. They, and especially the *liau*, the unclean body spirits of the dead, are often perceived (although this is not consistent) to see things inversely to people – night as day, left as right, small as large and so on – a faculty that is also sometimes attributed to spirits in general (this being given as the reason, for example, why they are predominantly contacted at night). The spirits of the dead also perceive graves and the bone repositories erected for them during secondary mortuary rituals as houses they inhabit in the afterworld, and water buffaloes and pigs sacrificed for them become their domestic animals there. As this indicates, their 'life' in their world basically differs little from life in this world, yet crossing the boundary between life and death involves a change of perspective, which may momentarily be adopted by the living in dreams about the dead, although this is dangerous, indicating impending transformation of the living, who should not maintain this perspective, or intimate connection with the dead, too long.

Invisibility and Originary Transparency

As in Amazonia, then, there is between humans and spirits both a 'subjective and social continuity', based on shared interiority or 'humanity as a condition' and a fundamental 'discontinuity', expressed, for example, through perspectivism (Descola 2006: 141; Viveiros de Castro 1998: 482). Although it is not stated or clear that it is, as Descola and Viveiros de Castro argue, primarily *because* of their different bodies – their 'bodily dispositions' or 'physicality' – that spirits are different, their difference is often prominently expressed by special physical characteristics. Some are monstrous and excessively hairy or corpse-like (*wok*), others extraordinarily beautiful with long fingernails (*bansi*), some huge (*kerataan, buta*) or tall as trees (*tontin*), others very small and child-like (*punyut*, some manifestations of *tontin*). Although the spirits are mostly anthropomorphic (but also sometimes zoomorphic, like *juata*, the water-dragon spirit, or *biang belau*, Ma Unsir's mammal-like protecting spirit), there is usually some distinguishing bodily attribute setting them apart from humans, as with *bongai*, one of the most important 'malevolent spirits' (*blis*) that has red skin and large canine teeth. Often, the spirits are in some ways deformed or incomplete, like *tentuwaja*, with pointed head, bent jaw, or several of the celestial *seniang* spirits acting as the custodians of the cosmic or social order, which lack one or several limbs (deformities reflecting their origins from the incestuous union of the first man and his daughter). The *liau*, even though not understood as different in appearance from the living, is also similarly incapacitated, lacking the capacity to speak, and to be seen clearly or otherwise than from the side or behind (when appearing in dreams). These deficiencies and aberrations suggest that spirits, at least generally, are not quite human, that a basic sense of alterity remains despite extension of human attributes and sociality to them.

Beyond these distinctive bodily characteristics and perceptual faculties, the difference between spirits and humans has an important general and bodily basis in the spirits' invisibility. Invisibility is often proposed as the principal characteristic of the spirits, as what distinguishes them from living people, and is shared by all of them, including the spirits of dead humans – of whom it cannot really be said, however, despite their 'disjunction from a [visible] human body', that they 'are not human' (Viveiros de Castro 1998: 482).[6] The spirits' invisibility has important consequences for human-spirit relations. It entails not only that they cannot be seen – which is important since it can never be known for sure where they are, or what they are up to, meaning that they should be treated a little as if continually present, with care taken so that they receive respect and are not offended by human behavior – but also that they cannot really be known, which is something Bentians often observe in response to questions about them. But it is also as if the condition of invisibility, of inhabiting or temporarily crossing over to the 'invisible realm' (*alam gaib*), by itself entailed an important ontological difference. First, invisible beings are attributed greater powers – superhuman abilities – than visible beings. The word *gaib* designates not only invisibility but also mystical, unexplainable phenomena. Second, the invisibles, although coeval, live somewhat as if in another dimension – or in Janowski's terms (this volume) a 'parallel world' – with which communication is not straightforward, although it once was, in mythical times, when different beings could still 'see each other' (*beketineng*), and readily shift form (*bebalik*), before visible living beings, which were then infinitely more powerful than now, became in a fundamental sense differentiated from spirits, which unlike humans have retained much of their primordial powers. As in Amazonia, myth describes the bifurcation of an 'originary transparency' – 'a 'chaosmos' where the bodily and spiritual dimensions of beings did not as yet reciprocally eclipse each other' – into a domain of 'relative invisibility' of spirits (and souls) and one of 'relative opacity' of visible living beings, which are under ordinary circumstances separated from each other (Viveiros de Castro 2007: 157–58).

More than a primordial, bygone state, however, this conception of originary transparency provides the ground for a shared underlying 'pre-cosmological virtuality [which] is indestructible and inexhaustible', which still enables – 'below the surface discontinuities separating the types and species' – occasional reversal, for shamans, souls, and spirits, of this *relative* invisibility and opacity (2007: 158–59).[7] Thus myth, as in Amazonia (but unlike many animistic societies), is central in reproducing a foundation for an animistic ontology, something which it is well-equipped to do since there is a large corpus of Bentian origin myths (*tempuun*) regularly recounted during larger rituals, and additionally sometimes told for entertainment, and invoked or quoted in discourse.

Shared Origins and Human-Spirit Integration

Another way in which Bentian myth sustains an animistic ontology is by postulating a near-universal human origin for non-human beings (and most everything else important to Man in the world), a condition often invoked in communication with these beings, and between humans, to stress mutual obligations and the kind of respect characterizing proper human sociality in interaction with them. According to the myth of origin of mankind, spirits are paradigmatically seen as the siblings of humans, originating from the incestuous union of the first man and his daughter as deformed, poisoned, or misbehaving children who were sent off or ran away (Herrmans 2011: 197–98).[8] Although this origination of spirits resulted in their departure from human society, and, especially for some of them, their estrangement from human ways and sociality, which motivates separation from them in some circumstances, and suggests that they are in a sense inferior to humans – incomplete quasi-humans – even while superior – supernatural superhumans – in another, their origin is most fundamentally taken to express the kinship bond which unites them with humans, and associated with a pledge for reciprocal assistance made upon their departure, involving regular presentation of offerings to them and calls for their assistance when needed.

Despite their separation, and the bifurcation of the world into a visible and invisible realm, there is a strong sense of continuous interconnection with the spirits, evident not only in the possibility of temporary or permanent metamorphosis, but also, and more continually significant, through influential notions that actions and events in the one realm affects conditions in the other. Here, as elsewhere, animism not only involves attributing interiority and human dispositions to other-than-human beings, but also, understanding conditions and events in the world with reference to the spirits' actions and relations with human beings – and how these are affected by human action.

As in Inner Asia (Pedersen et al. 2007: 145), this expresses a view that 'the not-directly detectable causes [to events in the world] tend to be "enpeopled"'; that is, seen to reflect spirit action and, typically, human action indirectly. This view spawns integration with the spirit world and the natural environment of which Bentian spirits, like the *devaru* of the Nayaka, are a 'constitutive part' (Bird-David 1999: 68), amounting to a socio-cosmic symbiosis in which more or less everything is connected, especially as influence between the human and spirit realms not only reflects action directly affecting human-spirit relations – such as spirit neglect or disrespect – but also social relations *between* humans, which spirits as elsewhere oversee and frequently sanction, such as through soul theft upon the breach of taboos. With Bird-David (2004a: 336), we may speak of 'a sophisticated sense of the world as expanding waves of social relatedness, a network of mutualities, where disturbance at one end reaches and affects the other'. Significantly, as with the Nayaka, the remedy prescribed for such disturbances, rather than identifying causes or culprits, most fundamentally consists of mending the spirit relations by doing the best to maintain and improve them – which above all means arranging rituals, inviting and presenting offerings to the spirits, and in the process calling on their superhuman resources.

This testifies to the relevance for the Bentian of Bird-David's understanding of animism as 'relatedness' – although here expressed in an idiom of siblingship, the paradigmatic idiom of Bentian relatedness, rather than parent-child relations – according to which it is based on the extension of kinship and sharing, particularly during ritual, to non-human beings, and it 'grows from and *is* maintaining relatedness with neighbouring others' (1999: 78, original italics). Ritual operates to construe an 'irreducible plurality constructed as "relatives" that transcends classes and boundaries, both human and non-human' (2004a: 337). Even though the Bentian are shifting cultivators, and highly ritualistic, much of what Bird-David has to say about the Nayaka hunter-gatherers of south India and their relations with spirits makes good sense for the Bentian. Like the Nayaka's yearly trance gatherings, and intermittent, small-scale healing procedures based on trance and divination, Bentian rituals essentially frame illness and misfortune 'relationally' in terms of ruptured relations with spirits or between people, and seek to alleviate such unfavourable conditions, and promote well-being, by 'engaging relationally' with the spirits.

Thus it is imperative for the Bentian, as for the Katu (see Århem, this volume), to maintain good relations with spirits, this being a goal of the rituals in its own right whatever more particular purposes they may have, as evidenced by the fact that they typically engage a multitude of spirits, rather than single out a few particularly relevant agencies. Even soul retrieval is usually extended to a variety of spirits, retrieving the soul from many 'suspects' (*tuduh*) being important, a *belian* told me, even though one would 'know' who has taken it, since such action is intrinsically beneficial by working to maintain good relations with the spirits. For the same reason, soul retrieval is usually not restricted to the particular patient(s) (*dongo*) for which the rituals may have been primarily initiated, but extended to the souls of family members and other present participants.

This is not to say, however, that a perfect union of unreserved closeness or unproblematic harmony with the spirits ever materializes, or that this is always desired. In the first place, there is an aspiration that the spirits, especially those predominantly acting as 'malevolent spirits' (*blis*), stay apart from people, at least between rituals. These spirits, in particular, are likely to steal people's souls or cause illness, accidents and misfortune, and their alterity and predatory nature is often stressed. The endeavour of relating to spirits, of course, plays out rather differently with different spirits and in different contexts, a fact which cannot be ignored when characterizing human-spirit relations. In the second place, there is a sense that the spirits in general are unpredictable and unreliable, reflecting a recognition that they, despite their common origin with Man, are very different in some ways, including invisible, and as such ultimately unknowable. As this indicates, there is indeed a sort of parallel or counter perspective on spirits to the one described by Bird-David (cf. Willerslev 2007: 46). Moreover, there is, as Bird-David acknowledges, an understanding that 'relatedness with the ... [spirits] is not a given, but has to be cultivated' (2004a: 336), that common origin, just as with people, amounts to little without fulfilment of the obligations that go with it, and that, notwithstanding the best of attempts to secure good relations with spirits, their satisfaction and goodwill cannot be guaranteed, as shown all too often by the outcomes of the rituals by which this may ultimately only be judged. Influencing the spirits is thus an essentially unpredictable endeavour, made not less uncertain by especially pertaining to conditions and processes which by their very nature are unpredictable or beyond the control of humans.

However, for the duration of the rituals, especially the larger ones to which a large, essentially open-ended collectivity of spirits are invited to partake of a rich variety of offerings, something approximating a harmonious union with the spirits – in which their relatedness and basic equivalence with Man is stressed – is at least ostensively realized, and there is an often-stated ideological aspiration to achieve this. This mode of relating to the spirits is congruent with a general social ideology of interpersonal solidarity and respect which holds a hegemonic position in public discourse, suggesting a homology between social life and human-spirit relations. Sharing and maintaining respectful relations indeed in both spheres express such an ethos, and is promoted by a number of elementary spirit-sanctioned categories of taboos (*tapen, pali, bunsung* and *sumbang*) – remarkably similar to the 'cosmo-rules' of the Chewong (see Howell, this volume) – which are central to local explanations of illness and misfortune. However, as among the Chewong, this ethos does not adduce to full equivalence and limitless integration – fusion – between different beings, anymore than between people. Interpersonal respect involves respect for the autonomy, different dispositions, and, to some extent, different statuses, of different beings and individuals, and thus implies recognition of a certain distance and separation. Also, as Howell observes for the Chewong, different beings in the world inhabit different domains and all have their own peculiar characteristics, and the general mixing of conceptual or social categories, which like failure to share or affirm relations is proscribed by the taboos, brings about cosmic upheaval and spiritual vulnerability.

Moreover, the taboos are not always relevant or invoked, and the spirits not always invoked. This draws attention to the fact that the Bentian, like other animists, often relate to the world and carry on with life without mediation of spirits, and that non-human beings are not continually subjectified, or fully integrated into the human order. Indeed, like the Batek of peninsular Malaysia, they would vacillate – often somewhat abruptly, it seemed to me – between two distinct modes of explaining and acting upon events and phenomena: a 'natural', or secular, and an 'anthropomorphic', or animistic, the latter essentially associated with the invocation of the spirits and 'brought in to help explain deviations from what is assumed to be the normal run of events' (Endicott 1979: 217–18). Rather, then, than something consistently animated or subjectified, the world in Bentian understandings calls to mind Morten Pedersen's (2001: 415) characterization of North Asian animist cosmologies as 'strangely reminiscent of a Swiss cheese', in which the holes, which make up much of nature, represent inanimate or at least asocial entities, devoid of interiority, or whose potential interiority is at least ignored in practice.

Oscillation between Subjectification and Objectfication

The variable nature of relating to spirits, and the oscillation between sometimes intensely relating to them and at times ignoring them and the sentience of non-human beings, suggests the relevance of Wazir-Jahan Karim's (1981) insightful study of a similar doubleness among the Ma' Betisék. She describes how relations with spirits, animals and plants express two distinct views, and two opposed but complementary sets of principles, labelled *kemali* and *tulah,* exemplified by certain taboos and cultural rules (*adat*), which explain a pendular movement between a subjectifying and objectifying stance to non-human beings, entailing, respectively, continuity and discontinuity with them. This scheme explains how the scope of the human order varies contextually, so that it is sometimes extended to plants, animals, and spirits, whereas at other times these are excluded from it. When procuring food (or other resources) from the environment through cultivation, gathering, hunting and fishing, the human-like qualities of non-human beings are ignored, or the latter are othered and subordinated to humans in hierarchic relationship based on a curse by the human ancestors on the non-human beings due to their supposed destructive qualities, and the acquisition of culture by the former which dissociated them from the latter. Conversely, when humans are affected by illness, misfortune or resource depletion, the anthropomorphic origins and subjectivity of non-human beings, and their greater mystical powers, are invoked. Thus, when humans exploit or stand in a position as predators to non-human beings or the non-human environment, the distinction between the human and non-human domain and the cultural superiority of humans is stressed, but when they occupy the position as prey or disempowered victims, the continuum between the domains, and the superior superhuman powers of non-human beings, are emphasized.

Even though the Bentian do not go to equally great pains to legitimize exploitation of the environment as the Ma' Betisék – the 'animistic dilemma' (see Århem, this volume) for some reason not requiring equal cultural elaboration – Karim's scheme is valid for them. In particular, it helps explain why and when spirits are invoked, and what role the incorporation of non-human beings in the human order plays. Like the Ma' Betisék, the Bentian sometimes hold a view of human cultural superiority over spirits and animals based on *adat* and maintain an instrumental, objectifying relationship to the non-human environment and then, and often in human social interaction, ignore the existence of spirits, while at other times a notion of human incompleteness and dependence on non-human beings takes precedence and they engage with spirits, and sometimes other non-human beings, according to what Bird-David (1999) calls 'responsive relatedness'. This occurs, as among the Yukaghirs, especially in situations 'when things go wrong' (Willerslev 2007: 153–54), such as when misfortune strikes or the moral order is violated, or as with the Batek, in 'attempts to manipulate their environment [or human conditions], beyond what they can do by direct physical means' (Endicott 1979: 219). This suggests that the spirits essentially represent what could be called the domain beyond human control – of natural forces, and of existential and political unpredictability associated with the human predicament. The animistic idiom thus essentially complements a secular and objectifying relationship, which the Bentian for much of the time maintain with the world, and does not represent an all-embracing paradigm continually influencing their worldview.

Multiple Modes of Relating to Spirits and People

It may be noted that the form of inclusive sharing taking place in major rituals when the spirits, along with human relatives and neighbours, are invited *en masse* to the organizing house or village, is only one of several modes of relating to the spirits, just as it is in relations between humans. Sometimes bartering and cajoling, often associated with threats and deceit, take prominence. During *sentous*, when buying back the soul in curing rituals, human-spirit interaction typically takes the form of relatively strictly balanced exchange rather than sharing, which is also true for the practice of making and fulfilling vows (*niat*) to spirits. Another basic activity in rituals serving to influence spirits, *besemah*, the presentation of offerings and respect, in turn exemplifies a pattern of submissive, devotional gift-giving to someone of higher status. In yet other contexts, spirits are likened to aggressive predators which the shamans' spirit helpers fight and try to drive away.

Although not all these different modes of relating to spirits conform to social relations in their most typical form in everyday life in Bentian communities, each resembles one or another form of interaction that either has been historically prominent or occurs in some present-day context. *Sentous* and *besemah* basically correspond to the two principal forms of interaction – trade and tribute – that the

Bentian historically had with Malay traders and sultanates, while the less decorous mode of approaching spirits through more straightforward requests, and stratagems such as trickery and wit, resemble the important practice of demand sharing and other informal ways of appealing for relatives' resources or services, and the efforts to fight and drive away dangerous spirits, in turn, calls to mind antagonistic relations with stratified, predatory upriver societies in the nineteenth century.

Relations with spirits and the non-human environment are obviously not uniform in animistic societies. From South America there are examples of animistic societies maintaining exchange relations with spirits in a range of different modes of 'reciprocity' and 'predation' (Descola 1992: 115–121). Bird-David (1990) describes for Nayaka (and Batek and Mbuti) foragers a system of mutual, compassionate and near-unconditional sharing with spirits likened to parents personifying a 'giving environment', which she distinguishes from the reciprocal exchange relations of neighbouring agriculturalists with spirits likened to ancestors. Willerslev (2007: 42–9), by contrast, describes how Yukaghir spirit and human social relations are organized by the principle of demand sharing, and characterized by manipulation and deceit.

Usually there is a strong correlation between human social relations and spirit relations, and animism has most typically been identified with hunter-gatherer or other egalitarian societies (but see Gardner 1991 on the Paliyan of south India where the former relations are egalitarian and the latter hierarchic, and Rousseau 1998 for the Kayan of central Borneo who describe animistic human-spirit relations as paralleling relations between commoners and aristocrats). Pedersen (2001: 416) suggests that the continuity between humans and non-humans constitutive of animism according to Descola 'seems to both imply and be implied by wider societal relations of a horizontal character' and that 'animism can only really flourish' in such contexts. Since animism in his view is based on the principle of 'analogous identification', involving 'the ability to imagine oneself in someone else's position, and the ability to imagine someone else in one's own position', he assumes it presupposes a relatively egalitarian social system, or at least a notion of basic ontological equivalence between all beings, allowing for their integration and immanent transformation within one regime of being (as opposed to totemism which presupposes a segmentary order of discrete ontological domains).

There is clearly a similarity between Bentian social life and spirit relations, corroborating Descola's (1996: 86) presumption that, 'whether it operates by inclusion or exclusion, the social objectivation of non-humans ... cannot be disjoined from the objectivation of humans; both processes are informed by the configuration of ideas and practice from which every society draws its concepts of self and otherness'. However, in this case relations in both spheres are multifaceted, and the spirit relations exhibit the same broad range of variation as the social relations, which encompass various sorts of relations with relatives and 'others' within and beyond local communities. Thus a wide variety of idioms and modes of interaction characterize human-spirit relations, including predation, exchange, tribute, demand sharing, and voluntary sharing, and in these similarity and difference, and relatedness and alterity, are variously stressed, just as in social interaction between humans.

A similar condition seems to characterize human-spirit relations also in other Southeast Asian societies (e.g., Rousseau 1998; Wessing 2006). It is particularly evident in Thomas Gibson's analysis of the Buid of the Philippines according to which: 'there is a sort of continuum in Buid rituals ranging from relations of extreme hostility and separation from certain spirit types at one pole to relations of absolute alliance and virtual fusion on the other' (1986: 180). Thus, rather than one relational mode exhibiting clear dominance in any particular society – or one at least ultimately 'encompassing' the others, as Descola would seem to imply (1996: 89–91) – the coexistence of multiple relational modes among which none is clearly dominant appears to be common in the region, suggesting the simultaneous importance in native spirit and human relations of both the 'relatedness' and 'alterity' idioms, and the simultaneous relevance of the corresponding theoretical perspectives for understanding them.

Conclusion

In Bentian animistic ontology, spirits articulate human society with the non-human world and are essential for the conceptualization and negotiation of various ontological, existential, and socio-moral dilemmas of being human and being-in-the-world. This ontology prevails in certain conditions, complementing a secular and objectifying relationship with the world which is maintained at other times. It is based on the attribution of human-like dispositions to unseen non-human agencies and the identification of such agencies as causes of conditions and events in the world. Consistent with Descola's understanding of animism as based on the extension of interiority to non-humans, but in contrast to a dominant understanding in the Southeast Asian ethnography, animation and potentiation by spirits, rather than the workings of an impersonal, all-pervading life force, represents the principle which explains the distribution and acquisition of life and power in the world.

Bentian human-spirit relations are regulated by two opposed but complementary sets of principles, sanctioned by taboos and precepts of *adat*, which explain oscillation between a mode of relation based on integration and similarity, and another based on separation and alterity. They demonstrate the simultaneous relevance of Bird-David's and Viveiros de Castro's perspectives on relations with spirits which respectively emphasize conjunction and disjunction. People are connected to spirits and through them to the natural environment and each other in a socio-cosmic web of relatedness in which actions and events have a distinctly moral quality and their influence transcends ontological boundaries. In accordance with Bird-David's understanding they actively seek integration within this web by affirming human-spirit relations through rituals, because they regard it as essential to human well-being, demonstrating the inadequacy of a tendency in Borneo studies to primarily characterize human-spirit relations by separation. Expressing this orientation, they postulate shared origins with spirits. Besides conjuring mutual obligations, these myth-reproduced origins invoke what Viveiros de Castro's calls an 'originary transparency' that persists in the invisible realm of spirits and souls as an underlying potentiality of metamorphosis and temporary transition across ontological boundaries. Yet spirits are separated from people by their invisibility and different corporal and affective constitution, inescapably entailing different points of view and an ultimately irreconcilable alterity. Despite extension of subjectivity and shared origins to the spirits, they remain unknowable, unpredictable, and intractable forces, which are invoked to explain loss of human well-being and events beyond human control, as often as to remedy or influence such occurrences.

Notes

1. By participating in rituals, virtually everyone in Kaharingan communities has acquired basic knowledge of a fairly large number of spirit categories, and everyone perceives that the spirit world is diverse and requires a differentiated approach. Thus it cannot be said, as Willerslev states for the Yukaghirs, that 'in most cases, they simply do not know the spirits well enough to say anything specific about them' (2007: 155). However, the gist of his findings on Yukaghir spirit knowledge is still valid for the Bentian since it is primarily in and from concrete encounters with spirits – and most importantly rituals for the Bentian – that spirit knowledge matters and derives. Spirit knowledge is thus acquired through practice as opposed to theory, from what Ingold, drawing on Heidegger, calls a 'dwelling' as opposed to 'building' perspective (2000: 172–89), or according to the principles of what Bird-David (1999) calls 'relational epistemology'. Like the Nayaka, the Bentian learn about spirits not so much by 'hearing about' them as by 'relating to' them in rituals – and what they above all learn from these encounters is 'how to engage' with them (Bird-David 2004: 415).
2. Although all living organisms are sometimes said to have *juus*, trees would not in practice be associated with one. However, large individual trees and particular forest groves are occasionally associated with *ruo* – a synonym for *juus* – or a particular spirit owner. This expresses a tendency, reported for the Malays by Kirk Endicott (1970: 49–50), to regard less salient and non-individualized life forms as collectively sharing a soul or, as more commonly with the Bentian, a spirit, and conversely, to attribute individual souls or spirits only to such life-forms that have distinct bodily boundaries, special salience, or practical importance to people as individual entities. An example of this, among both Malays and Bentians, is rice: the plants of a rice field are not each being associated with an individual soul or spirit but have one in common.
3. This may be seen to entail the 'hierarchical inclusion' of domestic animals in a 'mode of relation' with non-human beings which Descola terms 'protection', which he distinguishes from two other such modes of relation characteristic of animism, 'reciprocity' and 'predation', but with which he observes it may be articulated (1996: 89–91). Such a mode may indeed characterize Bentian relations with non-human beings in this particular context, at the same time as 'reciprocity' (or sharing) and 'predation' form dominant modes in others. In addition, this inclusion, albeit hierarchical, suggests a greater tendency to include domestic as opposed to wild animals within the human order. This sets the Bentian apart from hunter-gatherers, and it could be asked if this mode of relation has something to do with their tendency to attribute relatively little subjectivity to wild animals and wild-growing plants. Consistent with Descola's thinking in which relational modes serve as generalized models which imprint a particular ethos upon a society, 'protection' could be imagined to have spurred 'a reduplication of asymmetric relations' across different domains of relations with non-humans (1996: 91). It might also be hypothesized that the practices of shifting cultivation and animal husbandry, with which this mode of relation is associated, could somehow explain this tendency. However, Bornean hunter-gatherers share this tendency more than hunter-gatherers in general, while South American shifting cultivators generally

do not, cautioning against derivation of patterns of thinking from modes of subsistence. Another factor that may have contributed to this tendency is the development of an objectified tradition of *adat* legitimizing both the hierarchical inclusion of domesticated animals and plants, and the 'hierarchical exclusion' of wild counterparts, as aspects of a contextually recognized human superiority (cf. Karim 1981).
4. Spirit association subjectifies animals in many ways, association with master spirits being just one. The myth of origin of mankind describes the origination of various spirits and animals from the children of the incestuous union of the first man and his daughter who became their original ancestors. Other spirits are masters of several animal species, such as *juwata*, regarded as the master of crocodiles, monitor lizards, fish, frogs, water and land leeches, turtles and tortoises, scorpions, millipedes, and so on, and the *naiyu*, who has a similar relationship with pythons, pangolins, and certain house lizards. Animals also act on behalf of the spirit guardians or other spirits of particular localities, such as those of spirit-rich 'primary forest groves' (*simpung*) near villages, by which they may be tricked into hurting people. Malevolent spirits are often identified through divination (*perau*) to have possessed domestic animals and inflicted illness through them. Many birds and some mammals act as omens (*baya*), and are then seen as intermediaries of the *nyahu* omen spirits, while killed animals that transmit illnesses involving convulsions resulting from inadvertent imitation of their death throes act as intermediaries of the *abei* spirits. A bird with a master of its own is the Bentian bird from which the people take their name (*Erythura Prasina*, the Long-tailed Munia), a small bird – whose master is said to be large as a chicken – which supposedly inhabits crevices of mountains in their area, and sometimes attacks ripening rice fields in large swarms, whose flight is imitated in the practice of collectively planting rice (*mementian*).
5. These spirit houses are essential for the reproduction of Bentian spirit knowledge. There is an amazing variety of spirit-specific miniature houses and various other worship structures, such as suspended trays, upright altarlike constructions and different indoor and outdoor shrines, all made of specific plants or trees, which have to be procured from the forest or domesticised environment by special ritual assistants (*pengeruye*), and are often metonymic of the habitats of the particular spirits or spirit groups which receive ritual offerings in these houses.
6. Corroborating this, the spirits of dead humans, unlike other spirits, are consistently identified as humans (*senaring*). Unlike most spirits, they are never given offerings of blood and raw food, but only cooked food, and seen to continue living in the afterworld like humans by a specifically human *adat*. This indicates a stronger sociological continuity between living and dead people in Southeast Asia than South America, a condition giving a particular slant to Southeast Asian animism. Despite lacking association with a visible physical body, the dead are notably also, as in Amazonia, conceived of in bodily form – they 'are not immaterial entities [spirits in the sense of ethereal beings as in the common Western understanding], but equally types of bodies' (Viveiros de Castro 1998: 481). In Viveiros de Castro view, spirits, in general, are defined by an excess rather than lack of body, by a 'constitutive transcorporality, rather than by a negation of corporality' (2007: 161). However, unlike in Amazonia, Bentian spirits of the dead are quite consistently conceived of in *human* bodily form – they are not 'defined by their disjunction from a *human* body ... [hence] logically attracted to the bodies of animals' (1999: 482, italics added). This is consistent with a tendency for spirits, anthropomorphic in particular, to figure more prominently than animals in Southeast Asian cosmologies compared to other 'animistic regions' like Amazonia, North America, and Inner Asia. In Southeast Asia, it is not to the same extent true that 'the 'animic mode' is characteristic of societies in which animals are the 'strategic focus' of the objectivation of nature and of its socialization' (Viveiros de Castro 1998: 473, quoting Descola). Instead it is spirits which most centrally occupy this role, and they are moreover complemented in this by plants as often as animals (e.g., Karim 1981, cf. Descola 1992: 115).

7. This indestructibility of the connection between the visible and invisible world is symbolized by the 'iron pillar of the sky' (*orin besi langit*) which is located on top of Purei mountain, and which, although now invisible, still supports the sky and 'will not rust, will not topple' (*beau daki, beau tempong*). It represents a vestige both of the time when heaven and earth, and people and spirits, were not yet separated, and a symbol of the continuing connection, invoked in ritual, of people on earth with the spirits of the upperworld, and the superior powers of the primordial era of original creation, when 'what was uttered could become real' (*ye dulek tau jadi*), from which much of the magical power accessible today ultimately derives.
8. Different versions of the origin myth of mankind, and other myths, explain this separation differently. In one version, spirits originated already prior to this event, when several improper attempts to make the first man out of an anthropomorphic clay figure failed, and gave rise to spirits instead (this only succeeded after a *belian* ritual was held) (cf. Endicott 1970: 55) for similar origins of Malay spirits). According to other myths, many spirits, animals and plants came into being much later, typically arising from particular dying humans. There is evident in these myths an ongoingness or immanence of creation, things and beings (including humans) not originating all at once but repeatedly arising – often in multiple manifestations – and frequently transforming, in a process of continuous creation which Ingold describes in terms of 'incipience' and 'continuous birth' (2000). As typical in Austronesian mythologies (Fox 1987: 524), nothing is created *ex nihilo*: there were already some beings around before the first human beings, and even heaven and earth, whose origins are told in the 'oldest' (chronologically first) origin myth, were preceded by different sorts of small pieces of earth out of which they were made by becoming flattened into their current proportions by ontologically ambiguous human-animal-spirit beings pre-existing later orders of beings.

References

Anderson, B. (1972) 'The Idea of Power in Javanese Culture', in C. Holt (ed.) *Culture and Politics in Indonesia*, Ithaca, NY: Cornell University Press, 1–69.

Benjamin, G. (1994) 'Danger and Dialectic in Temiar Childhood', in J. Koubi and J. Massard-Vincent (eds.) *Enfants et Sociétés d'Asie du Sud-Est*, Paris: L'Harmattan, 37–62.

Bird-David, N. (1990) 'The Giving Environment: Another Perspective on the Economic System of Gatherer-Hunters', *Current Anthropology*, 31(2): 189–96.

—— (1992) 'Beyond "The Original Affluent Society": A Culturalist Reformulation', *Current Anthropology*, 33(1): 25–47.

—— (1999) '"Animism" Revisited. Personhood, Environment, and Relational Epistemology', *Current Anthropology*, 40 (supplement): 67–91.

—— (2004a) 'Illness-Images and Joined Beings: A Critical-Nayaka Perspective on Intercorporeality', *Social Anthropology*, 12(3): 325–39.

—— (2004b) 'No Past, No Present: A Critical-Nayaka Perspective on Cultural Remembering', *American Ethnologist*, 31(3): 406–21.

Chua, L. (2011) 'Soul Encounters: Emotions, Corporeality, and the Matter of Belief in a Bornean Village', *Social Analysis*, 55(3): 1–17.

Descola, P. (1992) 'Societies of Nature and the Nature of Society', in A. Kuper (ed.) *Conceptualizing Society*, London: Routledge, 107–26.

—— (1996) 'Constructing Natures: Symbolic Ecology and Social Practice', in P. Descola and G. Pálsson (eds.) *Nature and Society: Anthropological Perspectives*, London: Routledge, 82–102.

—— (2006) 'Beyond Nature and Culture: Radcliffe-Brown Lecture in Social Anthropology', *Proceedings of the British Academy*, 139: 137–55.

Endicott, K. (1970) *An Analysis of Malay Magic*, Singapore: Oxford University Press.

―――― (1979) *Batek Negrito Religion: The World-View and Rituals of a Hunting and Gathering People of Peninsular Malaysia*, Oxford: Clarendon Press.

Fox, J. (1987) 'Southeast Asian Religions: Insular Cultures', in M. Eliade (ed.) *The Encyclopedia of Religion, Vol. 13*, New York, NY: Macmillan Publishing Company, 520–30.

Gardner, P. (1991) 'Pragmatic Meanings of Possession in Paliyan Shamanism', *Anthropos*, 86: 367–84.

Gibson, T. (1986) *Sacrifice and Sharing in the Philippine Highlands: Religion and Society among the Buid of Mindoro*, London: The Athlone Press.

Gibson, T. and Sillander, K. (eds.) (2011) *Anarchic Solidarity: Autonomy, Egalitarianism and Fellowship in Southeast Asia*, New Haven, CT: Yale University Southeast Asia Studies.

Herrmans, I. (2011) *Towards the Breaking Day: An Ethnography of Belian Curing Rituals among the Luangans of Indonesian Borneo*, Research Series in Anthropology no. 19. Helsinki: University of Helsinki Press.

Ingold, T. (2000) *The Perception of the Environment: Essays on Livelihood, Dwelling and Skill*, London: Routledge.

Karim, W.J. (1981) *Ma' Betisék Concepts of Living Things*, London: Athlone Press.

Keesing, R. (1984) 'Rethinking Mana', *Journal of Anthropological Research*, 40(1): 137–56.

Kruyt, A.C. (1906) *Het Animisme in den Indischen Archipel*, Den Haag: Martinus Nijhoff.

Lambek, M. (1996) 'Afterword: Spirits and their Histories', in A. Howard and J. Mageo (eds.) *Spirits in Culture, History and Mind*, London: Routledge, 237–50.

Needham, R. (1976) 'Skulls and Causality', *Man*, 11: 71–88.

Payne, R. (2012) 'Agency and Ambiguity in Communication with the Ancestors: Spirit Possession, Ancestral Transformation, and the Conflicts of Modernity among the Benuaq', in P. Couderc and K. Sillander (eds.) *Ancestors in Borneo Societies: Death, Transformation, and Social Immortality*, Copenhagen: Nias Press, 313–35.

Pedersen, M. (2001) 'Totemism, Animism and North Asian Indigenous Ontologies', *Journal of the Royal Anthropological Institute*, 7(3): 411–27.

Pedersen, M., Humphrey, C. and Empson, R. (2007) 'Editorial Introduction: Inner Asian Perspectivisms', *Inner Asia*, 9(2): 141–52.

Rousseau, J. (1998) *Kayan Religion: Ritual Life and Religious Reform in Central Borneo*, Leiden: KITLV Press.

Viveiros de Castro, E. (1996) 'Images of Nature and Society in Amazonian Ethnology', *Annual Review of Anthropology*, 25: 179–200.

―――― (1998) 'Cosmological Deixis and Amerindian Perspectivism', *Journal of the Royal Anthropological Institute*, 4(3): 469–88.

―――― (2001) 'GUT Feelings about Amazonia: Potential Affinity and the Construction of Sociality', in L. Rival and N. Whitehead (eds.) *Beyond the Visible and the Material: The Amerindianization of Society in the Work of Peter Rivière*, Oxford: Oxford University Press, 19–44.

―――― (2004) 'Exchanging Perspectives: The Transformation of Objects into Subjects in Amerindian Ontologies', *Common Knowledge*, 10(3): 463–84.

―――― (2007) 'The Crystal Forest: Notes on the Ontology of Amazonian Spirits', *Inner Asia*, 9 (2): 153–72.

Wessing, R. (2006) 'A Community of Spirits: People, Ancestors, and Nature Spirits in Java', *Crossroads*, 18(1): 11–110.

Willerslev, R. (2007) *Soul Hunters: Hunting, Animism, and Personhood among the Siberian Yukaghirs*, Berkeley, CA: University of California Press.

9 The dynamics of the cosmic conversation

Beliefs about spirits among the Kelabit and Penan of the upper Baram River, Sarawak

Monica Janowski

This chapter looks at beliefs and practices associated with spirits among two peoples: the Kelabit of the Kelabit Highlands, Sarawak, who live at the headwaters of the Baram River, and the Eastern Penan[1] who live to the east of the Baram River in areas surrounding the Kelabit Highlands.[2] The Kelabit are rice-growers who also rely on the forest for hunting and gathering (Janowski 1995, 2003, 2004, 2007). The Eastern Penan were, until recently, all nomadic hunter-gatherers who relied entirely on forest resources, particularly wild pigs and the sago palm; some are still nomads, while others are semi-settled or settled, relying partly on rice-growing (Needham 1953; Langub 1989, 1993). My aim here is to explore what beliefs and practices about spirits can tell us about conceptualizations of the nature of cosmic reality among these two peoples, and how this relates to the different ways in which they relate to the environment in which they live. This relates in particular, I argue, to their relationship with rice-growing (Janowski and Langub 2011).

Philippe Descola has suggested that there are four modes in which humans relate to the environment – 'animistic', 'totemistic', 'analogistic' and 'naturalistic' (Descola 2009). Descola sees the 'naturalistic' mode – which conceives of humans as similar in 'physical' terms but different in 'interior' terms from other living beings – as characteristic of people who are often described as 'Western' or 'Euro-American', who live at a distance from the natural environment and have a sense of a gulf between humans and the part of the cosmos which is characterised as being 'nature'. He sees the other modes as characteristic of peoples from a range of different kinds of society but all closer to the natural environment in which they live. I would like to suggest that the distinctions between these modes is not easily mapped onto straightforward physical distance from the natural environment, and that people do not necessarily fit neatly into one or other of the modes, as is indeed suggested by Descola elsewhere (Descola 2013). I would further suggest that the relationship with the natural environment – conflated for many people with the cosmos itself – can be understood as a dynamic, exploratory and ongoing 'cosmic conversation'. The different quality of the conversation among Penan and Kelabit tells us something about the dynamics driving it.

Penan and Kelabit Perceptions of the Human Role in the Flow of the Cosmos

Both the Penan and the Kelabit have a dynamic and exploratory perception of, and relationship with, the environment in which they live (see Janowski 2012 for a discussion of this among the Kelabit). The flowing and dynamic nature of cosmic reality in the perception of people in the broader region was pointed to some years ago by Benedict Anderson in his seminal article on the Javanese idea of power (1972). Here, he suggests that there is a belief in life force or power in Southeast Asia, which is believed to have a natural tendency to flow around the cosmos, concentrating in certain spots and people. There are a variety of terms that express this belief, including the Javanese *kasektèn* and the Luwu (Sulawesi) *sumangé* (Errington 1990). The Kelabit term *lalud* and the Eastern Penan term *penyuket* (which derives from the word *sukat*, 'able to' [Mackenzie 2006: 183])[3] are other linguistic expressions of this belief, conveying a meaning of life force/ power/potency/effectiveness. The Kelabit concept of *lalud* and the Penan concept of *penyuket* are central to Kelabit and Penan views of the cosmos and how they should interact with it. However, I would argue that there is a significant difference in the way these two peoples actually interact with the *lalud* or *penyuket* of the cosmos, founded in a difference in the way they believe that humans should interact with the rest of the cosmos and the *lalud* or *penyuket* inherent in it.

For peoples like the Kelabit and Penan, all living entities have *lalud* or *penyuket*; its presence is an indication of being alive – *mulun* in Kelabit and *urip* in Penan. *Lalud* or *penyuket* coalesces, as it were, in living entities. All have consciousness, volition and direction. This reflects a sense that energy and life are in flow through the cosmos on a continuous basis. Within, and through, this flow, individual entities come into being. These individual entities, which can, to borrow Tim Ingold's term (Ingold 2008: 106; 2011: 70), be described as 'knots' of life, are entangled with each other in the tissue of life and power. Each has what are described as *ada'* in Kelabit, a term which can be glossed in English as 'spirit'. In Penan, a range of terms are used to describe what would be described in English as the spirits of humans, animals, trees and places: *beruen* or *sahe* for human spirits, *penakoh* for tree spirits and *bale* for other spirits. There are also specific terms used for certain spirits in both Kelabit and Penan.

A living entity, a knot of life, is, then, an enspirited entity. Any living entity in Kelabit is said to *inan ada'*, which means 'there is a spirit there'. Penan and Kelabit are watchful for signs in the environment of the presence of an enspirited entity and of how 'strong' (*kail* in Kelabit) its life force (*lalud/penyuket*) may be (Janowski 2012). For both Penan and Kelabit, the cosmos is to be discovered, and their cosmology and philosophy is founded in experience and onto-praxis; this echoes Ingold's analysis of the nature of life as movement and flow (Ingold 2008, 2011), something which Remme (this volume) argues is also evident among the Ifugao.

While careful and correct interaction with the flow of life force through the cosmos is vital among both Kelabit and Penan, the Kelabit take a much more proactive and controlling approach to that flow. While the Penan seem content to play a more humble role within the flow of life, the Kelabit attempt to direct and manage it. They not only do this in a generalized way, directing its flow, but through adopting a controlling and managing relationship with other entities carrying life force – in particular, rice.

Spirits and the Spirit World

Coexistent with the material world, Kelabit and Penan conceive of a parallel world containing more life force and more power and associated with spirits. This exists in the same space as the material world, but is not perceived in the same way as the material world. It appears not to be seen through the eyes but through what can be described as whole-body perception. Thus, the Kelabit say that it is possible to *kelit* (to be aware of, to perceive) spirits but not to *ne'ar* them (to see them with the eyes). Until the 1960s/1970s spirit mediums (*dayong*) were able to *kelit* this spirit world and entered it to cure the sick, retrieving their *ada'*, which had strayed into it. Nowadays Kelabit, as charismatic Christians, say that they *kelit* Christ or the Holy Spirit.

Spirits may be free-floating in the cosmos or may have a material embodiment, as what may be described as 'enspirited entities', including humans. Spirits which are free-floating appear to have more life force or power (*lalud/penyuket*) than enspirited entities. Many free-floating spirits are believed to have previously had a material embodiment.

The material world is seen as a kind of imprint of the spirit world and is infused with *lalud/penyuket*: power, life force, what we might term 'aliveness'. All material existence is an embodiment of *lalud/penyuket*, which is both biological and spiritual. The animation of the landscape is considered to be expressed through evidence of the activity and presence of free-floating spirits and enspirited material entities, and messages and signs from them, suggesting a social relationship between humans and the enspirited landscape of the kind Descola describes as 'animism' (Descola 2009). Birds were, in pre-Christian times, particularly important messengers, communicating with higher-level spirits. They flew in different directions to give positive or negative messages about enterprises in which people were engaged. Other animals also communicated messages; for the Kelabit, snakes, the barking deer and the civet cat transmitted a negative message about any enterprise, including journeys, new rice fields and marriages. Among the Penan similar beliefs and practices exist (Brosius 2001: 142).

The spirit world is associated with inversion; it is the other side of the material coin. In a story related to me by many people about the spirits of the dead moving the stones of the megalithic cemetery near the community of Pa' Dalih from one bank of the river to the other (because it was on a slope, which they didn't like), the spirits used grasses and creepers which are very weak in the material world but strong in the spirit world. Another story related to me, of how Pun Ngera became the spirit Pun Tumid (see below and Janowski 2014c), tells how his feet were inverted by a rock fall and how this triggered his becoming a spirit. Inversion is widely associated with the spirit world in Southeast Asia, and is also exemplified in other contributions to this volume; for example, in Sven Cederroth's contribution we are told of a man in Lombok who became an evil spirit or *sedaq* as was demonstrated by his desire to eat disgusting things, which to him appeared delicious. Inversion can perhaps be seen as due to the fact that the spirit world is a kind of mirror image of the material world; it is the other side of the same coin, as it were.

The distinction between the spirit and the material world was not always so clear. The Kelabit say that there was a time long ago, *getoman lalud* ('linking to *lalud*' – cosmic power) when the boundary between the spirit world and the human world was much more porous. At that time their ancestors were more regularly in contact with spirits and had more of the *lalud* now associated with the spirit world. Powerful heroes living at this time are said to have been 'partly children of Derayeh,[4] partly children of humans' (*opa-opa anak Derayeh, opa-opa anak lemulun*)[5], and as such were only partially visible, and shimmered with *lalud*. At that time it was possible to die and live in the world of the dead for a while, and then to return to the world of the living, as some of the followers of the mythical hero Tuked Rini are said to have done when his cousin Balang Katu sprinkled *pa' lalud* (water of power/life) on their bones. This was recounted to me as part of the legend of Tuked Rini, by Balang Pelaba of Pa' Dalih in 1987 (see Janowski 2014a).

Hearths, Rice and the 'Othering' of the Forest

Both Penan and Kelabit have cooking hearths at the centre of their dwellings, although the traditional shelter constructed by Penan hunter-gatherers is simpler than the Kelabit longhouse and more open to the forest. It is clear that fire is central to both groups in creating a human space. This is expressed in the fact that there is a clear opposition, for both groups, between fire and spirits. The Great Spirit (see below and Janowski 2014c) does not like fire or warmth. Kelabit told me that if people put their clothes to dry near the fire while they are in the forest, heat up rice which is already cooked at the fire, or put citrus fruit in the fire, this makes the Great Spirit's teeth and head hurt, and he will exact retribution by spearing you (invisibly), licking the blood from his spear and consuming your spirit, unless an older person, preferably someone who is friends with the Great Spirit, apologizes and explains that you didn't do it deliberately. Otherwise, you will sicken and die.[6] The Penan differentiate between the warmth of the shelter and the cool of the forest, and emphasise the need to keep these apart (Brosius 2001: 142). Penan informants in the upper Tutoh related to me in 2008 that the fire keeps spirits and wild animals at bay, as both fear the fire, and this makes humans feel safe. Thus both Kelabit and Penan create a human space through the hearth and fire, and in some sense 'other' themselves from the rest of the cosmos, since only humans generate fire and even the Great Spirit does not like it.

However, the Kelabit go much further in creating a specific human space, through their cultivation of rice. Rice creates, for the Kelabit, a much more explicit demarcation between human space and forest, extending that human space considerably both physically and conceptually. It also valorises this demarcation.

Success in growing rice was, in pre-Christian times, seen as an expression both of full adulthood and social status[7] and of an individual's and a group's ability to interact with the spirit world. Before the Kelabit became Christian, rice-growing was the most important focus of attempts to read messages from enspirited material entities within the environment.

I have argued elsewhere that the Kelabit, through rice-growing, engage in the management and control of *lalud* in a way the Penan do not (Janowski 2004). Rice-growing is a difficult, time-consuming and risky endeavour in the tropical forest and Kelabit say that rice cannot grow without human help. In growing rice, the Kelabit control and manipulate another enspirited entity as well as the flow of *lalud*. Before the Kelabit became Christian they, like other rice-growers in Borneo (such as the Iban whose rice cult was studied in some detail by Freeman – see Freeman 1972) and in Southeast Asia more generally placed great emphasis on retaining and placating the spirits of the rice, and the various stages in the rice year involved rituals focused on achieving this. Rice was seen by some tribes, including the Iban, as being explicitly kin to humans.

The growing of rice is associated with an 'othering' of humans from the forest surrounding them and its inhabitants, in the sense that a symbolic and a physical barrier is erected between the human world – incorporating rice, as kin – and other living beings. The cultivation of rice means the creation of a space dedicated to rice growing, processing and consumption. This space, which is associated with the hearth at which rice is cooked, with the longhouse, and with the rice fields, is contrasted to the space of the *polong*, which is described by the Kelabit as 'growing on its own' (*mulun sebuleng*).

The separation of the human world from the *polong* is symbolically stated and enacted through gender. The *polong* is seen as inhabited by powerful and frightening spirits, relations with which are the province of men, while the longhouse, rice granaries and rice fields are seen as inhabited by spirits which are under the (at least partial) control of humans, and particularly women: rice spirits and hearth spirits.

By contrast, the hunter-gatherer Penan have only the small area immediately around the hearth as their human space, and do not appear to associate the forest (*tana'*) with men, as opposed to women. The term *tana'* means not only forest but also 'earth' in both the Kelabit and Penan languages and can be glossed as referring in some sense to the entire cosmos in both Kelabit and Penan. The lack of any distinct term in the Penan language parallel to the Kelabit *polong* and the fact that there is only a vague sense among the hunter-gatherer Eastern Penan that the *tana'* is something distinct from the tiny human area around the fire indicates a significantly lesser sense of 'othering' of the forest from the human space among these Penan.

I have argued elsewhere that this 'othering' of the *polong* associated with rice agriculture is related to the generation of difference and hierarchy within human society (Janowski 2007; Janowski and Langub 2011). Kaj Århem, in his contribution to this volume, suggests that a similar 'othering' of the forest among the Katu of Vietnam is also rooted in hierarchy (in the Katu case, via asymmetric alliance patterns, extended to the relationship between village and forest). However, he does not link this to rice agriculture but sees hierarchy as fundamental to Southeast

Asian societies, contrasting this with the more equal relationship between people and forest spirits/animals which prevails in Amazonian societies. I would suggest that there is, in fact, the potential for a more equal relationship between people and forest spirits/animals in Southeast Asia too, as is demonstrated by the Penan case as discussed here. As Graeme Barker and I have discussed elsewhere, it can be argued that certain modes of life – in Southeast Asia, rice-growing – have the potential to generate a sense of 'difference' between humans and other life (Barker and Janowski 2011).

Power, Stone and Marks on the Landscape

Kelabit success in rice-growing was, until the 1950s, expressed through the making of stone or earth 'marks' (*etuu*) on the landscape at *irau* feasts, which are status-generating (Janowski 1988; Janowski and Langub 2011). The use of stone is linked to the belief that the flow of power and life force through the landscape expresses itself and can be read through stone, which is petrified power (Janowski and Barton 2012). Spirits are associated with stones and stony places in the landscape. Batuh Lawi, a mountain with twin stone peaks, is said to have once been a married couple, and the area around it believed to be inhabited by many spirits[8]. The mountain ridge Apad Ke Ruma' is considered to be have once been a longhouse, petrified when its residents laughed at a frog released by a young woman called Ronan whose child had been maltreated.[9]

Kelabit used to place their dead in megalithic cemeteries (*menatoh*). We know from carbon dating done recently that at least one of these cemeteries, that at the mouth of the Diit river, may be 1,200 years old (Barker et al 2009: 158). The Kelabit consider these cemeteries to have been established by their ancestors in the time of *getoman lalud* ('linking with power'). *Menatoh* are often focused on natural stone outcrops, with other stone added by humans in the form of slabs (*batuh nangan* – 'supported stones') and shaped stone jars (*lungun batuh* – 'stone coffins') inside which the dead were sometimes placed, although they might also be placed in wooden coffins or Chinese 'dragon' jars (*belanai*) sited near the stones. This underlines the association of stone with the world of *lalud* and the spirits, where the dead, as pure spirits (*ada'*) without material form, are located. Cemeteries, full of the spirits of the dead, are stony places.

Etuu include stone cemeteries, other stone and earth marks on the landscape made at *irau* feasts to commemorate prominent dead, and channels cut for wet rice growing in old channels of the river (Janowski and Barton 2012). The nomadic Eastern Penan, by contrast with the Kelabit, say explicitly that they do not make *etuu* marks on the landscape; they leave only *uban*, or 'footprints' (Janowski and Langub 2011). As nomads, they simply left their dead where they died (see below). Whilst they manage sago and other resources in the forest, they do not engage in the risky and difficult enterprise which rice-growing represents. Sago occurs naturally in the forests of the highlands and in managing it the Penan are as it were, 'going along with' the flow of *penyuket* through the landscape; they are doing only a minimal amount to divert it.

The Great Spirit

At the apex and origin point of the cosmos there is an ultimate and continuing source of *lalud/penyuket*. Among the Penan this was, before they became Christian in recent years, described as Tenangan or Pesolong Luan (Brosius 2001: 142). Among the Kelabit, before they became Christian, Baru' was said to have created the Earth[10] but the ultimate source of life and of power was Derayeh or Ada' Rayeh, two terms which appear to be etymologically the same, literally meaning 'Great Spirit'. The Penan have an equivalent belief in Bale Ja'au, also literally 'Great Spirit'. The Kelabit and the Eastern Penan say that the Great Spirit which they both know is the same spirit.

Among the Kelabit, people prayed to Derayeh before they became Christian in situations of crisis and ill health and the term '*Derayeh nok ngimat*' – 'Derayeh who holds/supports') is often used. The Penan prayed to Tenangan. In their attempts to bring together pre-Christian and Christian beliefs, older Kelabit associated Derayeh with the Holy Spirit in discussions with me in the late 1980s and early 1990s, and Baru' with the Christian God, the Father (who is described as Tuhan or Tuhan Allah, using the Malay/Islamic terminology)[11]. However, in the story of the Kelabit culture hero Tuked Rini,[12] Derayeh, there described as Sinah ('Mother') Purid Derayeh, is conceived of as an entity rather than a force.

The two terms which the Kelabit use for the Great Spirit are associated respectively with male (and forest) and female (and rice): Derayeh with the female and Ada' Rayeh with the male. The splitting of the Great Spirit along gendered lines may be understood in the context of the fact that in Austronesian societies the origin or source of power and life force is imaged as either dual-gendered or without gender but once it manifests in the flowing cosmos becomes gendered (e.g., see essays in Fox 1980). The term Derayeh is also used to refer to both aspects of the Great Spirit. Expressing a common complementarity in the wider region between female underearth/underwater and male sky, Derayeh is associated with both the sky (*lemunid langit* – 'within the sky') and the underearth (*puruk tanah liang* – 'the place where all is washed underground') in the legend of the culture hero Tuked Rini as recited by Balang Pelaba to me in 1987 (Janowski 2014a).

The Great Spirit described as Bale Ja'au among the Penan and Ada' Rayeh among the Kelabit is associated with high mountains and big forest and can perhaps be seen as embodying the enspirited animation of the landscape.[13] In one sense this is true in a holistic sense, in that people often talked of the Great Spirit as singular; but in other contexts they talked of individual Great Spirits associated with each mountain peak.[14]

Possession of large amounts of power confers the ability to shape-shift (Kelabit *balio*; Penan *paleu*). According to Balang Pelaba of Pa' Dalih, who himself used to be a 'friend' of the Great Spirit (and, later in his life, a spirit medium), the Great Spirit and the *menegeg* are the only entities that can shape-shift, although powerful humans including some of the heroes of the legend of Tuked Rini, which Balang Pelaba related to me in 1987 (see Janowski 2014a) also seem to have this capacity. I had a dream while living in the Kelabit Highlands in 1992, of a very small thing which became a buffalo and then a tall pole and fell on me, and the following morning, when I recounted my dream, I was told that I had dreamt of the Great Spirit; the Great Spirit is also known as the *ada' ranat* or 'expanding spirit' because of its ability to change shape and size rapidly. This can be said to express the Great Spirit's capacity to express any and all elements of the environment. One Penan, Asai Beret of Long Si'ang, called the Great Spirit the 'King of the Spirits'.

The Great Spirit, unlike spirits which are anchored in specific material entities, is not associated with any particular material form. However, to humans the Great Spirit appears in quasi-human form. To Balang Pelaba he appeared as a tall white man with black eyes, white hair and a beard to his waist, wearing a red bracelet (red, the colour of blood and life, is said to be the only colour that spirits can see; red beads, said to have come originally from the spirits, used to be placed on the wrists of the dead by the Kelabit, before they became Christian). To the Penan Moyong Usai he appeared looking like a government official, wearing glasses.[15] The Penan Asai Beret said that he may appear as a big black or red macaque monkey, with hair like white people, looking like a human from a distance.[16]

The Ada' Rayeh or Bale Ja'au, in its human-like manifestations, appears to be male. Many people, both Kelabit and Penan, told me that they had heard the Great Spirit hunting, and only men hunt. He hunts during both the day and the night; as humans do not hunt at night, when you hear someone calling their dogs at night it must be the Great Spirit.

The Great Spirit is believed to hunt human spirits; we are said to be 'his pigs' (*baka iah* in Kelabit); this can be seen as an example of what Viveiros de Castro describes as a 'perspectival' approach (Viveiros de Castro 2008) – also pointed to by Kaj Århem and Guido Sprenger in their discussions of the Katu and the Rmeet respectively in this volume – where the ontological status of an entity depends on its relation to other entities.[17] This relates to a Kelabit story in which the Great Spirit manifests as Pun Tumid, or 'Grandfather Heel'. The story goes as follows: Once there were two brothers who went hunting. They were called Pun Ngera' and Pun Luun. They took shelter under a rock overhang known as the Lepo Batuh. They had no fire so they sent their dog back to the longhouse to bring a burning brand. They laughed at the dog crossing the river, and it began to hail.[18] The hail caused the stone shelter to collapse on to Pun Ngera'. His feet were damaged and some say they were reversed – a form of inversion, often associated with spirits. Because of this he was embarrassed to return to the longhouse, and he told his brother to return to the longhouse and hunt 'hairy prey', while he would remain in the forest and hunt 'hairless prey' (humans).[19] He became a spirit, a manifestation of the Great Spirit (Ada' Rayeh), known as Pun Tumid, 'Grandfather Heel' (see Janowski 2014c for a full version of the story).[20]

Human-like manifestations of the Ada' Rayeh or Bale Ja'au can be dangerous if people misbehave, but they also aid humans. According to the Penan Asai Beret of Long Si'ang, the Great Spirit will help you if you ask him. He said that the Great Spirit will approach grown men; young people cannot see him.[21] The Kelabit also say that the Great Spirit, as Pun Tumid, approaches men to make friends and wants to help humans. Balang Pelaba of Pa' Dalih told me that Pun Tumid approached him when he was a young man – in the late 1930s – and invited him out to meet with him. At that time Balang Pelaba had a wound on his foot and Pun Tumid massaged it and it immediately got better; thereafter, they became friends. Pun Tumid would help him to find pigs when he was hunting. He also gave him powerful substances (*tabat*) in the form of small bottles containing liquid which could cure or kill, as well as three powerful stones – one black, one white and one red – which were enspirited entities. The black would kill, the red would make a person vomit blood and the white would cure. The spirits of the stones would do what Balang Pelaba told them to do, but he had to feed them with human blood, from one human each year. To do this, he told me that he used to kill faraway people, not people nearby whom he knew. Balang Pelaba remained friends with Pun Tumid until he was approached by *dayong* spirits and he became a spirit medium (*dayong*); when this happened he returned the stones and the liquids to Pun Tumid.[22] Later, he became Christian and abandoned his role as *dayong*.

Encounters with Pun Tumid still occur. Lian, Balang Pelaba's son, told me that he was approached by Pun Tumid (whom he described as his *tepo'*, or 'grandfather) in 2005, but he rejected his friendship, saying that he now had a spirit who was much bigger and more powerful than Pun Tumid – Jesus Christ. Ribuh Paran of the Kelabit community of Pa' Dalih told me that he met Pun Tumid in the forest when he was a young man, which would have been in the late 1970s. Telona Bala of Pa' Dalih actively sought to meet Pun Tumid in the 1980s, during a period when he was also in search of powerful stones and other powerful objects.

The importance of the figure of Pun Tumid appears to suggest an assertion of a closer and more controlling relationship with the environment on the part of the Kelabit. It is notable that the Kelabit see themselves as being related to the Great Spirit manifesting as Pun Tumid, since they are descended from his brother. The Penan are much more focused on relationships with small, localised spirits associated with individual trees and animals.[23] I heard of no close friendships with Bale Ja'au such as that which Balang Pelaba had with Pun Tumid. It has been suggested that the Penan have borrowed the very idea of the Great Spirit, at least as an entity which has a human-like manifestation, from the Kelabit.[24] Among the Western Penan, the Great Spirit is associated only with the Thunder God, who sends petrification if people laugh at animals, and there are no stories of meeting him in person as there are among the Eastern Penan (Brosius 2001: 142).

Spirits of Humans

Human spirits are called by the same term as other spirits by the Kelabit – *ada'*. The Penan call human spirits *beruen*. They use the term *sahe* for the soul which wanders when people sleep; here again the Kelabit simply use *ada'*. As is very common in Southeast Asia, spirit loss was believed to be an important cause of illness in the past, and people would seek the help of *dayong* or shamans/ spirit mediums, who sought to retrieve lost *ada'*, sometimes through travelling in trance. They might also pray directly to the Great Spirit.

Christianity introduced the idea that people would eventually go to heaven (*surga*) when they died. The location of heaven is not known but is thought by Kelabit to be likely to be in the sky since that is where the Supreme Deity and Jesus Christ are believed to reside. Most people told me, in discussions about this, that the spirits of the dead would enter heaven at the Last Judgement; until then it was unclear where their spirits would go, although some people were of the opinion that some of them – those who had not behaved well in life – might remain in the cemetery (here they are referring to the Christian cemetery; when they became Christian the Kelabit established new cemeteries, called *tanem*, 'burial places', to replace the pre-Christian megalithic and dragon jar cemeteries). Before the Kelabit became Christian they believed, according to Balang Pelaba of Pa' Dalih, that humans had ten *ada'* and that five of these remained in the vicinity of the place where their bodies were placed, in other words in the cemetery (*menatoh*), and five joined Derayeh, the source of *lalud* and life, above the sky (*luun langit*). There appears, therefore, to be some continuity between pre-Christian and Christian belief about the destiny of the dead, but in Christianity there is a greater emphasis on the continuing unity of the dead person's spirit after death (rather than its division into a number of constituents) and its destination in the sky with the Supreme Deity, now known as Tuhan Allah.

The land of the dead in which the spirits lived in the cemetery in pre-Christian times was considered to be just like the land of the living, but invisible to the living in normal circumstances. The dead lived as do the living. They had villages, and they carried out rice-farming, hunting, gathering – all the things that living humans do. Indeed, the pre-Christian dead are still considered to be living at the *menatoh* or pre-Christian megalithic cemetery closest to Pa' Dalih. I was often told while living in Pa' Dalih in the late 1980s that if you went near the old *menatoh* at the mouth of the Diit river, which was used until the 1950s as the cemetery for the whole area, you could still hear the dead, talking to each other and calling their animals. It was unwise, I was told, to go to the cemetery as it could make you ill, and when I became unwell shortly after visiting the cemetery for the first time this was attributed to my visit.

The existence of villages of the dead deriving from cemeteries all over the landscape is possibly linked to the fact that there are many instances recounted by Kelabit of meeting spirits in the form of humans in the forest. These may lead you astray and keep you away from the world of the living for many weeks or even months or years. Such spirits may be very friendly and hospitable, and appear to live like 'normal' humans. One can hypothesise that these are the spirits of dead people, who are living their lives as do the living.

As is common in Southeast Asia, the separation of the dead from the living among the Kelabit was carried out gradually in pre-Christian times. This was through the gradual breaking-off associated with secondary funeral practices. These were particularly important for powerful leaders, probably because their *lalud* (power or life force) was strong, meaning that their spirits (*ada'*) were potentially dangerous and/or helpful to the living. It was therefore important to 'manage' the breaking-off properly. The bodies of such leaders, and of all of those dead who had reached grandparental status, were kept in or near the longhouse, in wooden coffins or Chinese 'dragon' jars, for a significant period. For important leaders, this would be for at least a year; for other grandparents, it might be only a few months. Young people were kept for shorter periods. After this period, the dead were taken to the *menatoh*, the megalithic cemetery in the forest. This might either be that used by the community in which they lived or another, further away, where their close kin were buried; it was believed that the dead would not be accepted by the other dead in the *menatoh* if they were not their close kin. While the dead were kept at the longhouse, they were 'fed' every day, with food from family meals left near the coffin. The dead would take the essence of the food, which they shared with the living who ate the material aspect of it. Only when the dead person was taken to the *menatoh* did this cease.

Among the Penan the separation of the dead from the living was achieved through simple avoidance – something practised by the Kelabit too, who did not go to the cemetery except to take a dead person there, and who greatly feared the spirits believed to be concentrated there. The Penan, until recently, simply left their dead in the campsite where they died, and moved on. For many years after a death, they would avoid making camp at the same spot. They did not keep any of the dead with them for a period of time, as did the Kelabit. This appears to indicate that, unlike the Kelabit, they were not concerned to retain and draw on the *lalud* of the prominent dead. The Penan believed that the spirits of the dead had the capacity to do harm or to assist the living, but did not believe that certain people had more capacity to do this than others and did not believe that it was necessary to keep the dead close to the living for a period of time to ensure that their *penyuket* was retained.

The Kelabit were headhunters until the late nineteenth century, when the Brooke Rajas ended head-hunting in Sarawak. For the Kelabit headhunting was associated with introducing children to human life; at the ritual at which a child was initiated into human social life he or she received a shower of pig's blood and then of water which had been placed inside a human skull taken in head-hunting.[25] A human head was believed to carry within it the spirit of the person who had been killed.[26] Head-hunting was closely associated with the building up of status, which was closely linked, for men, with bravery and aggression. It represented the hunting of the *ada'* – the spirit – of other humans, and the bringing of the *lalud* of the dead person into the community, apparently strengthening it.[27] As we will see, for the Kelabit the Great Spirit (Ada' Rayeh) was also believed to hunt human spirits. The Penan, who by contrast, did not proactively make war on others, and they did not take heads. In other words they did not, through headhunting, attempt to accumulate *lalud*.

Spirits of Animals

All animals, birds and indeed even insects are believed to have spirits and *lalud/ penyuket*. The Kelabit call the spirits of animals *ada'*; the Penan use the term *beruen*.

Kelabit keep pigs, chickens and buffaloes for meat, killing pigs and buffaloes at *irau* feasts and chickens when visitors come. The Eastern Penan do not keep domestic animals except dogs for hunting. Many nomadic Penan informants told me that they cannot conceive of killing an animal with which they live. Many wild animals are killed for meat by both Kelabit and Penan, but the principal game for both groups is pigs, with deer a close second. I have argued elsewhere that pigs have a special status among the Kelabit (Janowski 2014b), being paralleled to or linked with humans in pre-Christian ritual practice. Wild pigs are greatly desired as food; they are meat *par excellence*.

While animals are regularly killed for food – wild animals by both Penan and Kelabit and domestic animals too by the Kelabit – this is not done lightly. Wild animals are believed to be given to humans – in the past by the Great Spirit and now by Jesus. Prayers are offered to ask for pigs before a hunt. When killing domestic animals in the past the Kelabit would speak to the spirit of the animal, explaining why they needed to kill it.

There are two animals that are considered to exist only in spirit form in the highland area and are considered to be very powerful because of this – the crocodile (*bayeh* in both Kelabit and Penan) and the tiger (*balang* in Kelabit; *tepun* in Eastern Penan).[28] Crocodiles live in the lower reaches of the Baram river but not in the highland area where the Penan and Kelabit live. Tigers may have once existed in Borneo, but they are no longer present. There is a special relationship between humans and the tiger in other parts of Borneo and indeed more widely in Southeast Asia (Hutton 1920; Karim 1981; Sellato 1983).

The Kelabit relationship with tigers and crocodiles relates to their attempts to harness the power of these animals for human purposes. While the Penan use systems of teknonymy and death names and do not take names with meanings, the Kelabit take names with meanings when they become parents and again when they become grandparents. These names are usually very boastful and part of this is the frequent use of the terms for tiger (*balang*) and for crocodile (*bayeh*) as name elements, particularly *balang* (Janowski 2005). A large proportion of Kelabit men take the word *balang* as part of their grandparental name, expressing the association between bravery and masculinity and the nature of the tiger.

The Eastern Penan word for tiger, *tepun*, expresses a different kind of relationship with the power of the tiger, one which does not attempt to harness its power but respects it as kin and as imposing rules of sharing. *Tepun* also means 'grandparent' and reflects an Eastern Penan myth of origin for both the tiger and the crocodile,[29] which states that they are the twin children of a human mother long ago, thus being related as 'grandparents' to humans now (the word 'grandparent' refers not only to lineal grandparents but to collateral relatives). Because they consider themselves related to the crocodile and to the tiger, the Eastern Penan would not, they told me, eat tigers or crocodiles (even if they could) and do not eat while in the river. Informants told me that the tiger will punish young people who do not share their food, something which emphasises kinship; the tiger, then, can be seen as promoting kinship.[30]

Spirits of Trees

While all plants are seen as enspirited entities, larger plants have larger and more important spirits. There is a particular awareness of the presence of spirits in trees. Cutting down trees is considered to be tantamount to killing another sentient being. Nomadic Penan do not fell large trees at all. It seems that in the past the Kelabit rarely cut down large trees of any kind as these were believed likely to contain spirits. When making dry swidden rice fields, Kelabit would only cut down the smaller trees, not the big ones – these they would leave in the field, where they would be burnt by the burning of the other trees but would not be killed.[31] As Nikolas Århem points out in his chapter, the Katu of Vietnam also do not cut down large trees, seeing them as persons or abodes of spirits.

The Penan have a specific word, *penakoh,* for the spirits of trees; the Kelabit use the more general word for spirits, *ada'*. I was specifically told by informants that there are spirits living in the tree known as *tele* (Kelabit)[32] or *telesai* (Penan); in that known as *tanid* (Kelabit) or *tanyit* (Penan);[33] in the strangler fig, known as *lonok* (Kelabit) or *mutan* (Penan); and in the *tutun* tree (Kelabit). Older Kelabit informants told me that, before they became Christian, cutting down the trees listed above was prohibited, *male*, and the spirit of the tree would make someone who cut such a tree down ill. Even physical contact with the strangler fig, in the branches of which the bodies of women who died in childbirth were placed in the past,[34] or the *tutun* tree, in which a spirit called Ba'o Budok lived, was believed to be dangerous since the spirit would get angry and make you ill, and people avoided walking under the *tele* tree or stepping on its leaves.[35] The *belaban* tree was not cut down as it is said to attract lightning. In his contribution to this volume, Nikolas Århem discusses the fact that among the Katu of Vietnam, too, big trees are considered to contain spirits, with the strangler fig also being particularly likely to contain a spirit.

Not only the species but the age and size of trees are significant. There is much less concern about cutting down small trees (of species other than those mentioned above). Both Penan and Kelabit cut down small trees regularly for firewood, the building of shelters and houses, and for craftwork. It is large trees whose cutting is considered problematic. With the adoption of a more sedentary lifestyle and rice agriculture the Penan are beginning to cut down more trees, but are still afraid of cutting down very large trees, as they fear the reaction of the spirits of the trees.

Both Kelabit and Penan saw, in pre-Christian times, a need to be cautious and respectful in relation to the cutting down – which meant the 'killing' – of enspirited entities in the form of trees. However, while the Penan never cut down trees, the Kelabit seem, judging from what people have told me, to have operated on the edge of danger, taking risks by cutting down trees and burning them for building and for rice-growing, risks which the Penan did not take. Once they became Christian, the Kelabit began to take greater and greater risks in cutting down trees, but the Penan are still very cautious. A group of Penan in Long Taha expressed surprise in conversation with me that the people working for the logging company working in their area do not become sick as they are constantly cutting down big trees.[36]

In the past, I was told, there was a prohibition on cutting down trees which were not really needed, reflecting a more general sense which is still current that it is not right to take resources from the forest that are not needed. I was told that if a tree was needed, for example for building, it could be cut down, but if you cut down trees that you didn't need, just to show how powerful and brave you were, then the spirit of the tree would make you ill.[37]

The Kelabit, immediately after they became Christian, began to cut down big trees after praying to Jesus to keep them safe from the spirit of the tree. The *belaban* tree in particular is frequently felled nowadays, as it is very useful both for building and for firewood, although there is belief that *belaban* attracts lightning, even as timber.[38] There remains a reluctance to cut down the strangler fig, although some people boasted to me that they had done this and nothing had happened to them. However, while a group of town-dwelling Kelabit were some years ago talking of building a longhouse at a grove of strangler figs upstream from Pa' Dalih, others declared that they would never go through with it. One informant, Bayeh Ribuh, told me that even the loggers are afraid of cutting down the strangler fig and pointed out that all the strangler figs along a certain stretch of forest being logged had been left alone.[39] However, he declared, in an assertion of bravery, that he had himself cut down some strangler fig trees for planks as there were so many around (presumably because other people were reluctant to cut them down). An older man, Balang Muned, had told him not to cut them down as it would be dangerous but Bayeh Ribuh said that so far he had not suffered any adverse consequences.

Spirits of Places

Watery places and places where the earth is disturbed are associated with spirits, reflecting beliefs about the spiritual and cosmological significance of underearth/underwater. Both Penan and Kelabit believe that there are spirits associated with any kind of turbulent area in the river, such as rapids (*paro'* in Kelabit; *o'ong* in Penan).[40] Pools are most closely associated with spirits. There is the potential for a spirit to be present in any river pool. If someone drowns in a pool, this is seen by the Kelabit as proof that there is a spirit resident in the pool, and it is described as *daka*, which can be glossed in English as 'cursed'. One of the previous longhouse sites which we excavated and discussed with informants as part of *The Cultured Rainforest* project between 2007 and 2011 was adjacent to such a pool, and for this reason was known as Ruma Ma'on Daka (Old Longhouse Site by the *Daka* Pool).[41]

In very deep pools, the Kelabit believe that a particularly powerful enspirited entity may reside.[42] This is the *menegeg*, a creature which starts off as a snake but becomes a kind of water serpent. A pool that forms part of the oxbow lake by Pa' Dalih, most of which is now being used for wet rice fields, is believed to contain a *menegeg*. This creature is presumably a form of what is known in Sanskrit as *naga*, known under different names throughout the whole of Southeast Asia. The *naga* expresses the importance of the underworld/underwater principle, often associated with the feminine principle.

Spirits are associated with places where the earth is disturbed or there is a break in the earth. The Penan in particular are concerned about such spirits, which are called *ungap*. People have to be very careful to be quiet and respectful, to avoid the anger of the *ungap*, when they are in the vicinity of salt springs/animal salt licks (*sungan*), landslides (*tana besale*), pig wallows (*lina' babui*), porcupine dens (*beseneu*), anthills (*pelemau*) and burial grounds. In the vicinity of such places, especially *sungan*, you may hear voices or meet what appear to be normal people; but they are *ungap* and will lead you away and cause you to get lost.

The Kelabit too believe that there are spirits – *ada'* – at places where the earth has been disturbed, including at landslides (*toran*) and salt springs (*ropan*). However, they appear to have been, even in pre-Christian times, much less concerned than the Penan about such spirits. The Kelabit have a long history of making wet rice fields, which involves the disturbance of the earth; braving the wrath of the spirits of the underearth is, then, part of their heritage as wet rice farmers. Since the 1960s, they have embarked on large scale conversion of areas into wet rice fields. As for the spirits of salt springs, which are so feared by the Penan, one Kelabit informant expressed the view that the spirits at salt springs are friendly, not dangerous.[43] The Kelabit and their Lun Dayeh cousins across the border in the Kerayan area in East Kalimantan, Indonesia, make salt from the brine at salt springs, which the Kelabit used as currency in trading with other peoples, including the Penan, and which is still used as currency in the Kerayan area. Making salt at these springs is something which the Penan would not consider, due to their fear of the spirits residing there.

Caves, which are of course inside the earth, are also associated with spirits. The (spirit) tiger (*balang*) which is said to have threatened one of the longhouses in the Kelapang area long ago at the time of *getoman lalud*, which was hunted down by a culture hero (see above) lived in a cave just below a ridge, a spot that can be pinpointed exactly by people living nowadays, which I have visited. The Great Spirit is also said to live in a mountain cave.

It seems likely that the fact that places associated by both Kelabit and Penan with access to the interior of the earth, and deep pools, are believed to contain spirits is an expression of the generalised *lalud/penyuket* which exists in the depths of the earth, associated with the feminine principle.

The Kelabit, like the Penan, also consider that where an accident has occurred is due to the spirits living at that place, and that they caused the accident. There was a series of vehicle accidents at a certain spot on a logging road running along a ridge near Pa' Dalih in 2000s, and it was concluded that there were spirits lurking around that spot which were hitching a ride with the vehicles and causing the accidents; the fact that it was on a mountain ridge made this even more likely. The Kelabit set up a temporary forest church at an old longhouse site nearby and held prayer sessions, praying to Jesus Christ to remove the spirits. The series of air accidents which have occurred in the past twenty years in the vicinity of Batuh Lawi mountain are believed to have been caused by the spirits of the mountain, unhappy with the logging and disturbance which has taken place around the mountain in recent years.

There are also spirits associated with the places where humans live. Mostly, these seem to be benevolent. These are particularly associated with the hearth itself, and may be fire spirits, although this is not explicit. For the Kelabit, who live in more complex structures than the Penan, there are also spirits associated with other parts of the longhouse. Most are linked with rice storage and processing, and are probably associated with beliefs about rice itself. In Pa' Dalih, there is also a spirit called the *ada' kok*, associated with the *tawa'* (the area associated with visitors and men in the past), with which very small children were threatened if they strayed too far from the hearth area where they are more easily watched, when we lived there in the late 1980s. My daughter Molly would frequently talk to me at that time about the *ada'kok*, which she said had big red eyes and made a howling noise.

Spirits of Hard Objects

The *lalud/penyuket* of the cosmos is believed to cohere and become hard. Unusual hard objects of any kind found in the environment – little nuggets of power, as it were – are believed likely to contain a spirit by both Penan and Kelabit, particularly if they are round and perfect. These were commonly collected and kept in the past, before Christianity arrived in the highlands, and individual Kelabit and Penan still sometimes collect them in an attempt to harness their power (Janowski and Barton 2012). Such an object might be an oddly-shaped antler; a strange stone; or what were described to me as 'crystals' by Telona Bala of Pa' Dalih. In Kelabit, such objects are known as *pub*. The objects described as thunderstones, *batuh pera'it*, fall into this category of small hard objects; many people told me that these are petrified *lalud/penyuket* which solidifies on hitting the earth.[44] Such objects need to appear whole and undamaged, as this means that they are inhabited by a spirit – that they are enspirited entities. Otherwise, they contain *lalud/penyuket* but do not have the individuated consciousness which allows them to be actors vis-à-vis the rest of the cosmos.

Among the Penan hard objects, including thunderstones, were kept to ensure success in finding pigs and sago. A person who owned one must, I was told, be very careful when taking a bath as it might cause thunder and he or she would need to speak to the spirit of the stone beforehand to avoid this.[45] Among the Kelabit, too, thunderstones were kept, in the past. Their most important use was as rice charms; they were, until the 1970s, kept in rice barns and were believed to increase the amount of rice in the store. The Kelabit also used hard objects to cure and to kill. The spirit of the object had to be fed blood in return for its services, and the possessor of the object was therefore believed likely to be seen as guilty of attacking other people to get their blood. Such attacks did not mean the physical wounding of the person; the blood concerned was invisible, as was the weapon used and the wound itself. However, the person attacked would, it was believed, become sick and might die.

The use of *pub* has almost died out among the Kelabit, although I know of at least one instance of a man who kept a collection of them as recently as the 1990s, although he has now discarded them. He is said to have himself become sick due to keeping the *pub*; if the keeper does not feed its spirit adequately with the blood of others it is believed that it will begin to feed on its owner. I do not know how common the keeping of such objects is among the Penan nowadays.

Christianity and Loss of Attention to the Flow of Power in the Landscape

The Kelabit converted to Christianity during the period from the Second World War until the so-called 'Revival' in 1973 (Lees 1979), and the Penan are also now at least nominally Christian, though some Western Penan have adopted the syncretic Bungan religion. The evangelical form of Christianity which both the Kelabit and the Penan have adopted implies a particularly emphatic abandonment of attention to the small-scale enspirited entities within the forest and the landscape, and an abandonment of any attempt to watch out for messages carried by these, or of any attempts not to break the rules which are imposed by them. This has, however, been taken up much more by the Kelabit than by the Penan. The Kelabit now say that they rely entirely on a higher-level source of *lalud* – Jesus Christ. The Eastern Penan, who continue to be largely nomadic and to grow little or no rice, continue to attend to smaller enspirited entities and to the more detailed animation of the landscape in which they live. I would suggest that the Kelabit, by contrast, have lost most of the depth of 'attention' to the environment (Gibson 1979) which they previously had.

Jesus Christ is not directly associated with forest or landscape. Success in life, with Christianity, is not founded in any particular way of behaving toward the environment. The only requirement associated with the 'deal' with Christ is to follow the rules laid out in the Bible and to pray hard. A good deal of effort goes into working out what these rules are; the Bible is, of course, notoriously difficult to interpret. But the Christian rules as interpreted by the Kelabit do not appear to include anything about behaviour toward the environment; indeed they seem to have included a willingness to abandon any pre-existing rules about such behaviour, which were underlined and imposed by the potential retaliation of spirits of enspirited material entities when humans over-used resources. Some people say that there are no spirits in the landscape anymore; perhaps, informants have mused in discussion with me, if people no longer follow (*maya'*) them, spirits cease to exist.

It is arguable that this loss of attention has meant that Kelabit are less closely embedded in the environment in which they live. They are much less concerned about the potential implications of cutting down trees or disturbing the soil than they were. The Penan, by contrast, remain profoundly concerned about these activities, and have been the most active group in Sarawak in resisting logging.

The Christian God, known as Tuhan Allah, is associated in Christianity as well as in pre-Christian religion with the sky. However, the sacred complementarity between sky and underearth/underwater associated with the Great Spirit appears to have been lost. The Great Spirit, in its manifestation as Pun Tumid, is now disregarded by the people of the Kelabit highlands. Our late neighbour in Pa' Dalih,

Balang Pelaba, who had been friends with Pun Tumid, told me that Pun Tumid is now lonely. Balang Pelaba's son Lian told me, after he met Pun Tumid in 2005, that Pun Tumid is seeking his relatives (in other words, humans).

It seems that for the Kelabit access to the life force or power – the *lalud* – of the cosmos has become concentrated at its source, with the Supreme Deity and through his son Jesus Christ, and this source has become more distanced from the physical cosmos. The landscape and the forest, already 'othered' through the practices of rice-growing, have become even more separated from humans. This process of focusing higher, looking towards the source of life force, *lalud*, began, I have suggested, with rice-growing, and has been built on and has grown since the adoption of Christianity. Compared to the Penan, the Kelabit have always focused less on smaller-scale enspirited entities within the landscape and more on an encompassing approach to the enspirited landscape, as represented by their relationships with manifestations of the Great Spirit as mediator with the source of life and power. With Christianity, Christ, who appears to have no association with the landscape, has taken over as mediator with the ultimate source of power and life force, God or *Tuhan*, enabling very powerful access to control over the flow of life force and power and a disassociation of power from the landscape itself. Mathew Amster has described this process as making power more 'portable' (see Amster 2009); but it also disassociates humans from the landscape in which they live.

As Matthew Amster points out in his chapter in this volume, Kelabit themselves often assert that this change is welcome, pointing out that their previous practices, which stemmed from a constant attention to signs and messages from enspirited entities in the environment, were onerous and often distressing. However, conversations within a Kelabit group on Facebook, and poems by a Kelabit using the pseudonym Maya Green often posted on that group, suggest that there is an increasing sense among some Kelabit that much has been lost, too, in abandoning close attention to spirituality in the natural environment. It is also noteworthy that the Kelabit continue to pray on hills and mountains, and many villages, including Pa' Dalih where I have lived, have their own local 'prayer mountain'. In 1987 the Kelabit and Lun Dayeh undertook a pilgrimage to the highly enspirited twin-peaked mountain of Batuh Lawi just north of the Kelabit Highlands (in which my husband Kaz participated), and since then there has been an annual pilgrimage to another nearby mountain, Mount Murud, organised by the Sidang Injil Borneo church (Amster 1999). This seems to suggest that the Kelabit continue to have a sense of a continuing enspirited-ness of the landscape, even if they do not focus on individual spirits within it or overtly recognize that they see the landscape as sacred.

Conclusion

How are we to understand the modes of relating to the landscape on the part of the Penan and the Kelabit? In one sense both groups could be categorised as 'animist'. Both Penan and Kelabit conceive of the cosmos as animated and see the same 'life force' or cosmic power, which they term *penyuket* and *lalud* respectively, as coursing through the entire cosmos. They see this as expressing itself in enspirited entities, including humans. They see consciousness of the same kind as their own in other animated beings. They see material reality as plastic, considering it possible for living beings to shape-shift, particularly if they have high levels of power. These are all modes of thought which are associated with 'animism' in a broad sense. However, the Kelabit conceive of humans as in some sense qualitatively different from other living beings, 'othered' from the rest of the living cosmos, controlling of other living beings. The Kelabit have always reached higher, relating to higher-level spirits than the Penan. With Christianity, this has gone even further. It would seem reasonable to describe this shift as a shift towards the kind of perspective which Descola describes as 'naturalistic', since something glossable as 'nature' is 'othered' and humans are attributed powers and abilities which other living beings – other enspirited entities – do not have. Through their special and direct relationship with higher-level spirits – and, with Christianity, with Jesus Christ – humans become even more separate from the rest of the environment.

However, it is worth noting that the germ of 'naturalism' can be found among the Penan too. In the making of fire, both Penan and Kelabit create a human space – albeit tiny in the case of the nomadic Penan – which other enspirited entities, and even the 'Great Spirit', will not enter. This suggests that, since the control of fire and cooking are apparently unique to the human species, all humans may in some sense be seen as 'naturalists' in Descola's terms. The fact that the Kelabit, and even the hunter-gatherer Penan, can also be seen as incipient 'naturalists' (as well as 'animists') makes evident that there is no clear-cut divide between 'animists' and naturalists'. Even those who live in close association with the natural environment can 'other' it and try to control it.

I would suggest that we need to look closely at the significance of the control of certain crops – particularly grain crops, including rice in Southeast Asia (see Barker and Janowski 2011) – in developing a better understanding of the foundations for the human inclination towards a dualistic 'othering' of humans from the rest of the cosmos. People partake of more than one mode of relating to the environment in which they live and of which they are ultimately part. While the positing of different modes of thought (or ontologies, in Descola's terms) is useful in helping us to understanding the dynamics propelling groups and individuals in different directions, these should not be seen as discreet boxes. The wonderings, wanderings and thought explorations of real people cannot easily be shoehorned into just one of them.

Furthermore, I suggest that the distinction between the 'physical' and the 'interior' upon which Descola's modes rest is questionable as a universal given. I prefer to attempt an understanding of the relationship which individual Kelabit and Penan people have with their surrounding environment through seeing it as exactly that – a relationship. For the Penan and the Kelabit, the relationship with the rest of the cosmos is a relationship between the individual enspirited entity and the flow and flux of the life-stuff of the cosmos, via relationships with other enspirited entities – knots of life, in Ingold's terms. One might describe these as 'conversations' both with and within the cosmos. Such conversations do not preclude the possibility that some enspirited entities – humans, in this case – may have the notion that they are in some sense 'special' and distinct, and that they can, even should, set up relations of control over other enspirited entities – as I have argued the Kelabit do. This remains part of the ongoing conversations with and within the cosmos in which each individual being – each enspirited entity – is engaged.

Notes

1. Rodney Needham divides the Penan into Eastern and Western Penan (Needham 1972); the Western Penan live around the watershed of the Rejang river and along the Silat river in Baram District.
2. I draw on material gathered through fieldwork in Pa' Dalih in the Kelabit Highlands carried out in 1986–88 and during numerous subsequent visits, including during the course of the interdisciplinary project *The Cultured Rainforest*, a collaboration between anthropologists, archaeologists and environmental scientists. Material on the Eastern Penan also draws on material gathered during the course of *The Cultured Rainforest* project, in collaboration with Jayl Langub of University Malaysia Sarawak. *The Cultured Rainforest* was funded by the UK Arts and Humanities Research Council and carried out between 2007 and 2011. I thank the funders and my collaborators on the project for discussions and comments, particularly Jayl Langub.
3. Spellings for Penan words are those used by Mackenzie (2006) and by Brosius (1992); pending a proper analysis of the Kelabit language and the development of an accepted orthography (yet to be carried out) I have used provisional spellings for Kelabit words based on a combination of Kelabit phonemics and the spellings used by Kelabit themselves now.
4. The Great Spirit, source of *lalud* and life, now equated by older people with the Holy Spirit. See below and Janowski 2014c for further discussion of the Great Spirit.
5. This description of the heroes was used in the story of the mythical hero Tuked Rini which I recorded as told to me by Balang Pelaba of Pa' Dalih in 1987.
6. Darin Lemulun of Pa' Dalih, 16 July 2007.
7. See e.g. Janowski 1995, 2007. I suggest that the Kelabit conceive of something I have called rice-based kinship (as distinct from biological kinship) within which adulthood is founded in the ability to feed rice to others. I have suggested elsewhere (Janowski 1997) that the Kelabit see forest activities – hunting and gathering – as most appropriate for young people without children. Kelabit are nowadays strongly encouraging nomadic Penan to grow rice, and appear to consider that an entirely forest-based lifestyle, which does not activate a rice-based kinship system or any status founded in rice, is not appropriate for humans.
8. Nikolas Århem and Sven Cederroth also discuss beliefs in enspirited mountains in their contributions to this volume.
9. Many older Kelabit informants said that laughing at animals triggers 'stone rain' (*udan batuh*), which leads to petrification. Among the Penan too laughing at animals is considered liable to lead to petrification (Brosius 2001: 142–3).
10. According to Balang Pelaba of Pa' Dalih.
11. Conversations with Balang Pelaba, Lawe Padan and others in Pa' Dalih in the 1980s and 1990s; and with Pun Nibu in Pa' Mada in 2011.
12. As told to me by Balang Pelaba of Pa' Dalih in 1987 (see Janowski 2014a for the full legend and discussion of it).
13. In many Southeast Asian societies, the original source of life is conceived of as either male + female or as sexless (because not-yet-sexed), with a hierarchy sometimes clear between a primary form which is not sexed and a secondary form which is male + female. However, there is a sense in which the female principle 'stands for' the original

The dynamics of the cosmic conversation 201

unity, before division into male and female. This means that there is sometimes confusion between – or conflation of – a female or sexless source of life and one which is already divided into male and female, as is the case among the Katu of Vietnam as discussed by Kaj Århem in this volume.
14. Among the Katu in Vietnam, as discussed by Nikolas Århem in his contribution to this volume, there are also beliefs in spirits associated with individual mountains or hills.
15. Moyong Usai of Ba Puak, 16 July, 2008.
16. Asai Beret of Long Taha, 15 July 2008.
17. The idea that spirits hunt humans, just as humans hunt game animals, is also present among the Katu of Vietnam, as discussed by Kaj Århem, in this volume. He argues that this is an expression of an hierarchical (and asymmetric) ontology which underlies the Katu sacrificial idiom and asymmetric exchange system.
18. As noted above, laughing at animals causes petrification.
19. Harrisson recorded a story in Belawit, just across the border, which echoes this story, telling also of stone rain leading to widespread petrification including the petrification and collapse of the house in which people were living, caused by laughing at a dog crossing a river carrying fire. A young man who had taken shelter in a hunting shelter had his feet reversed in the petrification and resulting rock fall and people became afraid of him (Harrisson notebook 'Boundaries in Fields of Various Kelabit Villages – August 1948' p. 54, National Archives, Kuala Lumpur, 2006/0035294).
20. Among the Katu of Vietnam (Kaj Århem, this volume) there is also a myth relating how the female spirit guardian of the animals of the forest, who gives meat to humans as does Pun Tumid, originates in laughter at an animal.
21. Asai Beret of Long Taha, 15 July 2008.
22. Balang Pelaba of Pa' Dalih, February and March 1988.
23. Jayl Langub, pers. comm.
24. Jayl Langub, pers. comm.
25. Balang Pelaba and Bayeh Ripug, March 1988.
26. Balang Pelaba, March 1988.
27. Reasons for headhunting in Southeast Asia have been much discussed, with different theories advanced for its practice. An early theory was that heads are believed to contain 'soul-substance' or fertility (e.g. see Hutton 1928); this approach was criticized by Downs (Downs 1955) and Needham (1977), but has remained part of more multifacetted approaches to understanding head-hunting.
28. Brosius (2001: 144) says that the Western Penan call the spirit tiger *saang*.
29. Told to me by Asai Beret of Long Siang, 15 July, 2008.
30. Asai Beret of Long Siang, 15 July, 2008.
31. Pun Nibu of Pa' Mada, 13 August 2008.
32. In which a spirit called the *ada' senaing* lives – Lugun Bala of Pa' Dalih, 30 December 2009.
33. The *tanid/tanyit* is one of the trees from which damar resin is taken, used for lighting fires and in the past to burn on lamps.
34. Those who die prematurely or suddenly are often seen as dangerous to the living in Southeast Asia. Kaj Århem discusses this for the Katu of Vietnam (this volume).
35. Merada Ulun of Pa' Mada, 12 August 2008; and Pun Nibu of Pa' Mada, 13 August 2008.
36. Sagong Jawa and others living in Long Taha, 15 July 2008.
37. Merada Ulun of Pa' Mada, 12 August 2008.
38. The parents of the Kelabit Yahya Talla told me this.
39. Bayeh Ribuh of Pa' Dalih and Bario, 12 August 2008.
40. Sagong Jawa of Long Taha, 15 July 2008; Pun Nibu of Pa' Mada, 13 August 2008.
41. There is a widespread association in Southeast Asia between spirits and water. David Hicks, in his contribution to this volume, points to the close association between

spirits and water in Eastern Indonesia. Such beliefs relate to the association between the *naga* spirit and water.
42. Nikolas Århem (this volume) points to a similar belief among the Katu in Vietnam in spirits living in pools which reach deep into the earth as they have no apparent source.
43. Pun Nibu Ulun of Pa' Mada, 13 August 2008.
44. Stones believed to derive from lightning/thunder are also kept for the same reasons in other parts of Borneo and more widely in Southeast Asia (Hose and McDougall 1912; Evans 1913; Hutton 1926). They all appear to be prehistoric stone tools. The ones found in the Kelabit Highlands are conically shaped, with an indentation at one end. They have been the subject of some discussion in recent years and Bernard Sellato has suggested that they may have been nutcrackers (Sellato 1996). Sago starch has recently been identified on those collected by Tom Harrisson and kept at the Sarawak Museum by Huw Barton, as part of the *Cultured Rainforest* project, and it would seem that they are ancient sago pounders (Barton and Janowski 2012).
45. Moyong Usai of Ba Puak, 16 July 2008.

References

Amster, M. (1999) 'New Sacred Lands: The Making of a Christian Prayer Mountain in Highland Borneo', in R.A. Lukens Bull (ed.) *Sacred Places and Modern Landscapes: Sacred Geography and Social-Religious Transformations in South and Southeast Asia*, Tempe, Arizona: Monograph Series Press, Program for Southeast Asian Studies, Arizona State University, 131–60.

—— (2009) 'Portable Potency: Christianity, Mobility and Spiritual Landscapes among the Kelabit', *Anthropological Forum*, 19(3): 307–22.

Anderson, B. (1972). 'The idea of power in Javanese culture', in C. Holt (ed.) *Culture and Politics in Indonesia*, Ithaca, NY: Cornell University Press, 1–69.

Arnold, G. (1956?) Unpublished field diary from visit to the Kelabit Highlands.

Barker, G. (2006) *The Agricultural Revolution in Prehistory. Why did foragers become farmers?*, Oxford: Oxford University Press.

Barker, G., H. Barton, et al. (2009) 'The Cultured Rainforest Project: The Second (2008) Field Season', *Sarawak Museum Journal*, 66 (87 (New Series)): 119–84.

Barker, G. and Janowski, M. (2011) *Why Cultivate? Anthropological and Archaeological Approaches to Foraging-Farming Transitions in Southeast Asia*, Cambridge: McDonald Institute.

Barton, H. and Janowski, M. (2010) 'Reading human activity in the landscape: stone and thunderstones in the Kelabit Highlands, Sarawak', Unpublished paper presented at the European Association for South East Asian Studies (EuroSEAS) conference, Gothenburg, Sweden.

Brosius, P. (1992) 'The Axiological Presence of Death among the Penan Gang of Sarawak', Malaysia, University of Michigan. PhD thesis: University Dissertation Publications.

—— (2001) 'Local knowledge, global claims: on the significance of indigenous ecologies in Sarawak, East Malaysia', in J.A. Grim (ed.) *Indigenous Traditions and Ecology: the interbeing of cosmology and community*, Cambridge, Massachusetts: Harvard University for the Centre for the Study of World Religions, Harvard Divinity School, 125–57.

Descola, P. (2009) 'Human Natures', *Social Anthropology*, 40(2): 145–57.

Descola, P. (2013) *Beyond Nature and Culture*. Chicago, IL: University of Chicago Press.

Downs, R.E. (1955) 'Headhunting in Indonesia', *Bijdragen tot de Taal-, Land- en Volkenkunde*, 111: 40–70.

Errington, S. (1990) 'Recasting Sex, Gender and Power: A Theoretical and Regional Overview', in J.M. Atkinson and S. Errington (eds) *Power and Difference. Gender in Island Southeast Asia*, Stanford, CA: Stanford University Press, 1–58.

Evans, I.H.N. (1913) 'On a Collection of Stone Implements from the Tempassuk District British North Borneo', *Man*, 13: 154–58.

Fox, J.J. (ed.) (1980) *The Flow of Life: Essays on Eastern Indonesia, Harvard Studies in Cultural Anthropology*. Cambridge, MA and London: Harvard University Press.

Gibson, J.J. (1979) *The Ecological Approach to Visual Perception*, Boston, MA: Houghton Mifflin.

Hose, C. and McDougall, W. (1912) *The Pagan Tribes of Borneo*, London: Macmillan.

Hutton, J.H. (1920) 'Leopard-Men in the Naga Hills', *Journal of the Royal Anthropological Institute*, 50: 41–51.

—— (1926) 'The Use of Stone in the Naga Hills', *Journal of the Royal Anthropological Institute*, 56: 71–90.

—— (1928) 'The Significance of Head-Hunting in Assam', *Journal of the Royal Anthropological Institute*, 58: 329–413.

Ingold, T. (2008) 'Bindings against boundaries: entanglements of life in an open world', *Environment and Planning A*, 40: 1796–810.

—— (2011) Being Alive, Oxford: Routledge.

Janowski, M. (1988) 'The motivating forces behind changes in the wet rice agricultural system in the Kelabit Highlands', *Sarawak Gazette*, 114(1504): 9–20.

—— (1995) 'The hearth-group, the conjugal couple and the symbolism of the rice meal among the Kelabit of Sarawak', in J. Carsten and S. Hugh-Jones (eds.) *About the House: Levi-Strauss and Beyond*, Cambridge: Cambridge University Press, 84–104.

—— (1997) 'The Kelabit Attitude to the Penan: Forever Children', *La Ricerca Folklorica*, 34: 55–8.

—— (2003) *The Forest: Source of Life. The Kelabit of Sarawak*, London and Kuching: British Museum and Sarawak Museum.

—— (2004) 'The wet and the dry: the development of rice growing in the Kelabit Highlands, Sarawak', in P. Boomgard and D. Henley (eds.) *Smallholders and stockbreeders. Histories of foodcrop and livestock farming in Southeast Asia*, Leiden: KITLV, 139–62.

—— (2005) 'Kelabit names and Kelabit 'titles': grandparenthood, prestige and kinship', in J.T. Collins and Hermansyah (eds.) *The Languages and Literatures of Western Borneo: 144 Years of Research*, Bangi: ATMA UKM: 373–404.

—— (2007) 'Being 'Big', Being "Good": Feeding, kinship, potency and status among the Kelabit of Sarawak', in M. Janowski and F. Kerlogue (eds.) *Kinship and Food in Southeast Asia*, Copenhagen: NIAS Press: 93–120.

—— (2012) 'Imagining the forces of life and the cosmos in the Kelabit Highlands, Sarawak', in T. Ingold and M. Janowski (eds.) *Imagining Landscapes, Past, Present and Future*, London: Ashgate.

—— (2014a) *Tuked Rini, Cosmic Traveller. Life and Legend in the Heart of Borneo*, Copenhagen, Denmark and Kuching, Sarawak: NIAS Press and Sarawak Museum.

—— (2014b) 'Pigs and people in the Kelabit Highlands', *Indonesia and the Malay World*, 42(122): 88–112.

—— (2014c) 'Puntumid: Great Spirit of the Heart of Borneo', *Indonesia and the Malay World*, 42(133): 120–22.

Janowski, M. and Barton H. (2012) 'Reading human activity in the landscape: stone and thunderstones in the Kelabit Highlands, Sarawak', *Indonesia and the Malay World*, 40(118): 354–71.

Janowski, M., Jones, S. and Barton, H. (2013) 'Culturing the Rainforest: the Kelabit Highlands of Sarawak', in S. Hecht, K.D. Morrison and C. Padoch (eds.) *The Social Life of Forests*, Chicago, IL: Chicago University Press.

Janowski, M. and Langub, J. (2011) 'Marks and footprints in the forest: the Kelabit and the Penan of Borneo', in G. Barker and M. Janowski (eds.) *Why Cultivate? Anthropological and Archaeological Approaches to Foraging-Farming Transitions in Southeast Asia*, Cambridge: McDonald Institute, University of Cambridge.

Karim, W.J. (1981) *Ma' Betisèk Concepts of Living Things*, London: The Athlone Press.

Langub, J. (1989) 'Some Aspects of Life of the Penan', *Sarawak Museum Journal*, 50(61), 169–84.

—————— (1993) 'Hunting and Gathering: A View from Within', in V.H. Sutlive (ed.) Change and Development in Borneo. Selected Papers from the First Extraordinary Session of the Borneo Research Council, August 4–9, 1990, Williamsburg: Borneo Research Council.

Lees, S. (1979) *Drunk before Dawn*, Sevenoaks, Kent: Overseas Missionary Fellowship.

Mackenzie, I. (2006) Dictionary of Eastern Penan (unpublished).

Needham, R. (1953) *The Social Organization of the Penan, a Southeast Asian People*, University of Oxford.

—————— (1972) 'Penan', in F. LeBar (ed.) *Ethnic Groups of Insular Southeast Asia*, vol. 1, New Haven, CT: Human Relations Area Files Press.

—————— (1977) 'Skulls and Causality', *Man*, 11: 71–88.

Rubenstein, C. (1973) 'Poems of Indigenous Peoples of Sarawak - Some of the Songs and Chants. Part II', *Sarawak Museum Journal*, 21(12): 723–1127.

Sellato, B. (1983) 'Le Mythe du Tigre au Centre de Borneo', *ASEMI*, 14(1–2): 25–49.

—————— (1996) 'Stone Nutcrackers and other Recent Finds of Lithic Industry in Interior Northeastern Kalimantan', *Sarawak Museum Journal*, 71: 39–67.

10 Animism and anxiety
Religious conversion among the Kelabit of Sarawak

Matthew H. Amster

Much of the anthropological literature on animism has been concerned with identifying the defining features of what constitutes an animistic perspective, rather than considering how *animistic* thought may not necessarily be that different from other religious and non-religious modes of thought. This paper will consider a case of religious change among the Kelabit of Sarawak, Malaysia and use the Kelabit example to ultimately question whether animism, as Kelabit experienced it, is really fundamentally different from how they relate to spirits and their natural environment as Christians. As the paper outlines, over many decades of change, the Kelabit have given up the rich array of practices associated with their former animistic perspective in favor of a deep and widespread conversion to Christianity. This conversion, I argue, occurs not just due to the appeal of Christianity and the social, political, and economic contexts of modernity that make conversion appealing, but likely also has something tangible to do with the perceived onerous nature of Kelabit animism and the perceived improvements Christianity seems to offer in spiritual terms.

Kelabit commonly describe their beliefs prior to conversion as being rife with various forms of anxiety with regard to their relationship to the world. I take up this indigenous claim and consider its validity as a factor in the conversion process, in conjunction with other reasons why Christianity appealed to Kelabit, especially in terms of seeking to participate in a wider world. The key questions I seek to address concern the motivations that propelled Kelabit conversion, and what this can tell us about the nature of their animistic beliefs and practices as a lived, everyday experience prior to, during, and after conversion. I highlight here how the conversion process was one of both powerful pushes and pulls and show how the Kelabit were drawn to new beliefs, and the instrumental value associated with conversion. An important element of my argument is that Kelabit animism was in many regards a source of entrenched fear and anxiety, as well as a system of belief with life-affirming values, clear notions of power, and a system of ethics, much of which remains as Christians.

In presenting this perspective on Kelabit animism, I am aware that I have been influenced by an overwhelmingly negative bias that contemporary Kelabit have with regard to their former animistic, pre-conversion past; indeed, many Kelabit describe the past as a time without religion, when they lived by superstition or—as they often say—under the influence (or *adat*) of Satan. Having noted this source of bias, I nonetheless believe it is worth taking seriously such post-conversion narratives, not just as after-the-fact justification, recognizing the possibility that conversion may indeed been meaningfully propelled by a combination of both push and pull factors: i.e., from a desire to escape a difficult to navigate system of beliefs and the impulse to embrace new ones that seemed simpler and less stressful. Through such an analysis, I hope to offer some insight into not just why the Kelabit converted, but also the issue of why people might seek to reject an animistic orientation when exposed to an alternative set of beliefs, and what this might help us understand about the nature of so-called animistic thought.

The Conversion Context and the Kelabit People

The Kelabit are an indigenous people numbering approximately 5,000 whose rural homelands are in the interior highlands of Sarawak, Malaysia on the island of Borneo. Conversion to Christianity among the Kelabit began more than seventy years ago, with the arrival of the first evangelical missionaries in the late 1930s (Southwell 1999), and conversion can be described as having become virtually complete in the 1970s, after a major Christian revival took place in the Kelabit Highlands (Lees 1979). Kelabit are known today throughout Sarawak for both their Christian zeal and successes in urban professions, having done disproportionately well in modern professions in comparison to other indigenous groups.

The Kelabit today have a strong urban orientation, with relatively few young people remaining in the rural longhouse-based communities of the interior. Roughly three-quarters of the Kelabit population today live in coastal towns, mainly concentrated in Miri — whose economy is centered on an offshore oil industry — a source of numerous jobs to many town-based Kelabit. Among those who remain or return to the remote rural communities of the interior, rural life continues to focus on growing rice as both a subsistence and cash — or, more commonly, remittance — generating crop regularly sent to family members in towns along the coast. Most of these rural communities, namely those in the Kelabit Highlands, are close to the international frontier with Indonesia, and this is a critical positive factor in support of their local economies, providing a source of cheap seasonal labor that allow rice farms to be maintained despite large-scale outmigration of Kelabit, and as a source of marriage partners for the handful of mainly male, younger Kelabit who choose to remain or return to the highlands today (Amster 2005). The neighboring indigenous people on the other side of the border, with whom Kelabit marry and who supply much seasonal labor, are also devout Christians with a nearly identical pre-conversion set of animistic religious beliefs.

Kelabit in both rural and urban settings today universally identify themselves, and are identified by others in Sarawak, as deeply committed Christians. Many Kelabit have occupied key leadership roles in the local evangelical church (*Sidang Injil Borneo* or SIB), and most Kelabit, in both rural and urban areas, are actively engaged in some form of church participation. In the typical rural community, church services are held daily in the early morning before sunrise; these services are modestly attended, with the dominant group attending consisting of most village elders. In addition to the daily service, there are a regular assortment of evening services and impromptu prayer gatherings held multiple times a week in most communities (typically about three evenings per week), as well as the conventional and widely attended Sunday church services, which are much longer and bring the whole community together. During holidays, such as Christmas, New Years and Easter, Kelabit will often also host or attend large-scale church gatherings, including multi-day events that bring together congregations from throughout the Kelabit Highlands (as well as drawing people from or to neighboring communities in Indonesia) for prayer, singing and dancing and communal activities.

In town, church involvement is much less intense than in the rural communities, largely confined to regular Sunday worship, the meetings of youth groups and other special events. Christian prayer is always included in periodic large-scale communal events hosted by various Kelabit ethnic associations and only a few Kelabit have converted to other religions — mainly a small number of Kelabit women married to Muslim men. Many Kelabit, especially rural people, regularly participate in large-scale multi-ethnic religious retreats. The most notable of these are multi-day services typically held every other year on a makeshift temporary village and large church located deep in the wilderness near the peak of Mount Murud, an important site that has emerged as a regional prayer mountain and place for Christian retreat during the past two decades (Amster 2003).

When discussing conversion with Kelabit elders — and especially those who claim to have some knowledge of prior beliefs — Christianity is typically described as linking them to a higher power which has freed them from the daily nuisances associated with their former beliefs. In mentioning this claim, I would also note that Christian prayer for these same elders is also a type of round-the-clock and daily source of engagement. Many of these elders also described continued belief in spirits that pre-date Christianity, but believed such spiritual entities are kept at bay by the power of prayer and belief in Jesus Christ. Despite such vaguely syncretic elements – what might be better labeled 'religious synthesis' or 'recombination' (Aragon 2000: 46) – pre-conversion beliefs are nonetheless typically categorized as 'superstitions' rather than religion, following a perspective that has been taught by missionaries. Hence, elder Kelabit tend to frame conversion as providing liberation from an anxiety-filled spiritual geography of their former beliefs, which included the existence of a host of spiritual forces beyond their control. Some would occasionally comment that those spirits are still lurking out there in the forest and, in general, fear of spirits remains a part of people's lives both young and old.

In speaking with these elders, as well as their children and grandchildren, I was regularly confronted with a well-formulated narrative of negativity regarding most aspects of prior beliefs. In light of this, I have to consider whether this bias is revealing of something legitimately reflective of life prior to conversion or whether the conversion process has introduced and crystallized this negative bias. In attempting to answer this question, I turn to a more explicit consideration of some of the contours of Kelabit animism, as reconstructed through conversations with Kelabit elders.

Kelabit Animism as a Source of Anxiety

Prior to conversion, Kelabit were guided to a set of understandings about maintaining good relationships with non-human persons and entities inhabiting their social and natural world, what Ingold (2006) and others have referred to as a relational epistemology (Bird-David 1999). Their main occupation was rice farming, and communities concentrated on large, multi-family longhouses, each of which had a headman, typically of hereditary high status. Their major ritual complexes centered on large-scale longhouse feasts, the most important being mortuary rites held in conjunction with secondary burial (*burak ate*) and protective initiatory rites for children (*burak ngelua'*). Both of these periodic multi-day events — *burak ate* and *burak ngelua'* — involved copious drinking of rice beer (*burak*) and a host of ceremonies of a protective nature. For the *burak ate* (lit. 'rice-beer death feast'), the events focused on helping the soul of deceased travel safely on its journey to the other world. With the *burak ngelua'* (lit. 'rice beer blood sacrifice feast') focused on protecting children by instilling them with the gender specific skills they would need to safely transition to life as adults.[1]

In essence, these major ritual complexes were events focused on creating safe transitions in an inherently dangerous world. They afforded the opportunity to protect whole communities and to reaffirm people's relationship with, and place in, their local environment and did so via a host of practices that symbolically reaffirmed these relationships. Outside of the major ritual complexes, more spontaneous and task-specific ritual activity would also take place more or less as needed. This included the use of shamanistic trance mainly for purposes of healing, the calling of birds to offer signs or omens, dream interpretation, and the regular propitiation of spirits in the course of daily activity.

In the most general sense, the Kelabit animistic epistemology promoted a close integration of the human and non-human arenas; however, as described by elders today, they were also sources of major anxiety. Maintaining harmony was a major theme of this system of belief, including maintaining harmony between people in the same community, as quarrelling was (and still is) considered potentially dangerous to everyone in the community in which it occurred as it created an opening for dangerous spirits to intervene. Virtually all dimensions of the physical and social world were potential sources of fear and spiritual concern, often manifest – visibly, audibly or in dreams – by signs communicated by birds, animals and forest-dwelling spirits. People were in constant dialogue with nature, spirits and the broad environment, and virtually all elements of this seemingly merged social/natural environment (including weather, rocks and water, as well as living beings and dreams) were seen as having communicative, or at least informational, potential.[2] Spirits (*ada'*) not only inhabited land, the underworld, and layers of the sky, but were capable of entering one's dream states as well. Daily life under this spiritual regime regularly engendered the need for ritual action and the need to pay constant attention to signs and omens, both positive and negative. As people navigated the world, rife as it was with information of spiritual consequence, many events necessitated ritual response, and usually immediate response.

For example, in the event of the death of a woman in childbirth, as well as the case of a stillborn child, it was considered an immediate potential threat to the whole community and, of necessity, to mount a ritual response to dangers that emerged from this particular spiritual disharmony (see also Metcalf 1982: 254–56). This kind of dangerous or bad deaths (what Janowski in this volume has documented as being labelled '*mate mata*', or 'unripe deaths') was viewed by Kelabit as risky to the whole community and requiring community-wide ritual action to cleanse and protect all individuals from the perceived risks associated with what might best be described as extremely angry spirits. This meant temporarily abandoning the entire longhouse and purifying all of the inhabitants through rituals by a nearby river or stream. An obvious explanation why this particular category of death was so problematic is that they brought into contact two opposing, and typically gender divided domains, of power and spiritual concern — that of life and death, or more pertinently birth and mortuary rituals — bringing them into dangerously close proximity to each other (Amster 2003a).[3] This created a sense of urgency in which no time was wasted in disposing of the deceased body and protective ritual action taken. As this example helps illustrate, breaches of perceived natural order were themselves inherently dangerous; and the more significant such breeches, the larger the perceived threat and need for ritual response.

Within the Kelabit animistic worldview, the world was fundamentally conceptualized as having many layers, with animals and birds able to communicate signs or information that portended both hazards and positive cues to people during their daily lives. Watching or listening for signs and omens, especially bird omens, was an ongoing part of daily life that was described as requiring vigilance and care. Among the signs most commonly cited by elders as daily concerns were those linked to the movement of birds, particularly the *ngae'* or spiderhunter. Whenever a *ngae'* crossed in front of people while walking, the direction of its movement, whether right to left or left to right, was viewed as significant, one being auspicious and the other inauspicious. Bad omens would inevitably force people to stop doing their intended task — whether working a farm, setting out on a journey or hunting — and to perform small rituals right on the spot with the aim of having the situation confirmed or disconfirmed, a process that involved further observation of birds and interpretation of their movements. Even more potent than common low-flying birds such as the spiderhunter, which appeared with regularity, were less commonly sighted birds such as eagles (*keniu*) and other large soaring birds, and these were considered especially powerful sources of information, including grave warnings of greater overall importance. This is probably due to their ability to transmit messages across larger layers of sky. Eagles would be ritually called in ceremonies by specialists to gain important information, such as confirmation about the spread of an epidemic or consulted before weighty decisions, such as with regard to the timing of holding of major rituals or prior to moving a longhouse.

In addition to birds, many other animals were considered capable of conveying warnings via their calls or linked to misfortune merely by accidentally sighting or hearing them. Features of landscape and weather were also meaningful too, and

Kelabit attributed dangers to entering particular geographic spaces, such as springs and salt licks where animals go to drink (*rupan*). They also had well-defined concepts of prohibited places, *tana da'at* or 'bad land', including places where people had died unnatural or untimely deaths, such as the aforementioned death of a woman in childbirth, would be placed. Other locations to be avoided included the homes of water spirits along the bends of rivers, certain anthills, and areas of forest used for the final placement of deceased (see Janowski, this volume). There were prohibitions and restrictions attached to many tasks and objects, particularly those objects considered to be for exclusive use by either females or males, and to break such taboos was considered hazardous, leading to death or disease. In this regard, hunting rituals, such as the ritual incisions made to newly hunted prey, were strongly taboo for women to witness, and, similarly, men were restricted from being present at the onset of harvest rituals when the first symbolic collection of rice took place. Even the objects associated with these activities were entirely prohibited from being touched or seen by the opposite gender. Food prohibitions were rife as well, and often connected with major life events such as birth, death and pregnancy – though the food taboos during pregnancy were considered somewhat special since they were not gender specific and shared by both expecting parents. In short, pre-conversion Kelabit life, as described by elders in the mid-1990s, was full of restrictions and the list of possible dangerous transgressions they could cite was quite long. Rousseau (1998) describes a similar spiritual context among the neighboring Kayan, who 'were burdened with a staggering number of taboos' (ibid.: 61) and for whom 'taboos and omens created a world in which one's actions were constantly regulated and scrutinized by supernatural beings, where the pervasive expectation of supernatural danger echoes the possibility of attacks by headhunters' (ibid.: 62).[4]

The essential underpinning of these practices was the understanding that one was engaged in intimate and ongoing conversation or dialogue with spiritual elements inhabiting local geography. If we are to take the perspective of the Kelabit elders with whom I collected this ethnohistorical material at face value, many of these engagements were indicative of the manifold interconnectedness of Kelabit with their surroundings, though often decidedly tinged with fear. As Ingold (2006) has astutely noted, there is a creative, constantly unfolding, element to such a worldview, one which he describes, borrowing a Cree phrase, is akin to 'continuous birth' (11). However, given what I have just described, one might amend this to add the caveat that living in such a worldview has many elements of continuous death as well. Forces of life and death were both always present in people's minds as they navigated this merged spiritual/natural world, rife as it is with the possibility of bountiful harvests and joyful births and the ever-present threat of poor crops, epidemics, and ill health. Thus, Kelabit were closely attuned to the natural world, and appear to have experienced it as a source of useful practical information, including information that offered both warnings and affirmations as people sought to make sense of, and respond to, a complicated web of information that permeated their daily lives. Kelabit were (and probably still are as Christians) deeply embedded in what Ingold (2006) has called a 'domain of entanglement' (ibid.: 14) and many of these entanglements were anxiety producing, just as others were (and still are) life affirming.

Kelabit today justify conversion in part by putting emphasis on the onerous aspects of their former beliefs, while downplaying examples that might be interpreted as positive.[5] Among elders, it was commonplace to speak about the daily annoyances of dealing with bird omens as a negative feature of pre-conversion life, whereas conversation with younger Kelabit, who have much more limited knowledge from which to draw, the tendency is to focus on a few well-trod examples of what they see as the most overtly *sinful* elements of their old culture. The two most common such examples given by younger Kelabit are headhunting and former practices of infanticide, the latter reportedly performed upon the birth of twins or in instances when certain prohibitions were not properly observed. For example, I was told about the former taboo restricting a pregnant woman from sighting a wild snake which, I was assured, would require she bury alive her child upon its birth. While this example is admittedly extreme (and likely unusual), it has helped reinforce the post-conversion perspective that their former beliefs were the work of Satan (and it would also have been an effective barrier from having a women wander too far afield into a potentially dangerous forest while pregnant). These practices were presented as evidence of the misguidedness of their former beliefs. However, even after infanticide ceased to be considered an option, it was still a common practice to try to separate twins at birth by adopting out one or both to another family, and/or to rename one or both of them to trick the 'spirits', as a means to avoid danger, suggesting that spiritual anxiety about twins persists even today. The larger point here is that in conversations about the past, virtually all Kelabit expressed views regarding the problematic and untenable aspects of their former beliefs, even as many such beliefs have not been entirely abandoned. While this orientation should not be surprising, given their zealousness as Christians, it also does not mean that there isn't an element of truth to fact that such beliefs were a source of anxiety in the past and a likely factor that helped motivate conversion.

The Lure of Christianity

Having briefly considered these onerous features of Kelabit animism — albeit through the biased lens of Christian converts — I turn to a more explicit discussion of factors that compelled Kelabit to embrace Christianity. I focus here on a number of potential advantages to conversion, both in terms of the social, political, and economic contexts of the conversion experience, as well as some of the ways that a newly conceived, and certainly more mobile and broader, spiritual relationship to geographic space was made possible by conversion. Animism, as the previous section has shown, created numerous connections to local geography, including relationships to spiritual forces that created a sense of restriction in terms of people's movement and activity in physical space. In contrast, Christianity provided a kind of mobile spiritual regime, allowing for a kind of *portable potency* in which people could better navigate a wider spiritual world, while facilitating the ongoing ability to imbue and re-inscribe local/regional spaces with potent spiritual meanings in new, Christian terms (Amster 2009).

Kelabit have naturally conflated being Christian with notions of progress, improvement, and engagements with modernity — a process that began most profoundly during World War II and has continued to the present. The earliest overt exposure to Christianity in the Kelabit Highlands dates back to the late 1930s, when the Australian, Protestant, evangelical missionary C. Hudson Southwell walked into the region and tried to convince some local leaders to convert, only to find that 'the people were not yet willing for a complete change from the old pagan ways' (Southwell 1999: 98). According to Southwell's account and that of elder Kelabit, there was initial resistance to Christianity, in large measure due to the belief that it would require giving up the drinking of *burak* (rice beer) — a crucial and valued component to Kelabit communal life, as well as a core feature of major rituals. Christianity was thus initially resisted by leaders (Southwell 1999: 190–1). During this same period, in the late 1930s, a group of Kelabit young men traveled to and attended a bible school in Belawit, across the border in Dutch (now Indonesian) territory. When they returned they attempted to convert people in their home communities, with only slightly better success. Then, a few years after this, allied troops dramatically parachuted into the Kelabit Highlands to organize the local population to fight against the Japanese, and during that period the desire to convert became more widespread, this despite being discouraged from converting by the Allied commanding officer, Major Tom Harrisson (Harrisson 1984 [1959]).

Oral accounts from elders who were present at the time indicate that Kelabit were impressed with the capabilities of these troops and that they were curious about their religion as well. One aspect of this curiosity toward these Western military airmen was their obvious disregard for omens and prohibitions that might have restricted movement and the fact that they could ignore such things with no ill consequences. Harrisson himself (who married into the community and maintained a home in the Kelabit Highlands after the war) was deeply opposed to Kelabit religious conversion, yet also aware of his own role in helping to inspire the mass-conversions that occurred during and after his occupying force was present in the Kelabit Highlands:

> There had already been some Christian missionary activity, most effectively from the Dutch side, before the Japanese occupation. But the great majority of inland people were much too afraid of the past to overthrow old superstitions. It was one of the inevitable and in some ways saddest repercussions of our sudden appearance that, almost overnight, these traditions had to be reconsidered and revaluated... I suppose I was one of the last people in the western world who wished to upset and alter other people's beliefs as such. But it would have been impossible to have conducted any operations had we followed local observances and determined the movement of our runners — or our aeroplanes — by the position of the first barking deer to sound off on the track in the morning, or the direction in which an eagle was last seen to be soaring over the mountains at sunset.
>
> (Harrisson 1985[1959]: 236)

While Harrisson (whose ego was apparently considerable) may overstate his own role in inspiring conversion — as clearly the motivations for conversion were multifaceted — there is no question that during that time Kelabit were deeply impressed with the weapons, planes, and supplies of his men, and logically saw them as connected to a superior regime of spiritual power. One of the more significant events of this period was the building of an airstrip in the Kelabit Highlands. After the war this provided much easier access to missionaries who frequented the Kelabit Highlands. Many Kelabit, men especially, were invited to enroll in bible school in Lawas, thus ushering in an era of nearly universal Kelabit conversion and internal missionization. Another facet of conversion that cannot be ignored or understated is that it helped to undermine, and eventually nearly eliminate, indigenous conceptions of hereditary class differences that were a critical aspect of former beliefs. Christianity, as a kind of equal opportunity religion, not only allowed commoners to become religious leaders, but it actively undermined and challenged a range of restrictions and expectations about longhouse behavior that had been linked to the authority of traditional leaders and their hereditary class positions.

Conversion, it must also be emphasized, was a gradual and ongoing process for the Kelabit. Practices, such as the drinking of *burak*, were reported to have persisted into the 1950s and 1960s, despite being labeled sinful. In the early 1970s, during the Christian revival movement that took place in the Kelabit Highlands, many of the lingering practices associated with former beliefs still in place — such as the use of magical charms and the keeping of skulls — were actively purged by this youth-centered movement. Speaking in tongues was also widespread during the revival, and people in the highlands, led by schoolchildren, became focused on what they saw as the advent of the Holy Spirit (Lees 1979). Certain aspects of this revival movement in the Kelabit Highlands subsequently spread to neighboring Lun Bawang people to the north, which eventually led to the emergence of Mount Murud as a prayer mountain in the mid-1980s, where Kelabit remain key participants today (Amster 2009).

In addition to Christianity's obvious association with powerful outsiders and the opportunities it provided as an escape from at least some of the anxieties associated with former beliefs, including the traditional class distinctions mentioned above, it also offered advantages in terms of facilitating participation in the wider world. As I discuss in depth elsewhere (Amster 1999), by embracing Christianity, Kelabit have adopted a set of beliefs that no longer depend on the local spiritual geography to generate spiritual meanings. In addition to linking them to broader structures of power from the outsider world, it provides new avenues to articulate important regional pan-ethnic ties with neighboring indigenous groups. Christianity has also proved flexible enough to generate new ways for articulating spiritual connection to local landscapes in a new Christian idiom, as phenomena such as the local prayer mountain movement illustrate (Amster 2003).

An important question that remains to be asked is the extent to which conversion changed the way Kelabit think about the world and if there are fundamental differences in the ways animistic practices and beliefs oriented them to their sense of place in and relationship to their natural surroundings. As Monica Janowski has argued in this volume, Kelabit animists (as rice farmers) exhibited a greater effort to control land than the neighboring, and nomadic, Penan. It may be as well that, as Christians, they have sought to extend this control even further. Certainly, there are examples of how conversion has changed the way Kelabit relate to the natural/spiritual world and others that show continuity with the past. As Aragon has noted in a study of Christian conversion among an indigenous group in Sulawesi, 'Tobaku highlanders have adopted Protestantism wholeheartedly and yet never banished themselves — or, significantly, the Christian God — from the realm of a single interactive cosmos' (2000: 243). As with many other indigenous people who have converted to Christianity, Kelabit obviously still tend to relate to notions of agentive spirits, whether that be the Holy Spirit or others.[6] Furthermore, the notion that disharmony or quarrelling in the community is a spiritual hazard clearly persists, though now the ill consequence would likely be something expressed in a Christian idiom, such as possession by evil spirits associated with the Devil, suggesting a kind of replacement of one spiritual anxiety for another. Furthermore, the intensity with which Kelabit in rural areas pray and hold church services suggests that, even if they have rejected beliefs relating to the vast array of omens and taboos that were part of pre-conversion life, they still see the need to be spiritually vigilant on a continual, daily, basis, and this resembles the kind of deep, interactive, immersive experience that is part and parcel of how an animistic orientation is typically understood. Hence, just as Kelabit paid close attention to birds and animal calls on the way to their farms in the past, it is typical now that people would instead pray when embarking on many of their daily tasks. And while Kelabit have tended to demonize animistic practices, suggesting that they perceive a fundamental break with the past, it appears that their brand of Christianity has, in many respects, replaced one set of all-consuming beliefs with another. Many Kelabit (rural elders especially) still go about their lives as if they are traversing the world as a kind of deeply meaningful spiritual landscape laden with potential danger and though the content of this spiritual engagement has radically changed, in many respects they're still living in a 'domain of entanglement' (Ingold 2006: 14).

Conclusion

In the recent book *Soul Hunters*, about a group of Yukaghir animistic hunters in Siberia, Willerslev (2007) critiques two extremes in the anthropology of animism. On the one hand are approaches of early theorists like Tylor and continued in the work of some modern contemporary anthropologists (Guthrie 1993), which discount the truth-value of animistic beliefs. At the other extreme are contemporary theorists who take animism more seriously in cognitive and symbolic terms, but whose work risks presenting a romanticized view of animists as uniquely in tune with their surroundings. While Willerslev appears to appreciate the current focus in anthropology, in that it draws attention to the relational elements of animism as a kind of cognitive perspective (within which he highlights the important role of mimesis as a key process), he also raises concern over how such an approach leads to undo emphasize on difference over sameness — i.e., the tendency to treat animists as having a more deeply immersive experience vis-à-vis the world they live in than others. Willerslev points out that a so-called Western perspective is presumed to be infused with a kind of Cartesian dualism, in contrast to animists who are (in his view, falsely) presented as having a 'basic affinity with the world,' something that 'Western society has supposedly lost' (2007: 187).

In drawing attention to this as a kind of false dichotomy, Willerslev argues instead that animists — or at least those among whom he has worked — are able to move back and forth between what we associate with as being an animistic relational experience in their surroundings, and one in which they are also capable of separating themselves and can clearly distinguish the human realm as separable from that of spirits and animals. He thus posits that Yukaghir hunters will only temporarily become like the elk they are hunting as a means to seduce and kill them, and that they move across this threshold of sameness and difference with ease. In essence, Willerslev argues that Yukaghir hunters are not trapped in a way of thinking marked by an immersive, relational epistemology but actively engaged in pursuing their own agency in relation to the world in which they live as humans (and thus separate from the non-human world).

> What I mean to suggest by this is that if we are to take animism seriously, we must abandon the idea of total coincidence (the Heideggerian tradition) or total separation (the Cartesian tradition) and account for the mode of being that puts us into contact with the world yet separates us from it.
> (Willerslev 2007:190–91)

Hence, rather than view the Yukaghir animistic epistemology as fundamentally exhibiting a kind of immersed harmony with nature, as Graham Harvey (2006) generally implies to be the rule among animists, Willerslev's argues that animists selectively move in and *out* of this kind of relational dialogue with the world around them, as can be the case for people in virtually any culture, and not just a characteristic of an animistic orientation.

The implication of Willerslev's argument is that animists do not live in a seamless world in which spirits, people, and nature are always inexorably interconnected and inseparable. As I have sought to show here, Kelabit animists were certainly deeply immersed in their beliefs, but at least in the context of the conversion process, they could also perceive of themselves as distinctly human and separate from the merged spiritual/natural world that they lived in close contact with. Furthermore, as I have attempted to show here as well, as Christians, Kelabit have not simply severed their ties to their immediate surroundings and abandoned the immersive experience of being religious, rather widened its scope to encompass a wider world and what they see as simply more powerful spiritual allegiances, all of which, I argue, serves as the basis for understanding a diverse and complex set of motivations helping propel an ongoing process of conversion and change.

It should come as no surprise then that, as Christians, Kelabit continue to seek out causal explanations for misfortune that resemble those of their seemingly rejected animistic past. One might argue it is entirely human to do so. As with Hallowell's classic study of Ojibwa ontology (2002 [1960]) — a group who was also already influenced by Christian concepts at the time of his writing — Kelabit continue to see links between bad behavior and fear spiritual consequences. Indeed one will often hear after the fact sorts of explanations for misfortune, including about the danger upsetting the harmony of a community, that seem to be consistent with the animistic logic they claim to have abandoned as superstitious as well as that of Christian teachings. Kelabit tend to also see Christianity as providing an overarching blanket of security, one that has not entirely displaced their way of thinking about their place in the world or the relational balance that life entails, but rather serves as an ever more powerful trump card. The fact that some of these primordial forces are still perceived to be out there by some, does not make them any less devout as Christians, but rather can further reinforce their commitment and belief (see, for example, Aragon 2000; Amster 2003). In this sense, I would argue, having a relational epistemology is not unique to Kelabit animism but can extend to Kelabit Christianity as well, just as having a more dualistic sense of engagement with the world is probably not unique to life as Christian moderns, but likely was part of the broad cognitive palette available to Kelabit as animists as well.

Perhaps it is overly simplistic to try to pigeonhole animism as fundamentally different from other modes of religious thought, at least as a kind of moral system. Harvey, for instance, has awkwardly asserted that '(i)nherent in animist distinctions between animate persons and inanimate objects is the notion that the ability to relate is definitive and brings with it the obligation to attempt to relate well' (2006: 48). As such, he emphasizes that 'respectful engagement is the central moral imperative of animism' (Harvey 2006: 99). However, there is a fine line between respect and fear, and it is hard to ignore Kelabit claims about their sense of anxiety and danger they recall as animists. The fact that Kelabit, or any group who converts, might actively choose to reject deeply held beliefs that are or were imbued with fear, anxiety and restrictiveness shows that they were both immersed in these beliefs, but also capable of choosing an alternative. While conversion to Christianity has by no means abolished fear – nor probably the tendency to be immersed in a kind of dialogue with one's surroundings – it has certainly given Kelabit a greater sense of agency and allowed them to take a more proactive role in asserting their place in a changing, and still deeply animated, world.

Notes

1. Headhunting was likely a third important source of major ritual activity, and likely fits into a ritual cycle with the *burak* feasts, as Metcalf (1982) has shown to be the case among the Berawan who articulate an explicit link between mortuary and headhunting. Skulls collected during headhunting were certainly used in the initiation of boys as part of *burak ngelua'*. However, headhunting was a subject about which the elders I consulted claimed to know very little and were also reluctant to discuss. Headhunting likely ceased in the Kelabit Highlands around the turn of the twentieth century, roughly thirty years prior to conversion, so it is also likely that those elders I worked with had limited first-hand knowledge, and were probably concerned about discussing the topic for fear of highlighting any perceived misdeeds of their ancestors.

2. Rousseau has noted an interesting distinction on this point regarding the neighbouring Kayan, who, he claims, 'do not perceive omens and divination as sources of information, but as indices about reality. In other words, omens and divination are not messages' (1998: 73). Given that my material is more reconstructed and ethnohistocial than it is observed and ethnographic, it is difficult for me to tease out whether such a distinction would have held for the Kelabit or not.
3. A similar symbolic logic is noted by Howell who documents the Chewong belief that a pregnant women 'must under no circumstances look upon a dead body' due to the fact that "while life... is in the process of being created, it must not be put in contact with death" (1989: 191).
4. Interestingly, the broader focus of Rousseau's monograph is on religious changes he observed among the Kayan in the 1970s, most notably their efforts to reform their indigenous religion in such a way as to do away with most of the taboos and omens that most plagued them, while trying to retain other features of their spiritual life (a movement known as *Adat Bungan*).
5. One obvious exception here concerns *traditional* practices of name changing that have been retained and modified to fit into their lives as Christian and still involve major ceremonies today. For a detailed analysis of how the Kelabit have selectively maintained these former practice see: Amster 1999.
6. I often heard people comment on the existence of angry spirits still feared in the forest, such as that of a young child who was shot in a hunting accident, and even occasionally traditional pre-Christian spirits, such as Pun Tumid (a mountain spirit) that more than one elder professed belief in. Even if such spirits can be rendered relatively powerless by Christian prayer, the fact that some still think of them as real is interesting, implying the possibility of holding dual beliefs, a concept taken up in depth by Robbins (2004).

References

Amster, M.H. (1999) '"Tradition", ethnicity, and change: Kelabit practices of name changing', *Sarawak Museum Journal*, 54(75): 183–200.

────── (2003) 'New sacred lands: The making of a Christian prayer mountain in Highland Borneo', in R.A. Lukens-Bull (ed.) *Sacred places and modern landscapes: Sacred geography and social-religious transformations in South and Southeast Asia*, Tempe, AZ: Monograph Series Press, Program for Southeast Asian Studies, Arizona State University, 131–60.

────── (2003a) 'Gender complementarity and death among the Kelabit', in W.D. Wilder (ed.) *Journeys of the soul: Anthropological studies of death, burial, and reburial practices in Borneo*, Philips, ME: Borneo Research Council, Inc., 251–307.

────── (2005) 'Cross-border marriage in the Kelabit Highlands of Borneo', *Anthropological Forum*, 15(2): 131–50.

────── (2009) 'Portable potency: Christianity, mobility and spiritual landscapes among the Kelabit', *Anthropological Forum*, 19(3): 307–22.

Aragon, L.V. (2000) *Fields of the Lord: Animism, Christian Minorities, and State Development in Indonesia*, Honolulu, HI: University of Hawai'i Press.

Bird-David, N. (1999) '"Animism" Revisited: Personhood, Environment, and Relational Epistemology', *Current Anthropology*, 40 (Supplement): 67–91.

Guthrie, S. (1993) *Faces in the Clouds: A New Theory of Religion*, New York, NY: Oxford University Press.

Hallowell, A.I. (2002) [1960] 'Ojibwa ontology, behavior, and world view', in G. Harvey (ed.) *Readings in Indigenous Religions*, London: Continuum, 17–49.

Harrisson, T. (1984) [1959] *World within: A Borneo story*, Singapore: Oxford University Press.

Harvey, G. (2006). *Animism: Respecting the Living World*, New York, NY: Columbia University Press.

Howell, S. (1989) *Society and Cosmos: Chewong of Peninsular Malaysia*, Chicago, IL: The University of Chicago Press.

Ingold, T. (2006) 'Rethinking the Animate, Re-Animating Thought', *Ethnos*, 71(1): 9–20.

Lees, S.P. (1979) *Drunk before dawn*, Southampton: Overseas Missionary Fellowship.

Metcalf, P. (1982) *A Borneo Journey into Death: Berawan Eschatology from Its Rituals*, Philadelphia, PA: University of Pennsylvania Press.

Robbins, J. (2004) *Becoming Sinners: Christianity and Moral Torment in a Papua New Guinea Society*, Berkeley, CA: University of California Press.

Rousseau, J. (1998) *Kayan Religion: Ritual Life and Religious Reform in Central Borneo*, Leiden: KITLV Press.

Southwell, C.H. (1999) *Uncharted waters*, Calgary, Canada: Astana Publishing.

Willerslev, R. (2007) *Soul Hunters: Hunting, Animism and Personhood among the Siberian Yukaghirs*, Berkeley, CA: University of California Press.

11 Boundaries of humanity

Non-human others and animist ontology in Eastern Indonesia

Timo Kaartinen

Animism refers to cosmological thinking which presupposes a common ground between different kinds of subjects, typically humans and animals. Nineteenth century anthropologists defined it as an early form of religion which attributed a soul to animals and objects and endowed them with imagined, human qualities (Tylor 1903: 247). When Émile Durkheim argued that the object of belief was not the spirit of animals but the sacred power of society (Durkheim 1965), he continued to support the idea that religious worldviews project the human, institutional order onto nature.

Recent efforts to move anthropology beyond its humanist, Enlightenment underpinnings has called into question this human-centric theory of religion, even as it has revived animism as an anthropological topic. This theoretical agenda is not entirely new: it rehearses the intellectualist approach to religion introduced by Claude Lévi-Strauss (Turner 2009). Nevertheless, it has produced new ethnographic descriptions and debate which point to animism as a valid epistemology (Bird-David 1999), an ontology in which people and animals differ in their bodily nature but share a human, spiritual essence (Descola 2006: 141; 2009), or a type of intentionality which is expressed in hunting, healing, and other actions that transmit life force from one species or cosmological domain to another (Viveiros de Castro 2004: 469).

In this chapter, I ask what elements of this new concept of animism apply to the ethnographic context of Maluku, the vast archipelago of Eastern Indonesia. This article is organized around three arguments made in the new animism debate: that animistic peoples attribute human consciousness to non-human beings (Descola 2006: 141), treat certain animals, plants and objects as persons (Viveiros de Castro 2004: 469), and sometimes assume their mode of perceiving reality.

The celebrated cases of animism are drawn from the ethnography of Amerindian peoples, who often frame the interaction between humans and animals as exchange, seduction or warfare. My ethnographic reference is to societies for which the commercial, social and political interaction with strangers presents similar ontological issues as hunters face in their encounters with animals. Among these is what Eduardo Viveiros de Castro (2004) calls 'perspectival exchange', the assumption of an animal perspective on humanity.

Spirit Guardians, Free Spirits, and the Spirits of the Dead

People in the Kei Islands often refer to the taboos and metaphysical punishments as an 'unwritten law'. This law does not pretend to be a universal moral code. Its rules and punishing agents are immanent in each local island, a local world which is centered on a real or imaginary mountain in the interior of the island. New visitors and settlers are warned that people who transgress the law risk being attacked by invisible beings which populate the forest. These beings guard springs, rivers, rocks and large trees. They dwell in places where an open beach changes into a bush, or around rocky capes which mark the boundary between two village settlements.

The unwritten law was also recognized by the people of Banda Eli, the coastal, Muslim community in the eastern coast of the Great Kei Island where I did fieldwork in 1994–1996. This village was founded by people exiled from the central Maluku Islands of Banda after the Dutch East India Company conquered their ancestral home in the early seventeenth century.[1] The descendants of the Bandanese have kept their own language and Islamic faith, but on settling in Kei four centuries ago they also promised to observe the taboos and rituals through which people in Kei manage their relationship to the invisible world of guardian spirits, ancestral shadows and other invisible agents in their environment.

Even if spirit is not an entirely satisfying word for describing such beings, I will use it as shorthand for different types of metaphysical entities. The word spirit has a connotation of immaterial existence and determined moral qualities, neither of which are central for Eastern Indonesian concepts for such beings (Valeri 2000: 24). For present purposes, the most important question about spirits is how they resemble humanity and what kinds of relations they form with humans.

The main clue to the human qualities of different spirits is the way they interact with humans. Spirits react to the breach of taboos, things that are forbidden and yet the objects of suppressed desire. This means that they respond to human intentions, and not merely to people's external acts or gestures. To do so, it seems, the spirits also have to be intentional agents. But how can we know if they have human intentions? One way of measuring this is to ask whether it is possible to establish and maintain relationships with them. A relationship with a spirit means that one gets a predictable response when one repeats a certain act or gesture in the spirit's presence. This response – imagined or not – is a sign of the spirit's awareness of rules, or positive schemes of action, an awareness which is one hallmark of human consciousness.

In this section, I discuss different types of spirits in the light of these diagnostics of their intentional and human qualities. Three kinds of spirits are worth mentioning because of their family resemblance to similar categories over a wide area. The first kind are the 'owners' or 'guardians' of trees, springs, and various sites in the forest and along the coast (see also Nikolas Århem and Janowski, this volume). In spite of their low status in Banda Eli society, shamans (*sewa*) are in a privileged position to communicate with such beings. As they divine the cause of illness or affliction they turn away from the human audience and speak to the 'people of the mountains'. People of Banda Eli also address spirit guardians with prayers and material offerings when they plant a garden, build a house or exorcise illness from their village. In these contexts, the spirit is called the 'lord of the land' (Ind. *tuan tanah*).

The widespread concept of landlord conveys the sense in which Eastern Indonesian places and landscapes are always already owned by spirits and people. A similar notion of spirit ownership is found in the highland societies of Papua-New Guinea (Robbins 2004: 168), and Janowski (this volume) reports it among the Kelabit of Sarawak. An imagined chain between present and former landowners extends beyond village boundaries and historical memory and connects particular groups and places to each other. The link to the original landowner is recognized explicitly in a house-building ritual which takes place just before sunrise and repeats the mythical event at which the spirit of the first human, together with a rooster, arrived in the village (Barraud 1979: 81).[2] I have witnessed this ritual on my very first visit to the Banda Eli village in 1992, and as late as in 2009 among villagers who had recently moved to an urban area in the Kei Islands. The residents of the new house present betel leaves and areca nut to the spirit owner of the land where their house will stand and smear each house-post with the blood of a young chicken offered on the site. After this they raise the central pole that will hold up the roof.

The relatively localized spirit owners or guardians stand in contrast with another main type of metaphysical agents: the free spirits. Free spirits is my gloss for entities known as *bel wab* in the Kei Islands, and also called 'satans' (*setan*) by Muslims and Christians. These potentially malicious entities are described as 'small, angry men who act quickly' to punish people for breaking taboos. They are a species of *hilang-hilang*, the 'disappeared' or 'unseen', which also include people who died on long travels or drowned in the sea, and therefore never received a proper burial. The forest teems with these beings, and people avoid bringing young children to garden sites because of their vulnerability to illness and affliction. They suspect that a person suffering from mental illness, unconsciousness or fever has been made to disappear by the *bel wab* in punishment of some major breach of taboo, such as marriage or sexual relations between siblings, or between a man and a woman who are kin and belong to different generations. When illness or death is attributed to such spirit attack, the remedy is a ritual called *hukum* in which a slight amount of material from a valuable object is scratched and dropped to a hole in a ground.[3]

A third type of spirit agents is associated with recently dead people. A properly conducted funeral localizes the dead permanently in the village. Over a few years' time they cease to exist as distinct personalities and become part of the anonymous community of ancestors which is seen a protective, benevolent power. The Keiese refer to the spirits of the dead as *nitu*, while the people of Banda Eli only refer to *tua-tua*.

All dead people do not become benevolent ancestral beings. People who die on a long voyage, or who for other reasons cannot receive a proper burial, join the beings called *hilang-hilang*, 'disappeared people'. In Banda Eli, this category also covered the free spirits (*setan* or *bel wab*).

The Kei Islands' concepts of different spirits are not clear-cut categories. People avoid making general statements about spirits, and usually mention them when they talk about a particular place. For instance, one is warned against defecating near the spirit's abode at the end of the beach or harvesting and eating the products from a garden planted less than forty days ago.

Following such rules and talking about them is a source of certainty and value. It is conceivable to be accepted by a spirit by showing respect to it, in the same way as one acts on one's obligations toward other people and recognizes the values of social life. As Signe Howell (this volume) suggests, proper behavior toward spirits of this kind is defined by rules by which people conceive of order in their world. The superhuman beings who cause misfortune to the Chewong 'do not move in mysterious ways' (Howell 1989: 207). In this sense, they are a source of stability, rather than of anxiety and hazard.

It is harder to see how the free spirits of Eastern Indonesia could have stable relationships with human beings. They threaten people with malign attacks and punishments. Often the cause of the attack is not the breaching of a taboo by the victim, but a transgression by some other person. If spirit guardians can be seen as an extension of the cultural order in which intentional beings recognize each other by following rules, free spirits show no sign of such ethical rationality. Human interaction with spirits includes, but is not limited to, moral relations between personal beings: the spirit world includes beings which people are not capable of addressing as persons. If, as I have suggested, free spirits are intentional beings, they reflect the potential of human intentionality to destroy sociality as well as to create it (Kapferer 1997: 264; Turner 2009: 31).

Invisible People

What might be called Kei Islands animism consists of practices for managing the tension between humans and non-humans in the immanent world (Remme, this volume; Scott 2007). Whereas some spirits, particularly those associated with land, house and village, can be engaged in benevolent association with humans (Forth 1998: 121), free spirits are potentially malign and morally ambiguous beings that may nevertheless provide benefits for particular people (ibid.: 147). The encounters with them signal access to a dangerous and illicit source of wealth and power (ibid.: 115; Hoskins 1993: 224), and the relations with them are often framed as marriage (Spyer 1997: 523). While the distinction between spirits and human souls may otherwise be emphasized (Forth 1998: 47), these categories overlap in the figure of the witch as an inverted human being (ibid.: 56).

It is tempting to think that the spirit owner or guardian, unlike other, wild types of spirits, stands for the stabilized relational system of human society and its given objective conditions of existence. This, however, is the view which Philippe Descola discards as 'sociocentric prejudice'. He defends the 'ontological' view of animism by arguing that 'social realities – i.e., stabilized relational systems – are analytically subordinated to ontological realities – i.e., the systems of properties that humans ascribe to beings' (Descola 2006: 139).

We should not underestimate the degree to which many Eastern Indonesian societies, including Banda Eli, are structured by social hierarchy and exchange. Whereas mobile hunting societies have fewer ways of objectifying social relationships, the structured village societies of the Kei Islands have a greater impulse to stabilize the identities of persons and groups. Descola's analytic priorities must therefore be compared to the sociological and ontological priorities found in the ethnographic context. But Descola's argument is helpful for recognizing that Eastern Indonesian animism involves human engagements with wild and angry taboo-guarding spirits (and animals and plants) as well as the spirit guardians who in some sense share people's moral perceptions and interests. I will therefore follow Descola's lead and take a closer look at what I have called free spirits.

By all accounts I have heard, free spirits in Kei are not reflective beings, but respond blindly to human behavior that makes them feel anger, fear, curiosity or desire. The risk of becoming a victim of their attack appears to be greatest in densely peopled places with a long history of settlement. Occasionally, travelers who face misfortune in a foreign land interpret it as the presence of evil spirits. Paradoxically, however, people are most concerned about the influence of free spirits when they are at home, in the familiar environment where social humanity is expressed in predictable movements, skills, habits and diet. This is the field of reproductive relationships, the domain in which different life forces flow together. The abundance of fertility, which many Eastern Indonesian myths associate with the autochthonous world, creates an abject sense of being in the presence of invisible others.

The broad lines of Eastern Indonesian spirit classification were present in the context of my fieldwork in the Kei Islands. Particularly the boundary between the world of visible, ordinary social experience and the world of 'disappeared', unseen and unseeing beings is of comparative interest. Versions of this parallel can be found across Maluku. Among the Buli of Halmahera, in the northern part of the archipelago, the greatest metaphysical risk posed by former human beings is witchcraft which deprives a living human being of his or her consciousness or 'shadow'. The victim is turned into a living dead, but other people do not recognize this immediately because he or she is animated by the shadow of the witch (*suangi*). An orderly transmission of the shadow from one person to another may involve the reincarnation of a grandparent in a small child (Bubandt 1998: 55). This is an indication that the alien quality of the unseen powers is related to the fundamental otherness which obtains between parents and children, in spite of their intimate, caring relationships.

In his ethnography of the Korowai society of West Papua, Rupert Stasch (2009: 96) argues that such intimacy with the 'other side' expresses a broader ontology of otherness. The most intimately connected people, such as parents and children, are fundamentally alien to each other because their formative experiences and social relations do not coincide. Children do not dwell in the same time and space as their parents: they marry off, build their own houses, and get friends who are their own age. The Korowai imagine that such experiences of otherness result from a circulation of personal identities between visible and invisible sides or territories. When a visible person dies, he or she is reborn as a baby on the invisible side. Later, after dying on that side, the person is reborn on the visible side as a successor to the earlier visible person (ibid.: 97).

The other side of the Korowai is reminiscent of the inverted reality of the disappeared in the Kei Islands. In both places, there is a notion of invisible people who inhabit the treetops and streams of the perceptible world. The Korowai sometimes identify these people with birds and fish. They also call them *xenanop*, 'angry people', further emphasizing their foreign, malign character. They are emotionally alien, in addition to being visually and socially separate (Stasch 2009: 98).

Certain spirits reflect the kind of human intentionality which is expressed and modeled by behavioral rules. It is easy to see why people identify such spirits with a rational consciousness which is similar to their own (Howell 1989: 131). It is possible to give a totalizing, rule-based interpretation to human relations by making offerings to such spirits, as I have argued, for land rights. But Eastern Indonesian spirit classifications point also to a different, chthonic, dark side of humanity. Disappeared people and similar, invisible agents do not respond when people follow rules, but when they break them. Their response is spontaneous: people in Kei say that they 'act quickly', without taking the time to reflect on their rules and reasons.

The invisible, angry men are different from spirit masters or guardians in that they do not support a sense of the social world as stabilized relations and practices. They respond to transgressions, and transgressors respond to their anger, in a pattern which is like repetition in the sense discussed by Gilles Deleuze (1994). Stasch's argument about the Korowai lines out otherness as an ontological condition which gives people a clean slate for constructing a shared experience of space and time.

One should always be cautious about making sweeping ethnographic statements about indigenous ontologies. Compared to the mobile Korowai people, the people of the Kei Islands have a far more structured sense of their local society. Many elements of their identity are determined by already existing institutions and relationships. Even so, the meaning of their personal life is not determined by this sense of order. The Kei Islands' concepts of personhood revolve around an ontological concern with strangers and travels to the outside world. This is an ontological concern because strange beings and foreigners do not play by our rules. We cannot relate to them socially without knowing their intentions and feelings, and when we do, we tend to respond to these intentions and feelings. This ontological interest in strangers is an important component of Keiese concepts of personhood, the topic of the next section.

The Elements of the Person

An important part of personal existence is based on the concentration and eventual dispersion of the natural energies and powers of the body (Turner 2009: 36). Bodies interact with each other in everyday practices and life-cycle rituals. Everyday human interactions – eating, nursing, sex, birth, and death – as well as massaging, warming, grooming and other nurturing treatments and gestures transmit concrete, material substances, energies, and feelings between human bodies.

One prominent argument of the new animism literature is that there is no fundamental difference between such social interactions and people's interaction with animals, plants and objects. Companionship with animals, plants and objects produces similar affective and moral rapports that we normally associate with social relationships. Another, more intense case of companionship is the shamanic journey which, like hunting, is a matter of life and death. All of these engagements with non-human agents fall under animism in that they generate kinship, exchange, enmity, sharing, and trust between people, animals and spirits (Bird-David 1999: 72; Fausto 2007: 498).

A point of theoretical disagreement is whether the interactions between human and non-human beings are enough to produce personal, subjective existence – the ultimate mark of humanity. By the account of Viveiros de Castro (2004: 477), the animistic 'paradigm of exchange' eliminates the need to produce social persons through the manipulations and modifications of their body. Humanity in this paradigm is not reflective self-awareness based on rules and categories imprinted on the body, but a consciousness that circulates between the bodies of different living beings who 'exchange perspectives' with each other.

Perspectival exchange relies on the idea that the body of each animal species has its own affective and perceptual stance towards its environment. Different animals desire different things. But because people are able to imagine the underlying humanity of animals, they can identify with animal desires and perceptions. For animists, by Viveiros de Castro's account, the 'bundle of affects' determined by the animal's body becomes the basis of generalized human identity.

What could be the comparable, exchangeable element of humanity in Eastern Indonesia? The notion of disappeared people in the Kei Islands, and the shadow among the Buli, point to a locus of human affects and desires which continues to circulate when it is removed from the body of its owner. They are analogous to Viveiros de Castro's 'point of view' which circulates between different forms of embodied existence. But it is an open question how people can imagine an alien point of view without an animal body. The Eastern Indonesian images of conscious, non-human beings are more ghostly and yet more human-like than Amerindian ones. Perspectival exchange means that animals see the same, real things as human beings, but perceive them as something else. The disappeared, on the other hand, do not necessarily see these things at all. Their ability to share a human reality is only partial, which suggests that they are not complete persons, but partially human at most.

Soul is the conventional word for the circulating element of personhood. In Eastern Indonesia, it is commonly thought that human souls can leave the body and manifest themselves in animals (Forth 1998: 51). An important clue of their continuing humanity is that the soul, in this separate state, is often associated with the visual properties of the human reflection or image (Landtman 1927: 269; Bubandt 1998: 60). Soul in this sense should not be confused with the Western notion of spiritual essence. Guido Sprenger (2006: 87) argues that 'soul stuff', the entity which constitutes or represents the value of the exchanged thing or person, does not exist outside the system reproduced by it. It is only meaningful to approach the soul as an element of personhood, a totality of relationships and images grounded in certain material and practical experience.

Another circulating component of personhood is the name. In Peter Metcalf's (1991: 51) account of the Penan of Eastern Sarawak, the name marks the 'conjunction of a particular body and soul'. The combination of soul and body in turn marks certain kinds of interiority, such as mannerisms and temperament (1991: 52). Names can and do change over a particular person's lifetime in reflection of parenthood, aging, marriage and friendship. Likewise, the combination of soul and body is not a constant but manifests the person's diverse, constituting relationships. Metcalf notes that this combination is vulnerable to breaking apart, particularly in small children and shamans undergoing trance (1991: 53). The same vulnerability is seen at death, a long-winded but potentially reversible journey in which the soul travels farther and farther away (1991: 66).

How are the components of personhood related to the circulation of life force? The most obvious answers point to the body, the site of consumption, growth, reproductive processes, social gestures, and sensory experiences and qualities. It is foremost as a bodily process that the circulation of life force becomes accessible to other people's perception. We know when a baby is hungry because we share its bodily impulses and signals. By looking into the eyes of a deer, a hunter can identify it as another subject and imagine that it offers itself to be shot out of good-will toward the pursuing humans (Ingold 2000: 13).

Bodily form alone, however, does not determine personal, subjective identity or perspective. Terence Turner (2009: 33) argues that we must also consider the 'meta-form of the social body', the social categories and relationships which are indexed by the modifications of the body and the clothes worn on it. More generally, subjective identity is built on those aspects of the body which indicate sensibility to other people's social expectations. Eastern Indonesians are concerned with the invisible or hidden aspects of human intentionality. For them, looking someone into the eye does not necessarily make his or her intentions transparent to us. As I will argue, mutual ability to see is an ability which emerges gradually as a child in the Kei Islands undergoes the social birth.

The Keiese model of internal experience emphasizes three senses: the ability to hear, see, and feel. In her article about childbirth rituals in Kei, Cécile Barraud (1990: 218) describes the assembly of seven beings called *inya* or *mat inya* in the body of each person before birth. These beings are said to be able to hear when the baby is still in the mother's womb, but they only gain the ability to see after the child is brought out to the sight of social others.

Hearing and seeing by this account are clearly more than natural, sensory faculties. Seeing in particular begins as a reciprocal event, when the baby is being seen by others. This does not depend on the child's autonomous consciousness. I have often seen a pregnant woman unfold her shirt or cloth, with the explanation that this will transfer my appearance (particularly my straight nose) to her unborn baby. I was thus expected to recognize the baby in her mother's belly and imagine it would look like me, so that, in a possible future encounter with the child I would recognize it was like myself.

Barraud is reluctant to translate *inya* as 'souls': she describes them as 'principles acknowledging the social value of things and beings'. The hierarchical constitution of Kei society means that value is not measured against a uniform, human substance. Persons are not valued as individual subjects: their human value is manifested in totalizing ritual exchanges in which they are encompassed by some larger category, such as their dead ancestors or their house of birth. The house and the person are 'sets of permanent relationships' between persons and non-human beings that must be re-established through long-lasting ritual exchanges (Barraud 1990: 228). Outside these totalizing rituals, *inya* do not represent human souls but an infinite number of living beings (ibid.: 218).

Overall, *inya* do not stand for human substance but a similarity between some aspect of a person's self-experience and those people, things, and categories that encompass his or her personal identity. This makes it understandable why *inya* can also be present in some animals and plants, as well as in sailing-boats and houses.

The difference between *inya* and the Western notion of *soul* is precisely that seeing another person, looking at him or her in the eyes, is not enough for intersubjective communion. On the contrary, *inya* stand for diverse possibilities of totalizing experience, and only some of those experiences are desirable and human-like. Images, visualized in trance or seen in a photograph (Kaartinen 2010: 19), make it possible to imagine the feelings of a distant traveler, even after his or her death. But looking at people from a distance does not create an immediate communion, any more than another person's presence reveals his or her true feelings. Instead, the gaze of other people anticipates a later moment of recognition and creates relations which continue over time.

The potential effects of other people's gaze on one's future intentions and self-perceptions create an obvious danger for personhood. Children are particularly vulnerable to disarticulated experiences and influences. What threatens a baby's *inya* during the early weeks of life are precisely other, free-roaming *inya* (Barraud 1990: 220). These beings belong to the other, unseen side of reality, and just as living people cannot normally see them, they cannot see us.

The organic linkage of the person with cosmological forces is also signified by the flow of wind, heat, odors, and liquid and solid substances flowing through the body. People of Kei take care to regulate these flows by touching the baby with a cloth heated over coals while the child and mother are secluded inside the house of birth. Divination rituals performed at this time ensure that the fragile connection between the *inya* and the body is not severed before the child is finally brought to the view of outsiders and given a name (Barraud 1990: 220).

In the Muslim village of Banda Eli, where I did fieldwork in the 1990s, these rituals followed the same overall pattern as in Barraud's account. In each case, rituals stress the house as the totalizing anchor of each person's differentiated relationships to other people in society, as well as to strangers and non-human others, which make up his or her fate in life.[4]

What is the broader significance of these concepts of personhood? In a comparative essay Barraud and other Dumontian anthropologists (Barraud et al. 1994: 118) have argued that the Kei society is 'cosmomorphic'. Even though its ideology recognizes the existence of an outside world, it claims that ordered social life is only possible within its limits. In other words, people can only realize their full humanity when they are visible to each other. When they travel and meet strangers they are at a constant danger of forgetting their relatives, being lost at sea, wasting their resources and libidinal energies: in a word, 'disappearing' as fully integrated social persons.

In spite of these dangers, the people of Kei, and particularly Banda Eli, value travels and interactions with strangers as transformative events. Long-distance trading voyages used to be a crucial phase in the life of men in the Kei society and helped them achieve a fully adult status in their own community. Men whose fathers have passed away are addressed as *amakaka*, 'elder fathers', who have the right to speak on behalf of their family in public meetings. In these meetings they cultivate a world-weary mien and mix their local-language speech with Indonesian words and quotes to underline their experiences from the outside world. While most young, married men live in their wife's household, these senior men aspire to rebuild their father's house and end their subordinate position among their wife's relatives.

The authority of men who turn from dependent sons-in-law into independent fathers (and eventually fathers-in-law) rests on being able to look at society from the outsider's perspective. In all former stages of their lives, their personal identity was encompassed by collective categories: relative age and membership in a house – either that of their father or their father-in-law. On returning from their travels, however, men effectively become the agents of creating such categories, often in the literal sense of building the house again. As Terence Turner (2012: 494) puts it, they are no longer the objects but agents of socialization. It is through them that elements of the outside world, such as disembodied soul-particles and free spirits, are integrated in the center of social space.

The senior men's outside perspective on society is not the opposite of humanity but an expression of its generalized cultural value. This is different from Viveiros de Castro's argument about perspectival exchange. In his view, the human perspective – or the embodied subjective stance towards the world – must either be validated by making a universal claim to its objectivity (the choice of modern, Western ontology), or by recognizing that the perspectives embodied by other species are so many other instances of humanity (the choice of animists) (Viveiros de Castro 2004: 469). In Turner's argument, the human perspective is grounded in the natural and social forces and qualities of the human body. Its subjective validity is based on cultural values which express the integration of these embodied forces and qualities (Turner 2009: 33; 2012: 500).

In spite of rejecting the notion of perspectival exchange, Turner is open to the concept of animism (Turner 2009: 37). Just like human beings, animals are capable of giving a sustained form to their life-process. The question is whether people who do not subscribe to the dualism of culture and nature will need to support their human identity by assuming an animal's perception of the world. As I argue in the next section, many Eastern Indonesian people see the human to animal metamorphosis as a real possibility. But in contrast to the Amerindian peoples discussed by Viveiros de Castro, Eastern Indonesians see this makeover as a nightmare. Why this should be so is the topic of the next section.

People and Animals

My discussion so far has focused on people of the Kei Islands who are only marginally involved with hunting. The exception for this is wild pigs, which some myths in the islands of Maluku represent as transformed human beings. Valerio Valeri's ethnography from another part of Maluku, the large central Maluku island of Seram, presents a case of a hunting society of similar scale and complexity as some of the Amazonian societies which have sparked off the new interest in animism. The Huaulu are a small community of about two hundred people who live in shifting settlements but identify with a single village, divided in four intermarrying clans (Valeri 2000: 33). When Valeri started his fieldwork in 1972, they were surrounded by a largely untouched rainforest. As late as in 1988, the Huaulu had converted to neither Christianity nor Islam (ibid.: 41).

Valeri's theoretical questions have more in common with perspectivism than with (standard) animism. He starts by pointing out that philosophical Christianity is almost unique when it claims that sin and defilement are two different kinds of evil (2000: 43). This claim points to an ontological opposition between God and the world, an opposition which also underlies the notion of the autonomous human subject (ibid.: 43). Anthropologists have reproduced this opposition when they have made a difference between religious and magical prohibitions (ibid.: 44). Some interpretations about animism point in the same direction: if people establish a reciprocal social relationship to animals or spirits, their life is oriented by certain rules of interaction which supports a generalized, moral sense of humanity. But as soon as we consider the different bodily constitution, affects and desires of people and animals, it becomes difficult to imagine them as part of the same moral community. The exchange of perspectives, as Viveiros de Castro describes it, certainly leads to an alien, if not inhuman sense of morality.

Perspectival exchange does not, in principle, exclude kinship with spirits and animals. Some examples of this can be found in the fishing and hunting magic of Melanesia. *Shark Callers of Kontu*, a film by Dennis O'Rourke, shows a New Guinean shark hunter attracting and capturing his pray with movements and noises which are precisely adapted to the shark's sensory field. This is not merely a matter of imagining the alternative perceptual world of the shark: the fisher depicted in the film makes clear that one must also establish a benign moral relationship to it through avoidances of speech, food and sexual contact. The shark fisher does not merely shift to the shark's point of view and pretend that it is real: he incorporates it in his own preparations and posture.

The shark fishers of Kontu identify their prey as relatives. In Eastern Indonesia, this mode of involving animals in the social structure is largely absent. Kinship implies a moral relationship with animals, and here it tends to be projected into the past. The Huaulu only recognize the humanity of animals in the domain of myths. Before people became mortal, their stories tell, animals could take off their skin and reveal their underlying humanity. To people their underground nests appeared like a human village. Today, however, most animals are what they look like: the possibility of an animal with a human-like awareness is a monstrous, false animal.

Instead of 'multiple natures' (as Viveiros de Castro would claim), such animals exemplify 'non-human occult beings' (*manusiassi*).

This terminology points to humanity (*manusia*) as the unmarked form of subjective existence. The world of invisible others is inhabited by a wide range of non-human or partly human beings. Women who die in childbirth turn into ghosts who seduce men and try to kill other women in childbed and make them share their fate (Valeri 2000: 27). The shades of dead people are envious of the living but also attracted to them: they want living people to die and become their companions (ibid.: 165). These are examples of perspectival exchange: affects which are recognizably human are manifested by the dead in a monstrous form. In addition to former humans, the Huaulu also recognize the possibility of perspectival exchange with game animals. In a story told by a hunter, *makalisafu* or the bewitching power of a hunted animal possessed the hunter who dropped his clothes and lost his ability to speak and keep track of time. Only the fact that he managed to hold on to his bush knife broke the spell, but he had to be taught to speak and eat cooked food again (ibid.: 185).

Whereas Viveiros de Castro (2004: 470) stresses the enabling, agentive potentials of animist ontology, people of Eastern Indonesia see perspectival exchange with animals and spirits as a dreadful possibility. People are morally superior to other conscious beings, and the only beneficial change is from non-human to human. This is possible through shamanic agency which may turn witches, ancestral shades, guardians of game animals, crocodile spirits in rivers, and the spirits associated with external state power, into helpers which act against similar powers which they used to be before turning 'good' (Valeri 2000: 29).

All of this points to a hierarchical relationship between human and non-human agents. That which can transit between a human and an animal body, according to the Huaulu, is organic and feeling life (*mattiulu*). *Hali*, the internal organ that signifies the powers of reflective thinking, is also possessed by people and animals alike. Yet it is only possible for humans to have *hali manusia*, the potential for love and compassion for other people (ibid.: 186).

The hierarchy between humanity and animals has similar implications as Turner's (2009, 2012) analysis of the Kayapó. Even if the Huaulu recognize the intentionality of non-human beings and animals, their subjective humanity is shaped by cultural values. The point where Valeri comes closest to the discussion sparked by Amerindian ethnography is his notion of a 'metamorphic potential', the suspicion and danger involved in encounters between humans and internally non-human beings in the forest. The embodied sense of self among the Huaulu means that it is always haunted by the 'inarticulate', or the threatening lack of a boundary between subject and object (Valeri 2000: 110). This may sound like the psychoanalytic theory of taboo, except that Valeri is careful to speak about a subject constituted by a broader sense of cultural order than that of the phallic. Taboos exist 'to protect the subject constituted by the entire spectrum of objectual relations' (ibid.: 109), in other words, everything that is relevant for the boundaries of the symbolic body.

The Huaulu do not see their moral superiority to animals as an original condition. According a Huaulu myth, people owe their superiority to animals to the dog, the animal which is essential for hunting. In this myth, the hierarchy between people and wild animals is established when all dangerous animals are killed by the first dog (ibid.: 191). It is only on the basis of this event that domestic animals, which the Huaulu do not eat, can assume cultural value as the metaphors of the house, forest and sexual difference (ibid.: 212–15).

The boundary of humanity is not supported by the dualism of mind and body but by the avoidance by the Huaulu of numerous substances, objects, actions, words, and events that threaten their subjective integration. The most conscious expression of this is their relationship to wild animals. Valeri suggests that when the Huaulu are hunting, they interact with animals on an equal footing: one intends to kill, but one can also be killed by the game. Laughing implies a degree of identification with the object of amusement; therefore, Huaulu avoid laughing at wild animals or in their presence (ibid.: 187). Just because animals are a privileged reference for humans, the Huaulu avoid expressing any identity with them.

Valeri is thus arguing that the Huaulu oppose animals to humans as a category. He goes to some pains to show that the Huaulu have an underlying category of animal, even if the word does not exist in their vocabulary. The closest approximation of the word, *peni*, refers to species which have meat (ibid.: 181). In contrast to Descola (Turner 2009: 17), Valeri avoids the interpretation that the Huaulu relate to animals as discrete cultural beings. This means that, for the Huaulu, killing an animal does not create the 'hunter's predicament' (Århem, in this volume): the moral debt or guilt that arises from killing a friend or ally. On another level, however, eating animals is a problem for them. Meat is the most valued food, and therefore a distinctive animal property, but at the same time it is the stuff which people ingest at the risk of fusing their own physical substance with it.

Aside from taboos, the Huaulu solution to this problem is to restore the category division and recognize the game animal as the property of its spirit master. After butchering the animal, they put its head on a stake as an offering to the spirit. By doing so, the Huaulu acknowledge the animal's form as a species before consuming its substance. Another practice through which the hunters reaffirm the category division is to abstain from eating meat from the animal they have killed. At the same time as the offering to the master spirit recognizes the animal as a cultural category, the individual hunter is excluded from the cultural practice of eating together.

Valeri's Huaulu ethnography traces a boundary around social humanity which, at times, resembles the structuralist division between nature and culture. Yet, the division is not clear-cut and certainly does not presuppose a transcendent human mind. By his account, the huge, omnipresent effort to maintain the boundaries of humanity testifies to its fragility as category and its resulting, ever-present metamorphic potential.

Conclusion

Southeast Asia does not fall readily in the comparative categories which have so far been proposed in the new anthropological debate about animism. The case for animist ontology has been made in a way that satisfies a general philosophical interest, but often at the expense of detailed ethnographic comparison, at least outside the field of Amazonian societies. Anthropologists – myself included – risk being carried away by the philosophical novelty of addressing people's relationship to animals, spirits, objects and the environment as an ontological rather than cosmological issue.

My approach here has been to use them as complementary points of view. While ontological questions encourage us to broaden our theoretical horizons, an attention to cosmological ideas forces us to maintain a holistic, ethnographic view of the subject. Eastern Indonesia, however, presents a challenge to the intellectualism which is inherent in the concept of animist ontology. Descola, Viveiros de Castro and Latour are together in rejecting the 'sociocentric prejudice' by which people's relationships with other people always have priority over their relationships to things. Once we have done so, we can begin a disinterested observation of how people attribute human, animal, physical, spiritual and other qualities to concrete things and mental experiences. The difficulty, however, is that things and experiences cannot have qualities unless they fall under cultural categories. It is only on this condition that they can be repeated and recognized by other people (Keane 2008: 114).

Anybody who comes from rural Eastern Indonesia will know what people talk about when they mention the disappeared. Clearly this is a cultural category. What is difficult to grasp, conceive and translate is the humanity of these invisible beings. It is far easier to imagine a parallel humanity in animals because they are attentive to regular, human behavior and therefore responsive to human intentionality. The angry men, occult powers, and disappeared people are a different case. They respond to those things which people share with animals: unthinkable actions, repressed desires, and the 'nonsense' produced by the body (Valeri 2000: 111).

The presence of such human-like beings raises questions that are answered by a *social* ontology. What makes society possible? Are there more kinds of people than one? What does it take to produce a human person? Far from secure in their human superiority, people have to affirm their humanity by social conventions. These demarcate their social being apart from the physical domains, life forms and bodily states and substances which correspond to the disordered domains of 'nature' (Ellen 1996). Even then, as Valeri puts it, 'social conventions exist against the background of a non-human world more powerful than the human one' (2000: 308).

One should exercise caution against overly generalizing statements about animism in Eastern Indonesia. Where Amerindian animism expands its notion of humanity to the entire lived world, the Eastern Indonesian societies discussed in this article are concerned with maintaining a differentiated social humanity. I am not suggesting that all societies of the area fall under this ethnographic type. The Kontu of Papua New Guinea, not very far away from Maluku, construct animals as their kin whereas Maluku societies assume a certain species superiority for humans. In the case of the Huaulu, this superiority can be seen as an ideological construct which is grounded in an underlying ontological continuity.

What general, theoretical interest is served by the comparative discussion about ontology? Bruce Kapferer (1997: 180) argues that the actuality of experience amounts to far more than the models and constructions by which human beings seek to grasp or control it. Accordingly, ontology is not a model of social and cosmic order but 'the outline of a dynamic identifiable in a diversity of practices' (ibid.: 288). Webb Keane (2003: 413) uses the Peircean notion of 'outward clash' for the new meanings which arise from contingent events rather than established significations.

We might expect, for instance, that people's way of dealing with the shock and responsibility of killing animals depends on their routinized livelihoods. Killing probably has a different utility and aesthetics for those people who live by hunting and to those who farm land (and mostly kill domesticated animals). Some of its effect is always bound to escape from such routinized domains of meaning. I have a lively memory of the troubled and helpless gesture that my Muslim friends in Banda Eli made as they watched a sacrificial goat die by their own action. Ontologies arise from the need to integrate such experiences when they cannot be resolved within a single moral or symbolic framework. In such ways, Kapferer argues, people organize their experience into determinate and repeatable patterns, which implicate specific modes of personal existence (1997: 288).

As Michael Scott (2007: 3) points out, any inquiry into ontology has to be sensitive to its historical and social context. Ontological ideas and practices are not the essence of culture but a way in which human life articulates with ongoing, ever-changing realities (Kapferer 2009: 219). In some places, we might find that people recognize several origins for humanity; in other places they think of humanity as having a common substance (Scott 2007: 10).

With this caveat in mind, I have tried to push the concept of animic ontology beyond the paradigmatic ethnographic case of hunting societies. I have suggested that the peoples of Maluku recognize a universe inhabited by diverse conscious beings, and at times they have to struggle to preserve their social humanity. Eastern Indonesian ideas and stories of this struggle are clearly concerned with spirits rather than animals as such. In many cases, the spirits appear simply as inverted or partial humans, and similar entities may also be recognized as elements of the person. In contrast to Renaissance Europeans whose imagination placed strange and monstrous things at an extreme distance, Eastern Indonesians see foreign, unseen realities as an intimate presence. We should not exaggerate the difference between these ontologies. They disagree less about the essence of humanity than the spatial and temporal frameworks in which it appears as a stable category.

Notes

1. For a summary of this history, see Kaartinen 2010: 35–53. Field research in the village of Banda Eli took place over fifteen months in 1994–96, with funding from the Academy of Finland and the Väinö Tanner Foundation and under the sponsorship of the University of Gajah Mada, Yogyakarta. In 2009 I did fieldwork in Ambon and the Kei Islands with funding from the Academy of Finland, sponsored by the Indonesian Institute of Sciences (LIPI) at Jakarta and Ambon. I would like to express thanks to these agencies and the Banda Eli community for their generous support to my research. Thanks are due to the editors and two anonymous readers of this article for their encouraging, constructive comments.

2. Although access to land usually involves contracts, sometimes based on a historical precedent of intermarriage or alliance in a war, the ultimate landowner is always the spirit guardian. Being relatively late arrivals to the Kei Islands, the Bandanese depend on their Keiese neighbors for their land rights. According to local historical narratives, they received land from local allies in return for helping them in warfare. By performing the house-building ritual, the Bandanese affirm that they have a direct relationship to the original spirit landowners.
3. Only special chiefs of high rank may perform the ritual called *hukum*. Their high rank is a sign of their origin outside the Kei Islands. Their ritual authority implicitly recognizes the encompassment of the Kei Islands society and spirit world to a larger cosmological order.
4. The people of Banda Eli differ from their Kei Islands neighbors in that they do not practice the matrimonial exchanges which, among the people of Kei, trace the differentiating effects of the body's movement from one house to another. Marriage is recognized as an exchange between entire houses, and this exchange recognizes the value of the bride, but there is not a systematic ideological subordination of this value to the exchanges (particularly in the context of funerary rituals) which establish the house as a source of life. For this reason, I cannot make the same conclusions about 'two orders of relationships' as Barraud (1990: 223, 228) draws from her material.

References

Barraud, C. (1979) *Tanêbar-Evav: Une société de maisons tournée vers le large*, Paris: CNRS and Cambridge University Press.

―――― (1990) 'Kei Society and the Person: An Approach through Childbirth and Funerary Rituals', *Ethnos*, 55(3–4): 214–31.

Barraud, C., Coppet D. de, Itéanu A., and Jamous, R. (eds) (1994) *Of Relations and the Dead; Four societies viewed through the angle of their exchanges*, Oxford: Berg Publishers.

Bird-David, N. (1999) '"Animism" Revisited. Personhood, environment and relational epistemology', *Current Anthropology*, 40: 67–79.

Bubandt, N. (1998) 'The Odour of Things: Smell and the cultural elaboration of disgust in Eastern Indonesia', *Ethnos*, 63(1): 48–80.

Deleuze, G. (1994) *Difference and Repetition*, London: Athlone Press.

Descola, P. (2006) 'Beyond nature and culture. Radcliffe-Brown Lecture in Social Anthropology, 2005', *Proceedings of the British Academy*, 139: 137–55.

―――― (2009) 'Human natures', *Social Anthropology*, 17(2): 145–57.

Durkheim, É. (1965) *The Elementary Forms of the Religious Life*, New York, NY: Free Press.

Ellen, R. (1996) 'The cognitive geometry of nature'. in P. Descola and G. Pálsson (eds.) *Nature and Society: Anthropological Perspectives*, London: Routledge, 103–23.

Fausto, C. (2007) 'Feasting on People. Eating animals and humans in Amazonia', *Current Anthropology*, 48(4): 497–514.

Forth, G. (1998) *Beneath the Volcano. Religion, Cosmology and Spirit Classification among the Nage of eastern Indonesia*, Leiden: KITLV Press.

Fox, J. (1980) 'Introduction', in J. Fox (ed.) *The Flow of Life*, Cambridge, MA: Harvard University Press, 1–20.

Hoskins, J. (1993) *The Play of Time: Kodi Perspectives on Calendars, History, and Exchange*, University of California Press.

Howell, S. (1989) *Society and cosmos: Chewong of Peninsular Malaysia*, Chicago, IL: The University of Chicago Press.

Ingold, T. (2000) *Perception of the Environment. Essays in livelihood, dwelling and skill*, London: Routledge.

Kaartinen, T. (2010) Songs of Travel and Stories of Place. Poetics of Absence in an Eastern Indonesian Society, Folklore Fellows' Communications 299, Helsinki: Academia Scientarium Fennica.

Kapferer, B. (1997) *The Feast of the Sorcerer. Practices of Consciousness and Power*, Chicago, IL: University of Chicago Press.

—— (2009) 'Afterword: Cosmological Journeys', in C. Sather and T. Kaartinen (eds.) Beyond the Horizon. Essays on Myth, History, Travel and Society, Studia Fennica Anthropologica 2, Helsinki: Finnish Literature Society, 215–19.

Keane, W. (2003) 'Semiotics and the social analysis of material things', *Language and Communication*, 23: 409–25.

—— (2008) 'The evidence of the senses and the materiality of religion', *Journal of the Royal Anthropological Institute*, 14: 110–27.

Landtman, G. (1927) *The Kiwai Papuans of British New Guinea. A nature-born instance of Rousseau's ideal community*, London: MacMillan.

Metcalf, P. (1991) *A Borneo Journey into Death. Berawan Eschatology from Its Rituals*, Kuala Lumpur: S. Abdul Majeed & Co.

Robbins, J. (2004) *Becoming Sinners. Christianity and Moral Torment in a Papua New Guinea Society*, Berkeley, CA: University of California Press.

Scott, M. (2007) *The Severed Snake. Matrilineages, Making Place, and a Melanesian Christianity in Southeast Solomon Islands*, Durham, NC: Carolina Academic Press.

Sprenger, G. (2006) 'Political Periphery, Cosmological Center: The reproduction of Rmeet socio-cosmic order and the Lao-Thailand border', in A. Horstmann and R. Wadley (eds.) *Centering the Margin. Agency and Narrative in Southeast Asian Borderlands*, New York, NY: Berghahn, 67–84.

Spyer, P. (1997) 'The Eroticism of Debt: Pearl Divers, Traders, and Sea Wives in the Aru Islands, Eastern Indonesia', *American Ethnologist*, 24(3): 515–38.

Stasch, R. (2009) *Society of Others: Kinship and Mourning in a West Papuan Place*, Berkeley, CA: University of California Press.

Turner, V. (1967) *The Forest of Symbols*, Ithaca, NY: Cornell University Press.

Turner, T. (2009) 'The Crisis of Late Structuralism. Perspectivism and Animism: Rethinking Culture, Nature, Spirit, and Bodiliness', *Tipití*, 7(1): 3–42.

Turner, T. (2012) 'The Social Skin'. Hau: Journal of Ethnographic Theory, 2(2): 486–504. Reprinted from J. Cherfas and R. Lewin (eds.) (1980) *Not Work Alone: A cross-cultural view of activities superfluous to survival*, London: Sage, 112–40.

Tylor, E. (1903) *Primitive Culture. Researches into the Development of Mythology, Philosophy, Religion, Language, Art, and Custom*. Vol. II, Fourth revised edition, London: John Murray.

Valeri, V. (2000) *The Forest of Taboos. Morality, Hunting, and Identity among the Huaulu of the Moluccas*, Madison, WI: The University of Wisconsin Press.

Viveiros de Castro, E. (2004) 'Exchanging perspectives. The transformation of objects into subjects in Amerindian ontologies', *Common Knowledge*, 10(3): 463–84.

12 Gods and spirits in the Wetu Telu religion of Lombok

Sven Cederroth

With its approximately 4.750 km², Lombok is one of the smaller in the arc of islands that start from the Asian mainland and run all the way to Australia. Together with its eastern neighbour, Sumbawa, it forms the present-day province Nusa Tenggara Barat of the Republic of Indonesia. The capital of the province, Mataram, is situated near the west coast of Lombok. The indigenous people of Lombok, known as Sasak, constitute some 90 per cent of the population and today they number approximately three million. Up until the early sixteenth century, the Sasak embraced a kind of Hindu-Buddhist religion with traces of animistic beliefs. After the formal conversion to Islam, a split occurred among the Sasak where one group, the *wetu telu*, incorporated many of the earlier beliefs in their practices of the new religion, while a second group, the *waktu lima* developed more orthodox practices. At first there was an overwhelming majority of *wetu telu* Sasak but gradually the balance shifted and today a large majority, maybe as many as 80 per cent of the Sasak are seen as *waktu lima*

There are several different stories of how Islam was brought to Lombok, but they all seem to agree that it took place sometime in the beginning of the sixteenth century. We have to rely here on narratives from indigenous palm leaf manuscripts, the reliability of which is difficult to assess. These manuscripts were often used as arguments in conflicts between competing royal houses, and their contents were manipulated so as to suit the arguments of either side. According to one of the versions, found in a manuscript named Petung Bayan, Islam entered Lombok by way of the Bayan kingdom where Pangeran Prapen, a grandson of Sunan Giri, one of the *wali songo*, the nine saints popularly believed to have converted Java to Islam, started to teach the new religion in 1540. In another palm leaf manuscript we are told that in 1640, a certain Sunan Pengging, a pupil of Sunan Kalijaga, another of the Javanese *wali songo*, arrived to the island. He was teaching Sufi practices mixed with Hindu-Javanese and pantheistic beliefs. At first he settled at the court of the Parwa kingdom where he married the daughter of the king. When Parwa was attacked by Macassarese forces who at that time had conquered the Lombok kingdom, Sunan Pengging fled to Bayan where he gained a huge influence and continued to preach his Sufi teachings.

The type of Islam, originating from Sunan Kalijaga and spread on Lombok by Sunan Pengging, seems to have been a highly syncretistic blend of original animistic beliefs, Hinduism and Islam. Belief in various supernatural beings and offerings made to these beings continued more or less as before. In the old belief system, mount Rinjani[1] had held a special position as a sacred place, inhabited by the High God. Also after the formal acceptance of Islam, reverence of the mountain continued as it was seen as the path of the soul when ascending to heaven after death. Thus, in the *wetu telu* cosmology, there is the idea of a High God, the name of which may not be mentioned and who is almighty and responsible for the conditions on earth. Below this High God there are a large number of lesser Gods, (*dewa*) and spirits, which so to say are the contact persons between the High God and man. These *dewa* carry out the commands of their master, and they have divided the tasks among them. Some *dewa* carry sickness and other plagues as measures of punishment from the High God whereas others provide and regulate the benefits such as spring water for the crops, fertility of the land, and so on. No ordinary man can contact the *dewa* and ask their favours; this may be done only by a special category of religious official, the *pemangku*, who is the only person who knows the proper name of the *dewa*, although he never pronounces it. Sometimes the *dewa* may descend to earth; when they do this, they dwell at certain well-known sacred places, *pemaliq*, such as a mountain top, a spring water, a large tree, a specific stone.

Thus, from the early beginning, two versions of Islam were propagated on Lombok. This dualism is reflected in the legend about Nurcahya and Nursada, two sons of Sunan Pengging who after his death had divided the island between themselves. In the palm leaf manuscript they are described as the originators of two versions of Islam, Nurcahya being the oldest is seen as the founder of *waktu lima*, Nursada, the youngest son founded the *wetu telu*. What can be said, with a fair amount of certainty, however, is that the introduction of Islam on Lombok was the result of military conquests which were combined with missionary campaigns from two directions, Java in the west and Sulawesi in the east. In the various Lombok kingdoms, the king was the first to convert whereupon his subjects also automatically adopted the new religion. It seems probable that the teachings proclaimed by the Sufi-inspired Javanese missionaries differed from the stricter Sunni creed spread by the Sulawesi Bugis. Here, then, is the background to the contemporary division of the Sasak into one orthodox Sunni Muslim sect, the *waktu lima* and one syncretistic animist Muslim sect, the *wetu telu*. It is extremely difficult to ascertain how many Sasak that belong to each of the two various religious groupings, but it has been estimated (Leemann 1989: 31) that at the time of independence around 25 per cent could be counted as adherents of *wetu telu*. On the basis of a survey carried out in the early 1970s, A.M. Hartong (1974: 22) estimates that in 1965 some 20 per cent or around 250,000 of the Sasak were *wetu telu*. The Bayan area, which comprises the region situated north of the Rinjani volcano, is nowadays a center for and a stronghold of *wetu telu*. It was also here that Islam, in its Javanese version, first entered Lombok and it is here that the oldest mosque on the island is situated.

The Bayanese

The Bayan area is situated north of the Rinjani volcano and is separated from the rest of the island by the mountain chain. Here live approximately 120,000 people who eek out their existence mainly from dry-land cultivation. Only in some limited areas has it been possible to convert the land into irrigated *sawah* fields. The largest such area is in and around Bayan itself, which consequently has developed into the population centre of North Lombok. Bayan is one of the oldest, if not the oldest, village in Lombok, and it is also here that the oldest Mosque is situated. In former times Bayan was also the centre of a kingdom which comprised most of North Lombok. Still today, you find in the village some of the places where the king and his family lived. The hamlets where the king used to live are still today populated almost exclusively by people bearing the highest nobility title, *Raden* for the men and *Denda* for the women.

Although officially an Islamic sect, the *wetu telu* religion has many basic features in common with not only Balinese Hinduism, but also – and perhaps above all – with Javanese Islamic syncretism (*agami jawi*). Among such common elements, the central role of the ancestors stands out as especially important. This is based on a philosophy which is rooted in a belief about life as a kind of continuous flow, in the course of which a powerful element, commonly labeled a soul, is generated.[2] During life, the soul is contained within the body and although it may leave its abode temporarily, for instance during sleep, it always returns to the person concerned. At death, the soul has to abandon the body but therefore does not cease to exist. It now feels deserted and homeless and starts to roam the surroundings at will. To placate and appease such, potentially dangerous, souls, a series of rituals is required, whereby the soul is guided to the hereafter. In this process the deceased is transformed into an ancestor.

But not only ancestors are thought to influence the living. To the Bayanese the whole nature is animated. These supernatural powers may dwell everywhere, but certain places like springs, hills stones and trees are thought to be especially favoured. Although some of the spirits thought to roam in the countryside are inherently malevolent and prone to injure and even kill people, most of them are not dangerous unless disturbed or harmed. Some of them, especially the ancestral spirits, even help people as much as they can. To contact the spirits, a secret formula called *mantra* is read by a religious official in the presence of certain power-transferring media such as betel, sacred water or sacred cloths. Together, these three objects form the highway for establishing relations between the human beings and the animated powers of the surrounding nature. The spirits are expected to react upon the petition and extend assistance or transfer some of their power to the people. Through the use of these media, the Bayanese will also be able to elicit protection from attacks by the really harmful, ill-willing powers, such as *bakeq*, or *anta boga*, and other spirits which also dwell in the nature.

The ancestor souls can be approached through their graves. For this purpose the grave is swept, a *mantra* is read and a bowl of sacred water and some chewed betel is placed on top of the grave. Whenever an important ceremony is to be celebrated it never happens that anybody neglects to call upon the ancestors to participate. Ordinary people cannot perform the necessary mediating acts between the living and the dead themselves. To handle these tasks, there is in Bayanese society two categories of religious officials, on one hand *pemangku* and *perumbaq* and on the other *kiyai*. The two former officials handle all relations with the spirit world while the *kiyai* handle the relations with the High God and the hereafter. Depending on the situation, either of these can act as a go-between.

The first mentioned group of officials, the *pemangku* and the *perumbaq* can be seen as a kind of mediators between the human world and the spirit world. As said, the creatures inhabiting the spirit world are most real to the Bayanese, and their powers are generally respected and sometimes also feared. In the *wetu telu* syncretism, the institution of *pemangku* represents a pre-Islamic Hindu tradition while that of *perumbaq* predates not only Islam but probably Hinduism as well.[3] According to the orthodox Muslims, both these offices are heretical and should be abolished – the sooner the better. In Bayan there are many *pemangku* with different tasks, but they all have in common an association of some kind with the world of the spirits. In this capacity they act as go-betweens, bridging the gap to the human world and invoking the spirits to protect and/or help the human beings.

Ancestral Spirits (*roh alus*)

In Bayanese society there is no clear–cut borderline between the society of the living and that of the dead. There is a firm belief that life does not end with death but the spirits of the deceased continue to live on and can in many ways communicate with and influence the lives of their descendants. It is, therefore, of great importance for the latter not to forget to pay attention to the needs of their ancestors. If they receive proper recognition they assist their descendants so that they are blessed with a happy and prosperous life, but if they are unduly neglected they can strike back by causing sufferings and sicknesses. The ancestral spirits are omnipresent, and are called upon again and again to participate in meals of celebration. It is especially the oldest ancestors whom the people hold in high esteem and think of as particularly powerful.

Veneration of the ancestors is thus an ubiquitous theme in Bayanese life and one may even say that it is a central focus in the *wetu telu* syncretism. The ancestors are always invited to participate in religious, personal as well as communal ceremonies of all kinds. In the village there is a strong preference for endogamous marriages.[4] This has led to a situation where almost everyone is related to everybody else in one way or another. The focus on common ancestors may then be seen as a reflection of the strong sense of communal spirit that characterizes the village.[5] The Bayan land is regarded as the navel of the world. It is a sacred land inherited from the ancestors and given to those now living to take good care of and to pass on to future generations.

It is above all in connection with ceremonies that the ancestors are approached and their blessing asked. For this purpose, a mixture of areca nut, lime and betel leaves (*lekoq buaq*) is used as a medium. A *pemangku*[6] offers the mixture to the ancestors by placing it overnight in his *bale beleq*, the grand house, or in his *makam*, the ancestor grave of his group. After he has removed the mixture, he applies it to the forehead of persons belonging to the same descent group as the spirit who has blessed the mixture. The magic substance is then believed to protect them from any kind of sickness or other danger.

If for a long time nobody has visited the graveyard and the ancestral spirits feel neglected and hungry, they may return to their former home. Here they make their presence known by striking their descendants with a minor sickness, which comes in the form of a constant headache. If someone in the family develops this kind of headache and one suspects that it may be caused by the ancestors, there is a way to find out. One of the women is sent to the graveyard where she sweeps the grave with a piece of hair. When this tuft of hair is drawn with the fingers and it gives a squeaking sound one can be sure that neglected ancestral spirits are behind the headache. To appease the ancestors as quickly as possible, the family has to prepare a plate of rice and meat and put in the house to share with the ancestors. Later, but as soon as possible, a special ceremony, *roah jumat,* has to be celebrated, or one has to visit the graveyard to sweep it.

There are two kinds of ancestral spirits. Firstly, there are the exalted ones, those who are buried in the *makam*[7] around the mosque or in the oldest graveyard, just to the north of the mosque. These graves are then cleaned with an *usap*, a kind of sacred cloth. To show one's respect, the souls of these graves are addressed in the same polite language that would be used towards a living king or noble aristocrat. Secondly, there are the ancestral spirits of all those that have been buried in ordinary graveyards. They are approached every time there is a celebration of some kind when *sembeq,* the healing betel quid, is put at the gravesite considered to be the oldest.

At the death of an individual there is an elaborate and expensive seven-day ceremony. This is required to transform the spirit of the dead person into a revered ancestor.[8] Also after this occasion there are ceremonies at regular intervals up to one thousand days after death. After that, the individual identity slowly fades away and the person becomes absorbed into a joint group of nameless ancestors. But also at this stage they will be remembered, and their descendants regularly place offerings at their graves.

All ceremonies in Bayan are accompanied by a sacred meal to which the ancestors are also invited to participate. The following case provides a vivid illustration of the reverence paid to one's ancestors:

> *Raden* Gagar was a respected member of the leading noble group in Bayan. One day when he had travelled to Lendang Awu, a village some 40 km east of Bayan, he suddenly fell ill and died. The circumstances did not permit his relatives to transport his body back to Bayan. He was, therefore, buried the same day in Lendang Awu. Now, each time that any member of his nobility group is to hold a ceremony of some kind (and that happens frequently) someone has to walk[9] all the way to Lendang Awu. There he informs the soul of *Raden* Gagar and invites him to attend the ceremony.

Those trips are time consuming as well as tiresome. Some people, therefore, began to consider moving the remains and carrying out a reburial in Bayan. During preparations for the celebration of a so-called thousand-day ceremony,[10] a delegation from Bayan came to Lendang Awu. Here, they dug up the bones of *Raden* Gagar and later reburied them in the Bayan cemetery. Soon afterward, strange and frightening things started to happen, and a lot of accidents occurred.

All these extraordinary events caused people to become upset and attribute the accidents to the reburial. Many people believed that the disturbance had caused the soul of *Raden* Gagar to become homeless and bewildered. Because of this change in the state of mind of the spirit, he had influenced the situation in the ward so that it had become hot, that is, abnormal and dangerous. The leading *pemangku* therefore decided to call a joint meeting of all the elders (*tua lokaq*) to discuss how to handle the situation. At that meeting, the elders decided that the only way to placate the spirit would be to arrange yet another burial ceremony followed by a seven–day celebration. It was also decided to stop all preparations for the thousand–day ceremony until this had been done.

After the prescribed ceremony had been held, the situation slowly returned to normal. Some people were still frightened, however, and foresaw further dire consequences of the sacrilege. A few weeks later the wife of the sub-district chief (*camat*), a leading member of the same nobility group, suddenly became insane. She started to wander around in the village, continuously rubbing her hands and mumbling to herself. One day, however, she spoke up and declared herself to be the soul of *makam Reaq*.[11] He had possessed her and now used her body as a medium to proclaim his will. The spirit was disturbed, he said, by what had happened to *Raden* Gagar. He now demanded that the villagers perform a cleaning ceremony (*pengasuh desa*).

This was promptly done and after that it seemed as if the curse had finally been lifted. Preparations for the thousand day ceremony were taken up again and everything proceeded smoothly. During the ceremony itself, however, a near fatal accident occurred. An accidental fire caused people to start worry again. However, since nothing more happened, the whole affair was slowly forgotten.

As this case shows, the fate of the ancestors is something which is of great concern to everybody. If they are neglected, or if something wrong is done, dreadful results might follow. If required, an ancestor soul might even take possession of a human being to make his will known. Summarily, we can conclude that the cult of the ancestral spirits is the central element in the *wetu telu* religion. It permeates all religious beliefs and is a common theme in all ritual celebrations. These spirits, however, are not the only supernatural beings; the Bayanese cosmos is also populated by many other spirits.

Local Spirits (*isin*)

The Bayanese believe that several places in the surroundings are inhabited by – mostly benign – beings. Referred to as the 'content' (*isin*) of the place concerned, such places are, for instance, ancestor graves, spring waters and hills. There are two hills at the southern and northern village borders respectively, which are specifically revered. On the top of these hills are placed a large number of stones around which a bamboo house has been erected. These two sacred places are known as *gedeng lauq* and *gedeng daya*. Each of them is guarded by a special kind of official (*perumbaq*), the office of which is certainly of pre-Islamic origin. The welfare of these beings is the concern of the various *pemangku* mentioned above. People regularly visit these places to pay their respects to its inhabitants and ask in return for a favour of some kind. The sacred places are also the foci of large communal ceremonies held at special occasions. At the spring waters, for instance, farmers celebrate a ceremony to ask the spirit inhabiting the place to bless the rice. This ceremony is held once a year, at the beginning of the rainy season, just before the rice is to be planted.

However, if something disturbs the peace of any of these beings, he may become upset and take possession (*kesandingan*) of a living person. The spirit then uses this person as medium to make his will known to the Bayanese *wetu telu* society. This was what happened when the soul residing in the holy grave *makam Reaq* took possession of the wife of the sub–district head as related above. In Bayan there have been a number of such cases, several of which took place during the unruly years following the 1965 coup d'état.

During the months following the 30 September 1965 coup d'etat when President Sukarno was deposed and PKI, the Indonesian communist party, eradicated, riots spread also to Lombok and, in late 1965, a mob of orthodox Muslims headed by the local military destroyed the *wetu telu* mosque in Anyar, a neighbour village of Bayan, and the sacred northern *gedeng*, putting fire to the house and shattering the stones. Shortly afterwards, two Bayanese women became possessed by the spirit of the *gedeng*. At first, one of the women became disoriented and began to wander around in the village asking everybody to give her new clothes and food. She did not accept gifts from everyone, if anyone whom she did not like tried to give her food, she just threw it away. During her wanderings she was always accompanied by another woman who assisted her and interpreted her wishes. Not long thereafter, the accompanying woman also became possessed and from now on they, together, visited the houses of religious officials and other locally influential persons, insisting on the urgent necessity to rehabilitate the ruined place of worship. Although the stones were recollected and returned to their former site, the proper ceremonies and subsequent reconstruction of the house could not be carried out, because of the very tense situation prevailing at the time. The two women continued to be possessed for more than a year and half until they finally came to their senses again.

At about the same time there was also another similar case, which took place in Anyar at which the spirit taking possession of a woman was said to be the *isin mesigit*, the deity that had been residing in the mosque when it burnt down. In a way similar to the case described above she behaved in an incoherent and unpredictable way and kept on complaining that '*balen kami sor senyareq rengan jari perekeang*', 'my house is destroyed and there is nobody who bothers to rehabilitate it'. At first, it was her family and immediate neighbours who heard the complaints, but soon the rumour about her possession spread around the village, and people began to have faith in her claims. Being possessed by such a mighty spirit, the woman came to be regarded as a diviner (*belian*), meaning that people came to her with betel ingredients asking for *sembeq*, the healing quid that is blessed by the residing spirit. Thus, what was assumed was that the blessing did not come from the woman, but directly from the spirit for whom she acted as a medium. Now and then a *saur ucap* ceremony, a ceremony 'to pay a promise', was also held at her home.

In this group of spirits there are also some beings known as *antaboga* and *gegenduq*, respectively. They are supposed to be the souls of people who have behaved in such sinful and evil ways during life that they were not allowed to enter heaven and therefore have returned as ghosts. People who during life have been *selaq pikir*,[12] i.e., have behaved arrogantly and been maliciously jealous, or have been *selaq ate*, poisoning or otherwise killing people are those who may return to become *antaboga* after death. My informants made it very clear, however, that *antaboga* is not a *selaq*, an evil witch, but was classified as *isin gumi*, which can be translated as 'the deity of the earth'. According to Riel (1941: 66) writing about the beliefs of *wetu telu* Sasak in southern Lombok, *antaboga* is the *naga*, the world snake, living below the ground. This could not be verified in Bayan, where people were well aware of the *naga* and took it into account before undertaking journeys but did not want to admit that the *antaboga* and the *naga* had anything to do with each other.

Antaboga can appear in two shapes, either as a *kurung batang*, i.e., the stretcher used to carry the corpse of a deceased to the burial site or as a deceased man and wrapped into the white cloth used in burial ceremonies. In its first shape *antaboga* has a fragrant smell, whereas in his latter appearance the smell is putrid. Many stories circulate about this being. People told me that they usually meet *antaboga* in or around graveyards. Sometimes he can also be seen at other places, carrying a dead body to the graveyard. In its appearance as a stretcher, the *antaboga* is actually not dangerous, he just wants to confront those that he meet to see if they dare to come close to him. If they do so he will give them a valuable gift. Usually people who see an *antaboga* get very frightened and run away as quickly as possible and when meeting an *antaboga* looking like a corpse wrapped in a white cloth they have good reason to do so. If actually coming close to a living person, *antaboga* in this appearance will embrace and try to eat and kill that person.

Gegenduq are the souls of people who used to go with slander and speak with double tongues. A *gegenduq* can be recognized by the fact that they have three feet. *Gegenduq* are not really dangerous; however, people claimed that this spirit never kills anybody, but he likes to confront people to see if they dare to stand up against him. If anybody has the courage to do so, he might even present him with some valuable gift.

Magical Spirits (*Tau Selaq*)

So-called *tau selaq* are ordinary human beings who have acquired magic of some kind. In Bayanese society, the acquisition of magic seems to be dependent upon knowledge of the proper *mantra*. These are — presumably secret — phrases in old Javanese, or a mixture of old Javanese, Balinese and Sasak.[13] They are handed down from father to son or acquired by a pupil from a teacher. There are many kinds of *mantra* depending upon the effect one wants to achieve. Anybody who knows the proper words can use the *mantra*. The desired effects seem to arrive more or less automatically if only the proper form is adhered to.

As an illustration, I will give here just one example of a *mantra*. This specific phrase is used by a diviner[14] when he tries to cure a person who has become sick because of an attack by a ghost:

Oh Inaq tempur lauq, daya, timuq, bat	Oh Goddess of north, south, east, west
Tetempuran dewa Agung	Overwin the God Agung
Tetempuran dewa Batara	Overwin the God Batara
Tetempuran dewa Bakeq	Overwin the ghosts *Bakeq*
Tetempuran dewa Bakeq melaun	Overwin the ghosts *Bakeq* wherever they are
Sekua ehe aran tetempuran tawar–tawar	Overwin them all wherever they are

The diviner mumbles this phrase in a low voice. After that, he chews some areca nut, lime and betel leaves. He then spits this mixture out over the body of the patient.

Sometimes, however, the use of *mantra* leads to unexpected effects, as in the following case:

> A certain *Loq* Lokasti from Bayan desperately wanted to learn some love magic, *senggeger*, to catch a girl he had fallen in love with. He therefore went to a teacher who promised to teach him the proper love magic phrase, *mantra senggeger*. What he did not know was that the teacher was himself a practicing *selaq*, an evil witch. He intended to recruit his pupil as a *selaq*. To do this, he gave him a false *mantra* instead of the correct one. This transformed the pupil to a *selaq*.
>
> When the pupil had learnt what he thought was a *mantra senggeger*, the teacher instructed him to take a bath in the river. He should take this bath at midnight on a Thursday evening at which there was also a full moon. For the occasion he should also be dressed in a specific white cloth. As soon as the pupil had finished taking the prescribed bath, he realized that something was wrong. The *mantra* he had acquired had the opposite effect on girls than the one he had expected. They ran away instead of becoming attracted.
>
> Since he was now a full-fledged *selaq*, he had acquired a liking for human excrements. To him they had the smell of cakes and tasted delicious.

Whenever he met someone with a large, infectious, running wound, its foul smell was to him like the taste of mouth-watering fruits. He could not resist to eat from it. Because of the *mantra* he employed, the wounded person did not notice anything. Only when he had finished and the fresh wound was bleeding profusely did the person become aware of what had happened. For several years he indulged in these habits. He also often went to the graveyard to eat the flesh of newly buried persons.

On one occasion, however, he was seen trying to sneak away with a stinking chicken carcass. He intended to hide it to eat later. The man who had seen him reported to his father, who was ashamed and angry. He threatened to kill his son unless he gave up his present activities. To save his life, the son promised his father to stop practicing as a *selaq*. To dissolve the magic, he was instructed to write down the words of the *mantra* in reverse order on a piece of *pustaka* made from palm leaves.[15] Then he was to throw this into the river at the same place, date and time as when he had first acquired the magic.

There is also another and more advanced form of black magic, known as *selaq bunga*. Persons mastering this knowledge have acquired the capacity to fly. Such *selaq* often fight each other at night and can then be seen as flickering lights. Actually they do not fight physically but through their respective knowledge. When someone loses such a fight he may survive once or even twice, but the third time he perishes. The Bayanese were able to tell many stories about such fights, but they invariably involved people said to be living somewhere else. No one in Bayan possessed the necessary knowledge to practice as a *selaq bunga*. There was one person, however, said to have been a *selaq bunga* a long time ago. He confirmed this, but added that he never practiced any more. Besides, he said, he had now forgotten almost everything he had once learned.

A special kind of magic is practiced by *selaq mopol*. These have acquired the habit of separating their head from their body. The head then leaves the body and flies around by itself, searching for carcasses from which to eat. People related that in another North Lombok village it had once happened that a man awoke at night. Beside him in the bed he had found the body of his wife with its head missing. He then took a pointed bamboo and planted it in (the remaining part of) her throat. Later, when the head returned from its nightly excursion, it tried to refasten itself to the body again. Then it was mortally wounded by the sharp bamboo. In the morning the dead body was found in the bed.

There is also a being known as *bebaiq* which have a *selaq* as their master. A *bebaiq* cannot be seen by ordinary people and can be ordered by his master to sneak into the houses of other people and catch their valuables. In case someone suspects that he is attacked by a *selaq* or that a *bebaiq* will be stealing his valuables, he can use some *mantra* to counter the magic. By reciting one such *mantra* it is possible to confuse the *selaq*. He will come to believe that he is surrounded by water or that he balances on the edge of a deep ravine.

Ghosts (*Bakeq Beraq*)

These are supernatural beings who with an umbrella term are known as *bakeq beraq*. There are many different kinds of *bakeq beraq*, and they can appear in various shapes. They like to cause trouble for people although most of them are actually more of a nuisance than a real threat. As an example, I can mention a *bakeq beraq* called *kengkong*. She has the appearance of a large woman and likes to steal children, whom she hides in a secluded spot.

> Late one afternoon, while I was in the village, a child disappeared. It was gone all night and only reappeared next morning. During the night a large search party had combed the surroundings without finding any trace of the girl. As an aid in the search, people brought out a gamelan gong and carried it around. A woman carrying a plate with areca nuts, lime and betel leaves headed the search party. People believe that the *kengkong* is attracted by the sound of the gong. She will then come forward to listen and eat of the betel.
>
> When the patrol finally found the girl, they asked her why she had run away and if she had not heard the calls of the search party. The child replied that she had been with her mother, who had taken care of her and fed her. Since her mother was already dead, people commonly assumed that *kengkong* was responsible for the disappearance. This being can change its appearance at will, so it looks like the mother of a child it intends to rob away.

Bakeq beraq are found everywhere, not only in the forest or other quiet places but also in rice fields and even in the middle of the village, oftentimes also in and around the houses. Here they live together with human beings, who are unable to see them although they are able to see the men. Occasionally, a *bakeq beraq* may incarnate himself in someone's dreams. In one such case, a man saw an old woman dragging a crying child along in his compound. Since he did not recognize the couple, he hailed the woman who then rapidly disappeared through the grass-thatched roof of his house. He then became scared, awoke and felt a terrible weakness in his entire body.

Usually, however, the resident *bakeq beraq* cannot be seen and it, therefore, sometimes happens that someone – a man or maybe a cow – unintentionally steps on and hurts or even kills a *bakeq beraq* or one of its children who have been playing in the house yard. In such cases the *bakeq beraq* gets angry and takes revenge by striking the man responsible with sickness of some kind. As long as the *bakeq beraq* remains sick, the man or the cattle responsible for the incident will not become healthy again. Therefore, when a diviner, a *belian*, has identified a *bakeq beraq* as the cause of someone's problems, he will first of all try to treat the *bakeq beraq*, usually by reciting a proper *mantra*. If the accident has been serious and caused the death of a *bakeq beraq*, the responsible man, or cow if that was the case, will also have to die.

When people believe that a *bakeq beraq* may have caused an illness, they will contact a *belian*. He approaches the ghost, tries to cure as described above, and then proposes to escort it out of the village to a new place of residence. To induce the *bakeq beraq* to follow the procession and move to a new spot, some careful preparations are required. The sick person has to prepare an offering meal (*periapan*) and invite the *bakeq beraq* to participate. During the meal, the diviner will explain its purpose to the participants. He then takes some rice and other ingredients and wraps them in a small package (*takilan*). After the meal, all participants join in a procession. They carry the package and a jar of water to the place where the *bakeq beraq* shall settle. Upon arrival, they hang the food package and the water in a large tree. The diviner then addresses the *bakeq beraq* with a few words, saying that this is the place selected. He urges the *bakeq beraq* to remain here so that nobody will hurt him anymore.

As said, most of the various *bakeq beraq* are not dangerous, but they are fond of disturbing and cheating human beings. Therefore, whenever something inexplicable happens, people will immediately suspect that a *bakeq beraq* is involved. To prevent *bakeq beraq* from disturbing people when working with the rice, planting, cleaning or harvesting, packages with food and other ingredients are prepared and left at the corners of the field. This is supposed to keep the spirits inhabiting the field happy and they will then abstain from doing naughty things to the farmer while he is working in the field.

When someone approaches for the first time in his life a forest which is regarded as especially haunted, such as the forest around *gedeng daya* or the forests of Rinjani, just at the entrance to the forest the eldest person in the group takes some rice grains and grinds them between two stones. A small amount of water is added and the resulting mixture is then collected and used to make a protective sign in the forehead of the child, just as one uses to do with betel paste during ceremonies. When distributing the protection the person recites a mantra known as *pendede* as follows:

Yong leleq - yong leleq,	Listen all – listen all
leleq ku cemparing gunung,	All you beings living on the mountain
endang embe bunut merambiq.	We are coming here to visit your mountain
gunung sino	
Sangkareang	Sangkareang (name of the mountain)
Yong leleq - yong leleq,	Listen all – listen all
dua telu dandan bakeq,	Twenty-three different witches (*bakeq*)
sisopo'no dandan tondong,	We are not coming to disturb you
dua telu anak bakeq,	Twenty-three witch children (*anak bakeq*)
sisopoq no piaq ku polong,	We are not coming to disturb you
bareng, bareng, bareng	Excuse us, excuse us, excuse us

The purpose of the *pendede* is to win the sympathy of the resident *bakeq beraq* and, as said, it is usually recited before entering an area that is considered specifically haunted. If a small child is often crying in the daytime, it is believed that this is caused by disturbances from *bakeq beraq,* and to stop the crying the verse can then be recited.

There is one kind of *bakeq beraq* who appears to be dangerous, however, and he is known as *boro–boro*. People describe him as a giant man whose entire body is covered with hair. He lives in mountainous areas. When he meets a man who walks alone at night, he will attack and kill him. There is a certain hill at Gunung Sangkarean, close to Rinjani itself, where *boro–boro* assemble. Here they hold feasts on newly killed men and animals. Anybody who dares to approach the place during the daylight hours can easily find the leftovers from these gruesome feasts.

To protect against future problems with *bakeq beraq* it is important to take some preventive steps. Therefore, before a new house is inhabited for the first time, or a new rice field begins to be cultivated, a ceremony has to be carried out whereby a so-called *bangaran*, which consists of a heap of stones, is erected. The central concern of this ceremony is to inform all the spirits inhabiting the place about what is going to take place. A request is thereby made to all spirits, who happen to have their dwelling place at the site, to move to another place. It is believed that unless this ceremony is properly celebrated, the spirits will get annoyed at the intrusion of the area they inhabit and may strike the people who are going to live there, or the rice which is to be grown, with sickness.

A ceremony with a similar purpose, but without the erection of a heap of stones, takes place once a year just before the onset of the monsoon, at the spring water from which the rice fields of a certain *subak*, an irrigation society, receives its water. The purpose of the ceremony is to protect the growing rice and the farmers, both of whom subsist by the water, from sicknesses caused by the resident *bakeq beraq*, here known also as *penunggu aiq*, the guardian of the water. Each springwater has its own *pemangku*, known as *inan aiq*, the mother of the water, who is the leader of the ceremony.[16]

To start with, he places some rolls of *lekoq buaq*, betel ingredients, at a stone close to the spring water, and reads a *mantra*, a secret phrase, whereupon nine pieces of *kepeng bolong*, Chinese copper coins with a square hole in the middle, are scattered into the water. This is to inform all the resident spirits about the coming ceremony and its purpose. As the main offerings, a couple of chickens have been brought to the spring water. When the performing religious official, the *kiyai,* have cut their throats,[17] they are immediately thrown into the water, as close as possible to the source of the spring, where they are left to bleed to death. After they have died and the food been prepared and arranged on an *ancak*, a small platform made of plaited bamboo and covered with a banana leaf, this is placed close to the spring whereby the food is offered to the spirits.

All the owners of fields receiving water from this spring have contributed some *nasiq*, cooked rice, to the ceremony and a small portion of the rice from each participant is now placed on the *ancak* offered to the spirits. Some 15 minutes later the *ancak* is brought back to the place of the ceremony where it is used for the *periapan*, the communal meal in which the performing *kiyai* and the *pemangku* participate, facing each other and eating from the same *ancak*.

Before the meal starts the responsible *pemangku*, the *inan aiq*, invites the participants.

After the invitation, the *kiayi* reads two prayers, *doa sentulak* and *doa serabat*, which go as follows:

DOA SENTULAK (version from *lebe*)
Allalahuma janibis merasa kena tobat kukuning yang Allah.

Sunangambah putjuking gumi suka gumi badan sempurna hing awal harane tawar Allahuma putjuking langit suka langit badan sempurna kang awaling usesa tawar.
Sunangambah putjuking serengenge suka serengenge badan sempurna allal angsal ing usesa tawar.

Sunangambah putjuking ulan suka ulan badan sempurna hing awaling usesa tawar lintang

Sunangambah putjuking lintang suka lintang badan sempurna awaling usesa tawar
Sunangambah juluking angin suka angin badan sempurna ing usesa tawar

Sunangambah putjuking geni suka geni badan sempurna kang awaling usesa tawar.
Sunangambah putjuking banyu badan sempurna awaling usesa tawar. Laillahaillalah Mampan aku nganggoq Sinasuha tawar berkat laillahaillalah Muhammaddarrasullulah. Amin

Translation:
Oh Lord, I ask forgiveness if there is anything wrong that we have done, in the name of the Lord we ask forgiveness. If I have ever done any bad things on this earth, we ask that the body be forgiven and cleaned of those weaknesses.

If there are any bad things below the sky, we pray that the sky will return happy and the body cleaned of its weaknesses.

If there are any bad things arriving from the naktu,[18] make the naktu happy, the body happy and free from all weaknesses.

If the bad things come from the moon, make the moon happy, the body happy and free from all weaknesses.

If the bad things come every week, make the week happy, the body happy and free from all weaknesses.

If the bad things come from the wind, make the wind happy, the body free from all weaknesses.

If the bad things come from the fire, make the fire happy, the body free from all weaknesses.

If the bad things come from the water, make the water happy, the body free from all weaknesses.

Oh Lord, let all this happen because I make use of the Sentulak prayer.

DOA SERABAT
Allahuma eh wong sang raja srabat tawar penyakit siu satus tunggal sira hanglarani: sira hanambani tawar.

Translation:
Oh Lord, Lord that guides my living Please take away a hundred sicknesses, a thousand sicknesses, all sicknesses that grow in man.

Alungguh ing mulut kalu arane tawar.	If it is you Lord who has sent the sickness, we ask you to diminish or take away the sickness.
Alungguh ing cangkam alungguh ing lidah halakune arane tawar.	If the sickness comes from the mouth of man, please make it disappear.
Alungguh ing lambung kananne janah arane tawar.	If the sickness is within the mouth and tongue of man, please make it disappear.
Alungguh ing lambung kiri tawar. Alungguh tengah wati, rasa pati arane tawar.	If the sickness is within the right side of the body, please make it disappear.
Alungguh ing suku tengen jempe arane tawar.	If the sickness is within the left side of the body, please make it disappear.
Alungguh ing suku lungguh, neda berkat doa serabat.	If the sickness grows within the wind, make it pure, make the dirty elements disappear.
Tawar-tawar penyakit siu satus tunggal berkat lailahailelah aku nganggoq doa serabat.	If the sickness comes from the power of spirits and devils, make it disappear.
	If the sickness comes from the hands or feet of man, make it disappear.
	Take away a hundred sicknesses, a thousand sicknesses, all sicknesses that grow in man. Oh Lord, let all this happen because I make use of the Serabat prayer.

The two prayers are meant to salvage the village after a natural calamity of some kind, for instance an earthquake or an excessive drought. They can also be employed, as in this case, to ask for sufficient monsoon rains during the months ahead.

When the prayers have been read, the communal meal takes place. The leftovers are divided among the *inan aiq* and the *pekasih*, the official in charge of dividing the water among the *subak* members, to take home and offer to the spirits (*ngengolang*) in their respective houses.

The Stone Cult

As already mentioned, besides the mosques there are two more important sanctuaries in the Bayan region, known respectively as *gedeng lauq* and *gedeng daya*. Both of them consist of a great number of smaller and larger, *lingga*-shaped stones. Both sanctuaries are situated on the top of a steep hill. One of the worship places, the *gedeng lauq*, is located close to the sea and the other, *gedeng daya*, is found high up on the mountain slope. The stones of each of the two *gedeng*[19] are supposed to be protected by a bamboo house, just like the ancestor graves around the old mosque in central Bayan. The roof of the house is supposed to be covered with thousands of 40–50 centimetre-long split bamboo sticks, known as *santek*. In all of Bayan there are only two more buildings with this kind of roof: the old mosque and the nearby ancestor grave *makam Reaq*, in honour of which the *alip* ceremony described by van Baal (1941) takes place. Just to the west of the *gedeng* itself there is supposed to be another house, known as *bale gaung*. During the periodic *alip* ceremony in which the house is renewed, this is the place of a flute orchestra who plays all the time while *perumbaq*, the guardian of the stones, says his prayers (*penabe*) at the stones. This building does not have the same kind of roof as the *gedeng* itself but is covered in its entire length with bamboo poles split lengthwise in two halves and with every other pole turned upside down, hooked into its neighbours on both sides.

It is believed that the stones that are collected at the two *gedeng* are representatives of the ancestor souls and that they have magical powers. The number of stones vary in mysterious ways depending on the conditions in the world. When the times are unruly, much fighting and maybe even armed clashes occur, the number of stones at the *gedeng* diminish. The stones then move to the place where there is conflict and war, where they take the shape of human beings (*penyamar*) to guide and lead the people into restoring peace and order. When the world has again become quiet and peaceful, the human beings are again transformed back into stones who then return to their respective *gedeng* whereupon their numbers may increase manifold.

I once visited the house of *amaq* Ratnilem, one of the eldest men in the hamlet Luang Godek, the hamlet where also *perumbaq lauq*, the guardian of *gedeng lauq*, lives. We came to talk about the significance of the stones that could be found in the *gedeng* and at the house of *perumbaq*. He then told me that formerly, when the traditions, the *adat,* were still honoured properly and the house around the *gedeng* was in good shape, there were lots of stones in the *gedeng*.[20] Indeed, the place was so crammed that there was not room enough for all the stones inside the house and some of them were, therefore, found on the outside. There were so many stones that it was sometimes difficult even to count them. Some people who tried said that there were more than five hundred, whereas others claimed that the number was less. According to *amaq* Ratnilem those who counted fewer stones did so because they were impure at heart when they approached the *gedeng*. At that time the number of stones rose and fell all the time, but there were always lots of them.

In late 1965, the year of the coup d'état and three days after the local military and the mob accompanying him had burnt down the house of the *gedeng* and thrown the stones away, *amaq* Ratnilem and two more people dared to approach the *gedeng* where they encountered only six stones. All the others had been shattered, most of them thrown into the nearby sea. During the following night, *amaq* Ratnilem had a dream in which he met with six old men with long beards. One of them came close and said to him:

Epe uah takut, uah ketejut timaq baleng kami soweq julat anak jaring kami soweq buang laguq piran2 kumpul ampoq. Sangkaq rengan siq ketoang kami nono soraq nya dait selamat.	Brother, do not be afraid, do not be startled even if our house has been burnt down and our grandchildren have been thrown away. Go ahead and reassemble them where they belong. Because of these misdeeds, he will not be safe.

The men appearing in his dream were the spirits of the six remaining stones and they now told *amaq* Ratnilem not to be afraid but go ahead and reassemble all the shattered stones. In the last sentence of his speech the old man also prophesized that the person responsible for the deed should be duly punished. And indeed within a year the military who had led the mob died. When I visited the *gedeng lauq* in early 1996, there were perhaps some 120 stones assembled at the place where the house used to stand. According to *amaq* Ratnilem, the low number now compared to earlier was due to the bad times with less attention being paid to the tradition, the *adat*.

Communicating with the Spirits: the *Bao Daya* Ceremony

In Bayan there are two kinds of ceremonial performances that have magical purposes and through which the spirits can be called and come to possess those performing. These are known as *bao daya*. The *bao daya* ceremony, calling the spirits or the deities, can be performed for many different purposes and occasions. One of the uses is connected to the yearly agricultural cycle and should be performed before work starts in the fields, whether on the *bangket* (irrigated field) or on the *oma* (dry field) and also just before the harvest is finished. Moreover, if the owner stages a *selamat bangket*, a ceremony to bless the fields, it is obligatory that this is accompanied by a *bao daya* performance.

When a person, for instance a child, is seriously ill, it also often happens that the child's parents promise to stage a *bao daya* performance as a means to get supernatural assistance to help the child recover. In the *bao daya* group there are *belian* who can perform miracles on behalf of sick persons if they are treated in connection with a *mendewa* performance. They possess a specific *mantra* which when read during a *mendewa* performance causes the deity to arrive and possess the belian (*kedewaan*) who then, acting on behalf of the deity, can assist in curing the sick person.

The concept *mendewa* has connections with the stones (*peaci-aci*) that are assembled at certain places known as *pedewaan*, the most prominent ones being the two *gedeng* mentioned above. These are sacred stones that are thought of as containers for the gods and that have the power to strike with sickness as well as to heal the same. According to the beliefs in Bayan, these stones can disappear and come back by themselves, depending on the situation in the world. In some of the isolated Bayan hamlets such as Telaga Banyak or Bon Gontor, worship by the *peaci-aci* in the forest or at the spring waters is still being carried out and is directed toward the stones in the *pedewaan*, which are seen as a symbol for the spirits.

During this ceremony, the participants are entertained by the *bao daya* group, which consists of a lone flute played by a blind flutist (*jero gamel*), and two elderly women (*inan gending*), who sing the songs. Those dancing to the songs of the *bao daya* flute are a man (*Maki*) and a woman (*Ini*). Before *Maki* and *Ini* start to dance, the person who has invited to the ceremony address (*penabe*) them and the spirits and deities (*dewa*) that have assembled as follows:

Tabeq, tabeq, tabeq, naq Ini, naq Maki, naq patih Panji bini laki agung alit Nyata samar, kulakoq Nugraha melekongin, mentandang kolan pegundeman pelendangan epe, buat salaq tertip tingkah ku, lan semalih timpal ku nene aku tunas ampura, seribu kali ampurayan, silaq.	Excuse, excuse, excuse *Ini, Maki, patih Panji*, all beings in the forests and the mountain, all beings known and unknown, seen and unseen, all who have arrived to the calling I have sent around, please join in the celebration help me to regain my health. I invite you all to join me and if I have done any mistakes, I ask forgiveness, I ask forgiveness a thousand times.

This is answered by *Maki* and *Ini* with another formal speech, whereupon the performance may start, usually around ten o'clock in the evening. The performance begins with a long session of flute playing and singing which is followed by dancing, then more flute playing and dancing. Slowly, the tempo increases, the flute becomes more and more insistent and, together with the effect of the droning yet mesmerizing singing, the spectacle builds up towards a crescendo. At the peak of the performance, usually deep into the night or even in early morning, the deities, the *dewa*, will appear and possess *Maki* and/or *Ini* and occasionally also one or more of the other actors.

The deity feels attracted by the sound of the flute and the accompanying songs, but he must come voluntarily, he cannot be forced to appear. The circumstances and the atmosphere must be right, otherwise nothing will happen. As an example, the *Maki* told that occasionally his group has performed during independence celebrations on 17 August and also for the tourists at the big hotels in Senggigi. Although the circumstances in the form of flute playing and singing are exactly the same during such occasions, he feels that the whole performance is enforced and thus the *dewa* refuses to appear.

The outward signs of possession are a stiffening of the body, interrupted by violent shaking, acting in irrational ways, talking incomprehensibly, crying, asking for food, and so on. To wake the possessed from his trance it is necessary to burn incense while sprinkling the body with young coconut water (*nyur gading*) in which has been put white flowers from the *Jepun* tree (*kembang jepun*) and dark-red flowers from the *Serinata* plant. According to the *Maki* he is totally unaware of what is happening when he becomes possessed, the deity takes over completely and he becomes another person.

If a sick person is brought forward, he may proceed to speak incoherently and strangely, blessing the sick person and distributing *sembeq*, the healing betel quid to the sick. On another occasion which I watched, three persons laid down, faces toward the ground, while *Maki* began to massage their backs, legs and arms using first his feet walking on their bodies and finally massaging with his hands. Immediately after the treatment was finished, the *Maki* greeted each of them in the way described above and swung a jar of burning incense in front of each of them. Afterward, when I was talking to one of the patients, he said that he had suffered a severe attack of lumbago, but after the treatment it was completely gone and he felt totally refreshed.

Is it possible to say what deity is entering the body of *Maki*, *Ini* and others? *Maki* himself was unable to tell, but other people voiced various opinions; many claimed that it was either the *isin awak*, 'the deity of the body' or the *isin gubuk*, 'the deity of the hamlet'. Others suggested that the deity came from places such as Gunung Batua and Gunung Rinjani (two of the Lombok volcanoes) or Lokoq Getaq and Gedeng Daya (two sacred places in the Bayan area). It seems that once in possession of a body, the deity in question never identified himself as an individual entity. Since the person being possessed is not aware of what is happening, he has no way of knowing and the deity never tells anything about himself. People have very vague ideas about these deities and cannot tell much about them; they don't know what they look like or what their characters are. It rather seems that they conceive of them as a kind of ephemeral substance that inhabits and somehow empowers certain places. During *bao daya* performances this substance enters the body of the person being possessed and with this body as its medium it is able to communicate and perform miraculous, healing actions.

Summary

We have found that among the *wetu telu* Sasak in the Bayan region there are two groups of religious officials – *kiyai* and *pemangku*. An understanding of the symbolic representations of their offices is basic in the *wetu telu* syncretism. As already indicated, the former office is associated with heaven and with the perpetuation of the human life essence, the soul, while the latter is connected to the earthly realm and to the spirits dwelling upon it.

It is interesting to note that this duality of functions between two kinds of religious officials seems to be a pre-Muslim phenomenon among the Sasak, and as such it is intimately connected to the w*etu telu* syncretism. Among the supposedly 'heathen' Boda[21] of Northwest Lombok, the institution of *kiyai* is unknown and in that society burials are led by a *pemangku gumi* (lit. *pemangku* of the earth) while among the orthodox Muslims the opposite situation prevails and the institution of *pemangku* has been abolished altogether in favour of the *kiyai*. The argument for this rejection among the orthodox is that the *pemangku* is a Hindu office which, as such, has no place in a Muslim society.

And indeed, among the Hindu-Balinese we find a similar opposition between two religious offices, *pemangku* (temple priest) and *pedanda* (high priest) respectively (Covarrubias 1937: 270). As among the syncretist Sasak, the Balinese *pemangku* may deal directly with the spirits and the ancestors, while the

Gods and spirits in the Wetu Telu religion of Lombok 255

pedanda handle the relations with the high Gods, either Batara Guru (Siwa) or Batara Budha.[22] The Bayanese ancestor genealogy starts with Batara Guru, and van Eerde (1901: 205) also reports Batara Guru as one of the Boda Gods. All these indications make it reasonable to assume that before Islam came to Lombok, when the Sasak were still animist/Hindu, a similar opposition as the one presently existing between *pemangku* and *kiyai* was already there, and when the new religion came, the names of some officials (and Gods) changed, but the symbolic content of the relations continued to exist more or less in the same way as before.

Notes

1. The mighty Lombok volcano, which is still active and rises more than 3,700 meters above sea level.
2. The Bayanese make a distinction between two different kinds of souls, which are called *roh* and *njawa,* respectively. The latter may be described as a kind of life essence, while the former is the soul proper. At death, *njawa* is dissolved, whereas *roh* undertakes a journey to the hereafter. The term *roh* is of Arabic origin and was probably introduced together with Islam.
3. See for instance Bakker (1938), Bousquet (1939) and Goris (1936).
4. See Cederroth (1981).
5. Internally the village is divided into a number of factions, which trace different origins. Externally they consider themselves to be one big family, as opposed to the orthodox Muslim migrants now moving into the area.
6. In Bayan there are lots of *pemangku*, all with different tasks assigned to them.
7. There is a total of six *makam* scattered around the old mosque. Each of them is protected by a bamboo house and dedicated to the oldest ancestor of the various nobility groups in Bayan.
8. See Cederroth (1988).
9. At that time there was still no road connecting Bayan with Lendang Awu.
10. In theory, this ceremony ought to be celebrated one thousand days after death. In practice, it is rarely held, mainly because of the excessive costs involved. Sometimes, it is decided to hold the ceremony, nevertheless. Then it is usually celebrated for many souls simultaneously irrespective of when they happened to die. See Cederroth (1988) for a description of the ceremony.
11. The most sacred of all the ancestor graves and the one in honour of which the *Alip* ceremony, described by van Baal (1941), is celebrated.
12. The *selaq,* witch, is common in Indonesia and closely resembles, for instance, the Balinese *leyak.*
13. Among orthodox Muslims, *mantra* are often in Arabic and may consist of a verse from the Koran.
14. The diviners *(belian)*, is a group of officials who can contact and communicate with the spirits. Because of such magic powers, they are often engaged to cure sicknesses. For more information, see Cederroth (1996). The term *belian* is commonly found throughout the archipelago and often denotes ritual specialists of an androgynous character who can contact with the world of spirits.
15. These are the dried leaves from a kind of palm tree. For many centuries they have been used as a kind of paper. Stories written on the leaves have been gathered into books.
16. Although the official is a man, he is known as 'the mother of the water'.
17. Since the *kiyai* officials are in charge of the hereafter they are consequently ritual butcherers.
18. A system used to calculate if the spirits are favourable or not to a certain activity on a certain day or time. There are several different modes of calculation available.

19. According to the dictionary of Goris (1938) the Sasak word *gedeng*, which is used in high speech, translates as palace and Goris mentions a sacred place in the village of Ketangga where a king of the east Lombok kingdom of Selaparang is said to have had a house.
20. By this he meant the period between the 1956 celebration of *alip luir gama*, the ceremony during which the houses of the two *gedeng* are repaired, and the events that led to the destruction of the house and the shattering of the stones in 1965.
21. In Goris (1938: 57), the general meaning of the term *buda* is translated as 'people without religion'. This term has been applied to the small group of non-Muslim Sasak, still living in some isolated parts of Lombok.
22. There are two groups of *pedanda*, Siwaites and Buddhists, respectively. However, these are not representatives of two religions, but aspects of one religion (cf. Covarrubias 1937: 295).

References

Bakker, J.B. (1938) *Memorie van Overgave van de Onderafdeling Oost Lombok*.
Baal, J. Van (1941) 'Het Alip feest te Bajan', *Mededeelingen van de Kirtya–Liefrinck van de Tuuk*, Afl, 16: 1–42 (Djawa 21:6).
Bousquet, G.H. (1939) 'Recherches sur les deux sectes Musulmanes (Waktou Telous et Waktou Lima) de Lombok', *Revue des etudes Islamiques*, 13: 149–77.
Cederroth, S. (1981) *The Spell of the Ancestors and the Power of Mekkah. A Sasak Community on Lombok*. Gothenburg Studies in Social Anthropology, no. 3: Acta Universitatis Gothoburgensis.
——— (1988) 'Pouring Water and Eating Food. On the Symbolism of Death in a Sasak Community on Lombok', in S. Cederroth, S. and C. Corlin and J. Lindström (eds.) *The Meaning of Death. Essays on Mortuary Rituals and Eschatological Beliefs*, Uppsala Studies in Social Anthropology, no. 10: Acta Universitatis Upsaliensis.
——— (1996) 'Return of the Birds. Revival of Wetu Telu Religion in the Village of Bayan', paper presented at the 1st EuroSEAS Conference, Leiden, July 1995.
Covarrubias, M. (1937) *Island of Bali*, New York, NY: Alfred A. Knopf.
Goris, R. (1936) 'Aantekeningen over Oost-Lombok', *Tijdschrift voor Indische Taal- Land- en Volkenkunde,* 76: 196–248.
——— (1938) *Beknopt Sasaksch-Nederlands Woordenboek*, Kirtya Liefrinck van der Tuuk: Singaradja.
Hartong, A.M. (1974) *Het adatrecht bij de Sasakse bevolking van Lombok,* Mimeo: University of Nijmegen.
Leemann, A. (1989) *Internal and External Factors of Socio-cultural and Soci-economic Dynamics in Lombok (Nusa Tenggara Barat)*. Anthropogeographie, Vol. 8, Zürich: Geographisches Institut der Universität.
Riel, A.C.J. (1941) 'Enkele Mededeelingen over de Heilige Weefsels van Poedjoet', *Mededeelingen van de Kirtya-Liefrinck van der Tuuk*, 16: 89–95 (*Djawa* 21:6).
van Eerde, J. C. (1901) 'Aantekeningen over de Bodha's van Lombok', *Tijdschrift voor Indische Taal-, Land- en Volkenkunde*, 43: 240–310.

13 Impaling spirit

Three categories of ontological domain in Eastern Indonesia

David Hicks

> It is in the penumbra, between the clear visibility of things and their total extinction in darkness when the concreteness of appearances becomes merged in half-realized, half-baffled vision, that spirit seems to disengage itself from matter to envelop it with a mystery of soul suggestion.
>
> (Caffin 1910)[1]

It will be recalled that Tylor proposed 'as a minimum definition of Religion, the belief in Spiritual Beings' (1883: 424) and that '... under the name of Animism [he sought] to investigate the deep-lying doctrine [as he called it] of Spiritual Beings, which embodies the very essence of Spiritualistic as opposed to Materialistic philosophy' (1883: 425). In the region that concerns us here, the contrast between the 'Spiritualistic' and the 'Materialistic' offers us lessons in how certain societies seek to come to terms with the ineluctable fact that the two ontological domains, or statuses, by their very natures, are inaccessible to each other. Intrinsic to their endeavour is the notion of conjunction, i.e., the process by which the two ontological statuses are subsumed in a relationship of proximity or even syncretism, since some sort of relationship is implied by the very existence of this duality. Furthermore, although this conjunction may have a destructive aspect, it has its beneficial aspect as well, and studies in comparative religion show that more often than not the conjunctive interaction of human beings and their spirits is mutually beneficial, and from the human perspective, especially the paramount benefits accruing from involvement in the world of the spirit are life and plenitude. Securing these benefits comes about in ritual, of course. As Arthur Maurice Hocart (1954: 19) has put it:

> Rituals have as their purpose to produce or increase the necessaries of life. They are acts of creation. They create more witchetty grubs, more buffaloes, more clouds, or whatever the desired objects may be. The cosmic rites create more of everything that man may need, and as the food supply depends upon the proper working of the whole world, such ceremonies create the world.

Myth, too, fulfils this function, and one purpose of the present chapter is to demonstrate how[2]. This much having been said, the question arises: how can what is insubstantial interact with what is substantial; how can invisible and intangible spirits be brought or – as I shall attempt to demonstrate in this essay, more properly, 'thought' – into a relationship with visible and tangible human beings? Certain narratives in the textual repertoires of peoples of eastern Indonesia juxtapose specific motifs that recur with sufficient regularity to define them as a set. There are seven of these motifs: (a) water; (b) life and plentitude/abundance; (c) an instrument of impalement or entrapment, an arrow, sword, rope, fishing line, or – most typically – a fishing hook;[3] (d) the quest, usually circular; (e) the social relationship of elder brother/younger brother; (f) deception (successful or unsuccessful) or an error; and (g) visibility/invisibility, as indexed by the opening and/or shutting of the eyes.[4] In the final section of his first volume of *Primitive Culture* Edward Tylor re-emphasizes his evocation of the duality he remarked earlier by referring to it as 'the deepest of all religious schisms, that which divides Animism from Materialism' (1883: 502), and it is clear from his words he identified the distinction between spirit and matter as central to discussions about religion. Given his awareness, therefore, it is interesting Tylor paid little consideration to the possible interfaces where the two ontological domains interplay with each other, nor discuss in a more comprehensive manner how the realm of the visible and the realm of the invisible are brought into relationship in different systems of belief. In eastern Indonesia one such interface for this kind of interplay and visible/invisible dialectic is water, whether fresh or salt[5] and by an analysis of the seven narratives summarized here it becomes possible to see how the indigenous imagination deploys a material artifact, the aforementioned fishing hook, to convey its comprehension of the interdependence of the two ontological domains.

Current explorations of animistic thinking among populations living in other parts of the world highlights predation as a pervasive motif in their thought. Among Amerindians in Amazonia (Århem 1996), the relationship between predator and prey functions as a central motif that gives coherence to affinal bonds, ritual, and cosmology, as well as their attitudes towards the natural environment on which they depend. Among the Wari' in western Amazonia, '[h]umans provide the Water Spirit Society with new members who marry and bear children, enhancing the reproduction of Water Spirit Society. The Water Spirits provide the living Wari' with life-sustaining animal food. For Wari', this exchange not only reproduces the primary human/non-human relations of their cosmology but also promises an enhancement of ecological resources important to their subsistence. White-lipped peccaries and fish are the only foods encountered in dense concentrations in this environment ...' (Conklin 1995: 90).

These seven narratives may be seen to constitute a coherent 'set' in the sense established by Claude Lévi-Strauss (1979), in which the same few motifs are worked and reworked, at once diverse and constant, in the advancement of certain ideas important to the tellers and hearers alike. Given the desiccated nature of that region of Southeast Asia, it is understandable that water, whether fresh or salt, should come to occupy a prominent place in many narratives of eastern Indonesia. Nor, given the widespread belief in all manner of animistic forms is it at all surprising that spirits also figure recurrently. In the set of narratives identified in this analysis water is cast as the essential mediating agency for engaging the two ontological modes of spirit and matter in a reciprocal relationship in which benefits accrue to at least one or – more commonly – both parties. These benefits include life, health, fertility, elevation in social status, and plentitude. So vital is this motif that it may be regarded as the 'fulcrum' of the tales and of the entire set while the other six motifs, combining and recombining, serve as lenders of support to this central motif. As a natural substance its cultural counterpart is the hook, which functions as a 'connector', so to speak, functioning to conjoin the two metaphysical domains. In these works of imagination this connector is an instrument of impalement or capture which makes its appearance in diverse forms, most typically that of a fishing hook,[6] the owner of which is, more often than not, a superior elder brother whose inferior younger brother, after losing the artifact, engages in a quest to retrieve it, the outcome of his venture typically inverting the terms of their relative statuses.[7]

The narratives analyzed here are truncated synopses of their originals and derive from the corpus of stories that form part of the verbal traditions of Sumbawa, Flores, Kei, the Alor Peninsula and Timor.

Some summary remarks concerning the ethnographic contexts in which the narratives discussed in this article are recited are in order. The island inhabited by the people of eastern Bima defines the western geographic boundary of the societies mentioned; the populations of the Kei islands define the eastern boundary. In between are Flores, where live the Nage; Timor, to the east, where the Atoni, Makassai, and Naueti live; and just north of Timor a small island cluster dominated by Alor. The people who incorporate the fishing hook into their corpus of oral literature are not necessarily fisher folk, indeed, the majority of ethnic groups whose narratives we consider in this article generally live at some remove from the sea, e.g., the Naueti and most Makassai and Atoni, though, locally, there may be rivers, streams, springs or lagoons from which they may take fish and crustaceans. The subsistence of these societies is based for the most part on the swidden or irrigated cultivation of rice, maize, sweet potatoes, yams and fruits of different kinds, among other cultivars; and raising chickens, pigs, buffalo and cattle. Local environmental cultural differences make for variation, of course; but the alternation of wet and dry season has an immense influence on all of them. Roughly speaking, the wet season runs from about October to April while the dry season occupies the period, May to September. Again, however, local variations occur and the rainfall regime is never to be counted on. Patrilineal descent and patrilocal residence tend to be the preferential modes governing social order, although the Bimanese are cognatic, accompanied by the giving of bridewealth. Matrilineal descent/matrilocal residence, though, sometimes prevails in the absence of bridewealth, and there is invariably scope for a variety of permutations in between. With the exception of the Bimanese, perhaps the most definitive feature of their social organization, however, is that they practice asymmetric exchange, whether of a prescriptive or non-prescriptive character (see Hicks 2007a). Prominent, also, in the social order is the superior status conferred upon the elder brother to whom the younger brother is expected to display deference. This relationship, as we shall see, is the fulcrum on which almost all the plots depend. The spirit world is, for virtually all these groups, a domain populated by an array of diverse elementals which include sky gods, earth goddesses, nature spirits, agricultural spirits, and most influential of any in daily life, the ghosts of the ancestors. The appellation 'god' or 'divinity' in the case of these societies may denote a high god or a lesser manifestation of divinity, such as an animistic power residing at the bottom of the sea or some such aquatic habitat, or a local immaterial power resident at the top of a mountain or in a grove of trees. Rituals, whether of a communal nature, such as the rites of passage of birth, marriage and death, or rituals carried out at the more restricted level of the household control much of the religious life, which in some communities is centered around a sacred building – part reliquary, part church – that provides a suitable forum for communication with the ancestors. Throughout eastern Timor this edifice is called the *uma lulik* or *uma luli*. The corpus of oral and among the Bimanese, written literature is rich, with many categories of genre finding verbal expression in their respective cultures. These include myths, legends, folktales, fables, poems, songs, and ritual speech. In these the animistic interaction with human beings are recurrent themes.

The Narratives

Narrative One

The following narrative comes from the Nage people who live in the central part of Flores. It is one of many texts that comprise their extensive oral literature and was collected by Gregory Forth (1998: 38–42).[8]

Lalo Sue, a younger brother, asked his elder brother, Siku Sue, if he might borrow his fishing hook and line. Although Siku refused, Lalo borrowed them anyway. While he was fishing at night in a pool along came a large eel which broke the fishing line, taking the fishing hook with it. Siku was furious and ordered Lalo to retrieve it. Lalo then went to his garden, which was located near the pool in which he had lost his hook and line. Remaining there for some days he noticed that the flowers on his pumpkins were being plucked, and to find the culprit he hid himself very early one morning at the top of a tree. Just as dawn was breaking he glimpsed two fish emerge from the water in the pool. They wriggled up the bank and after shedding their skins proved to be two women. Actually, they were spirits that lived in a village beneath the waters of the pool, and as they were plucking the flowers Lalo demanded to know what they were doing. They said they were collecting a flower called *runu* (*Wedelia* species) to make a medicine to cure their father who had an injured jaw. Their father had been hit by a 'god's tooth'. Lalo instantly realized the father must be the eel and advised them that the flowers would not cure him. But he knew a medicine that would. They said that if he did so they would reward him. Lalo entered the water and the two women told him to hold onto their backs and keep his eyes closed. When he arrived at the gate of the underwater village Lalo opened his eyes. Arriving at the father's house Lalo saw his fishing line wrapped around a house post. He tugged the line and heard a cry of pain and as he unraveled the line saw the old man rocking back and forth. Lalo had brought some dried coconut with which, after he had chewed it, he used to massage the invalid's jaw. When the jaw was sufficiently soft Lalo extracted the fishing hook and the man asked Lalo how he might reward him. After some time, Lalo told him all he wished were vine seeds he had seen children playing with in the village plaza and an old piece of rope tied around the village gate with which to tie up the basket in which the seeds would be placed. Puzzled though he was that Lalo wanted such worthless things the old man agreed. Lalo also asked for a set of four daggers called *kamu ke'o*, and these were also granted. The two fish women took Lalo back to the dry land. When he arrived at the edge of the pool near his garden Lalo peered into the basket and instead of the vine seeds he saw great round pieces of gold. Back in his village Lalo was reunited with Siku who was full of remorse for having made his younger brother look for his lost hook and line. He had thought him dead and was about to hold a wake. Lalo returned the hook and line, and showed his elder brother the gold.

Narrative Two

This narrative – of which there are a number of versions – was collected by Michael Prager (2010) from Bima regency in eastern Sumbawa. The motif of the quest is not elaborated in the form of a journey, explicitly undertaken, but a journey between dry land and sea would seem clearly implied. The deception/error motif appears. The younger brother lies to, and then tricks, his elder brother; and the elder brother fails to pick up all the scattered sesame seeds.

In Bima lived two royal brothers. The elder brother was called Indera Kemala. The younger was called Indera Zamrut. Kemala resided in the west; Zamrut resided in the east. Because he loved to fish Kemala's palace was located near the sea. He owned a golden fishing hook. Because he loved agriculture Zamrut's palace was located near the fields and mountains. He owned a golden tray that contained seeds. One day Zamrut visited his elder brother and asked if he could borrow his fishing hook. Kemala assented but told his younger brother to take care of the fishing hook and not lose it. However, while Zamrut was fishing in the sea the prince of the perch (*ikan kerapu*) swallowed the fishing hook and broke the line. When Zamrut told Kemala what had occurred he was ordered to go and find it. Zamrut travelled to the sea where he found the fish in a state of great agitation. They were looking for a healer and a medicine with which to cure the perch prince whose throat was injured. He had swallowed a hook. Zamrut extracted the hook whereupon the perch prince told him he would grant any wish the younger brother might have. Zamrut told him that he was content to have cured the perch prince and asked permission to leave. He arrived ashore accompanied by a swarm of fish. Zamrut gave his brother the hook and returned home. There, he filled his golden tray with white sesame seeds, which he placed above the ground at the entrance to his palace. On the ground, he sprinkled some white sand and sent word to his elder brother that he was seriously ill. Kemala did come, but upon entering his younger brother's palace the golden tray fell to the floor and the white sesame seed spilt out and mixed into the white sand. Zamrut ordered his elder brother to restore the tray to its original state by separating the sesame seed from the sand. Kemala tried and looked like he had succeeded in filling the tray with the every one of sesame seeds. But in fact he had failed to do so because when Zamrut came and poured water over the sand three sprouts of sesame emerged from the ground. Realizing he had failed in his task of restoring the sesame seeds as they had originally been in the golden tray, Kemala, after wandering about aimlessly, decided to go into exile. He finally disappeared in a pond leaving his younger brother king of Bima.

A much shorter variant of this narrative is given by Michael Hitchcock (1996: 47). The perch is replaced by a whale; the fish in a state of agitation are now shrimps; they tell him their king, the whale, is sick; and Zamrut (here called 'Jambrut') realizes that it is his elder brother's hook that is the culprit; and a fish known as *pari*, agrees to take him to the king on condition Zamrut's descendants will never eat *pari*;[9] and when he reaches the afflicted king whale's court 'craftily' persuades the courtiers of the king that his cure will only work if they close their eyes. He removes the hook, conceals it, and holds up a piece of seaweed as the agency responsible for the impalement. Zamrut is observed, however, by a fish known as the *tampoli*, which, unlike the other spectators, kept its eyes open, and so today is considered by the Bimanese as hard to catch.

Narrative Three

This narrative lacks the motifs of the hook and the fraternal relationship, and the quest is undertaken by a woman, not a man. And she is seeking, not a fishing hook, but water, with which to provide her community with life and pentitude. Furthermore, her quest into the spirit realm, via water, is not of a cyclical character. The woman ultimately fails to return. Nevertheless, her quest is undertaken through the initiative of a man, her father, who would appear to take on the role of elder brother that we see in the other narratives; his daughter meanwhile filling the role of younger brother. The means to life for human beings and spirits alike is this woman for it is her bridewealth that makes possible the life and abundance her community and the deity need. Another singular feature of the tale is that the deity is wife-taker to humanity. The text was collected on the island of Pura, in the Alor Peninsula, by Susanne Rodemeier (2009).

While out hunting a huge wild boar (which was in reality the mountain/water deity metamorphosed), Olangki, father of a girl named Bui, grew very thirsty. And so, as he was passing the mountain home of the local deity, he asked it for water. He did so by thrusting his arrow into the earth saying, 'If I get enough [water] for the fields also, I promise to give my daughter in exchange'.[10] At that moment water began emerging from the earth, clouds formed, and heavy rain began falling. Olangki realized he should not have said what he did and hurried home, only to learn the rainfall had caused a huge landslide that threatened his village. To avert this disaster Olangki told his wife to take Bui, their daughter, up the mountain next day. Giving her to the god was the only way to prevent calamity. The following day, as the two women were ascending the mountain, the rain ceased.

As they approached a mountain pool Bui told her mother she could see smoke on the slopes. This was due to the slash-and-burn carried out by the mountain spirits preparing their fields. Bui pointed towards the smoke and the woman looked, but because she was human and the smoke was of spirit essence she could not see it. When she glanced back to where Bui had been, she found that her daughter had disappeared into the pool. Before starting to walk down the slippery path home Bui's mother looked for a stick with which to support her and saw, floating on the surface of the pool, a number of bamboo sticks. She picked up one and upon reaching home thrust it beneath the floor of her house and fell asleep. Next morning Olangki looked at what had been a bamboo stick and saw instead a sacred sword. He immediately realized the bamboo sticks was the bridewealth from the deity. Bui's mother had left most of the bridewealth; but at least she had taken something. Now, as owner of a sacred sword, he could summon up fresh water from the earth with a stab of his sword. Water would flow – or cease – as he willed. The following year, before the harvest ritual, Olangki asked his wife to invite Bui. She arrived, accompanied by her recently born infant, which, since it was carried in a cloth, was invisible to human eyes. Bui hung the cloth containing the baby in her mother's house and ordered her mother not to look into the cloth even she were to hear a cry issue from it. Her mother fell asleep but was woken by a strange noise that sounded somewhat like a fish. The mother was confused and looking inside saw a big red fish with a pair of appetizing eyes. Without thinking she removed an eye and ate it. Bui felt a pain in her breast and ran back to her mother's house. She saw what had happened and became most angry. She decided she could no longer stay with her parents. Nor could she ever enter the human domain again. The relationship was over for ever. Bui walked uphill to a cave. This she entered and then used a boulder to seal it up. Later, Bui appeared to her father in a dream. She explained what had occurred but promised that no one from her human family would ever suffer thirst or experience hunger.

Susanne Rodemeier (2009: 472, 476) emphasizes the extreme environmental pressure the people of Pura faced in the period in which the events described here are supposed to have occurred. They had no source of permanent fresh water, which was assured only for the three to four months the rainy season lasted. Moreover, not only had villagers to endure the 'life-threatening lack of water' they were subject to 'its equally dangerous abundance'. Rodemeier characterizes the god as a composite mountain and water deity. When rain begins to fall, it seems to villagers the mountain and the clouds surrounding it are merged and that the water itself arises out of the earth – rather than falls from the sky – before cascading down the slopes. In pre-Christian times villagers credited the mountain deity with regulating the flow of water and creating the rainfall. The author remarks that on Pura the inferior status of wife-taker, a common feature of asymmetric alliance systems in eastern Indonesia, is intensified if it has not been completely discharged. Hence, even though it was Bui's mother who failed to collect the entire 'bridewealth' from the deity, the deity becomes so delinquent in his obligation as wife-taker he is obligated for evermore to provide water for his wife-giver's family and protect them from its excess. Another point of interest is the fashion in which Bui transforms into spirit for she metamorphoses from a material entity into an animistic entity only gradually (page 478). Her ability to see the spirit smoke is the first indication her transformation is beginning to take place and her ontological status now becomes ambiguous because human beings cannot normally see spirits. Bui's metaphysical ambiguity continues for some time, even after she has disappeared into the pool. 'She was still able to meet her father in his dreams and give him advice [and] could even physically meet her family', i.e., on the occasion of a ritual'. During this ritual, while human beings could not actually see Bui's spiritual in-laws, they could glimpse 'shadows that remained in the shade of trees'. But as for Bui's baby, since it was hidden in the cloth, there was no proof it really existed until, by infringing Bui's taboo, her mother saw with her own eyes final proof her daughter was married and by virtue of her granddaughter being a red fish confirm the fact her father was the water deity. Because of her mother's error in catching sight of the hidden baby, a *faux pas* made more heinous by her eating her granddaughter's eye, 'Bui had to carry out the final step in her metamorphosis into a fuller member of the supernatural world'. She effaces herself to the human eye and will never again return to the material domain.

Bui's transformation from human being into spirit was, it will be obvious, a process rather than an event, and a somewhat lengthy process at that. Indeed, it is the verbal equivalent of a rites of passage. Bui's initially vanishing into the pool was her stage of separation; her disappearance for good into the cave, her stage of incorporation; and the period when she moved between the two worlds, the transitional period or 'betwixt and between' stage, that of liminality.[11]

Narrative Four

The tale that follows was collected by Mr. José Maria Mok (Palmer 2010) and comes from the Naueti, an ethnic group living in the Uato Carabau district of Timor. This narrative, too, has the motifs of the fishing hook and the motif of the protagonist's deception: but the fishing line substitutes for the fishing hook in the mouth of the afflicted aquatic animal, which here is a 'sacred eel', while the hook itself is impaled in its gills. The protagonist is not described as a younger brother and the king would appear not to be the only eel afflicted by the fishing hook. The error motif, represented in this instance by a failure to take complete advantage of the deity's/spirit's gift, appears, and like Bui Hangi's mother, the protagonist fails to take all the proffered gifts. A further point of interest is that the gift, when it has been transformed, turns into a herd of buffaloes (cf. Narrative Seven), a species of animal typically included in bridewealth.

The narrative tells of a fisherman whose palm wine kept being stolen. The culprit used to come out of a spring each night and help himself to the wine. The owner of the palm trees set a trap and caught the man responsible. He turned out to be the assistant of a king, who was a 'sacred eel' (*tuna*). The thief said he only wanted the wine to take back to his king who was sick. The king could neither eat nor drink; but after drinking the wine he was able to sleep. He owner of the palms did not believe him but the thief convinced him to follow him to the edge of the spring. The thief persuaded the man to shut his eyes and together they both entered the water. When the man opened his eyes he found himself in an underwater kingdom where he saw girls with scaly skins working hard. The owner of the wine was taken to the sick king and saw that he had swallowed the fishing hook and it was caught in his gills. This was why he was ill and could not eat. The owner had secreted a sharp stick, which he used for tapping the palm wine, in his sarong and he asked the king to shut his eyes and for everyone else to leave the room. He removed the hook and the king recovered his health. Before returning home the king presented the fisherman with a necklace with twelve strands, among other things, and told him that when he returned home he was to place these objects outside his house and under some leaves and to wait until the following morning when he would find many buffaloes. The fisherman did not believe him, though, and after he had emerged from the spring he took only a few of the items and left the remainder. Next morning he found buffaloes everywhere. He searched diligently for the objects he had left behind but could not find them. Nor could he enter the spring.

Narrative Five

This story from the Kei islands, published by Heinrich Gottfried Langen (1902: 55–57), is less explicit than the majority of 'impalement' narratives discussed here, even to the point that one might claim it is too marginal to be included in our set.[12] However, as I shall argue below, the motifs it resorts to serve as sufficient justification for its inclusion within the set.

There were three brothers, Hian (the eldest), Tongiil and Papara. Papara went fishing in the cloud-sea and lost his elder brother's fishing rod. Hian became very angry and ordered Papara to go in search of it. Papara dived down into the clouds. There he encountered a fish called Kaliboban who asked him what he was looking for. Papara told him the truth: he explained what had happened. Kaliboban promised to find the missing fishing rod and he proved as good as his word because he found the fishing rod inside the mouth of another fish, whose name was Kerkeri, extracted it, and gave it to Papara. The story does not state that Papara actually returned the implement, but it does go on to state that Papara schemed to take 'revenge' on his eldest brother (apparently for being angry and ordering him to go on the quest). So one day as Hian lay sleeping Papara hung a bamboo tube, filled with palm wine, a very expensive commodity in what the narrative describes as 'heaven', on his brother's bed, in such a fashion that the tube would immediately drop and spill the palm wine as soon as Hian got up. This duly happened, and Papara ordered Hian to fetch some palm wine to refill the container. Hian commenced his search by digging a hole in the sky in an excavation that reached the earth. But Hian did not find any palm wine.[13]

In this story the impalement motif is absent; the fraternal group consists of three brothers, not two; and the fraternal trio resides in the sky rather than on the land. Nor is an instrument of impalement as such mentioned; instead, it is a fishing rod that has ensnared the victim. Life and plenty are not included as a motif; clouds instead of water constitutes the medium that mediates between the two worlds; and the contrast visible/invisible is absent. Despite these deviations from our pattern, I think the tale can just about be said to qualify for inclusion. Water appears in the form of clouds (cf. Narrative Three); the male sibling relationship pertinent to the loss of the fishing rod involves the elder brother, and since in the sequence of named brothers the actions of the brother listed in the ultimate narrational position, Papara, are consistent with those of the younger brothers described in the other tales, one is justified in so identifying him. The motif of the elder brother/younger brother can therefore be argued to occur and the lost fishing hook replaced by it metonym, the fishing rod, while the motif of the quest appears, as does that of deception. The status relationship reversal of the elder and younger brother, it should be remarked, also occurs.

Narrative Six

This myth, which explains the origins of those members of the Makassai ethnic group living in the fishing settlement of Laga-Soba, ten kilometers east of Baucau Town in Timor-Leste,[14] is less clear than the other stories presented here (Spillet 1999: 277–80). It includes the motif of the fishing hook, the line ('rope'), the deceitful protagonist (whose name is Bertiti) and an ailing fish. But we are not informed whether the protagonist even cures the invalid, and in any case he goes unrewarded. Even more puzzling, we are not informed whose fishing hook impales the victim. The protagonist hits his wife with an arrow, not the victim he eventually cures, i.e., his mother-in-law. Furthermore, he is not described as having any brothers and he is the husband of a fish.

One day Bertiti shot an arrow at a fish and accidently shot his wife in the ribs. She fled home to her parents. Bertiti went into the sea to search for his missing arrow where he met a crocodile[15] whom he tried to deceive by pretending he was not on a quest. The crocodile, however, was well aware of what had occurred. The creature told Bertiti that his wife had taken the arrow back with her to her parents' home and that the artifact was on a shelf [presumably in her parents' house]. Bertiti sat on the crocodile's back and they dived below the sea to the wife's residence. Bertiti discovered that his mother-in-law was ill and despite the ministrations of the local doctor and the application of all their medicines the inhabitants of the underwater world had been unable to cure her. After his wife had confided the problem to him, Bertiti went into the room where the woman lay ill and said that it were better if everyone left the invalid and himself alone in the room together. Bertiti had understood the sickness as being caused by a fishing hook impaling the woman's mouth and [for some unstated reason] took a piece of rope and tied it to her neck and began to try to remove the hook. But when he left the room to pass the rope to the people [perhaps so they could help him extract it] he realized that it was the rope and not the hook that was in his mother-in-law's mouth. Eventually, Bertiti climbed on the crocodile's back and went to Laga where he founded (i.e., gave life to) the social group which looks upon this narrative as their myth of origin. The crocodile, who is the enabler for Bertiti as well as performing the function of being a mediator between the animistic world and the world of matter, became his group's[16] 'grandfather'.

Narrative Seven

This narrative was collected among the Atoni people of western Timor by P. Middlekoop (1958: 401–2).[17]

A man called But Ba'u was fishing with a fishing hook that belonged to a man called Ome. A crocodile came along and swallowed it, taking it with him into the sea. Learning what had occurred Ome became very angry and told But Ba'u he must go in search of it. But Ba'u could not find the hook. Then he spied a turtle on the seashore who inquired what he was looking for. But Ba'u replied that he was merely going to and fro. The turtle was not deceived. He said But Ba'u shouldn't just go hither and hither: the crocodile-king's body was 'badly hurt'. But Ba'u climbed on top of the turtle's back and the creature ordered him to close his eyes. 'Suddenly' they arrived at the palace of the king, whom they found sleeping. The turtle awoke the king and called to But Ba'u, who saw the king's 'beak' wide open and the fishing hook. He took a twig of *kusambi* (*Schleichera oleosa*) and told those present to close their eyes. He retrieved the fishing hook, which he had hidden, and said 'Open your eyes'. When those present had opened their eyes they saw that their king had recovered. But Ba'u displayed the twig, which he had moistened with his tongue and was red all over. The king wished to pay him but But Ba'u refused because of orders the turtle had given and although the king kept importuning him But Ba'u kept declining. The king finally said, 'This man has bewitched me to kill me, we want to pay him, but he refused me once and for all'. Those present tried to find a way to kill But Ba'u but the turtle took him on his back and fled with him and brought him up to his 'ceiling'. The turtle gave But Ba'u four papayas and told him that when he arrived ashore he was to place the papayas on the edge of a pool he would find there and that after four nights should come and look 'after them'. But Ba'u did so and then returned the fishing hook to Ome. Four nights passed. He went to see the papayas and found four buffalo in the pool together with the turtle who told him to go home and return after a further four nights. Four nights later he discovered eight buffalo in the pool. He 'drove them up' from the water in the pool and took them home. Out hunting later, Ome discovered But Ba'u milking buffalo. Ome's dog spilt But Ba'u's milk. But Ba'u became very angry and told Ome he must replace his milk because when he had lost his fishing hook Ome had been furious with him and that he had forced But Ba'u to go searching for the missing fishing hook until he found it. Accordingly, But Ba'u told Ome him that because he had spilt the milk he must dig into the ground and that if he found the milk it would be Ome's; but if he found water it would be But Ba'u's. Ome found water, and so it belonged to But Ba'u.

Motifs

Table 13.1 illustrates the frequency with which the seven motifs occur in these seven narratives, and it shows that five of these motifs occur in every text: water, life and plenitude, the fishing hook or its various surrogates, the quest and the deception/error motif.

268 *David Hicks*

Table 13.1 The seven narratives: motifs, occurrences and frequencies.

Motifs		One	Two	Three	Four	Five	Six	Seven	Frequency
1	Water	yes	yes	yes	yes	yes	yes	yes	7
2	Life and Plenitude	yes	yes	yes	yes	no	yes	yes	7
3	Instrument of Impalement	yes	yes	yes	yes	no	yes	yes	6
4	The Quest	yes	yes	yes	yes	yes	yes	yes	7
5	Deception/Error	yes	yes	yes	yes	yes	yes	yes	7
6	eB/yB	yes	yes	no	no	yes	yes	yes	5
7	Visible/Invisible	yes	yes	no	yes	no	no	yes	4

eB = elder brother   yes = motif present
yB = younger brother no = motif absent

Visible/Invisible

The alternation between the opening of the eyes and closing of the eyes is a motif commonly occurring in eastern Indonesian narratives. Closing the eyes serves as a marker indicating the escape from the confines of the material world to the 'half-baffled vision' of the spiritual world and from the spiritual world back to the material world. Opening the eyes indicates entrance into the opposite domain. The condition of eyes-closure corresponds to the period during which the protagonist in the tale is in a state of liminality engaged on a journey of greater or lesser duration. He/she is neither in the material world nor in that of the animistic world. As such, the closing of the eyes corresponds to the rites of separation, while the opening of the eyes corresponds to the rites of integration. Another situation in which the act of closing the eyes occurs is when a protagonist is engaging in an act of deception.

The opening/closing of the eyes serves, in addition, to convey the contrast between visibility/invisibility.[18] In the world of matter the protagonist closes his eyes and it becomes invisible to him; while they are closed he remains enclosed in a transient condition or stage of liminality; when he opens them he finds that he is in the domain of spirit. Later, he closes them again, and the animistic world vanishes; the liminal stage returns; finally, upon re-opening his eyes he once again confronts the material world. In Narrative Three the spiritual domain is visible to Bui but invisible to her mother and all prospects of it ever being visible to her vanish consequent upon her plucking out her grandchild's eye. Unlike the other instances of visibility/invisibility, which are temporary, this is a permanent condition of invisibility. Both child and Bui remain invisible to human beings. By contrast, within the world of the spirit the motif of visible/invisible is resorted to in two distinct situations: (a) When the protagonist asks the attendants to first close and then open their eyes (Narrative Seven), and (b), when he asks them to go out of the king's room and remain outside (Narrative Four and Narrative Six) outside the victim's room.

Elder Brother/Younger Brother

The motif of elder brother/younger brother is a common one throughout eastern Indonesia and as I have shown elsewhere (Hicks 2007b) in some narratives their relationship hinges on the motif of the fishing hook. It will not have escaped notice that Narratives Three, Six and Seven appear to lack the motif of elder brother and younger brother. In the first two stories the affinal relationship replaces, to some degree, that of the fraternal relationship. In Narrative Seven the respective protagonists are simply referred to as 'the man But Ba'u' and 'the man Ome'. In a previous article I called specific attention to this anomaly and noted that the plot in this story 'apparently' excluded this particular relationship (Hicks 2007b: 5). However, situating this narrative within the context of a semantic set whose definition includes interactions between elder brother and younger brother that demonstrably accord with similar actions in the other tales, we are able to infer that this story, in fact, describes yet another adventure of these two siblings (cf. Lévi-Strauss 1978: 2–33). Ome owns the fishing hook; But Ba'u loses it; Ome orders But Ba'u to recover it; But Ba'u, the socially inferior, succeeds, and after being transformed by his interaction with the spirits in an aquatic realm ends up with a very desirable material bounty Ome lacks. Ome's failure to rectify his mistake – made by his canine surrogate – obtains for But Ba'u ownership of that most precious valuable, water, and denies it to Ome. The spilling of milk in this tale and its irretrievable mixing into the earth repeats in a slightly different way the incident in which the elder brother in Narrative Two spills his younger brother's sesame seeds into the earth and is unable to retrieve them. In both cases whereas the previously subordinate younger brother succeeds in his mission the erstwhile superordinate elder brother fails. In his article Prager (page 450) remarks the relevance for Narrative Two of the common theme of 'stranger outsider', famously identified in its Austronesian context by Marshall Sahlins (1985). This is given expression to in various ways, among them narratives in which the younger brother travels, or is transported to, the spiritual world and upon his return finds himself assuming the office of king (Hicks 1988: 812–13). In the above group of stories the same sort of transformation occurs in the younger brother's role in society. He begins, of course, in his native context, but travels to an alien world and comes back transformed by his encounter with the spirits and affects changes in his old world. His native context may also be interpreted as the inner or interior world and his transient destination as the outer or exterior world, another common Indonesian dualism, and one discernible among the Tetum-speaking peoples of Timor (Hicks 1984: passim).[19]

Deception/Error

The motif of the successful deception or error plays a pivotal role in the plots in which it appears, for had the ploy failed the narrative would have had a radically different outcome. In Narrative One the protagonist requests as his reward what seems a trifle, but this humble gift transforms itself into (literally) gold and in Narrative Two the younger brother devises a trap into which his elder brother falls. In Narratives Four, Six and Seven the younger brother deceives the deity who thereby fails to realize the younger brother's culpability in bringing about his injury. In Narratives Two, Five and Six the mistake made inverts the status relationship between the erstwhile superordinate elder brother and his erstwhile subordinate junior while in Narrative Three it further intensifies the inferiority of the deity. Were this motif absent the aquatic deity would have been under no obligation to the younger brother. Exactly the opposite, in fact. Nor would the water/mountain deity have been required to provide the life-essential benefit of water. Two plots make use of what might be called 'negative' deception, in the sense the ploy fails. In Narrative Six the crocodile is not deceived by Bertiti and in Narrative Seven neither is the turtle deceived by But Ba'u.

The Quest

In three of the tales the quest involves a journey undertaken by a younger brother into the animistic world followed by his successful return (see Hicks 1988). In these narratives a protagonist undertakes a quest to fulfill an obligation and returns – the cycle completed, duty to his social superior discharged, and freely given life-sustaining help rendered a deity – with benefits accruing to himself. In one tale (Narrative Three) an unmarried girl *qua* intended bride for the deity travels to the spiritual domain where she marries him, provides the source of life for his descendants, and eventually remains in the realm of the spirit: a cycle unfulfilled. In all the narratives, however, male and female protagonists are the means by which human beings obtain life and plentitude.

Instrument of Impalement

The motif of the instrument of impalement, whether in its most characteristic form, the fishing hook, or one of its surrogates, serves as a cultural device for 'hooking', as it were, the world of matter into that of the spirit and securing the benefits that accrue from their reciprocal relationship. Enhanced by the support of the other motifs, this is accomplished within the natural medium of water which thereby acts as the procreative agency that makes life and plentitude possible.

Life and Plentitude

While we may assess Hocart's claim to lie somewhat on the hyperbolic side, the plangency of his prose emphasizes the extent to which the quest for life, fertility and abundance in general – essential elements of the human experience – finds aesthetic expression in action and – if only by implication – involves interaction between two metaphysical existences. As in ritual, so, too, in text. Not only can life and plentitude be obtained in the first; it can also be pursued in the second. But whereas fertility rituals enact or bring about rapport between spirit and matter, texts verbalize the experiences of those who entertain them and permit us a glimpse into how people conceive their relationship with their animistic counterparts.

Water

In these stories water furnishes an environment conducive to the intermingling of spirit and matter and thereby facilitates their reciprocity. Although of a material nature, water, because it shares a proximate identity with the animistic domain, shows itself to possess a more ambivalent character, one that is consistent with its role as an agent of transformation. As an enabling agency, water is the natural correspondent of the fishing hook. An artifact of culture, and moreover one that is unambiguously of the material world, the fishing hook, by contrast, makes possible a fertile interaction with spirit by facilitating its 'capture'.

Conclusion

In the foregoing narratives the spirits victimized, as it were, by the hook of the predator from the material world, are water-dwellers that are harmless to human beings. All, that is, except for the victim in Narrative Seven, who proves to be a crocodile. Hence, the protagonist in all the stories, except in that tale, accepts gifts from his victims whose sickness he has cured. To do so, however, when his gift-giver is a crocodile would place him in a relationship created and sustained by an exchange of gifts with a creature every bit as much a predator as himself. To avoid placing himself in a gift-relationship that is balanced, and therefore equal, the human protagonist fends off the opportunity to establish a relationship with a fellow-predator and spurns the gift offered by the crocodile. Not that he goes unrewarded, for the mediating turtle, which reconciles the worlds of the spiritual and material, provides him with his compensation. The gift comes from a non-predator.

These seven narratives portray a pair of interdependent ontological domains mutually engaged in sustaining each other in a reciprocal relationship. Spirits require homage and food from human beings, while human beings, for their part, need life and plentitude, a dialectic described for other ethnographic regions including South America and North Asia.[20] In the imaginations of the eastern Indonesians, therefore, I suggest that water may be construed as corresponding to the aforementioned 'penumbra' of our epigraph, an ambiguous substance by whose very ambiguity 'the clear visibility of things material' and 'their total extinction in the spiritual' merge, as spirit envelops matter with the mystery of 'soul suggestion'.

This conclusion suggests a possible answer to a question that necessarily arises. It will not have escaped attention that – with the exception of Narrative Three – all these narratives depict an alternative world inhabited by animals. Only in that story is the spirit (the god of the mountain) intangible and invisible, and not reified in material form. The 'penumbra', as it were, consists of the underwater denizens themselves. The hero of these tales does not confront spirits as such. This penumbral quality raises an interesting issue of ontological classification when the deployment of animal imagery in these narratives of eastern Indonesia is compared with the ways in which societies in other ethnographic regions, such as South America and Northeast Asia, incorporate the world of animals into the respective domains of human beings and spirits (cf. Århem 1996; Conklin 1995; Pedersen 2001). In the classificatory thought of these eastern Indonesian societies are these underwater animals, in fact, spirits or are they only creatures of the material world? Put another way, should we regard these narratives as depicting three worlds (spiritual; animal; human) or only two (spiritual/material)? In the latter case, the material world would be binary: human/animal. According to this interpretation these seven tales describe a spiritual world and a material world, but the latter contains a human sub-world and an animal sub-world. The case for regarding the animals as animals is clear enough, for there is nothing especially immaterial in their behaviour or in the environment in which they live, and the physical pain the instrument of impalement inflicts on the creature implies a material affliction hardly consistent with an ontological mode of immateriality.

At the opening of this essay, I raised the question of how can the insubstantial engage with the substantial or how can invisible and intangible spirits be 'thought' into a relationship with visible and tangible human beings? The foregoing analysis suggests a possible answer. If water, in these tales, is seen as an ambiguous medium that conjoins, indeed syncretically intermixes the material and spiritual, the ontological status of these underwater denizens becomes evident enough. These water animals possess the qualities of both spirit[21] and creature. They are, at one and the same time, spirits and animals, immaterial and spiritual, and visible and invisible. Fish are denizens of an opaque medium. They are present, yet invisible, to those outside, and therefore have the potential to serve as representations of an animal kingdom that might be conceived as a third mode of existence. For its part, the eel provides a natural link between the worlds of the spirit and the realm of the material, as does the cultural device of the instrument of impalement.[22] By the process of alternatively closing and opening his eyes a human being, typically a younger brother, can gain access to this material/immaterial world and so empower himself to engage with the source of life and plenitude. In collusion with the eyes, the instrument of impalement makes it possible for the human being to see what remains invisible to his fellows as he enters into an engagement with the third ontological domain. Water is the opaque or semi-opaque window[23] through which human beings may, on occasion, just catch a vague glimpse of the indefined, penumbral world that is the home of the spiritual entities their imaginations, furnished by experience and knowledge of the world, have conceived. Through it, the mysterious can be almost caught sight of; and the imminence of the unknown becomes, if only for a brief moment, palpable.

Notes

1. Art and photography critic Charles Caffin's comment on Edward Steichen' celebrated photograph, 'The Pond-Moonlight', which shows a pond in a wooded area with moonlight glinting between the trees and casing reflections on the water.
2. I wish to thank the following for their help in preparing this paper: Dr. Lisa Palmer, Dr. Michael Prager, Dr. Susanne Rodemeier, Miss Francesca Calarco, Dr. Sachiko Murata, Dr Michael Ashkenazi, a reviewer of a previous version, and Professor Kaj

Árhem and Professor Guido Sprenger who invited a contribution from me for the Panel and subsequent suggested improvements to my initial draft. Thanks, too, to Ms. Katharina Stöhr for her translation of Narrative Five. A special word of gratitude to José Maria Mok who, through the considerate offices of Dr. Lisa Palmer, generously permitted me to include a synopsis of the unpublished Naueti text he collected and which makes its appearance here as Narrative Four.

3. To avoid cumbersome locution, from this point onwards, unless otherwise remarked, I shall use the term 'fishing hook' or 'hook' to include all these surrogates.
4. Each of these seven motifs appears sporadically in other narratives of the archipelago, either in conjunction with certain other motifs considered in this article or alone. However, in the class of narrative discussed here they conjoin into an identifiably cohesive set of tales, bound together by the repetitions of plot device and play their respective parts in imparting meaning to the entire set.
5. Dr. Michael Prager (personal communication) notes that water as interface between spirit and matter is also a recurrent theme throughout Southeast Asia and the Pacific, as it is in the pre-Islamic cosmology of Bima.
6. The symbolic semantics of the fishing hook in the comparative context of eastern Indonesia I originally discussed in Hicks (2007). The present study is intended as a second step in the investigation of this motif and its congeners. It might be noted that the motif of the elder brother and the lost fishing hook is not restricted to the Indonesian archipelago. The oldest surviving Japanese book, the *Kojiki*, which dates to 712 A.D., contains a story that fits into the corpus of narratives analysed here were it not for the fact that it comes from outside the ethnographic region we are considering (see Anon. 1983). I am indebted to Miss Francesca Calarco for bringing this source to my attention. In another reference to Japan, Dr Michael Ashkenazi sent me in response to my earlier article on the younger brother and the fishing hook (Hicks 2007b). He remarked: 'The "younger brother loses the fishing hook" myth is not confined to the Indonesian archipelago. I came across it as one of the founding myths of the Japanese imperial house. In the Japanese case, at least, it forms a complex with a Japanese version of the Melusine myth, which spans Asia from east to west'.
7. It may be recalled that Christopher Booker has identified 'The Quest' as one of the seven 'basic plots', which he considers universal themes common to the human imagination. Of distinct interest for us is his discussing all seven basic plots under the rubric 'The Seven Gateways to the Underworld'.
8. As with most narratives summarized here, Forth's original text is longer and contains motifs additional to the ones I include in the present article.
9. A taboo observed by the Bimanese royal family (Hitchcock 1994: 47).
10. Parallels may be found in Lombok (Bosch 1961: 155–6) and among the Atoni of western Timor (van Wouden 1968: 50). The Lombok story involves a guru who displays extraordinary powers when he thrusts his trident into the earth and makes a spring gush forth. For its part, the Atoni story describes how the eldest of a group of brothers thrusts his sword into the ground and a spring issues from it.
11. Bui's transformation into a spirit is a variation of the myth of how Ali-iku, the youngest brother, transformed himself into a spirit eel (*'tuna'*) among the Viqueque Tetum (Hicks 1984: 24–5). Both describe metamorphoses from the material into the spiritual and their transformations are brought about gradually rather than instantly. In both texts, too, the final departure from the world of matter to that of spirit is permanent. Of supplementary interest is the fact that both transformations suggest an identity between the statuses of younger brother and that of female (see Hicks 1984: 100–2) and while this is not the occasion to develop the analytic possibilities suggested by this convergence it should be remarked that it does tend to confirm my earlier suggestion regarding the correspondence between Olangki and elder brother and between Bui and younger brother in Narrative Three. The same deserves to be said of the process

of transformation, a striking motif throughout Indonesian narratives, and one that recurs in the set of narratives discussed here. It is, in fact, this omnipresent character it reveals that prevents it being including as a defining component of the narrational set analyzed in this article.

12. I am indebted to Professor Guido Sprenger for making a copy of the original Langen text available to me and for Ms. Katharina Stöhr who was so kind as to provide me with a translation of the narrative.
13. The narrative continues to relate how the brothers, their sister and their four dogs descended to earth. The failure of the elder brother to redress a mistake he makes recalls the failure of the eldest brother, Kemala, in Narrative Two, to successfully fulfill his obligation of restoring the sesame seeds to the golden tray.
14. In addition to the Baucau sub-district, the Makassai are found further west in the sub-district of Viqueque.
15. In Southeast Asian literature crocodiles are often thought of as having a kingly status and classed as predators endowed with the capacity – like turtles – to transverse boundaries, such as the sea, or that separating the underwater world from the world above. I am indebted to a reviewer for suggesting I include this observation.
16. Most likely, this group is a clan, and the crocodile its totemic culture hero.
17. Middlekoop includes another text featuring a fishing hook and the protagonist, But Ba'u, who together with the turtle undertakes a sea voyage to the realm of a king. But the sibling relationship is absent and the combination of motifs that give the story its integrity places it outside the genre considered here.
18. I am grateful to Professor Guido Sprenger (personal communication) for pointing out how the mofit, visible/invisible, rather than that of opening eye/closing eye, might help to stress the continuity of the myth set analysed here.
19. I thank Professor Guido Sprenger for reminding me of this analogy.
20. See Conklin (1995); Pedersen (2010).
21. The inhabitants of the underwater world present themselves in such a way as to be described as spirits, as among the Nage, for example, who refer to them as *nitu*, a term denoting 'spirit', and their ethnographer, Gregory Forth (1998:42), so designates them.
22. Like crocodiles and turtles, eels and snakes are, of course, in the literature of Southeast Asia, common mediators between the world of the spirit and the human realm. In the foremo turtles myth told by the Tetum-speaking peoples of Viqueque, the eel, called Ali-Iku, a part-human/part-deity, appears in a stream as a cultural hero who establishes a descent group, before disappearing into the depths (Hicks 1984: 24–7). The same population have tales that tell of demons from the underworld appearing as snakes in the material world and initiating an ambiguous relationship with human beings. As I remarked in an earlier work, *A Maternal Religion* (1984: 96), some psychoanalysts have suggested that the snake image mediates in the unconscious mind between this world and the other world (Henderson 1964: 154–6). Applying to Timorese symbolic thought the insight of Endicott (1970: 136) about magical thinking among the Malays, I further argued that in Tetum culture, also, because water weakens the boundaries that keep categories discrete, it facilities passage between different domains. To that earlier conclusion I would now add that water serves as an exemplary medium for establishing relationships between the human domain and that of the spirit domain.
23. 'Water seems to weaken the boundaries between many kinds of category, facilitating passage across them. … Even spirits cross boundaries with the aid of water. … The quality that gives water the ability to weaken boundaries is probably its fluidity, the complete lack of "hardness". It will sustain no divisions or boundaries of its own' Endicott (1970: 136).

References

Anon. (1982) 'The Luck of the Sea and the Luck of the Mountains', XXXIX–XLII, in *The Kojiki: Records of Ancient Matters*, Transactions of the Asiastic Society of Japan. 10, suppl. Yokohama. Translated by Basil Hall Chamberlain.

Århem, K. (1996) 'The Cosmic Food-web: human-nature relatedness in the Northwest Amazon', in P. Descola and G. Pálsson (eds.) *Nature and Society: Anthropological Perspectives*, London; New York, NY: Routledge.

Bosch, F.D.K. (1960) *The Golden Germ: an introduction to Indian symbolism*, The Hague: Mouton.

Brooker, C. (2004) *The Seven Basic Plots: why we tell stories*, London and New York, NY: Continuum.

Caffin, C. (1910*) Camera Work*, New York: Alfred Stieglitz. Number 31, July.

Conklin, B.A. (1995) '"Thus are Our Bodies, Thus was Our Custom": mortuary cannibalism in an Amazonian Society', *American Ethnologist*, 22: 75–201.

Endicott, K. (1970) *Malay Magic*, Oxford: Clarendon Press.

Forth, G. (1998) *Beneath the Volcano: religion, cosmology and spirit classification among the Nage of eastern Indonesia. (Verhandelingen van het Koninklijk Instituut voor Taal-, Land- en Volkenkunde)*, Leiden: KITLV Press.

Henderson, J.L. (1964) 'Ancient Myths and Modern Man', in C. Jung and M. L. van Franz (eds.) *Man and his Symbols*, New York, NY: Garden City, Doubleday & Company, Inc.

Hicks, D. (1984) *A Maternal Religion: the role of women in Tetum myth and ritual*, DeKalb: Northern Illinois University, Center for Southeast Asian Studies. Monograph Series on Southeast Asia. Special Report No. 22.

—— (1988) 'Literary Masks and Metaphysical Truths: intimations from Timor', *American Anthropologist*, 90(4): 807–17.

—— (2007a) 'The Naueti Relationship Terminology: A New Instance of Asymmetric. Prescription from East Timor'. *Bijdragen tot de Taal-, Land- en Volkenkunde*, 163. (2/3): 239–62.

—— (2007b) 'Younger Brother and Fishing Hook on Timor: reassessing Mauss on hierarchy and divinity', *Journal of the Royal Anthropological Institute (new series)*, 13(1): 39–56.

Hitchcock, M. (1996) *Islam and Identity in Eastern Indonesia*, Hull: The University of Hull Press.

Hocart, A.M. (1954) *Social Origins*, London: Watts & Company.

Langen, H.G. (1902) *Die Key-oder Kii-Inseln des O.I. Archipelago: aus dem Tagebuche eines Kolonisten*, Vienna: Gerold, pp. 55–57.

Lévi-Strauss, C. (1979) *Myth and Meaning: cracking the code of culture*, New York, NY: Shocken Books.

Middlekoop, P. (1958) 'Four Tales with Mythical Features Characteristic of the Timorese People', *Bijdragen toot de Taal-, Land- en Volkenkunde*, 114: 384–405.

Palmer, L. *Water Relations: Customary Systems and the Management of Baucau City's Water*, unpublished manuscript.

—— (2010) Personal communication.

Pedersen, M.A. (2001) 'Totemism, Animism and North Asian Indigenous Ontologies'. *Journal of the Royal Anthropological Institute*, 3: 411–27.

Prager, M. (2010) 'The Appropriation of the 'Stranger King': polarity and mediation in the Dynastic Myth of Bima', in P. Berger, R. Hardenberg, E. Kattner and M. Prager (eds.)

The Anthropology of Values: essays in honour of Georg Pfeffer, New Dehli: Pearson, 447–70.

—— (2011) Personal communication. 24th February.

Rodemeier, S. (2009) 'Bui Hangi – the Deity's Human Wife', *Anthropos*, 104: 469–82.

Sahlins, M. (1985) 'The Stranger King; or Dumézil among the Historians', in *Islands of History*. Chicago, IL: University of Chicago Press.

Spillet, P.G. (1999) *The Pre-Colonial History of the Island of Timor Together with Some Notes on the Makassan Influence in the Island*, Darwin, Australia: Museum and Art Gallery of the Northern Territory.

Sprenger, G. (2011) Personal communication. February 24.

Tylor, E. (1873) *Primitive Culture, Vol. 1*. 2nd edition. London: John Murray, Albemarle Street.

Part IV
Concluding

14 Southeast Asian animism

A dialogue with Amerindian perspectivism

Kaj Århem

This chapter develops themes outlined in Chapter 1 with a view to substantiate what I take to be the prototype of Southeast Asian animism. I do so by systematically contrasting characteristic features of Southeast Asian cosmologies with Amerindian perspectivism as expounded by Viveiros de Castro, drawing also on my own work in the Colombian Amazon and the uplands of Vietnam and Laos. The examples from the Katu in the following carry my analysis of Katu hunting ideology from Chapter 5 one or two steps further in order to illustrate general features of the Southeast Asian prototype.

In Southeast Asia, the religious and cosmological landscape in the shadow of the great world religions – Buddhism, Hinduism, Islam and Christianity – is generally characterized as animist. But it is animism of a quite different hue from the type known from Amazonia and the circumpolar and circumboreal regions of the world that has been highlighted in the recent literature on animism and perspectivism.

Not only does animism in Southeast Asia exists side by side with world religions and has developed in contact with these religions but the typical animist societies in Southeast Asia which we deal with in this volume are – with the significant exception of the Chewong – agricultural societies, either upland swidden cultivators or wet-rice cultivators (Ifugao), in which domestic livestock play an important role in socioeconomic and religious life. All of them have for millennia maintained contacts through trade or tribute with petty kingdoms or powerful states formed by a dominant majority population. Usually, animist populations constitute enclaves within, or inhabit the margins of, these centralized state societies.

Historically, the contact – often hostile – with neighboring or encapsulating state societies has fundamentally influenced the cosmology and social institutions of the indigenous societies in focus in this volume. Nevertheless the internal structure and dynamic of these societies tend to conform to a distinctive societal pattern quite different from the typical tropical forest groups in South America and the hunting and pastoral societies of Northern Eurasia and the circumpolar region which have been at the forefront of recent studies on animism.

The predominant socio-political type in indigenous Southeast Asia is, or was until recently, a moderately ranked society.[1] Leach's depiction of Kachin political system ranging along a scale from egalitarian (democratic) to hierarchical (autocratic) structures most probably applied widely among pre-colonial upland groups in mainland Southeast Asia – many of which were, and still are, centered around the principle of asymmetric exchange. The accumulation and redistribution of material wealth, including livestock and ritual objects, through ostentatious sacrifices and feasting, are constitutive of these societies. Warfare and headhunting (or varieties of both) were common among the hinterland communities as well as between the autarchic hinterland groups and the dominant chiefdoms or kingdoms from which many of the former groups have splintered off (cf. Scott 2009).

The cosmological and religious articulation of these socio-political and economic forces amounts to a particular type of animism. The distinctive features of this type include: the centrality of animal sacrifice; a preponderance of divination and other mantic practices; spirit possession, ancestor worship, conspicuous funerary rituals and, generally, great attention paid to a panoply of nature spirits, and the now obsolete practice of headhunting. All these features distinguish the Southeast Asian type from the characteristic Amerindian and North-Eurasian forms of animism. I refer to this predominant form of animism in indigenous Southeast Asia as transcendent or hierarchical animism (cf. Chapter 1).[2]

In order to illuminate its ontological premises, it is instructive to contrast the prototypical form of Southeast Asian animism with Amazonian perspectivism (Viveiros de Castro 1998). In doing so, I borrow the expository strategy used by Viveiros de Castro – but instead of contrasting Amerindian ontology with Western naturalism I exploit the contrastive tension between Amazonian perspectivism and Southeast Asian transcendent animism to highlight the distinctive properties of the latter. For reasons discussed in Chapter 1 and reiterated in the following, I consider Amerindian perspectivism and the current standard notion of animism as varieties of what I call immanent animism.

The Human-Animal Relationship: Hunting, Livestock and Sacrifice

On Viveiros de Castro's account, Amerindian perspectivism is intimately associated with shamanism and hunting. In its North-Eurasian and Amerindian form, shamanism is essentially a venatic ideology (ibid.: 472); accordingly, perspectivism basically expresses a hunting point of view on reality. In perspectivism, the human-animal relationship is fundamentally conceptualized in terms of predation, the relationship between hunter and prey. The relation of predation is itself construed as a reciprocal exchange with the animal master whom Viveiros de Castro understands as a hypostasis of the animal person – the subject-aspect of the animal – where the direction of predation is continuously contested and reversible. The threat of retaliation and counter-predation is ever present. The relation between the human self and the animal other is commonly molded on the pattern of affinity in the human realm – that of direct or symmetric exchange between kin and affines in the human *socius* (Århem, K. 1996).

In Southeast Asian animism, however, the dominant role of game animals in Amazonian cosmologies is replaced by that of domestic livestock.[3] The relationship between the human master and his livestock is one of control and protection, nurture and identification. From the stock owner's point of view, his livestock forms a part of his social self. As opposed to Amazonian cosmology where the wild prey animal represents the other as body, domestic animals in Southeast Asian cosmology represent the self as body – a difference that gives Southeast Asian animism a very distinctive character.

This intimate association between the human livestock owner and his domestic herd in Southeast Asia forms the basis of the institution of sacrifice and the complex of ideas and ritual practices associated with it. The sacrificial complex in Southeast Asia, in many ways, performs the same function as shamanism in Amazonia.[4]

*

In indigenous Southeast Asia, domestic animals – pigs, cattle, buffalo and/or other large bovines – are ostensibly and almost universally kept for sacrifice. Their cosmological role is to be sacrificed to the spirits. They constitute ritual wealth; as such they also form part of elaborate exchange systems. As a supreme gift object, buffaloes represent part of the giver's social self; they objectify the corporal aspect of the self and serve to create alliances with social others. As sacrificial objects, livestock create alliances with the spirits as ontological others. This transcendental alliance amounts to a transaction involving the sacrifier's self and the superior spirits to which the sacrifice is dedicated, and has the character of an asymmetric exchange. It presumes submission to the spirits on the part of the human sacrifier and requires continuous and unconditional giving in the hope of gaining spiritual blessings and earthly rewards in the form fertility and prosperity.

Wild animals, by contrast, play a relatively modest role in Southeast Asian cosmology. The wild animals of everyday concern in indigenous Southeast Asia – just as among forest-living people everywhere – are the animals hunted for food. Other animals, such as the large predators, the elephant, wild buffaloes and human-like primates, are cosmologically and ritually important for their powers and extraordinary properties (Århem, N. 2007). Significantly, among Katuic peoples in Laos and Vietnam, the tiger is referred to by the same term as that used generically for the powerful and predatory 'nature spirits'.

Game animals are in some cases attributed with soul, in others not, but in all cases they are believed to be controlled by one or several typical Animal Masters – the spirit owners or guardians of animals. The figure of the Animal Master in Southeast Asian cosmologies, just as in Amazonia, is probably best understood as the hypostasis of the spirit or soul of the individual, physical animals – but of a quite different kind than in Amazonia.

Thus, there are important differences between Southeast Asia and Amazonia with regard to the intersubjective field between the human hunter and his prey. In Amazonia, game animals are widely and explicitly referred to as 'people'; they are spoken of as human-like persons 'dressed in animal cloak' – persons who are human on the inside and animals on the outside (cf. also the Chewong, Chapter 3). While perceived by the human hunter as animals, the animals 'see' themselves reflexively as humans, living in a society organized on the same pattern as the human society – visible as such by powerful shamans (Århem, K. 1996; Viveiros de Castro 1998).

This notion of 'humanized' animals, which is at the basis of Amerindian perspectivism and standard animism generally, is lacking in prototypical Southeast Asian animism. Except in the case of hunting-gathering societies such as the Chewong, there is in Southeast Asia no notion of a 'human interiority' in game animals. Wild animals are just that, animals, categorically different from humans. They constitute a distinct ontological category, subordinate to humans and belonging to a separate cosmological domain – the forest, as different from the human domain of the village.

However, they are animals with an owner – the Animal Master. In its generic Southeast Asian form, this notion points to another significant difference as compared with the corresponding Amazonian notion: the typical Southeast Asian relationship between Animal Master and his animal protégés is molded on the relationship between the human livestock owner and his domestic stock. From the point of view of the Animal Master, the animals are his livestock. In other words, the relationship between Animal Master and physical animals is here translated into the idiom of herd owner-herd according to what may be called the 'domestication paradigm'.

The Katu hunting ritual (Chapter 5) makes this symbolic logic explicit. Success in hunting is understood as a gift (of livestock) from the Animal Master.[5] The kill is followed by an elaborate public ritual in the village's community house involving the careful preservation of the skull of the slain animal and the communal feasting on its meat. The ritual converts the hunt into a religious act – a sacrifice of sorts. The hunt – from the actual kill to the postmortem treatment of the animal and the communal feasting on its meat – is structured as a sacrificial feast, only that the sacrifying agent is the Animal Master, not the human hunter. The hunter emerges in this sacrificial drama as the executor of the sacrifice, immolating the sacrificial animal on behalf of the Animal Master.

In fact, the successful hunt and the ensuing hunting ritual can be read perspectively from the point of view of either the animals (in their subject-form, the Animal Master) or the humans who enact the ritual (the villagers). From the perspective of the former, the hunt emerges as a sacrifice where the animal subject offers up its vitality ('livestock') to the human villagers (who act as 'spirits' killing and consuming the sacrificial animal); from the point of view of the villagers, the live game animal is a gift from the Animal Master which, according to the logic governing Katu asymmetric gift-exchanges, must be consecrated, immolated and offered up to the spirits before being consumed by the villagers.

*

The consumption of game meat is generally highly ritualized in both Amazonia and indigenous Southeast Asia, but in very different ways. In Amazonia, the meat is shamanized in a private ritual act involving only the household. The concern is to make the food safe for consumption; the act of shamanic food blessing purports to desubjectify the meat, i.e., remove the potentially lethal 'humanity' of the slain animal – the soul or spirit released by the act of killing – and thus complete the transformation of the animal from a powerful person capable of killing the human eater into harmless and invigorating food (Århem, K. 1998). This seemingly obsessive concern with the ingestion of food in Amazonia, particularly of animal food, points to what Viveiros de Castro has called the ever-present 'specter of cannibalism' in native Amazonian cosmology – the menacing prospect of a reversal of the hunter-prey relationship: the hunter becoming prey and the prey becoming hunter, killing and 'consuming' the human eater (cf. also Århem, K. 1996).

In Southeast Asia, the ingestion of animal food does not generally have the menacing connotations it has in native Amazonia. However, the killing of animals, both domestic and wild, is indeed the subject of cosmological concern and ritual elaboration. Death and the taking of life, implying the release of the victim's soul and an encounter with the spirit world, confront the living with serious metaphysical danger. The hunting ritual (as among the Katu) is a way of handling this metaphysical peril.

A prominent feature of the Katu hunting ritual, which it has in common with the regular livestock sacrifice more generally, is the ceremonial attention given to the head of the animal. In the case of the Katu hunting feast, the ritual treatment of the head and its ensuing consumption by the male villagers literally amounts to a communion with the spirit of the slain animal and its incorporation into the social body of the village in a manner that echoes both Amazonian warfare cannibalism and, as will be discussed below, the historical practice of headhunting in Southeast Asia at large.

Moreover, the fact that the meat of domestic animals can only be eaten in the context of a sacrifice and after the head and a sample of the body parts of the sacrificial animal – representing the whole animal – have been offered up to the spirits, just as the meat of game animals is consumed only after its head and body have first been offered to the spirits in a vicarious sacrifice – all these ritual practices regulating the consumption of meat do suggest a close parallel with Amazonian food shamanism: they are Southeast Asian variations on the same metaphysical theme – the need to carefully handle the soul of the animal released by the act of killing.[6]

*

The communal ritual following on a successful hunt among the Katu, briefly reviewed above, reveals, I believe, certain fundamental features of the sacrifice and the relationship between humans and animals in Southeast Asia more generally – features that bring out the distinctive character of Southeast Asian transcendent animism in sharp relief against the immanent animism of native Amazonians.

In the context of everyday life, animals seem to be attributed with little or no independent agency, let alone 'interiority' or autonomous subjectivity. Livestock, quietly grazing on the outskirts of the village, are seen as valued property on foot and a tangible measure of the prosperity and well-being of its owner. Entirely dependent upon the care and protection provided by their owner, they constitute a sort of extension and sign of their owners' power and agency – the object-aspect of the owner's personal and social self. To use Viveiros de Castro's formulaic language, livestock represent 'the self as body'. Herein lies their value as exchange objects and their efficacy as sacrificial beasts.

Game animals as such are given little metaphysical attention. They are *not* conceptualized or spoken of as 'people' or 'persons' in their own right – as they are in native Amazonia or among the Ojibwa. Just like domestic animals, they are understood to embody or objectify their owner, the Animal Master. Indeed, they are conceptualized as the livestock of the Animal Master. From the human point of view, they are food – the object-form (body) of the animal subject (spirit or owner being). Their cosmological role is to feed humans – just as the cosmological function of livestock is to feed the spirits.

However, this mundane role played by animals in everyday life changes dramatically in the context of animal sacrifice and hunting. Through the violent death at the hand of the hunter, the animal turns into its spirit form – hypostatized as Animal Master. Thus, through the killing, the human hunter enters into a person-to-person relationship with the animal spirit. The animal changes from object into subject. This transformation comes out particularly clear in the Katu hunting rite: the animal carcass is treated with utter care and, at the climax of the ritual, the cleaned and painted skull is addressed as the female animal guardian, Komorbarr, now present in the ritual house. In effect, the animal spirit is incorporated into the spiritual community of the village, thus affirming the alliance between villagers and the (male) Animal Master.

The same transformation from object into subject occurs during the regular livestock sacrifice – but in this case the consecrated animal is identified with its human master, the sacrifier, who offers himself up, as it were, to the spirits. Again the head and skull is given reverent ritual treatment, now as an objective sign of the sacrifying human subject and a relic of the transformative event. During the sacrifice, the spirits are the unseen participants, virtually consuming the sacrificial beast – who, in effect, becomes one with the human sacrifiers. In the view of the spirits, the sacrificial animal is the human person as food – the human subject as object. The real eaters are the spirits.

The sacrifice and the hunt, then, stage the same transformative drama but involve different actors and play up the act from different points of view; they are perspectival versions of the same sacrificial process. In the case of the ordinary sacrifice, the drama is seen from the human givers' point of view; in the case of the hunt, the process unravels from the spirit's – the receivers – point of view – enacted, as it were, by the villagers.[7] In either case, the sacrificial drama transforms the animal from object to subject, and creates an intersubjective relationship between the human and other-than-human persons involved – between spirits and humans in one case, between humans and animals in the other. In both cases, livestock, real and virtual, function as the mediating agent between the two parties of the relationship.

Ontological Predation: Warfare, Cannibalism and Headhunting

The relation between the social self and social others takes a particular and precarious form in prototypical animist societies where there is no absolute boundary between human and non-human beings. Accordingly, the boundary between humans and animals is unstable and often – as in Amazonia – reversible. Just as animal persons are desubjectified – turned into objects or 'food' – through food shamanism in Amazonia, human others can also, under certain circumstances, be transformed into their object- or prey form – indeed, into food, as past practices of warfare cannibalism in Amazonia and elsewhere show (Fausto 2007, Viveiros de Castro 1992: 273–305).

However, this practice of consuming a human being in its 'food form' – as a body divested of its soul by a process of shamanic desubjectification – is better called anthropophagy, reserving the concept of cannibalism for the distinct process of appropriating the soul of a human victim – the 'consumption' of a human person in its subject-form – since this was the rational for the practice in most of the cases where it occurred, certainly so in Amazonia. Warfare cannibalism and the ritual killing of war captives in Amazonia thus involved not the desubjectification of the victim but its hyper-subjectification – a process by which the killer turns his victim into spirit in order to re-incorporate the enemy spirit into his own person. Viveiros de Castro calls this process semiophagy to contrast it with anthropophagy. Hunting and warfare in Amazonia thus involved opposite strategies of predation. To distinguish the two modes of predation from one another, Amazonian scholars refer to the former as alimentary predation (hunting) and the latter as ontological predation (warfare).

Warfare cannibalism, as Fausto and Viveiros de Castro have shown, is a distinctively Amazonian form of ontological predation. As such, it aims at the sublimation and immortalization of the self and the reproduction of the sociocosmic whole. Indeed, cannibalism is not really cannibalism from the point of view of the animist subject; just like prey animals, enemies and strangers are conceived of as bodily others, different species of people.

Killing and being killed in war were for Amazonian warriors, notably among the Tupi-Guarani, the ultimate purpose of life – a way of becoming one with the divinities. Cannibalism, the endpoint of warfare, was the logical consequence of a perspectivist cosmology investing all its intellectual force in the notion of the body as the locus of self-identity and agency, and the idea of bodily metamorphosis as the road to self-transformation and transcendence. Hence the excessive concern with the metaphysics of food and predation.

*

Ontological predation as a form of ritualized violence was also an intrinsic feature of Southeast Asian animism – but here in the form of headhunting, an institution widespread in the region until the late nineteenth century. In its generic form, headhunting corresponds to its Amazonian counterpart; it was premised on the same fundamental idea – that of appropriating potency from the outside and convert it into vitality and fertility within. Like the Amazonian cannibal warrior, the Southeast Asian headhunter sought to capture the victim's person (soul) and incorporate it into his own personal and collective self – thus enhancing his and his community's power and potency. Like Amazonian warfare cannibalism, headhunting implied a form of self-renewal by other-becoming. Ultimately, it can be argued, headhunting and warfare cannibalism were distinct but analogous ways of maintaining and reproducing the animist cosmos.

Though similar in conceptual form and metaphysical rationale, headhunting in Southeast Asia differed in several significant ways from its Amazonian counterpart – the most obvious being that it involved the taking of heads rather than killing and consuming war captives. Cannibalism, alimentary or ontological (semiophagy), appears to have been rare or absent from native Southeast Asia although the imagery of cannibalism – the consumption of human beings – is salient throughout the region but reserved, as it were, for man-eating spirits – ontological predators by nature and definition. Thus, across the region people hold that powerful nature spirits feed on human persons and their substitutes, livestock – who from the spirit's point of view seem to be equivalent (Sprenger on the Rmeet, Chapter 4).

This difference in the articulation of ontological predation between the two regions is deeply significant. While warfare cannibalism in Amazonia was directly related to the Amerindian concern with the body and, hence with literal and semiotic ingestion and bodily metamorphosis, the elevation of cannibal predation in Southeast Asia to the exclusive realm of the spirits points to a corresponding concern with spirits – the transcendent subject-form of beings and things. In this light, it is not incidental that heads are the focus of Southeast Asian 'soul hunters'; the head is the privileged seat of the soul and the prototypical objectification of the spirit-aspect of human and other-than-human persons in Southeast Asian animist imagery.

Both forms of ontological predation, cannibalism and headhunting, are concerned with the destiny of the victim's soul. However, while the cannibal warrior seek to incarnate the enemy soul through semiophagy and thereby gain immortality and extra-human powers (Viveiros de Castro 1992: 304–5), the headhunter literally carries the victim's soul, encapsulated in his head trophy, back to his village where it is kept among other head trophies in a specially consecrated place (head tree, skull gallery or skull house) from which it mysteriously empowers the killer and his community. The fact that the victim's person (soul) is objectified in the head or skull trophy suggests a certain measure of detachment of soul from body. As a material object, the skull, like livestock, mediates the inter-subjective relationship between self and other to a degree and extent that is not present in Amazonia.

There is however another and more fundamental difference between the Amazonian and Southeast Asian modalities of ontological predation: in cannibalism, the victim is consumed –literally or figuratively – by the killer and his community; in headhunting, by contrast, the victim's soul is ritually offered up as 'food' to the (cannibal) spirits, before being spiritually appropriated by the killer and his community. As such, headhunting amounts to a supreme form of sacrifice.

Structured as a sacrificial process, the headhunt is an augmented form of the regular hunt and a paradigmatic expression of the distinctive Southeast Asian variety of animism. As Needham has pointed out (1976), it is the spirits, having been fed with the human victim, that convey power and potency to the killers' community. The sacrifice of the human victim is the necessary 'causal' link between the taking of enemy heads, on the one hand, and its assumed outcome – the prosperity expected to befall the head-taking community, on the other.[8]

Headhunting and Related Practices of Ritualized Violence

Until late nineteenth century and early twentieth century, headhunting was widespread in the remote parts of Mainland and Insular Southeast Asia – indeed, in some parts rampant until the mid-twentieth century. 'Blood-hunting' was a related practice prevalent in the central Annamitic Cordillera in pre-contact times. Both forms of ritualized violence were premised on the notion of ontological predation discussed above and forming what might perhaps best be referred to as the headhunting complex.

The purpose of these practices was similar across the region, and well summarized by an old Kayan warrior quoted by McKinley (1976: 95):

> [Head taking] is an ancient custom, a good, beneficent custom, bequeathed to us by our fathers and our fathers' fathers; it brings us blessings, plentiful harvests, and keeps off sickness, and pains. Those who were once our enemies, hereby become our guardians, our friends, our benefactors.

This quotation concisely summarizes the basic motive for the custom: to bring fertility, well-being and prosperity to the head-takers' community. It also makes explicit what seems to have been a universal feature of headhunting, one which it has in common with Amazonian warfare cannibalism: to convert the soul or spirit of the victim, objectified by the captured head, into a guardian spirit – a spirit ally and benefactor of the head takers' community.[9]

Headhunting raids were carried out to avenge the death of an important relative and/or to end the mourning period of the deceased (McKinley 1976). Thus, the Toraja needed to justify the taking of a head before their ancestors by claiming it to be retaliation for a grievance – real or imagined – committed against a deceased relative (Jacobsson 1992). More generally, however, headhunting was occasioned by sudden or prolonged misfortune – severe disease, multiple deaths or pervasive crop failure – interpreted as a loss, on the part of the community, of vitality and spiritual protection. The community had to be revitalized by capturing potency – human heads – from without. This is the reason universally given for head-taking raids and 'blood hunting' among Mainland groups (e.g., the Naga and Katuic groups) but also by many insular groups (Downs 1955: 54).

The connection between headhunting and crop fertility is universally evident in the region. Davison and Sutlive (1991) have shown how, among the Iban, head-taking was conceptualized in an agricultural idiom, closely associated with female identity and female fecundity: captured heads were compared to fruits, and head-taking to the harvesting of tree fruits in the Otherworld where the harvested fruits turn into babies nurtured by female spirits. Downs (1955) quotes mythical narratives from the Solor Archipelago in Eastern Indonesia suggesting that head-taking was conceived of as a male form of agriculture.[10] In one myth, the hero is exhorted by the gods to: 'take these weapons [...] in order to till my field and fill my barn [...] with human skulls'. The myths were used to justify the practice; if there were no wars (headhunting), the myths implied, granaries and barns would remain empty; there would be no rain, no vegetation or crops. 'For these reasons the [...] hostile parties never *dare* to make peace' (P. P. Arndt, quoted in Downs, ibid.: 54–5; my italics). Headhunting, then, just as warfare cannibalism in Amazonia, were sustained to evade a much greater calamity and more devastating destiny – cosmic cataclysm.

Headhunting involved raids on enemy groups – usually distant groups of people unrelated by kinship or alliance. Nevertheless, as Viveiros de Castro (1992) has argued for traditional warfare in Amazonia, ontological predation implied a form of intense social relationship rather than the absence of one. 'Enemies' was a well-defined social category; it referred to people who existed beyond the sphere of ordinary social interaction and, in a cosmological sense, were neither proper humans nor familiar non-humans (animals or spirits). As such they belonged to the prescribed category of potential targets for headhunting attacks. Rephrasing the Iban notion of prospective headhunting victims, 'people that are not people', McKinley (1976: 108, 120) coins the term 'counter people' for the category of 'enemies'.

The ultimate purpose and implied function of headhunting, the transformation of enemies into spirit allies, was expressed in various ways: the killer obtained a new or additional name, specific privileges and special adornments – all marking the new status of the head-taker and involving seclusion and restrictions on the typical pattern of transition rituals. The heads or skulls were treated with deference, as persons – indeed as close relatives; they were treated with food and drink, all suggesting the full incorporation of the victims-turned-spirit relatives into the community of their killers and head-takers. Killer and victim became one, permanently united by virtue of the act of killing. They become, as it were, relatives by death, giving the notion of 'blood relatives' – particularly in the case of blood hunting – a new and palpable meaning.[11]

*

In his now classical paper on the topic, Needham (1976) showed that headhunting as an institutional practice conforms to a sacrificial logic – a fact that, at the time, was curiously overlooked in the literature. He showed that headhunting was an ultimately religious practice in that it involved not only a ritualized killing and a consecrated victim but also and principally a divine, transcendent agent to whom the sacrificial person was dedicated. The captured head, representing the consecrated and immolated human victim, is offered to the spirits. In other words, it is the spirits who ultimately grant the head takers' community life and prosperity (cf. Hoskins 1996: 24–8).

In this way, the violent killing of a categorical enemy and the capture of heads becomes a life-giving act from the point of view of the head-takers' community. By positing the whole headhunting venture as a sacrificial project, the killing becomes for the perpetrators an exemplary moral act, the opposite of mere predation. The enemy-turned-self is converted into a transcendental gift to the spirits. In this light, the headhunting institution emerges as a maximal sacrifice, the most potent of human prestations to the spirits: a human sacrifice – in principle no different from the prototypical human sacrifices of war captives in pre-modern chiefdoms and states in different parts of the world.

What *is* different, though, and what makes the Southeast-Asian region special in this regard, is that headhunting continues to be evoked by many groups in the region, now as an image of a glorious past or, inversely, to account for the irresistible power of the state and foreign corporations penetrating into formerly indigenous lands. Many groups continue to perform rituals that were once associated with headhunting but now using old relics or substitutes for the trophy heads of the past. Hoskins' volume (1996) provides several examples of such contemporary imaginings of headhunting in Southeast Asia. One striking example is that of local people representing international development actors as headhunters, believed to take heads and burying them at new building sites to make the emerging constructions strong and durable (ibid.: 31–2).

This last example is interesting in light of the abundant archaeological evidence showing that, in pre-modern states and chiefdoms worldwide, slaves, war captives and ordinary citizens were often ritually killed and buried at the foundations of temples and the sumptuous dwellings of powerful chiefs. Apparently, the remains of the sacrificed victims – bones and skulls – were understood to lend the buildings qualities of strength, hardness and durability, just as the skulls, symbols of immortality and transcendence, kept as heirlooms by the more recent (literal or figurative) headhunters in Southeast Asia (cf. Hoskins 1996: 39–40).

The Living and The Dead: Ancestorship

Amazonian and Southeast Asian animist cosmologies differ – indeed contrast – with regard to the relation between the living and the dead. In Amazonia, the dead are generally conceived of as entirely disconnected from the living; there is no perceived spiritual continuity between the living and their deceased relatives. Viveiros de Castro (1998: 482–3) puts it thus: 'if [standard] animism affirms subjective and social continuity between humans and animals, its somatic complement, [Amerindian] perspectivism, establishes an objective discontinuity, equally social, between live humans and dead ones.' Dead relatives turn into 'others' – animals or celestial 'spirit affines'. Accordingly, ancestor worship and the phenomenological category of 'ancestors' in the conventional anthropological sense are entirely absent from the Amazonian religious and cosmological panorama. Mortuary ceremonies in Amazonia, spanning a spectrum from inconspicuous and private rituals involving only the closest relatives (as among Tukanoan peoples in Northwest Amazonia) to more elaborate and communal rituals involving a wider circle of kin and affines, all seem to have the purpose of bringing about the separation of the dead from the living, and to erase the memory of the dead among the living.

The case of the mortuary ceremonies of the Wari in Southeastern Brazil (summarized in Fausto 2007: 510) is typical in this respect. It highlights a further feature of Amazonian onto-praxis: the intense concern with the postmortem destiny of the body as expressed in the widespread practice of mortuary anthropophagy. The Wari funerary rites involve a process of 'othering' in which the dead is ritually transformed from consanguine to affine and from human to animal – culminating in the ritualized eating of portions from the corpse on the part of the attending relatives. The mortuary anthropophagy forms part of the 'work of forgetting' the dead – the active disposal of any physical basis for remembering the dead.

Among the Tupi-Guarani-speaking Arawete (Viveiros de Castro 1992), the soul of the dead is said to be devoured by celestial spirits and reborn as divine beings, themselves transformed into cannibal gods – celestial others and 'enemies' of the living. As the process of other-becoming is completed, there no longer exists any relationship between the living and the dead. Among the Tukanoan Indians of Northwest Amazonia, the names of the dead can never be mentioned, lest misfortune would befall the living, and every trace of the place where a dead relative is buried (usually inside the longhouse) must be erased so that the living must not be reminded of the dead. Even their memory must be dispelled.

*

In Southeast Asia the situation is very much the opposite: the dead are socially and metaphysically continuous with the living. Through the institution of ancestorship, implying the transformation of the dead into socially significant ancestors (Couderc and Sillander 2012: 5–12), the living maintain a relationship of social and metaphysical continuity with their deceased relatives. Mortuary rituals are usually conspicuous, public rituals. Family tombs and ostentatious lineage or clan ossuaries are visible manifestations of the rank and wealth of the deceased's family or lineage/clan, and ancestors play a supremely important role in people's everyday life and conduct.[12]

Whether we want to subsume this ritual attention to ancestors and the benevolent agency attributed to them under the broad label of ancestor worship or not, the universal importance of the institution of ancestorship in Southeast Asia is premised precisely on the fundamental notion of continuity – a bond of kinship and identity – between the living and the dead. The dead remain related to the living; they turn into 'hypersubjectified' relatives (to use a term coined by Viveiros de Castro for the enemy soul-turned-part-of the killer's self in Amazonian warfare). In many ways, the ancestors are the principal interlocutors in the life of Southeast Asian villagers, addressed and invoked to assist and guide the living in every aspect of life (see Chapter 1).

Commonly imagined as an anonymous collectivity, the ancestors are conceptualized as benevolent protectors of their living descendants but also as stern guardians of community moral and the traditions bequeathed to the living. Above all, they seem to function as familiar spirit-interlocutors mediating between the living humans and the powerful and unpredictable nature spirits. The ancestors are the most familiar and the least menacing of the spirits. People turn to the ancestors for help when afflicted by misfortune and illness – usually believed to be caused by angered or neglected nature spirits.

In their important volume on the phenomenology and significance of ancestors in Borneo societies, Couderc and Sillander (2012) criticize the conventional definition of ancestors as individualized and genealogically defined forebears known from classical studies of West African and Chinese ancestor worship. Couderc and Sillander refer to this, in their view, narrow concept of ancestors as the Sino-African type or model. They consider it an unproductive analytical category in the context of Borneo societies (and indigenous Southeast Asia more broadly) and call for a broader approach to ancestorship. Thus they favor a concept of ancestors which includes not only genealogically specified and unspecified forebears but also influential predecessors of continuing significance for the living whose assistance is actively sought and from whom people trace social or genealogical ancestry.

It seems to me that this inclusive notion of ancestors is unnecessarily diluted to the point of losing analytical precision, and potentially creates as many problems as it solves. I prefer to reserve the notion for stipulated genealogical forebears who, either as individuals (Sino-African model) or an anonymous collectivity (common in indigenous Southeast Asia), are of continuing significance for the living. Often individualized ancestors, after three or four generations, pass into the collective category of anonymous and depersonalized ancestors. This somewhat pruned concept of ancestors is usefully distinguished from the notion of 'divinized heroes' – persons of prowess elevated to the status of idolized divinities – a phenomenon typical of Sino-Vietnamese religious traditions and, apparently, common in animist societies of Borneo but absent from many other parts of indigenous Southeast Asia.

*

Funerals in indigenous Southeast Asia tend to be grand events, reflecting the continuous significance of the dead in the life of their living descendants. Secondary funerals are common, involving the exhumation of the bones or ashes of the dead from lesser individual graves and their transfer to a larger, communal, tomb or ossuary containing the sacred remains of deceased members of an entire, lineage or clan. Such communal tombs and ossuaries are often richly decorated house-like wooden buildings or megalithic structures. The complex mortuary rites, often extending over many years, have the important function of transforming the potentially harmful ghosts of the dead into benevolent and protective ancestors. The funerals accomplish this vital work; they literally serve to produce ancestors and, in the form of ancestors, reintegrate the dead into the community of the living.[13]

Related to the significance of ancestors, and the instrumental role of mortuary rites in their production, is another salient feature of Southeast Asian eschatology – one absent in Amazonian cosmologies: the explicit distinction between 'good' and 'bad' death (or their cognate vernacular renderings). This dichotomy refers to a conceptual distinction between 'natural', ordinary or auspicious death and 'unnatural', extraordinary and inauspicious death – sudden, violent or accidental death and death involving profuse bloodshed. Prototypical examples of bad death include suicide, murder and death in childbirth.

The social and cosmological significance of this distinction derives from the fact that the two opposed modalities of death produce entirely distinct postmortem destinies of the deceased's soul: in general terms, good death is followed by the full range of mortuary ceremonies including secondary funeral in a family or lineage tomb while bad death results in a simple mortuary treatment – little or no ritual, burial in a location far away from the village which henceforth will be avoided by the relatives and villagers, usually associated with harmful and malevolent spirits and surrounded by strict taboos, particularly on swidden burning.

The unfortunate soul of a person dying a bad death is condemned to eternal solitude and restlessness; being an outcast from the world of the living, the bad-death soul turns into a harmful and malevolent predatory spirit, forever on the hunt for the souls of living people to devour. Accordingly, bad-death spirits are believed to roam the outskirts of the village in search for human prey or their substitute – domestic animals (see Chapter 4 on the Katu concept of bad death).

The bifurcation of the postmortem destiny of the human soul, reflected in the notions of good and bad death and the radically different funerary practices associated with them, accentuates the different approaches to death and afterlife in Southeast Asia and Amazonia. Whereas death in Amazonia sets in motion an active process of forgetting and 'othering' – often involving the affinalization and, indeed, animalization – of the deceased, a 'good' death in Southeast Asia is celebrated as the apotheosis of life and the transformation of the soul of the dead into transcendent and potentiated kin. Only when afflicted by violent or sudden – bad – death is the unfortunate victim's soul, like the estranged ghost in Amazonian eschatology, for ever severed from his or her living relatives.

Shamanism and Possession

The differences between Amazonian and Southeast Asian varieties of animism also come to the fore in an apparent dichotomy between shamanism and spirit possession. Viveiros de Castro (1998) observes that spirit possession is conspicuously absent in Amazonia while shamanism is ubiquitous and, indeed, integral to Amazonian perspectivism. In what amounts to a general hypothesis about the mutually exclusive relationship between shamanism and possession, he implies that spirit possession becomes institutionalized only in a cosmological context that affirms continuity between the living and the dead and, therefore, tends to go with the idea of ancestorship and the cultic practices associated with it. Accordingly, he writes, '[We] have superhuman ancestrality and spiritual possession on one side,

[and] animalization of the dead and bodily metamorphosis on the other' (ibid.: 485, note 19).

In a context such as that of Amerindian perspectivism where the dead turn into ontological others and become socially and metaphysically severed from the living, spirit possession is unlikely to occur – perhaps even unthinkable. The dead turn into animals – the model of the other as body/object – and shamanic interaction with the spirits take the form of bodily metamorphosis. What might be called the 'possession complex' is predicated on the opposite premise – the social and metaphysical continuity between the living and the dead (ancestorship) – which, as we have seen, is a foundational feature of Southeast Asian cosmology.

Now, Viveiros de Castro's hypothesis seems at first a promising vantage point for exploring the similarities and differences between Amazonian perspectivism and Southeast Asian animism since it, on the one hand, affirms a phenomenological connection between the institutions of ancestorship and spirit possession (characteristic of Southeast Asian animism) and, on the other, points to a significant difference in the character of the intersubjective field defining the varieties of animism in the two regions. Together, these observations suggest that we are dealing with two quite different cosmological complexes – one in which the body is at the center of cosmological attention (Amerindian perspectivism), the other where the spirit is the focus of conceptual elaboration (Southeast Asian animism).

As it stands, however, the hypothesis fails to account for the apparent coexistence of both shamanism and spirit possession in Southeast Asia. Numerous regional ethnographies (see Atkinson 1992 for an overview) suggest (a) that shamanism takes a different form in Southeast Asia (for one, female shamans are common and even predominant in various parts of the region), and (b) that there is no clear-cut break or separation between the two phenomena in the region. Shamanism and possession occur side by side and, indeed, a single ritual specialist alternately performs the functions of both shaman and spirit medium – even in the context of a single performance (such as a healing session). Clearly, to account for the continuity between the two phenomena in Southeast Asia, we need to modify Viveiros de Castro's sketchy hypothesis. I propose here that shamanism in Southeast Asia, as described in the regional literature, should be considered a specific variety of spirit possession – an active or agentive form of possession subsumed under what I tentatively refer to as the possession complex.

*

According to Viveiros de Castro, shamanism in its generic Amazonian form fundamentally involves a process of voluntary and temporary other-becoming. A shaman is a person – almost invariably a man – who has the capacity to take up the position of an extra-human 'other' and, by adopting the other's point of view, harness the power of the other for the good of his community. Possession, on the other hand, generally involves a human subject – often a woman – who serves as a bodily vehicle (medium) for an alien spirit (although one that may include a deceased relative). The role played by the subject/medium, and his/her alleged skills, vary with the degree of control over the spirits he/she embodies.

Thus, possession in the active mode is associated with recognized ritual specialists, men and women, performing the function of shaman-healer – mobilizing and impersonating tutelary spirits to cure patients afflicted by alien spirits. In a more passive but yet instrumental and controlled mode, the typical medium acts as the mouthpiece and messenger of a possessing spirit. Recognized mediums are seen as privileged instruments of the spirits; they have the capacity to convey messages from the spirits to the community. Mediums are, in local understanding, given this capacity by the spirits – a capacity which can be activated by their own volition. At the extreme passive pole of the possession continuum is the victim of spirit affliction; here possession is perceived as a state or condition of illness. The victim-patient has no control whatsoever over her situation or the outcome (Fig. 14.1).

Active mode ←	→	Passive mode
shaman - healer	spirit medium	victim of spirit affliction
full control; mobilizing helping spirits to combat afflicting spirit	some degree of control; mouthpiece of afflicting spirit	no control; invaded by afflicting spirit
	high-status medium (routinely possessed) low-status medium (occasionally possessed)	

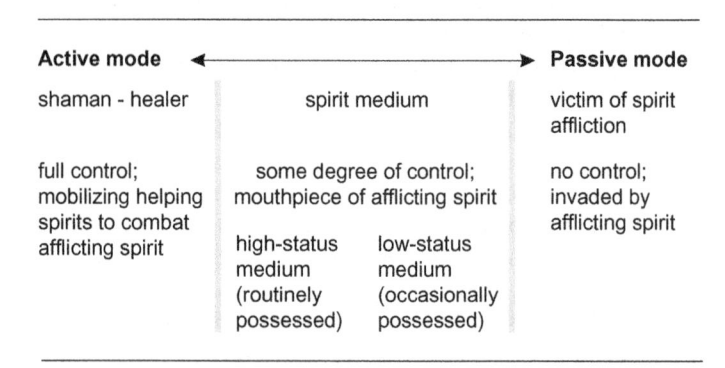

Figure 14.1 The spectrum of possession.

Evidently, shamanism in Southeast Asia is in important respects different from shamanism in Amazonia. While the Amazonian shaman is construed as a shape-shifter who acquires his extraordinary knowledge and power by bodily metamorphosis, his Southeast Asian counterpart is a powerful medium whose body serves as a vehicle for multiple spirits, and through which the powers and agency of the auxiliary spirits may be harnessed for curing purposes – combatting and expelling invading spirits and retrieving the soul of the afflicted patient (cf. Luu Hung 2012). In either case, the shaman acquires his/her powers from spirit others – animals, plants or ancestors.

In this light, and on a structural level, the two types of shamanism converge: they are both strategies of other-becoming. However, while the Amazonian shaman achieves this end by way of bodily metamorphosis, his Southeast Asian counterpart attains the same end through spirit possession. In other words, the different types of shamans achieve their common end by different roads and from opposite directions, as it were: the Amazonian shaman transcends his human limitations by temporarily adopting an extra-human body, the Southeast Asian shaman-healer by incarnating powerful tutelary spirits.

Interestingly, there exist in Southeast Asia the exact (structural) equivalent of the Amazonian shaman, but he – and he is generally a man – tends to play a quite different role from his Amazonian counterpart: I am referring here to the widespread phenomenon of lycanthropy, involving the figure of the were-tiger (or were-leopard).[14] The were-tiger (or other powerful were-predator) is usually a sinister and unhappy figure; a man whose soul every night takes up its abode in the body of an ordinary tiger who thereby transforms into an extra-ordinary animal – in fact, a vicarious human, an animal medium hosting a human spirit. In other words, the were-tiger is a tiger abducted by a human soul or, conversely, a human spirit who takes an alien, predatory body – a metamorphoser.

This formal equivalence between Amazonian shamanism and Southeast Asian lycanthropy – between the shaman and the were-tiger – suggests that metamorphosis and spirit possession, in structural terms, refer to the same process of transformation from different points of view. Thus, in Southeast Asian animism, possession from the medium's point of view is metamorphosis from the spirit's point of view to the same extent that, in Amerindian perspectivism (shamanism), metamorphosis from the shaman's point of view is possession from the animal's point of view – as when the shaman adopts an animal body. Thus, the virtual shamanic metamorphosis into an animal implied by a shamanic cosmology is so only from the shaman's point of view; from the point of view of the animal whose body has been abducted, what happens is best described as possession.

The notion of the metamorphic shaman (agent) thus requires an extra-human 'medium' (patient) whose body is abducted as clothing or enabling equipment by the shaman's soul/self. Conversely, the phenomenon of possession in its typical Southeast Asian rendering shifts the agency toward the possessing spirit who, by abducting the body of a human medium, acts as an Amazonian shaman – that is, metamorphosing into human form. In the case of the Southeast Asian shaman-healer, the tutelary spirits – typically including deceased relatives (ancestors) – act as 'true' shamans in the sense that they contextually and situationally tend to take the form of animals working for the shaman-healer who, from the tutelary spirit's point of view, is their human medium – their human body, as it were. In other words, the role of the Amazonian shaman-as-metamorphoser is, in Southeast Asia played by ancestors-as-tutelary spirits.

*

These two alternative conceptualizations of the shaman – one as master of metamorphosis, the other as mistress (or, less frequently, master) of possession – form part of two distinct ideological contexts which we, for consistency, may call the (Amazonian) shamanic complex and the (Southeast Asian) possession complex. The shamanic complex centers on the notion of bodily metamorphosis. The shaman as shape-shifter constitutes a generic and multi-functional ritual expert, fulfilling a whole series of ritual services to his community – protector of the living, healer, guardian of life and well-being, world maintainer and cosmic politician, and mediator between human beings, animals and spirits.

In the shamanic complex, illness and curing are conceptualized in terms of bodily metamorphosis. Thus, illness is understood as an uncontrolled and malignant change of body. Disease etiologies are usually formulated in a predatory idiom: the patient is thought of as a victim of animal predation – literally a prey 'eaten' by an animal subject (Århem, K. 1996). The afflicted victim finds him- or herself in the process of becoming an animal other. Curing, therefore, involves the reverse process – the unmaking of the malignant body change, metamorphosis in reverse. In a manner analogous to biomedical thinking, curing in the context of the Amazonian shamanic complex implies a change of body – returning the altered body to its normal, 'natural' state, literally a reconstruction of the patient's body.

The possession complex, on the other hand, revolves around the notion of the body as a medium and vehicle of alien spirits: a stable bodily form which may harbor or be occupied by more or less transient spirit agents. People and animals – notably domestic livestock – are frequently possessed by spirits, including the spirits of deceased familiars, producing a change of identity and behavior – and, thus, a change in bodily functions. Such a mental and/or physical alteration, induced by spirit affliction (possession), is interpreted as a state of illness – just as it would be in the context of the shamanic complex. However, the arrow of causation is reversed in the two cases. In both, bodily change is accompanied by a change of subjectivity (spirit), but while in one (shamanism) the change of body causes a change in spirit (point of view), in the other (possession) it is the spirit invasion that produces a malignant change in the victim's body.

Accordingly, curing in the possession complex involves a change of spirit – the expulsion of the afflicting spirit and the retrieval of the lost or displaced soul.[15] Interestingly, illness induced by involuntary possession or spirit affliction, just as illness interpreted in the metamorphic (shamanic) idiom, is formulated in a predatory idiom as 'being eaten' by an extra-human other (subject) – but a subject in its transcendent spirit form rather than its somatic animal form.

The Village and the Forest: Domestication as Ontological Project

The distinction between village and forest as different cosmological domains is typical of indigenous societies in Southeast Asia. Superficially, the distinction is reminiscent of the dichotomy between cultural and natural landscapes in Western tradition but, at a deeper level, the village/forest distinction in Southeast Asian society is a metaphysical dichotomy between what is perhaps best rendered as the Inside and the Outside – between the protected realm of the village ancestors and their living descendants on the one hand, and the distant and unfamiliar domain of nature spirits, wild animals and enemy peoples on the other. The full significance of this cosmological distinction becomes evident in the human project of settlement and domestication, epitomized by the establishment of a village and the clearing of land for cultivation and pasture.

Before the land is claimed and cleared for human settlement, the forest with its animals and plants is assumed to belong to the spirits. Every hill, stream and forest patch, and every other distinctive or conspicuous landform has a spirit owner. Hills and mountains in particular, but also springs and old tall trees, tend to be identified with specific owner spirits. This panoply of nature spirits are, in turn, refractions of superior and generic spirit categories often identified in the ethnographic literature as Lords of the Land (and/or Water). As the village is established, typically in the legendary past, the village founders ritually claim the village land from its original spirit owners (and/or ancestral human occupants – which comes to much the same effect).

Through elaborate founders' rituals (cf. Tannenbaum and Kammerer 2003), the first human settlers obtain legitimate control – a conditional tenure, as it were – over the land and its animals and plants. This covenant with the spirits typically involves regular and continuing sacrifices to the spirits who, though having ceded tenure to the human settlers, continue to dwell in, and ultimately rule over, the land and monitor its proper use and the moral behavior of its human occupants.

The founders of the village, on their part, venture to gradually 'domesticate' the land. In the process, the villagers progressively bring the forest and its animals under their dominion. By annually clearing the forest for cultivation, sowing the first rice and engaging in the ritualized first hunt, the covenant with the spirit owners is continually affirmed and renewed. The civilized order and socialized space of the settlement are thus expanded to comprise the whole of the village land, including settlements, fields and forest within the boundaries of the village territory. In this way, the land is occupied and its beings ritually domesticated – brought under vicarious human control.

As long as the villagers honor the contract with the spirit owners of the land, this 'civilized order' continues to govern the relations between humans and animals within the village domain. Beyond the village bounds, however, danger and insecurity lurk. The Outside is the uncultured domain of predatory spirits and enemy peoples where the safe and stable order of the village does not apply. Between strangers, unbound by ties of kinship and alliance, enmity was in the past the prescribed form of social relationship, and headhunting its maximum and legitimate expression.

Two Modalities of Animism

By way of conclusion I shall attempt to pull together some of the threads in the foregoing analysis. The shamanic complex and the possession complex outlined above are diagnostic of two quite different cosmological landscapes which I provisionally call immanent and transcendent animism respectively, the former referring to Amerindian perspectivism (and animism in its current standard form) and the latter to the typical form of indigenous animism in Southeast Asia.[16] While the shamanic complex implies a metamorphic cosmos in which subjectivity (spirit) is immanent in physical beings and things, and varies with bodily affects and behavior, the possession complex posits a universe in which beings and things have an essentially stable bodily form which serves as a vessel, abode or medium for an unstable and evanescent soul or spirit – which, therefore, must be ritually tied to its body. If not, it may escape or be displaced by an invading, alien spirit.

Immanent animism is intimately related to a hunting way of life in which people entertain a close, intersubjective relationship with their immediate surroundings, particularly the principal game animals on which they depend for a living. Engagement with wild animals and their living habitat is a daily activity. The hunter's life depends on his knowledge of animal life and behavior. To know the life-ways – the culture and subjectivity – of the game animals is of utmost importance. A venatic ideology (in Viveiros de Castro's terms) is likely to develop, one in which the animals are perceived and/or conceptually construed as autonomous, bodily subjects and agents.

The probing interest in the animal point of view and the elaborate depiction of the species-specific worldview or Umwelt (von Uexküll 2010) of the animal subjects characteristic of perspectivism, would seem to derive from this empathic concern with the animal other. The live animal is perceived and conceptually construed as a person dwelling in a world which, in its contours, is homologous with the human world and the human *socius*. This larger trans-human life-world shared by humans and animals is, in native Amazonia, commonly structured in terms of the elementary food chain governing the hunter's reality – the relationship between predator and prey (Århem, K. 1996, 1998).

This venatic world, in which both hunters and prey are figured as human-like persons, is fundamentally egalitarian, symmetric and reversible. Prey animals may turn into predators, food become eater. The knowledge to control and manage the predator-prey relationship is fundamental to survival. Shamanism as a mode of knowledge – of taking up the animal's point of view – becomes crucial for survival and, in cultural terms, the privileged mode of knowledge. In its active, practical aspect, shamanism seeks to ensure a stable trophic universe – the world as seen from the human hunter's point of view – and thus preventing the reversal of the predator-prey relations. Food and eating becomes the object of shamanic concern. The predatory idiom of the venatic cosmology makes the figure of the shaman in Amazonia almost invariably a man, and shamanism a male concern.

The symmetric and egalitarian cosmos of Amerindian perspectivism in which all living beings are ontological equals (or, in Viveiros de Castro's words, 'human at bottom') mirrors an egalitarian socio-political context, a hunter's society and sociality, with little social and economic differentiation (although ritual life may be subtly differentiated). This, I believe, is the formative context of a perspectivist cosmos: a symmetric and reversible multiverse where predation and counter-predation constitute the organizing template of the living world – a venatic cosmology articulated in an immanent modality of animism where the corporal diversity of life-forms is the focus of attention and intellectual reflection.

*

Transcendent animism, exemplified by indigenous cosmologies in Southeast Asia, is quite different and must be understood, I suggest, against the background of the shift from a hunter's world to a more complex and differentiated reality in which settled village culture, crop cultivation and livestock rearing have gained importance and become sources of cosmological elaboration. The domestication paradigm and the sacrificial idiom take precedence over the venatic ideology and predatory idiom of Amerindian perspectivism. The living environment beyond the human settlement is no longer at the center of cultural concern. Metaphysical speculation has shifted to the transcendent otherworld – the ancestors and the 'unincorporated dead', the spirits of the heavens and the earth – rather than animals and plants.

While immanent animism denies any social or metaphysical continuity between the living and the dead, Southeast Asian animism centers precisely on the continuing relatedness between the living and the dead and the transcendent powers of disembodied spirits. The idea of continuity between the living and the dead propels the notion of superhuman ancestrality and the concept that the ancestors form a society mirroring that of the living; thus, the conspicuous attention to, and elaboration of, funerary rituals and eschatological beliefs. The image of animals inhabiting a social world isomorphic with the human life-world which characterize Amerindian perspectivism is here replaced by the imagined society of the ancestors inhabiting villages and houses (cemeteries and tomb houses) modeled on the houses and villages of the living. From these otherworldly villages, the ancestors continue to influence the affairs of the village and to monitor, protect and punish their living descendants (cf. Waterson 2009: 207–8, 227–8).

This shift of cosmological attention in Southeast Asian animism from the living, biotic environment to the world of spirits and the dead implies a concomitant shift from body to spirit – from immanent to transcendent forms of subjectivity and personhood. In Southeast Asia, it seems, only humans and spirits are regarded as complete and autonomous persons, attributed with agency and subjectivity of their own. Wild animals in their tangible, embodied form are not considered subjects in their own right but as vessels or vehicles of spirits who, as transcendent persons, stand in relation to them as masters and owners. Agency is shifted from the living physical being to its transcendent subject-form – its owner or master. And spirit possession replaces bodily metamorphosis as the paradigm for shamanic other-becoming; the ancestors – the principal metamorphosers of Southeast Asian animism – take over major functions of the Amazonian shaman.

In sum, Southeast Asian animism in its prototypical form should, I suggest, be understood in this light: as an ontological development associated with the transition from a hunting mode of life to a more settled, agricultural way of life in which livestock keeping has progressively reduced the role of hunting and where the village-centered domestication paradigm and its attendant sacrificial ideology rather than the venatic ideology of shamanism constitute the organizing cosmological template – in short, as a transcendent permutation of immanent animism.

Notes

1. Southeast Asian upland societies were traditionally often subdivided into crosscutting and ranked categories of 'rich' and 'poor' people, the latter commonly including slaves and war captives. In the hierarchical lowland chiefdoms and valley principalities, the society was often hierarchically ordered in ranked classes of nobles, commoners and slaves.
2. The relationship between the Southeast Asian type of animism and analogism is also discussed in Chapter 1.

3. It does not mean, however, that hunting and game animals are not important (see Chapters 4 and 5, this volume).
4. Significantly, the reindeer-herding peoples in Siberia combines sacrifice with shamanism – the term itself originally deriving from the Tungus – thus literally occupying an intermediary cosmological space between the cultural worlds of Amazonia and indigenous Southeast Asia.
5. In the Katu case, the Animal Master is a complex, dual figure, contextually represented as male owner and a caring, female guardian spirit (cf. Chapter 5, this volume).
6. Analogously, among the Katu, the new rice at the beginning of the harvest season can only be consumed after first having been offered to the spirits in a first-fruit ritual presided over by the women of the household.
7. Significantly, at the height of the Katu hunting ritual, the men of the village consume the cooked head of the slain animal; as eaters of the animal offered them by the Animal Master, the villagers act as the recipients of the sacrificial food. From the animal's point of view, the human villagers are spirits.
8. Nevertheless, and qualifying Needham's thesis, some of the spiritual potency of the victim, just as in the case of the regular hunt, is evidently assumed to rest in the preserved skulls and to continue to bless the community in between predatory expeditions and the accompanying sacrificial rituals.
9. Guido Sprenger (pers. comm.) has pointed out that this contention contradicts Michelle and Renato Rosaldo's (1980) accounts of headhunting among the Ilongot in so far as they were not able to uncover any structural meaning in the practice (but cf. Hoskins 1996: 25–6).
10. There is a similar imagery among the Katu expressed in their harvest rituals: as the ripe rice is harvested, the sheaves of the last standing rice plants are cut and taken whole to the granary to protect the stored grains. The rice sheaves are compared to the head of the plant, and the act of cutting them is metaphorically equated with the taking of (enemy) heads. I hope to develop this theme in a coming paper.
11. Guido Sprenger suggests that the act of killing, rather than creating a relationship of identity – a fusion of identities – between the headhunter and his victim, creates a relationship of 'necessary difference' (pers. comm.).
12. The Mon-Khmer speaking Khasi of Meghalaya (Northeast India) is a particularly instructive case (Århem, K. 2000: 95–137; cf. also Århem, K. [2010: 234–6] on the Katu).
13. The Khasi megalithic complex provides an illuminating example (Århem, K. 2000). This process of ritual transformation of the dead is apparently not a necessary requirement for ancestorship in Borneo (Couderc and Sillander 2012: 9).
14. Guido Sprenger has called to my attention the existence of female were-tigers in the region, including among the Rmeet (pers. comm.).
15. Soul loss is also a frequent diagnosis in Amazonia.
16. I refer here to the distinction between standard (immanent) animism and hierarchical (transcendent) animism discussed more fully in Chapter 1.

References

Århem, K. (1996) 'The cosmic food-web: human-nature relatedness in the Northwest Amazon', in P. Descola and G. Pálsson (eds.) *Nature and Society: Anthropological Perspectives*, London: Routledge.
―― (1998) 'Powers of place: landscape, territory and local belonging in Nortwest Amazonia', in N. Lovell (ed.), *Locality and Belonging*, London: Routledge.
―― (2000) *Ethnographic Puzzles: Essays on Social Organization, Symbolism and Change*, London: The Athlone Press.

—— (2010) *The Katu Village: An Interpretive Ethnography of the Avuong Katu in Central Vietnam*, Katuic Ethnography Project Report, Papers in Social Anthropology 11, Gothenburg University.

Århem, N. (2007) 'Dangerous and powerful animals in Katu cosmology', in K. Århem (ed.) *Vietnamese Studies: Special Edition on Katu People in Vietnam*, (Hanoi) No. 1–2, 167–68; 73–98.

Atkinson, J. M. (1992) 'Shamanism today', *Annual Review of Anthropology*, 21: 307–30.

Couderc, P. and Sillander, K. (eds.) (2012) *Ancestors in Borneo Societies: Death, Transformation, and Social Immortality*, Copenhagen: NIAS Press.

Davison, J. and Sutlive, V. (1991) 'The children of Nising: images of headhunting and male sexuality in Iban ritual and oral literature', in V. Sutlive (ed.) *Female and Male in Borneo: Contributions and Challenges to Gender Studies*, Shanghai, VA: Borneo Research Council Monograph Series.

Downs, R. (1955) 'Headhunting in Indonesia', *Bijdragen tot de Taal-, Land- en Volkenkunde*, 111(1): 40–70.

Fausto, C. (2007) 'Feasting on people: eating animals and humans in Amazonia', *Current Anthropology*, 48(4): 497–530.

Hoskins, J. (ed.) (1996) *Headhunting and the Social Imagination in Southeast Asia*, Stanford, CA: Stanford University Press.

Jacobsson, B. (1992) 'Heads, buffaloes, and marriage among the To Pamona of Central Sulawesi (Indonesia)', in G. Aijmer (ed.) *A Conciliation of Power: The Force of Religion in Society*, Göteborg IASSA.

Luu Hung, A. (2012) 'Magical curing among the Katu', unpublished manuscript.

McKinley, R. (1976) 'Human and proud of it! A structural treatment of headhunting rites and the social definition of enemies', in G. N. Apell (ed.) *Studies in Borneo Societies: Social Process and Anthropological Explanation*, N. Illinois University: Center for Southeast Asian Studies, Special Report 12.

Needham, R. (1976) 'Skulls and causality', *Man*, 11(1): 71–88.

Rosaldo, M. (1980) *Knowledge and Passion*, Cambridge: Cambridge University Press.

Rosaldo, R. (1980) *Ilongot Headhunting*, Stanford, CA: Stanford University Press.

Scott, J.C. (2009) *The Art of Not Being Governed: An Anarchist History of Upland Southeast Asia*, New Haven, CT: Yale University Press.

Tannenbaum, N. and Kammerer, C.A. (eds.) (2003) *Founders' Cults in Southeast Asia: Ancestors, Polity, and Identity*, Monograph 52, Yale Southeast Asia Studies, New Haven, CT: Yale University Press.

Viveiros de Castro, E. (1998) 'Cosmological deixis and Amerindian perspectivism', *Journal of the Royal Anthropological Institute*, 4: 469–88.

—— (1992) *From the Enemy's Point of View: Humanity and Divinity in an Amazonian Society*, Chicago, IL: The University of Chicago Press.

von Uexküll, J. (2010) [1934] *A Foray into the World of Animals and Humans. With a Theory of Meaning*, Minneapolis, MN: University of Minnesota Press.

Waterson, R. (2009) [1990] *The Living House: An Anthropology of Architecture in South-East Asia*, Singapore: Tuttle Publishing.

15 End comment

To conclude in the spirit of rebirth, or, a note on animic anthropo-ontogenesis

Tim Ingold

I have often wondered, as I read ethnographic accounts from here and there in which people are credited with one or another ontology, cosmology or – as we used to say in our earlier days of philosophical naivety – 'worldview', how do children grow up with them? Are babies born in Western societies, to secular and scientifically enlightened parents, as budding naturalists? Are babies born in Southeast Asian societies such as those described in this book, to spirit-fearing omen-watching parents, as budding animists? Or are all babies, everywhere, born with a predisposition either to animism or to naturalism? If the former were the case, then Western societies would have to educate them into naturalism; if the latter, then south-east Asian societies would have to educate them into animism; in both cases against the grain – so to speak – of innate tendency.

The Western scientific establishment has long cleaved to the first alternative, believing that infants and young children are universally predisposed to animism – being innately inclined to attribute life and mind to ostensibly inanimate objects – and have to be weaned off it as they mature (Guthrie 1993). From this perspective, the persistence of animistic beliefs and practices in other cultures only goes to show that people in such cultures have never really grown up. Their mistake, it has been said, is to extend to the phenomena of nature an intelligence that has evolved to handle relations with beings of one's own kind, in the domain of society. Treating inanimate entities as 'people', they are bound to go astray (Humphrey 1976: 313). More recently some anthropologists, anxious to build bridges with cognitive science, have opted instead for the second alternative. They claim that children are universal dualists, primed to make a very clear distinction between persons and things, and between social and natural phenomena, and that any beliefs they may come to profess as adults that seem to blur or override these distinctions amount to an elaborate cultural or ideological overlay, to be rolled out on occasions of ritual or crisis which call for the reassertion of public values, and that contravenes what they know from ordinary, quotidian life. Even as grown-ups may insist, for example, that the world around them is alive with spirits with which they have to deal, in their heart of hearts they know it is really a world of nature that is entirely indifferent to their concerns. What people say is one thing, this argument goes; what they know is another: thus they may say that things are alive and enspirited even when they know that they are not. Indeed perversely, their assertions are likely to be all the more emphatic, the more they fly in the face of everyday realities (Astuti 2001).

Not that this reasoning accords any more credence to animism. Far from claiming that adults have got things wrong because they think like children, the counter-argument is that children – by and large – have got things right because their thought and practice has yet to be shrouded in the mystifications of adulthood. However, the attribution of childishness to the ways of others, as Claude Lévi-Strauss (1969) pointed out many years ago, can cut both ways. If the Westerner sees in others the persistence of a naive belief in the animacy or spirituality of things that in his own society – both historically and in the education of every individual – has been eclipsed through the cultivation of reason, a grown-up from one of the societies documented in this volume would be equally entitled to express some astonishment at the way in which Western thought not only prolongs into adulthood, but also enshrines as a higher form of knowledge, a naive presumption concerning the fundamental inanimacy and insentience of things. In truth the child's mind, according to Lévi-Strauss, comes exclusively pre-equipped neither with a propensity towards animism, nor conversely with a propensity towards naturalism, but rather with the seeds of both animism and naturalism, and indeed of every conceivable means that has ever been available to humanity 'to define its relations to the world in general and its relations to others' (Lévi-Strauss 1969: 93). Every newborn human child is a budding naturalist *and* a budding animist, and whether one or the other comes to prevail in adulthood, or something entirely different from both, depends on which of the seeds is nurtured, and which are left to wither.

Thus it is just as deluded to compare the mentality of adults in south-east Asian societies to that of Western children as it is to compare the mentality of Southeast Asian children to that of adults in Western societies. In every society, Lévi-Strauss insists (1969: 92–3), adult thought and practice differs from that of children in so far as it represents a particular, culturally selected crystallisation from a range of possibilities common to all. Yet while, at first blush, this conclusion seems eminently reasonable, there is one problem with it. For it is couched unequivocally in the language of naturalism. In this language, as John Tooby and Leda Cosmides put it in their manifesto for the brave new science of evolutionary psychology, 'infants are everywhere the same' (Tooby and Cosmides 1992: 33). They comprise a homogeneous substrate, pre-primed for the subsequent take-up of variable cultural content. So when we say that children will grow up to be animists or naturalists, depending on the social or cultural context, we are being naturalists ourselves.

Indeed ever since Alfred Kroeber, almost a century ago, declared that human nature is to culture as paper is to what is written on it, anthropologists have conventionally sought refuge in the comfortable idea that a new-born baby is a veritable blank slate so far as his or her future onto-praxis is concerned. Beginning, as Clifford Geertz famously put it, 'with the natural equipment to live a thousand kinds of life', each of us is supposed to 'end in the end having lived only one' (Geertz 1973: 45, see Kroeber 1917: 178–9). So this baby, born and raised in the West – perhaps even as the son or daughter of an anthropologist (and one can hardly get more Western than that) – ends in the end living the life of a naturalist, but that baby, born and raised among one of the societies documented here, ends in the end having lived as at least a part-time animist. But had the Western anthropologist been so careless as to leave her baby behind in the field and accidentally return home with someone else's child, then of course the former will end up no less an animist, and the latter no less a naturalist. It is all a matter of socialisation or enculturation, we used to say, implying of course that it has nothing whatever to do with heredity.

Such a top-down view of socialisation, however, leaves children without voices of their own. It is left to their seniors, self-appointed spokespersons for their respective cultures, to determine the directions that their maturing minds and bodies should take. In reality, do not children socialise grownups as much as vice versa? Do young people and elders not learn from one another, in the conduct of lives that they lead together? It is indeed puzzling that children's voices are so conspicuously absent from ethnographic studies of animism. Much has been written about how children are thought to be conceived and about how they grow, both before and after birth. Their health and general prosperity, too, are an abiding concern. But we hear adults talking about children, not from the children themselves. There may be good practical, methodological or even ethical reasons for this; yet with a typical demographic of a relatively high birth-rate and relatively low life expectancy, to exclude the voices of children is to leave out more than half the population. If only we knew how thought and practice matures over the years of growing up, and what changes it undergoes, we would be better placed to move beyond the crude dichotomy between innate capacities and acquired cultural content that underwrites orthodox theories of enculturation and socialisation. And we could find a way out of the duplicity entailed in, on the one hand, positing naturalism and animism as radically distinct and mutually exclusive ontologies while, on the other, sweeping under the carpet the default assumption as to how they come to be reproduced across generations, namely as culturally particular actualisations of universal capacities.

It could be objected, of course, that every life-cycle is a continuous process and that divisions between childhood and adulthood, if drawn at all in the society in question, are bound to be somewhat arbitrary. Birth, growth and ageing are facts of life; demarcated status divisions of childhood and adulthood are not. But this objection, which is entirely apposite, can point the way towards a solution. For it forces us to acknowledge that neither animism nor naturalism, nor any other candidate for ontological prevalence, is a systematic and coherent conclusion to which maturing thought and practice, starting from an original baseline, eventually arrives. It is not that innately animistic infants are eventually educated (in the civilised West) into naturalism or, conversely, that innately naturalistic infants (in societies such as those described in this volume) are inducted into animism. Quite to the contrary, we must be talking here about developmental pathways, not about beginning and end points. One does not, in short, become an animist, or a naturalist, nor are children of a certain age half-way there, in whichever direction of travel. But perhaps there are *ways of becoming*, identifiable in the educational practices of different societies, which incline along one course rather than the other, or even along alternative courses within the same society.

The point has often been made, and bears repeating here, that the suffix *-ism* assigns a false doctrinal rigidity and completion to what in truth are patchworks of ideas and practices that are continually subject to improvisation, experimentation and revision, and that may be as much idiosyncratic as shared within a community. This is what happens, for example, when science becomes scientism. Scientists (unlike their more zealous popularisers) are not the high priests of scientism. No more are shamans the officiants of shamanism. Everywhere, and at every age, people are in the business of figuring things out and, so far as they are able, of keeping well. And everywhere, and at every age, they do so in the company of others. Their understandings of the world are continually grown and re-grown, or shaped and re-shaped, within this process. My suggestion, then, is that terms like 'natural' and 'animic' might be better deployed to denote ways of becoming in the world, ways of conducting your life, which are not so much transmitted as *carried on*, as generation follows generation, alternately led by its predecessors and leading its successors.

There are, let us say, natural and animic ways of carrying on. They may lead you to different things – different discoveries, different experiences. But it is not the discoveries and experiences that are either natural or animic; it is the ways of coming by them. In short, with natural and animic, preferably with their -isms removed, *we are referring not to ontologies but to ontogenies*, not to philosophies but to generations of being. Practices of learning and teaching, long and unjustly marginalised in an anthropology that remains obsessed with the shapes and forms of mature thought, should be restored to the centrality they deserve. The challenge, then, is to establish whether there is a distinctive way of learning that could be called 'animic', and if there is, to identify how it differs from a 'natural' way. And one approach to address this challenge might be to look at alternative senses of the word *education* (Craft 1984). One sense, familiar to all of us who have sat in a school classroom as pupils, or who have stood up before the class to teach, comes from the Latin *educare*, meaning to rear or bring up, to instil a pattern of approved conduct and the knowledge that supports it. A variant etymology, however, traces the word to *educere*, from *ex* (out) + *ducere* (to lead). In this latter sense, education is a matter of leading novices *out* into a world in formation rather than – as it is conventionally taken to be in western societies today – instilling ready formed knowledge *in* to their minds. It seems to me that this 'leading out' is precisely what an animic ontogeny seeks to accomplish.

It is, fundamentally, an education of attention. I believe that contemporary anthropological discussions of animic becoming have got it wrong, in so far as they have been overwhelmingly couched in the language of intentionality. In animism, according to Carlos Fausto, 'intentionality and reflexive consciousness are not exclusive attributes of humanity but potentially available to all beings in the cosmos' (Fausto 2007: 497). Not just humans, then, but beings of manifold kinds – including diverse animals, gods, spirits, the dead, thunder and the winds, plants, artefacts – harbour the potential to make their presence felt as the bearers of intentions towards others. To harbour such intentions, we say, is to be a subject. And when the subject-being acts with an intention in mind, that action is said to be an expression of its agency.

'The capacities of conscious intentionality and agency', writes Eduardo Viveiros de Castro in this vein, 'define the position of the subject' (Viveiros de Castro 2012: 99). Thus intentionality, subjectivity and agency are linked in an indissoluble triad of mutual implication. What is implied is an *interiority* – a shared social space in which beings meet as fellow subjects and address one another by means of personal pronouns – as against the *physicality* of the object world. From this follows Philippe Descola's celebrated characterisation of animism: as similarity of interiority and difference in physicality (Descola 2013: 232–3).

I am not convinced, however, that these terms are the right ones. Does the movement from the quotidian to the numinous really take us into a hidden world of intentions as distinct from their outward effects or manifestations? Does consciousness necessarily rebound inwardly and reflexively on the self? Save in a mirror-saturated culture such as our own, as Peter Sloterdijk asks (2011: 197), how could anyone ever suppose that consciousness is an inner attribute of beings rather than a medium which, like the breath of life itself, envelops us in its folds? And if consciousness is the ocean in which we sail, how can it also be the harbour for our intentions or the launch-pad for our actions? Moreover in this numinous world, are beings really addressed with pronouns (Viveiros de Castro 2012: 97)? Not to my knowledge. For the movement is not from the outside to the inside of being but from being to becoming; not from the objective to the subjective but from a world in which beings are already positioned as subjects and things already cast as objects, to one in which the positioning and the casting are, so to speak, work in progress. It is to move upstream in the process of world-formation, to that moment of continual birth, or incipience, at which things are about to reveal themselves for what they are. Here, subjects and objects have yet to emerge from the generative currents that give rise to them; and so long as this emergence is in train, there is no separating the doer from the deed or the thinker from the thought. Agency has yet to fall out from action, and intentionality from consciousness.

The grammatical form of the personal pronoun implies that this separation has already been achieved. Where it has not – that is, in a world populated not by beings but by becomings (Ingold 2013: 8–9) – the grammatical form they take is neither of nouns (objects) nor of pronouns (subjects) but of *verbs*. In southeast Asian societies, as many of the contributions to this volume show, spirits are becomings; you encounter them in their going on, or in their continual emergence. Every encounter is different, and cannot be known in advance. Just as you cannot step twice into the same waters of a flowing river, so too, no experience of spirit is ever precisely repeatable. To move upstream is to relinquish one's stand on the banks and to beat a path into the current. It is not to assume a position in the world but to be led or pulled out of it. And this is precisely the meaning of education in the second of the two senses adduced above. As the philosopher Jan Masschelein explains, it is 'about putting this position at stake; it is about ex-position, about being out-of-position' (Masschelein 2010a: 276). Or in a word, it is a movement of *exposure*. It is not that exposure affords a different perspective; to the contrary, it does not disclose the world from *any* perspective – that is, from any fixed subject position – at all.

This is quite unlike the kind of switching of positions that Viveiros de Castro describes under the rubric of 'perspectivism'. In a simple switch or exchange of perspectives, as in a figure-ground reversal, nothing actually moves or goes on: the lines remain drawn as they always were; only the positions are reversed. Viveiros de Castro (2012: 58, 101) opposes the anthropo*morphism* entailed in the perspectivist attribution of human form to the pronominal subject, in the exchange of positions, to the anthropo*centrism* of the hylomorphic model of production, which has come down to us moderns as a legacy from classical Greece, according to which designs of human invention are cast upon the object world. Yet neither the reversal of perspectives nor the one-way transference of form onto matter – neither transformation-in-exchange nor creation-in-production – leaves any room for growth or becoming. Without growth or becoming, an animic ontogeny (not ontology) would be a contradiction in terms. Thus the animic way is not anthropomorphic, like perspectivism, and it is not anthropocentric, like creationism. It is rather *anthropo-ontogenetic* (Ingold 2015: 120–4).

In an animic education, positions themselves lose their definition. One does not look, or see, from this position or that, or with this body or that. One rather sees or looks along a way that always overtakes any position – that is beyond here or there – with a body that is to some degree unsettled and disturbed in its affects. The kind of exposure that results, and the existential threats and anxieties it entails, are a persistent theme in the literature on animism, not least in the contributions to this volume. Out of position, one is more than usually vulnerable to loss of bearings, metamorphosis and spiritual attack. Yet one can also be more than ever alive, and this vitality can contribute not just to one's own well-being but to that of one's entire community. But why should exposure entail attentionality? If the 'instilling in' of *educare* is intentional, then in what sense is the 'leading out' of *educere* attentional? Not, it must be said, in the sense in which the phrase was first coined by the psychologist, James Gibson (1979: 254). Pioneering his ecological approach to visual perception, Gibson had proposed that we do not perceive our surroundings from a series of fixed points, but rather that perception proceeds along what he called 'paths of observation' (ibid.: 19). The more practised we become in following these paths, according to Gibson, the better able we are to notice and to respond fluently to salient aspects of our environment. That is what he meant by an 'education of attention'. This, we might say, is the natural way.

The animic way is quite different, however. Recall that the verb *attendre*, in French, means 'to wait', and that even in English, to attend to things or persons carries connotations of looking after them, doing their bidding, and following what they do. In this regard, attention abides with a world that is always incipient, on the cusp of continual birth (Ingold 2011: 69). In a 'natural' education, the world waits for the learner to become practised in its ways, and to acquire the skilled mastery to bear him- or herself with confidence in it. Doubtless this occurs in the ordinary course of life, in non-Western societies as in Western ones. People become skilled in all kinds of everyday tasks. But the animic education is very far from a process of routine enskilment, and it does not lead to mastery. Entering into a world-in-formation rather than coming upon one that is already settled, it is a practice of submission in which one is continually at the mercy of what transpires. Here it is not the world that waits for the novice; rather it is the novice who must wait upon the world. To follow this path, as Masschelein (2010b: 46) puts it, is to be commanded, not by what is given but by what is *on the way* to being given. It is not an easy path to follow, and it does not lead to security.

Animic ontogeny is exemplary of what Masschelein (2010b: 49) calls 'poor pedagogy'. Contrary to the popular image of the indigenous person as one whose head is packed with traditional ecological knowledge, to be passed from generation to generation, the animic way is one without content to transmit. There is nothing to learn, and nothing to teach. To the consternation of their ethnographers, people who follow this way often seem to have little by way of systematic knowledge of their environment, and to care for such knowledge even less. What they do have, however, is an exceptional sensitivity and openness towards what is going on around them, and a capacity to respond with judgment and precision. Following on where others went before, they can keep on going, without beginning or end, pushing out into the flux of things. They are, in that regard, truly *present* in the present. The price of such presence is vulnerability, but its reward is an understanding, founded on immediate experience, that goes beyond knowledge. Perhaps it is an understanding on the way to truth.

References

Astuti, R. (2001) 'Are we all natural dualists? A cognitive developmental approach', *Journal of the Royal Anthropological Institute*, 7: 429–47.

Craft, M. (1984) 'Education for diversity', in M. Craft (ed.) *Education and Cultural Pluralism*, Philadelphia, PA: Falmer Press, 5–26.

Descola, P. (2013) *Beyond Nature and Culture*, trans. J. Lloyd, Chicago, IL: University of Chicago Press.

Fausto, C. (2007) 'Feasting on people: eating animals and humans in Amazonia', *Current Anthropology*, 48: 497–530.

Geertz, C. (1973) *The Interpretation of Cultures*, New York, NY: Basic Books.

Gibson, J.J. (1979) *The Ecological Approach to Visual Perception*, Boston, MA: Houghton Mifflin.

Guthrie, S. (1993) *Faces in the Clouds: A New Theory of Religion*, Oxford: Oxford University Press.

Humphrey, N. (1976) 'The social function of intellect', in P.P.G. Bateson and R.A. Hinde (eds.) *Growing Points in Ethology*, Cambridge: Cambridge University Press, 303–17.

Ingold, T. (2011) *Being Alive: Essays on Movement, Knowledge and Description*, Abingdon: Routledge.

——— (2013) 'Prospect', in T. Ingold and G. Pálsson (eds.) *Biosocial Becomings: Integrating Social and Biological Anthropology*, Cambridge: Cambridge University Press, 1–21.

Ingold, T. (2015) The Life of Lines. Abingdon: Routledge.

Kroeber, A. L. (1917) 'The superorganic', *American Anthropologist,* 19(2): 163–213.

Lévi-Strauss, C. (1969) *The elementary structures of kinship* (revised edition), trans. J.H. Bell, J. R. von Sturmer and R. Needham. Boston, MA: Beacon Press.

Masschelein, J. (2010a) 'The idea of critical e-ducational research – e-ducating the gaze and inviting to go walking', in I. Gur-Ze'ev (ed.) *The Possibility/Impossibility of a New Critical Language of Education*, Rotterdam: Sense Publishers, 275–91.

—— (2010b) 'E-ducating the gaze: the idea of a poor pedagogy', *Ethics and Education*, 5(1): 43–53.
Sloterdijk, P. (2011) *Spheres, Volume 1: Bubbles: Microspherology*, trans. W. Hoban. Los Angeles, CA: Semiotexte.
Tooby, J. and Cosmides, L. (1992) 'The psychological foundations of culture', in J.H. Barkow, L. Cosmides and J. Tooby (eds) *The Adapted Mind: Evolutionary Psychology and the Generation of Culture*, New York, NY: Oxford University Press, 19–136.
Viveiros de Castro, E. (2012) *Cosmological Perspectivism in Amazonia and Elsewhere*. (Four lectures given in the Department of Social Anthropology, Cambridge University, February-March 1998, introduced by Roy Wagner). Hau Masterclass Series, Volume 1.

Notes on contributors

Matthew H. Amster is professor of anthropology at Gettysburg College in Pennsylvania. In addition to long-term research in Borneo on the Kelabit, he has recently begun work on contemporary Norse paganism in Scandinavia, and done research on reenactment in both the US (Civil War) and Denmark (Viking). He is both an anthropologist and a filmmaker.

Kaj Århem is emeritus professor of social anthropology at the University of Gothenburg. He has worked for many years in the Colombian Amazon and among the pastoral Maasai in East Africa. Since 2003, he has pursued anthropological research among the Katu people in Laos and Vietnam. His publications include several books – notably *Pastoral Man in the Garden of Eden: The Maasai of the Ngorongoro Conservation Area, Tanzania* (1985); *Makuna: Portrait of an Amazonian People* (Smithsonian, 1998, reprinted 2003); and *Ethnographic Puzzles: Essays on Social Organization, Symbolism and Change* (Athlone, 2000). A monograph, based on his recent and ongoing work among the Katu in Vietnam, is under preparation for publication.

Nikolas Århem has a PhD in cultural anthropology from the University of Uppsala. He has carried out fieldwork among ethnic minority peoples in Laos and Vietnam with a focus on the relationship between indigenous knowledge, local religion and the natural environment. His publications include *Forests, Spirits and High Modernist Development: A Study of Cosmology and Change among Katuic Peoples in the Uplands of Laos and Vietnam* (Acta Universitatis Upsaliensis, 2014), *In the Sacred Forest: Landscape, Livelihood and Spirit Beliefs among the Katu of Vietnam* (2009), and consultancy studies for WWF in Vietnam and SUFORD, Laos.

Sven Cederroth is associate professor in social anthropology and retired senior lecturer at the School of Global Studies, University of Gothenburg. He has also been senior researcher at the Nordic Institute of Asian Studies, Copenhagen (1989–1998). He has specialized in the anthropology of religion with a focus on Indonesia and Malaysia. His publications include *Survival and Profit in Rural Java: the Case of an East Javanese Village* (1995) and *Managing Marital Disputes in Malaysian Syariah Courts: Islamic Mediators and Conflict Resolution in the Syariah Courts* (1997).

David Hicks is professor of anthropology at Stony Brook University and life member of Clare College, University of Cambridge. His research region is Indonesia and Timor-Leste where he has carried out nearly three years of field research. His books include *Tetum Ghosts and Kin* (1976, 2004); *Structural Analysis in Anthropology* (1978); *A Maternal Religion* (1984); *Cultural Anthropology* (with Margaret A. Gwynne) (1994, 1996); and *Ritual and Belief* (editor) (1999, 2002, 2010). He is the translator of *Povos de Timor, Povo de Timor: vida, aliança, mort* by Henri and Maria-Olímpia Campagnolo; the English translation is entitled: *Peoples of Timor, People of Timor: Life, Alliance, Death* (1993). Lisbon: Fundação Oriente. Instituto de Investigações Cientifica Tropical. His papers have appeared in the *American Anthropologist*, *The Journal of the Royal Anthropological Society*, and the *Bijdragen tot de Taal-, Land- en Volkenkunde*.

Signe Howell is professor of social anthropology at the University of Oslo. Her initial fieldwork with the Chewong of Peninsular Malaysia was undertaken 1977–79 for her D Phil thesis at Oxford. She has subsequently returned many times in order to follow-up her studies among the Chewong. She has also undertaken fieldwork with the Lio of Eastern Indonesia. Her publications include *Society and Cosmos: Chewong of Peninsular Malaysia* (Oxford University Press 1984), *Societies at Peace* (with Roy Willis, Routledge 1987), *Returns to the Field: Multitemporal Research and Contemporary Anthropology* (with Aud Talle, Indiana University Press 2012) and more than forty articles.

Tim Ingold is professor of social anthropology at the University of Aberdeen. He has carried out ethnographic fieldwork in Lapland, and has written on environment, technology and social organisation in the circumpolar North, on evolutionary theory, human-animal relations, language and tool-use, environmental perception and skilled practice. He is currently exploring issues on the interface between anthropology, archaeology, art and architecture.

Monica Janowski is a research associate and senior teaching fellow at the School of Oriental and African Studies, University of London. Recent publications include *Why Cultivate? Anthropological and Archaeological Approaches to Foraging-Farming Transitions in South-East Asia*, co-edited with Graeme Barker and published by the McDonald Institute, University of Cambridge (2011); and *Imagining Landscapes, Past, Present and Future*, co-edited with Tim Ingold and published by Ashgate (2012).

Timo Kaartinen received his PhD in anthropology from the University of Chicago in 2001. He has taught anthropology at the University of Helsinki since 2001 and presently works at the Helsinki Collegium of Advanced Studies as Core Fellow. His former publications on Maluku history and culture include the monograph *Songs of Travel and Stories of Place: Poetics of Absence in an Eastern Indonesian society*, published in 2010 by the Finnish Academy of Sciences. His latest fieldwork focuses on natural resource politics and perceptions of the environment in the Indonesian Borneo.

Jon Henrik Ziegler Remme, PhD, University of Oslo, is an anthropologist whose principal interests are religion, rituals and philosophy. His work deals primarily with the animistic religion of the Ifugao of Northern Luzon, the Philippines, but also includes studies of Pentecostal denominations in the same area. He has published several articles in *Norwegian Journal of Anthropology* related to inter-cultural encounters, management of ritual knowledge and to an anthropological understanding of causality. His most recent publications include 'Separating Encounters: Tangency in an interreligious encounter in Ifugao, the Philippines', *Anthropos*, 2012.

Kenneth Sillander is senior lecturer in sociology at the Swedish School of Social Science, University of Helsinki. He received his PhD in social anthropology from the University of Helsinki in 2004. He has done fieldwork among the Bentian of Indonesian Borneo since 1993 and published articles on Bentian social organization, rituals, naming practices and ethnicity. He is editor of *Anarchic Solidarity: Autonomy, Egalitarianism and Fellowship in Southeast Asia* (Yale, 2011) with Thomas Gibson, and of *Ancestors in Borneo Societies: Death, Transformation, and Social Immortality* (NIAS, 2012) with Pascal Couderc.

Guido Sprenger is professor at the Institute of Anthropology, Heidelberg University, since 2010, after positions at the Academia Sinica, Taipei and the University of Münster, Germany. He has done research in the uplands of Laos since 2000. His published works include *Die Männer, die den Geldbaum fällten (The Men who cut the Money Tree: Concepts of Exchange and Society among Rmeet of Takheung, Laos)* (2006) and numerous articles in international journals and edited volumes. His research interests include ritual, exchange, kinship and social morphology, human-environment relations, animism, cultural identity, gender and sexuality.

Index

abundance 20, 40, 127, 223, 258, 262–3, 270, 289
accidents, consequences of 95, 143, 161, 172, 195, 209, 241, 246, 266, 292, 304
actualization 45, 64, 83, 138, 140, 144–6, 148–50
adat (customary law) 163, 165, 173–4, 176, 178, 206, 251–2
affect 7, 24, 43, 100, 160, 171, 173, 177, 225, 229–30, 269, 297, 307
affines 74, 77, 79, 88, 94, 106, 126, 280, 289–90; affinity 35–6, 41, 44, 77, 84, 93–4, 105, 107, 108–9, 215, 262–3, 280; affinalization 292
affordances 145
afterlife 15, 292; afterworld 25, 167–8, 178
agency 3, 10, 20–2, 25, 35, 37–9, 42, 57, 74–5, 77, 108–9, 115, 165, 215–16, 230, 259, 262, 283–5, 290, 294–5, 299; harmful 92; impersonal 24; intentional 5, 24, 305–6; non-human 42, 44, 73, 87, 270–1; personalized 6; predatory 81, 92; social
agriculture 13, 34, 76, 185–6, 193, 261, 288; *see also* shifting cultivation, swidden
Alor 259, 262
alterity 31–6, 43–6, 157, 159, 169, 172, 176, 177
Amazonia 6–7, 17, 20–1, 27, 34, 59, 68, 91–2, 108–9, 110–12, 151, 157, 169–70, 178, 186, 229, 232, 258, 279, 280–90, 292–6, 298–301
America 3, 6, 20, 76, 85, 109, 112, 115–16, 118, 120, 175, 177, 178, 181, 271–2, 279
ambiguity 152, 264, 271
analogism 8, 13–16, 21, 23–4, 26, 58, 70, 140, 181

ancestors, Sino-African model 291; spirits 18–20, 33, 35, 46, 74, 76, 80, 91, 94–6, 98, 141, 161–3, 167–9, 178, 183, 186, 190–1, 221, 230, 239–41; 289–90, 292–3, 299; worship 16, 280, 289–90; as anonymous collectivity 15, 20; superhuman 241, 291–2
Anderson, Benedict 23–4, 37, 166, 182
animacy / animation 22, 160, 165–6, 176, 183, 187, 197, 303
animal: animal guardian 97, 99–100, 106, 109, 201, 230, 281, 284; master 19, 81, 99–101, 104–5, 107–10, 178, 280–2, 284, 300; animal people 56–7, 61, 63, 92, 108–9, 141, 167–8, 179, 281, 284–285; sacrifice 15, 19–20, 27, 34, 42, 44, 73–4, 76–84, 87, 92, 94, 97–8, 103–5, 107–8, 110, 116, 125, 128, 139, 149, 162, 168, 280–4; animal world 7, 17, 19, 56, 76, 79, 87, 111, 139, 209, 215, 271–2, 298–9; animal alters 12, 17, 20; cosmological role of 12, 19, 34, 97, 108, 219, 232, 280–1, 284, 296, 299; domestic 19, 25, 34–5, 42, 44, 73, 76, 79–80, 82, 84, 93–5, 97–8, 103, 109–10, 120, 139, 143, 158, 165, 168, 177–8, 192, 231, 233, 281, 283–4, 292; food 35, 41, 65–6, 76, 92, 97, 104, 143, 165, 173, 192, 231, 258, 283, 285, 298; game 19, 42, 44, 73, 75–6, 78–9, 81–3, 92–4, 97, 99–105, 107–9, 111, 230; head, ritual treatment of 78, 81–2, 99, 101–4, 231, 283–6, 300; humanized 6–7, 282; keeper of 19, 84, 100, 107; killing of 15, 63, 81, 83, 92, 104–5, 107, 110, 120, 136, 142, 192, 231, 233, 282–4; laughing at 106, 186, 188–9, 200–1, 231; person 5, 7, 10–12, 27, 41–2, 58, 61, 74, 77–9, 83–4, 87, 92, 100, 108, 111, 141, 143–6,

151, 159, 219, 280–1, 285, 298–9; prey 7, 25, 34, 63–4, 78–9, 81–2, 84, 105, 107–8, 229, 281, 283, 285, 298; wild 12, 19, 25, 34, 44, 73, 76, 83, 91–2, 95, 99, 101, 104–5, 109, 143–4, 177, 184, 192, 231, 281–3, 296, 298–9; *see also* human-animal relationship, lycanthropy, metamorphosis, shape-shifting
animism; Amerindian 41, 219, 232, 282, 293, 297; debate 3, 6, 26–7, 31, 34, 40, 44, 58, 111, 143, 151, 219, 231; egalitarian 4, 12–13, 16, 25, 175, 298; hierarchical 4, 13–16, 18–19, 24, 25–7, 40, 109, 112, 230, 280, 300; horizontal 4, 12, 17, 25, 175; immanent 12, 16–18, 21, 25, 222, 280, 283, 297–300; new 3–6, 12–13, 26–27, 34, 58, 76, 111, 157–8, 219, 225, 229, 231, 297; North Eurasian (Siberian) 19, 20, 27, 111, 141, 150, 280; phenomenological approach to 4, 6, 9, 11–12, 27; prototypical 13, 15, 17, 21, 25, 280, 282, 285, 299; sacrificial 19, 25, 34–5, 281, 287, 298–9; standard 4–6, 12–13, 15–17, 22, 25–6, 45, 111, 229, 280, 282, 289, 297, 300; structural approach to 6, 8, 12; transcendent 15–16, 20–1, 25–7, 280, 283, 297–300; venatic 12, 16–20, 25, 34, 280, 298–9; vertical 4, 18, 25, 27; asymmetric 16, 19, 25, 33–4, 39, 41, 91–2, 107–11, 177, 281–2; symmetric 7, 19, 25, 108, 110–11, 280, 298
animistic dilemma 63, 92, 110, 158, 174
Annamitic Cordillera/Mountain Chain 238, 287
anthropo-ontogenesis 302
anthropology 3–5, 9, 32, 35, 57, 152, 214, 219; of animism 140; 214; of religion 58
anthropomorphic 6, 14, 22, 62, 166, 169, 173, 178, 179; anthropomorphism versus anthropocentrism 307, anthropomorphization of nature 5, 12, 17, 26
anthropophagy 20, 21, 285, 290; *see also* cannibalism
anxiety 164, 205, 207–8, 211, 214, 216, 222
army 97, 120
arrow 258, 262, 266, 296
Aru Island 36
Asai Beret 188, 201
asymmetric (marriage) alliance 33–4, 41, 93–4, 107–8, 263

Atoni 259, 267, 273
attention, education of 45, 305, 307
Austronesian: *see* doxa; *see also* polity
autocratic 4, 23, 26, 279–80; autocratic-democratic 16, 23, 26, 279–80;
autonomy: personal 159, 172; political 159

bale (Penan general term for spirit) 182, 188–9
Banda Eli 220–1, 223, 227–8, 233–4
Baram River 181, 192
barking deer 183, 212
Barton, Roy Franklin 139, 186, 196, 202
Batak 152
Bayanese 238–9, 241–2, 244–5, 255
becoming 12, 44, 145, 286, 290, 293–4, 299, 304–7
Benjamin, Geoffrey 21–2, 33, 37, 40, 165
Bentian 19, 38, 45, 157–61, 164–7, 169–71, 173–8
betel nut 138, 144, 146, 246–8
bile sac 146–7
Bima 259–62, 273
Bird-David, Nurit 6, 9, 11, 27, 38, 74, 141, 146, 157, 160, 171–2, 174–6, 177, 208, 219, 225
birds; as omens 39, 45, 145, 178, 208–9, 214
blessing: of food 104, 253, 283; spiritual 20–1, 96, 103–4, 149, 239, 243, 281
blood 7, 18–19, 35, 56, 64, 66, 76–7, 81, 95, 97, 102, 149, 162–4, 178, 184, 188, 189, 191, 196, 197, 208, 221, 292; blood hunting 112, 116, 287, 288
blood relatives 288, 290
boar 99, 101, 164, 262
body 7, 12, 17–19, 21, 24–7, 31–2, 40, 44, 58–9, 61–2, 65–8, 70–1, 74, 77, 81–2, 92, 96–7, 99, 101, 103–4, 130, 139, 140, 142, 147, 149, 161, 166–9, 178, 183, 225–8, 230, 232, 234, 244–6, 248–50, 253–4, 281, 283–6, 290, 293–7, 307; corporality 59, 177–8, 281, 298; bodily affects 7, 24, 177, 229, 297; deceased 209, 217, 238, 240–1, 243; external 24; mind-body 31, 32, 46 55, 58, 231; natural 7, 18, 24–5, 224, 228, 296; social (socially achieved) 24, 225–6, 283; symbolic 230; *see also* metamorphosis, shape-shifting
Borneo 32, 36, 41, 45, 157, 158–9, 164, 175–6, 185, 192, 198, 202, 206, 291, 300
boundaries 33, 57, 67, 71, 75; cultural 37; between human and non-human worlds

56, 160, 167, 171, 274; of humanity 219, 231; maintenance of 65, 69; ontological 176–7; village 83, 221, 297
bride 34, 105–7, 234, 270; bridewealth 36, 44, 84, 85, 94, 105, 108, 111, 139, 259, 262–4
Buddhism 16, 32, 42–3, 279
buffalo: symbolic identification with 36, 74, 79, 83, 98; as sacrifice 77–8, 82–5, 93, 105, 158, 162–3, 168, 281
Bugis 16, 18, 23–4, 41, 237
Buli 223, 225
Bungan religion 197, 217
burial, *see* funeral
Burma, *see* Myanmar

Caffin, C. 257, 272
cannibalism 42, 63, 283, 285–8; alimentary 285–6; mortuary 38, 43, 98, 167–8, 208–9, 216, 289–92; ontological 20, 21, 63, 157, 285–8; warfare 92, 280, 283, 285–8, *see also* anthropophagy
Carrithers, Michael B. 146, 148
causation: impersonal 24, 166, 176; intentional 3, 5, 14, 24; magical 14, 24; natural 5; physical 3, 5, 14
cemeteries, Christian 190; megalithic 183, 186, 190–1
ceremony (*see* ritual)
chain of being 13, 87
chanting 92, 143, 147, 162, 165, 168
charm 165, 196, 213
Chewong 4, 17, 35, 44, 56, 58–9, 60, 63, 66, 87, 136, 217, 222, 279; animism 18, 20, 55, 61, 65, 67–71, 172–3, 282; cosmo rules 57; exchange 64, 85; mythology 62
chicken 76–8, 101, 125, 143, 145, 147, 168, 178, 192, 245, 259; offering 138, 146, 221, 248; sacrifice of 129, 149, 158, 164
chiefdom 14, 16, 26, 280, 289, 299
children, development of thinking in 302–4
Christianity 16, 32, 45, 162, 164, 183, 185, 187, 189–90, 196–9, 205–7, 211, 212–16, 229, 235, 279
circumboreal region 109, 279
circumpolar region 279
civet cat 183
clans 43, 93, 229, 274, 290–1
classes: of beings 75, 95, 140, 171; of people 18, 38, 92; ranked (*see* rank)
cloth 94, 97, 101, 226–7, 238, 240, 243–44, 263–4; loincloth 128, 130–1

coffins 186, 191
collective 8–9, 14, 20, 70, 140
colour 78, 146, 147, 188
community house 81, 93, 99, 101, 103, 118, 126, 282
communion 227, 283
Communist cadres 116, 119–20
conjunction 142, 149–50, 157, 176, 226, 257
consciousness 5, 22, 55, 59–61, 63–4, 69, 165, 182, 196, 199, 220, 223, 226, 306; perspectival 225; potential 151, 219, 224, 305; shamanic states of 87
continuum: animism-analogism 16, 23, 26; model 26; phenomenal 4, 16, 45; tribal 13; of phenomenal forms 4, 16
conversion 236–7; among the Kelabit 197, 205–7, 211, 214–6
coolness 56–7, 62, 65, 162, 184
corpse 67, 98, 141, 169, 243, 290
Corsín-Jiménez, A. 150
cosmology: [*see also* ontology] analogical 8, 14–15, 21, 23, 26; animic 7, 37, 178, 305; hierarchical 15–16, 18–20, 23, 41, 43, 46, 94, 112; hill-tribe 19, 23, 26; indigenous 4–5, 12, 15, 17, 20–1, 60, 92, 108, 279, 281, 296–8; intermediate type of 16, 109; perspectival 17, 24, 167, 285, 293, 298; prototypical Southeast Asian 15, 17, 19, 21, 279; western/non-western 10, 46, 57, 302
covenant: with the spirits 297
crocodile 168, 178, 192, 230, 266, 267, 270–1, 274
cultivation 126, 149, 184–5, 238, 296, 303; of crops 298; of difference 46, 75; *see also* rice, shifting cultivation, swidden, wet-rice cultivation
culture vs. nature, *see* nature vs. culture
curing 111, 252, 294–6; curing rituals 161–2, 167, 174; *see also* shaman, spirit medium

danger 18, 67, 71, 92, 106, 138, 140, 142, 148, 209–11, 227–8, 230, 241, 297; dangerous spirits 37, 80, 82, 85–6, 95, 100, 134, 163–4, 175, 190, 193, metaphysical 283; of spirit actualizations 149
dayong, *see* spirit medium
death 20, 22, 37, 39, 43, 66, 74, 85, 87, 128–9, 133–4, 147, 149, 164–8, 178, 190–2, 217, 226–7, 237–40, 246, 238,

255, 260, 283–4, 287–8, 292; bad/good death 95–6, 105, 107, 114, 166, 209, 292; in childbirth 95, 209–10, 292; as counter predation 34, 92; death names 192; rituals 67, 162; of shamans 17, 67
debt 94, 231
deception 62, 66, 258, 261, 264, 266–8, 269, 270
democratic 23, 280
Descola, P. 6–7, 10–11, 27, 32, 34, 38, 43, 46, 55, 58, 68, 70, 74, 76, 84, 92, 111, 140–1, 144, 150, 158, 169, 175–8, 183, 199, 219, 222–3, 231–2; schema 8–9, 12, 16, 59; typology 8, 13–15, 26–7, 181, 306
desubjectification 6, 108, 165, 283, 285
differentiation: spiritual 22, 25; bodily 25
differentiator 12, 26
disappeared beings 223–5, 232, 264
disease, *see* illness
disjunction 142, 149–50, 169, 176
divination: related to land/forest 103, 123, 178, 280
divinity, *see* gods, Supreme Being
divisions, *see* boundaries
domestication 45, 109, 112; as ontological project 296, 299; paradigm 282, 298–9
dominance 15, 25, 176
Down, R. 201, 287–8
dowry 94, 101
doxa: Austronesian 21; doxic view 22; regional 4; scholarly 22
dragon jars, Chinese 186, 191
Dreaming 78, 130, 139
dreams 5, 39, 62, 74, 78, 86–7, 99–100, 112, 114, 120, 123–4, 128, 130–1, 134, 139, 142, 149, 161, 164, 167–9, 187–8, 208, 246, 251, 263–4
duality 254, 257–8
dwelling 9–11, 177, 298

Eastern Indonesia 32–3, 36, 45–6, 202, 219–20, 222–6, 228–30, 232–3, 257–8, 263, 268–9, 271–3, 288
eels 260, 264, 272–4
egalitarianism 12, 17, 41, 159
Endicott, K. 21–3, 33, 35, 37, 40, 44, 173–4, 177, 179, 274
enemies: as social category 285, 288
entrapment 258
epistemology: relational 9, 58, 177, 208, 215–16, 219
Errington, S. 18, 27, 33–4, 182
eschatology 292, 299

Eurasia: Northern 3, 109, 111–12, 279–80
Evolutionism 3–5, 57, 91
exchange: asymmetric 33–4, 44, 91–4, 107–11, 201, 259, 280, 281–2; direct 93, 108, 280; generalized 92–3, 108–109; gift- 34–6, 82, 84–6, 94, 107, 110, 147, 174, 271, 281, 282; object 78, 81, 84, 94, 168, 281; reciprocal 34, 36, 86, 94, 108, 111, 152, 175; ritual 34, 36, 38, 40, 44, 73, 75, 77, 82, 84, 86–7, 93, 99, 105–6, 108–9, 142, 147, 148, 174, 227, 234; symmetric 107–8, 110–11
exposure 212, 306, 307
eyes 17, 39, 56–58, 61, 62, 65–8, 81, 183, 226–7, 263, opening and closing of 258, 260, 262, 265, 267, 268, 272; *see also* seeing, visibility, invisibility

FCSP (Fixed Cultivation and Sedentarisation Program) (?) 115, 119, 135
feast: hunting 100, 104–5, 108, 216, 282–3; sacrificial 20, 83, 97, 103, 105, 280, 282–3; of merit 20, *see also* sacrifice
feathers 147, 164
fire 23, 65–6, 102, 130, 184–5, 188, 196, 199, 201, 241–2, 249
fish 94, 119–20, 133, 136, 168, 178, 224, 260–6, 272; fishing 20, 92, 118, 158, 173, 229, 258, 261, 266; hooks 46, 258–62, 265–71, 273–4; fishing line 258, 260–1, 264, 266
Flores 259–60
food 7, 41, 58, 60, 63–4, 76, 84, 168, 173, 191–2, 229–31, 242, 247, 248, 253, 257, 258, 271, 281, 283–5, 288, 298; chain 298; consumption/ingestion of 60, 92, 97–8, 108, 111, 151, 231, 283–6; cooked 92, 101–2, 163, 178, 230, 248, 300; crops 35, 158, 210; cosmo-rules 66, 71; offerings 91, 97, 101, 104, 129, 163, 178, 248; preparation 44, 65, 151; raw 71, 78, 102, 178; taboos 67, 125, 164, 210; shamanism 108–9, 285
forest churches 195, 207
forest: as cosmological concept/domain 60, 76, 95, 282, 296–7
Forth, Gregory 42, 222, 225, 260, 273–4
founders' ritual 297
Fox, J. J. 21–3, 32–3, 37, 94, 179, 187
French 115–16, 120, 130
funeral 77, 96, 98, 128–9, 221, 291; secondary 38, 96, 190, 292; *see also* cemeteries, tomb

Gibson, J. 197, 307
Gibson, T. 36, 41, 75, 143, 159, 176
gift, of livestock 281–2; object 82, 84, 94, 105, 168, 281; *see also* exchange
gods 15, 76, 151, 163, 236–7, 244, 252, 255, 260, 262–3, 271, 288, 290, 305; goddess 244, 260, *see also* Christianity, Islam, Supreme Being, thunder god
gold 18, 36, 261–2, 269, 274
gongs 20, 94, 97, 101–2, 132, 147, 167
government policy 111, 114, 116, 121, 130
Great Spirit, *see* Supreme Being
groom 94, 105–7
gumlao and *gumsa* 23

Hallowell, Irving 6, 73, 91, 216
Hantu 21–2
Harrisson, M. T. 201–2, 212–13
harvest 60, 65, 98, 121, 149, 222, 247, 252, 288; ritual 210, 263, 300
head: human 19, 167, 191, 286–8, 308; tree 286, 288; trophy 286, 289; *see also* animal head, skull
headhunting 20, 112, 166, 201, 211, 216, 280, 283, 285–9, 297; in contemporary imagery 289; *see also* ontological predation; blood hunting
healers, *see* spirit medium
health 14, 20, 41, 65, 138, 149, 166, 187, 210, 253, 259, 265, 304
hearing 125, 209, 226
hearth 77, 102, 147, 184–5, 196
heirlooms 27, 289
hierarchy: ontological 14, 18–19, 26, 42–3, 112, 201; of being 14, 16, 23, 25, 42, 97, 230
hill-tribes 4, 19–20, 23, 24–6
Hinduism 16, 32, 159, 237, 238–9, 279
Hitchcock, M. 262, 273
Holy Spirit 183, 187, 200, 213–14
Hoskins, J. 222, 288–9, 300
houses 17, 20, 62, 77, 85, 93, 102, 118, 121, 128, 143, 145, 159, 164, 168, 193, 223, 227, 234, 245–6, 250, 256, 299; of influential persons 236, 242, *see also* spirits: houses
Howell, Signe 3–4, 17, 34–5, 37, 39, 44–5, 56, 58, 60–2, 64, 68–9, 71, 76, 78–9, 85, 87, 91, 136, 142, 152, 172–3, 217, 222, 224
Huaulu 229–32
human-animal relationship 27, 34, 42, 67, 73, 76, 78–9, 98–9, 111, 165, 192, 229–30, 280, 282–3, 298

iron 18, 179
Islam 16, 32–3, 42, 187, 220, 229, 236–9, 242, 255, 273, 279

Japan 63, 212, 273
Java 166, 236–8, 244; Javanese concept of power 23–4, 182
jars 20, 94, 96–7, 167, 186, 191

Kachin 23, 109, 110, 279
Kaharingan (religion) 159, 164, 177
Karim, W.-J. 41, 173–4, 178, 192
Katu 19, 33, 44–5, 71, 80–1, 91–100, 104–5, 110–11, 114–16, 118, 120, 122–4, 126–7, 129, 132–6, 171, 184–5, 188, 193, 201–2, 292, 300; cosmology 108–9; notion of hunting 106–7, 112, 279, 282–4
Katuic groups 120, 281, 287; languages 112
Kayan 175, 210, 217, 287
Keesing, R. 166
Kei islands 220–6, 229, 233–4, 259, 265
Kelabit 19, 45, 163, 166, 181–2, 184–6, 189, 191–3, 195–6, 198–202, 215–17, 221; animism as source of anxiety 208–15; Christianity 183, 185, 187–8, 190, 194, 197, 205–7
killing 81, 83, 104, 127, 193, 300; of animals 63, 92, 105, 107, 110, 120, 136, 142, 192, 231, 233, 282, 284; of humans 115, 243, 283, 285–6, 288–9; *see also* sacrifice, war
king 85, 236–8, 240, 256, 262, 264–5, 267–9, 274; divine 15, 19
kingdoms 4, 22–3, 25, 32, 74, 236–8, 256, 265, 272, 279–80
kinship 33, 36, 80, 93, 110, 112, 152, 159, 168, 170–1, 200, 225, 229, 288, 290, 297; bilateral 71, 159; classificatory 93, 159; kinning 152; *see also* affinity, blood relatives
Kirsch, T. A. 19–20, 23–4, 27, 41, 75
Kontu 229, 232
Korowai 223–4
Kruijt, A. C. 31, 37

lagoons 259
Lambek, M. 160
Lamet, *see* Rmeet
land of the dead, pre-Christian 190
land: tenure 297; village- 121–2, 125, 297
Laos 39, 42, 44, 73, 93, 98, 111, 120, 135, 279, 281

laughing, *see* animals
laws of nature, *see* nature: laws of
Leach, E. 23, 27, 33, 41, 74–5, 279
leadership 168, 206
lennāwa 37, 45, 141–4, 149, 152, *see also* life force
Lévi-Strauss, C. 6–8, 15, 27, 34, 88, 93, 110–11, 219, 258, 269, 303
life 19–20, 43, 57, 66, 69–70, 77, 87, 91, 95, 98, 138, 162, 164, 172–3, 205, 210–12, 226–8, 283, 302–7; conditions of 110; life-cycle 163; essence of 254–5, 270; daily life/everyday life/practical 65, 67, 134, 174, 260, 284, 290; destruction of 86; flow of life 33, 38, 60; -giving 59, 94, 96, 107, 109, 289; knots of 199; ontological life 138–40; reproduction of 35, 37, 41, 44, 75; social life 34, 39, 64, 175, 191, 222; source of 15, 187, 200–1, 234, 272; ways of 10, 232
life force 18, 21–2, 32, 37–8, 40, 45, 141–2, 152, 165, 176, 182–3, 186–7, 198, 210, 219, 223, 226; *see also lennawa,* potency, power, *semangat,* vital force
lightning 86, 96, 193, 202
lineage 23, 82, 93–4, 96, 98, 105, 290, 291–2
livestock 13, 16, 19–20, 26–7, 75, 93, 95, 97–8, 99, 105, 107–9, 110, 112, 279, 280–4, 286, 296, 298–9; owner (*see* owner)
lizards 65, 145, 178
Lombok 46, 184, 236–8, 242–3, 245, 254–6, 273
longhouse 184–5, 188, 191, 194–6, 206, 208–9, 213, 290
Lord of the Land/Water 221, 297
Luzon 138
lycanthropy, *see* metamorphosis

Ma'Betisék 41, 49, 174
magic 14, 21, 92, 192, 229, 240, 244–5, 251–2, 255, 274; sympathetic and contagious 14; *see also* causation
magical leaves 99, 101, 112, 244
Makassai 259, 266, 274
Malay 21–2, 33, 35, 37, 44, 161, 175, 177, 179, 187, 274; Peninsular 18, 41
Malaysia 35, 44, 55, 85, 205–6; peninsular 17, 136, 166, 173
marriage 33, 41, 60, 71, 92–5, 107–12, 151, 168, 183, 206, 221–2, 226, 234, 239, 260

marriage alliance 33, 41, 93–4, 107, 112, 234; system 41, 93–4, 112; *see also* sister exchange
Masschelein, J. 306, 308
material artifact 21, 40
matter 31, 35, 37, 56, 60–1, 96, 258–92, 266, 271, 273, 307; world of 268, 270
McKinley, R. 39, 85, 287–8
meat; consumption of 97, 282–3
mediation 168, 173
medium; spirit medium 15, 20, 25, 27, 183, 187, 189, 241–3, 293–7, 306
megaliths 183, 186, 190–1, 291, 300
metamorphosis 59, 64–5, 67–8, 70–1, 149, 167, 170, 176; of souls 176; into animals 228, 295; of shamans 17, 25, 68, 167, 293–5, 296, 299; bodily 17, 25, 61, 67, 286, 293–5, 299; in reverse 296; spiritual 264, 307; *see also* shape shifting
metaphysics: of food 60, 111, 285; of hunting 99, 111; of predation 111, 285; warfare 63, 92, 108
misfortune 96, 98, 108, 112, 160, 171–4, 209, 215–16, 222–3, 287, 291
missionaries 206–7, 213, 237
Mon-Khmer languages 73, 93, 136, 300
monism 5, 10, 44, 46
moral ecology 115, 135
mortuary ceremonies, *see* funeral, ritual: mortuary,
Mount Murud 198, 207, 213
mountains 74, 114, 138, 178, 187, 198, 200–1, 212, 220, 261, 296
Myanmar 33
myth 36, 42, 44, 46, 55–7, 60–8, 71, 106–7, 112, 145, 170, 179, 201, 223, 229–30, 231, 257, 260, 266, 273–4, 288; Elephant myth 57, 61, 62, 67, 70; origin 18, 42, 85, 106, 170, 176, 178–9, 192, 266

naga (mythic water serpents) 194, 202, 243
Nage (Flores) 259–60
names 33, 71, 97, 122, 139, 141, 146, 161, 192, 194, 226, 255, 290; nicknames 64, 71
narratives 57, 64, 114–5, 122, 134–5, 146, 148, 206–7, 234, 236, 258–74; mythic 106, 288; narrative discourse 57, 67–8, 71
natural kinds 7, 57–8, 64, 70–1; of people 17, 18
naturalism 3, 5–8, 13–14, 91, 140, 199, 280, 302–4

nature: animate 5, 11, 55, 57–8, 238; concept of 5–8, 9–12, 76, 228; humanized 7; laws of 6, 86, 91; sentient 5, 91; nature vs. culture 3, 7–11, 57, 63, 76, 231, 303, *see also* spirits: nature-
Naueti 259, 264, 273
Nayaka (India) 11, 171, 175, 177
Needham, R. 35, 166, 181, 200–1, 287–8, 300
non-human 5–6, 8, 10–14, 17, 25, 34–6, 38–46, 55–60, 63, 71, 75, 91, 97, 109, 138, 140–2, 144, 149, 150–2, 165–8, 222, 258, 288; actors/beings/entities 73–4, 84, 87, 139, 157–8, 170–1, 173–4, 177, 219, 225, 227, 230, 285; persons 208; species 65–6; world 69, 176, 125, 232
Novellino, D. 152–3
nyawa 22

object-subject transformation 20, 108–9, 151, 284–5
objectivation (objectification) 26, 151, 175, 178, 286; *see also* desubjectication
offerings 40, 81, 101, 112, 133, 138, 142, 146, 170–2, 174, 178, 221, 224, 237, 240, 248; food 91, 97, 104, 129, 162–3
Ojibwa 6, 216, 284
omens 39, 127, 164, 178, 208–12, 214, 217; inauspicious omens 209
onto-praxis 55, 60, 138, 151, 182, 290, 303
ontogeny; vs. ontology 12, 307
ontological: domains 175, 177, 257–9, 271, 296; effects, life-forms 139–40, 151; equivalence 14, 25; hierarchy 43, 112, 201; ontological predation 20–1, 25, 92, 157, 285–8 (*see also* cannibalism; headhunting); schemas 9
ontology: analogical 13–16; animic 141, 233; animistic 55, 59, 61, 71, 134, 140–1, 151, 170, 176; dualist 10, 13, 57; monistic 5, 10; naturalistic 5–6, 85, 302; non-naturalistic 13; non-Western 10, 46; sacrificial 15–16, 19, 25, 79, 108, 201, 281; totemistic 8, 58, 140, 175; venatic 12, 19, 25; of engagement 10, 13
operational dynamics 139
originary transparency 169–70, 176
ossuary 96, 291
other: ontological 13, 17, 38, 42, 281, 293; social 91, 108, 226, 281, 285; other-becoming 144, 286, 290, 293–4, 296, 299; otherness 100, 157, 168, 175, 223, 224

outside, as cosmological concept 41, 74, 296
owner being 143, 284; of animals 19, 35, 42, 44, 77, 82, 84, 100, 104, 143, 284, 296, 299; of livestock 19, 281–4

Palawan 152
Papua New Guinea 221, 232
patrilineage 74, 84, 93, 259
Pedersen, Morten Axel 27, 43, 59, 63, 144, 150, 171, 173, 175, 272, 274
Penan 45, 181–9, 191–201, 214, 226
Peninsular Malaysia 17, 136, 166, 173
penumbra 257, 271–2
perception 10–11, 57, 62, 66, 110–11, 145, 160, 166, 183, 223, 225–8, 307; of animals 12, 17; of the environment 9, 29, 182; of spirits 148; relativity in perception 58–9, 68
permutations 25, 27, 106, 167, 259, 299
person-environment relations 10, 91, 175
person: other-than-human 11–12, 25, 38, 77–8, 91–2, 284, 286
personalization 3, 5–6, 11, 14, 24, 37, 40, 42, 82–3, 104, 144
personhood 10, 24, 26–7, 37–8, 43–6, 55, 57–60, 68, 74, 80, 85–7, 143–5, 224–7, 299; attributes of 79; degrees of 84; graded 42, 73, 78; human 77; ontological status 12; potential 138, 141; relational 11
perspectivism 4, 6–8, 19, 27, 58–9, 68, 76, 140, 157, 167–8, 169, 229, 279–82, 292–3, 295, 297–9, 307; perspectival exchange 19, 219, 225, 228–30
petrification 189, 200–1
phenomenological: approach to animism, *see* animism
Philippines 32, 45, 138, 176, 313
physicality 8, 13–14, 25, 46, 55, 59, 68, 76, 91, 140, 144, 169, 306
pigs 78, 82, 138–9, 142, 145, 147–9, 168, 189, 191–2, 195–6, 259; domestic 76, 93, 94, 139, 143, 158, 165, 168, 192, 281; wallow 195; wild 62, 64–5, 76, 78–9, 87, 103, 139, 143, 181, 192, 229
pilgrimage 198
placenta 165
plants 3, 5, 7, 10–11, 19, 22, 25, 42, 64, 99, 112, 142, 168, 177–9, 223, 225, 227, 294, 296–7, 299–300, 305; as beings 56, 58, 61, 68, 151, 193; cultivate 34; as food 41; personhood 74, 91–2, 159, 165, 193, 219; relationship with 35, 173

policy 111, 114, 116, 130, 135
polity: centralized (Austronesian) 19
porcupine 65, 195
pork 148
possession *see* spirits: possession
postmortem: destiny (of person) 290, 292; treatment (of animal) 282
potency: graded 18, 24; as rank 18, 25; scale of 24; spiritual 20–1, 23, 25, 166, 300; fertility 14, 23–4, 286; *see also* life force/vital force
power 169, 182, 184, 198; Javanese idea/concept of 23–4, 182; as metaphor of causality 24, 166; powerful substances 189
Praet, Istvan 6, 27, 39, 85
Prager, Michael 261, 269, 272–3
predation 20–1, 25, 35, 45, 63, 96, 98, 107, 109, 111, 152, 157, 175, 177, 258, 280, 285–8, 296, 298; counter-predation 34, 92, 108–9, 111, 280, 298; *see also* cannibalism, hunting, predator-prey relationship
protection 14, 20, 23, 42, 77, 95, 104, 162, 177, 238, 247, 281, 284; spirit 112, 287
Pura 39, 262–3

quest 258–9, 261–2, 265–8, 270, 273

rank: high 18, 234; low 18, 24; naturalized 18, 24–5; of nobles, commoners, slaves 18, 24, 299
rationality 58, 61, 143, 222
reciprocity, *see* exchange
red (colour) 64, 78, 169, 188–9, 196, 267; animals 103; clothes 147; fish 263–4
relatedness 14, 57, 59, 79, 91, 157, 159, 171–2, 174–6, 299; human-spirit 157, 159, 269, 171, 175–6; *see also* kinship, relationalism
relational: cosmology 92, 108; epistemology 9, 11, 58, 177, 208, 215–16; ontology 11, 59, 91, 141; world 11–12, 141, 215
relations: modes of 9, 169, 178, 290, 292, 299; schemas of 9
religion: elementary 5; indigenous 3–4, 159, 217; local 3, 32; world 3, 16, 32, 43, 279, *see also* Christianity, Islam, Hinduism, Buddhism
resettlement 70, 115, 118–19, 121, 124, 135
revival 197, 206, 213, 219
revolution 119–21

rice 40, 65, 74, 95, 98, 101–2, 142, 145, 148, 165, 181, 183, 185–7, 190, 196–9, 200, 206, 208, 210, 212, 214, 240, 242, 247, 259, 297, 300; field 86, 115, 177–8, 193–5, 246, 248; rice wine 138, 142, 146–7; *see also* shifting cultivation, spirits: rice, swidden, wet-rice cultivation

ritual: communal/public 19, 93, 101, 103, 260, 282–3, 289, 290; mortuary 43, 105, 167–8, 208–9, 234, 280, 290, 292, 299; hunting 80–3, 88, 92–3, 99–101, 103–8, 112, 209–10, 216, 282–4, 300; specialists 15, 26, 138–9, 141, 146, 161, 209, 255; wealth 20, 44, 84, 93–4, 97, 105, 108–9, 280–1; economy 20, 24, 36, 75; healing, sacrificial 19, 34, 41, 82, 84, 87, 95, 97, 112, 143, 146–9, 171, 208, 219, 293, 300, *see also* funeral, sacrifice

rivers 20, 115, 118, 210, 220, 224, 230, 259

Rmeet 19, 33, 42, 44, 73–7, 79, 80–1, 83–8, 98, 188, 286, 300

Rodemeier, S. 39, 46, 262–3, 272

rope 78, 258, 261, 266

ruler 15, 18–19, 85

rules 37, 71, 115, 151, 162–3, 192, 197, 220, 222, 225, 229; behavioral 224; cosmo-rules 35, 44, 55, 57, 60, 62, 65–7, 69–71, 172; cultural 173; of rituals 34

sacrifice; animal 15, 19, 20, 27, 34, 42, 73–4, 77, 80–4, 87, 92, 94, 97, 103–5, 108, 110, 116, 125, 128, 142–3, 147, 149, 162, 164, 168, 280, 282–4, 300; complex 281; drama 104, 282, 284; human 19, 77–8, 84, 107, 281–2, 284, 289; logic 98; model 34–5, 77, 87; person 27, 44, 78, 84–5, 87, 164, 284; process 82, 284; project 289

sago 181, 186, 196, 202

Sahlins, M. 13, 16, 26–7, 33, 91, 269

Sarawak 45, 181, 191, 197, 200, 202, 205–6, 221, 226

Sasak 236, 237, 243–4, 254–6

seeing 55, 71, 193, 199, 226–7; a spirit 39, 193; *see also* eyes, invisibility, visibility

segmentary societies 12–13, 16–17, 26

self: as body 27, 281, 284–5; social 70, 175, 225, 281, 284–5

semangat 21–4, 37, 166

semiophagy 285–6

sense experience 38, 226

sentient ecology 10, 91

shadows 39, 220, 223, 225, 264, 279

shaman: Amerindian 20, 65, 280, 293, 295, 297; Amazonian 27, 92, 283, 292–6; -healer 20, 27, 294, 295; as master of metamorphosis 295, 299; mediumistic 20, 27, 183, 189; metamorphic 295–7; as mistress of possession 295; North-Eurasian 280

Shan 23

shape-shifting 41, 187, 199, 294–5; *see also* metamorphosis, lycanthropy

sharing 11, 34, 157, 171–2, 174–5, 177, 192, 225; demand 175; of essence 8; of meat 103

shifting cultivation 93, 116, 118–19, 121, 127, 130, 135, 158, 177; *see also* agriculture, swidden

shrimps 262

Siberia 19–20, 59, 110, 141, 150, 214, 300

singeing 63, 101, 147

sister exchange 93, 108

skull: gallery 99, 102, 286; animal 81–3, 99, 102–5, 112, 282, 284, 288

sky 74, 80, 82, 94, 96, 101, 107, 179, 187, 190, 197, 208–9, 249, 260, 263, 265

smell 63, 97, 147, 243–5

snakes 64, 183, 274

social organization 16, 159, 259

socialization 178, 228, 304

sociality: shared 138–9, 143–6, 148–50; proportional 150–1; common 80, 141, 143–4

society: egalitarian 12, 109, 175; moderately ranked 279; hierarchical 18, 109, 227, 299

solidarity 159, 172, 313

soul; conceptions of 73, 165–6; animal 5, 74, 78, 105, 159, 167, 219, 281, 283, 295; human 5, 24, 74, 95–6, 98, 165, 167, 189, 222, 225, 227, 285, 292, 295; retrieval 171, 172, 286; 'soul stuff' 37, 166, 225; substance 166, 201, 271; theft 161, 167, 171; loss 161, 165, 189, 300

Southeast Asia 3–4, 12–13, 15–17, 19–25, 27, 31–45, 68, 73–6, 92–5, 108–12, 148, 157, 166, 176, 178, 182, 202, 231, 273–4, 279–83, 285–7, 289–300, 303

speaking in tongues 213

spear 56, 64, 67, 138, 147, 164

spirits; affines as 77, 289; affliction 112, 220, 294, 296; alien 20, 224, 269, 293–7; ally 105, 287; ancestral, *see* ancestors: spirits; animal 19, 20, 44, 82–3, 88, 92, 97, 99–100, 102–5, 107–8, 112, 139, 151, 159, 165, 178–9, 191–2, 201, 219, 231, 281–2, 284, 295–6; bad-death 95–6, 105, 209, 292; change of 296; domain 35, 37, 39, 46, 76, 83, 86, 95, 139–40, 142, 147, 149–50, 170, 214, 257, 260, 268, 270, 272, 274, 282; dreams 39, 74, 78, 86–7, 123, 142, 161, 164, 167–9, 208; free spirits 17, 21–2, 183, 220–3, 228; as guardians 97, 114, 123–4, 132–3, 136, 161–3, 169, 178, 220–4, 230, 281, 294–5; of hearth 184–5, 196; hierarchy 18–19, 41, 97; hills 11, 123–4, 133, 296; houses 17, 85, 159, 168, 178; human 15, 20, 182, 188–9, 191, 219, 295; human-spirit-relationship 38–40, 44–5, 77–80, 85, 87, 94, 98–9, 108, 124, 150, 157, 160, 163, 174, 176, 220, 222, 234, 271–2, 274, 284; invasion 296; landscape 109, 114, 118, 122, 125, 135, 142, 183, 187, 190, 197, 213–14, 221; man-eating 286; medium *see* medium; of nature 11, 19, 33, 37, 91, 95–6, 109, 114, 163, 208, 260, 280–1, 286, 291, 296; outside spirits 83, 228, 272, 296–7; owner 19–20, 35, 42, 44, 82, 84, 104, 165, 177, 221–2, 281, 296–7, 299–300; pantheon 96, 139; pools/ponds 130, 132, 161, 194; possession 15–16, 20, 25, 43, 60–1, 109, 142, 147, 163, 187, 214, 241–3, 253–4, 280, 290, 293–7, 299; predatory 7, 95, 97–8, 172, 281, 292, 295, 297; and water 46, 136, 169, 194, 201–2, 210, 242, 250, 258, 271–2, 274, 297; world 22, 36, 39, 46, 87, 91, 138–9, 141–2, 162, 167, 171, 177, 183–5, 211, 214, 222, 234, 239, 255, 260, 268–9, 271–4, 283, 288, 299; malevolent 129, 160–1, 164, 169, 172, 178, 238, 292; of rice 42, 75, 82, 97, 142, 149, 162, 165, 185, 242; superhuman 61 169, 171, 174, 222, 299; tiger 98, 192, 195, 281, 295; of trees 80, 129–1, 133–4, 136, 142, 165, 182, 193–4, 220, 296

state: formation 16, 23, 26; modern 3, 135; pre-modern 14, 16, 23, 26, 46, 289; proto- 16

status 185, 259; hereditary 23, 208; and ritual privileges 23

stone 11, 14, 22–3, 40, 46, 62, 142, 145, 147, 161, 165, 183, 186, 188–9, 196, 202, 237–8, 242, 247–8, 250–2, 256; stone rain 200–1, *see also* megaliths

strangers 6, 20, 106, 219, 224, 227–8, 285, 297; *see also* enemies

subject 3, 7, 15, 19–20, 24–5, 27, 38, 56, 63, 73, 86, 140–2, 144, 151, 157, 202, 219, 226–7, 229–30, 232, 237, 293, 305–6, 307; animal 92, 100, 108–9, 280, 282, 284, 296, 298; autonomous 5, 229, 283, 298, 299; immanent 17; modern 45; potential 55; spirit 166; transcendent 12, 286, 299; unstable 16, 285, 297

subjectification 91, 151, 165, 173, 285

subjectivity: anthropomorphic 6, 22, 26, 173; change of 296; diffused 14; graded 25; universalized 7, 12–14, 16, 25, 26

submission 19, 25, 82, 174, 281, 308

substance 8, 13, 38, 92, 166, 189, 201, 224, 227, 231–3, 240, 254, 259, 271

Sulawesi 16, 18, 166, 182, 214, 237

Sumbawa 236, 259, 261

supernature 12

Supreme Being 14–5, 19, 21, 46, 96–7, 110, 190, 237; Great Spirit 184, 187, 198

swidden 39, 73, 82, 93, 125–8, 130, 143, 158, 193, 259, 279, 292; *see also* shifting cultivation

sword 167, 258, 263, 273

taboos 114, 116, 149–50, 162–4, 172–3, 176, 214, 217, 230–1, 292; break of 171, 210, 221; food taboos 67, 125, 210; environmental taboos 150, 220

talking as powerful practice 146

Thailand 39, 85–6

thanksgiving 162

Thunder God 35, 189

thunderstones 196

tiger, *see* spirit: tiger

Timor 37, 259–60, 264, 266–7, 269, 273–4

Tobelo 39, 50

tomb 96, 290–2, 299

Toraja 16, 18, 23–4, 37, 41–2, 287

totemism 6–8, 27, 58, 70, 140, 175

trade 34–6, 40, 45, 82, 174, 279; maritime 31

trance 39, 68, 171, 189, 227, 253; shamanic 65, 208, 226

transcendent: subject 12, 15, 19, 25, 286, 296, 299; transformation 292; *see also* animism,

transition, from hunting to agriculture 299

transitional period, *see* liminality
trees 14, 23, 57, 62, 80, 127–33, 136, 142, 161, 165, 169, 177–8, 182, 189, 193–4, 197, 201, 220, 238, 260, 264, 272, 296; fig trees 131–2; poisonous trees 131, 134, 136; *see also* spirits: of trees
tribal society 26
tribes-species 18
Tupi-Guarani 285, 290
turtle 178, 267, 270–1, 274
Tylor, E. B. 4–5, 12–13, 21, 31, 55, 57, 214, 219, 257–8

underearth/underwater complementarity 187, 197

valuables 20, 27, 34, 36, 85, 167, 168, 245
values 41, 43, 60, 63, 74, 205, 222, 228, 230, 302
venatic: cosmology 298–9; ideology 280, 298–9; idiom 298; world 298; (*see also* animism, ontology)
Vietminh 116, 120
Vietnam 91–3, 111, 114–6, 120, 126, 135, 185, 193, 201–2, 279, 281
village: as cosmological concept 16, 23, 76, 298; establishment of 126, 296; founder 297; village/forest dichotomy 96, 296
virtuality 160, 170, 176, 208, 295
visibility 37, 38–9, 257–8, 268, 271, *see also* eyes, invisibility, seeing
vitality/vital force 14–15, 21–2, 24, 83, 99, 104–5, 107–8, 138, 160, 165–6, 282, 286–7, 307; *see also lennawa*, life force, potency, power, *semangat*

Viveiros de Castro, Eduardo 6–8, 12, 27, 32, 34, 36, 55, 58–60, 63, 68, 70–1, 74, 76, 79, 92, 140–1, 148–50, 157, 168–70, 178, 188, 219, 225, 228–30, 232, 279–80, 282–6, 288, 289–90, 292–3, 298, 306–7

Waktu Lima 236–7
war 39, 63, 85, 107, 115–16, 118–22, 125, 191, 197, 212–13, 219, 234, 280, 299; in Amazonia 20–1, 283, 285–8; metaphysical 63, 92, 108, 283, 285–6
Wari 258, 290
water 64, 115, 127, 130, 132–3, 136, 143, 161, 184, 194, 202, 208, 237–8, 242, 248, 252, 267–74, 306; supply 118, 121; *see also* rivers
wealth 14, 24–6, 44, 93, 97, 99, 109, 222, 280, 290; as objectivized spirit power 20
Wessing, R. 161, 176
wet-rice cultivation 116, 127, 130, 135, 259, 279
Wetu Telu 46, 236–9, 241–3, 254
whale 262
wife-giver, wife-taker, *see* affines
Wilken, G. A. 31, 51
Willerslev, R. 27, 34, 59, 63, 91, 139, 141, 150, 160, 172, 174–5, 177, 214–5
witchcraft 14, 152, 223, 230, 255, 267
world religion, *see* religion; Hinduism; Buddhism; Christianity; Islam

Yukaghir 141, 150, 160, 174–5, 177, 214–15